EU ENVIRONMENTAL LAW, GOVERNANCE AND DECISION-MAKING

A vast and diverse body of EU law addresses an enormous range of environmental matters. This book examines a number of areas of substantive EU environmental law, focusing on the striking preoccupation of EU environmental law with the structure of decision-making. It highlights the observation that environmental protection and environmental decision-making depend intimately on both detailed, specialised information about the physical state of the world, and on political judgments about values and priorities. It also explores the elaborate mechanisms that attempt to bring these distinctive decision-making resources into EU environmental law in areas including industrial pollution, chemicals regulation, environmental assessment and climate change.

Volume 43 in the series Modern Studies in European Law

EU Environmental Law, Governance and Decision-Making

Second Edition

Maria Lee

·HART·
PUBLISHING
OXFORD AND PORTLAND, OREGON
2014

Published in the United Kingdom by Hart Publishing Ltd
16C Worcester Place, Oxford, OX1 2JW
Telephone: +44 (0)1865 517530
Fax: +44 (0)1865 510710
E-mail: mail@hartpub.co.uk
Website: http://www.hartpub.co.uk

Published in North America (US and Canada) by
Hart Publishing
c/o International Specialized Book Services
920 NE 58th Avenue, Suite 300
Portland, OR 97213-3786
USA
Tel: +1 503 287 3093 or toll-free: (1) 800 944 6190
Fax: +1 503 280 8832
E-mail: orders@isbs.com
Website: http://www.isbs.com

First edition published 2005

Hart Publishing is an imprint of Bloomsbury Publishing plc.

British Library Cataloguing in Publication Data
Data Available

ISBN: 978-1-84946-421-5

Typeset by Compuscript Ltd, Shannon
Printed and bound in Great Britain by
CPI Group (UK) Ltd, Croydon CR0 4YY

Preface

Over a period of more than four decades, environmental protection has become an important part of mainstream political debate, and governments around the world have accepted responsibility for the environment. The EU has been part of this movement. It has developed a vast body of environmental legislation, applying to an enormous market and a population of well over 500 million, across 28 Member States. That the environment should be actively protected is almost entirely uncontroversial; that the EU plays a central role in this, fairly uncontroversial. But quite what this means in practice contains the seeds of real conflict; we disagree on what we value about 'the environment', and to what extent and by what means it should be 'protected'. Environmental law and governance is based on values that relate to the way we want to live, as well as on facts about the world, 'an unstable blend of science-informed ethical postulates'.[1] This blend of facts and values creates challenges for EU environmental law and governance, since it demands the decision-making resources of both expertise and politics, of science and democracy. 'Political' is sometimes used in this context as a synonym for 'arbitrary' or 'self-interested' decision-making, and it should be noted from the outset that the term is not intended to be derogatory in this book. Political decisions are normative decisions, based on values (as well as facts), which might properly be subjected to debate in a political forum. There is no choice between expertise and politics—both are necessary. But the tension between these two refrains, and how that tension manifests, is perhaps the central theme of this book.

I had underestimated the pleasure of preparing a second edition of this book, and re-engaging with this rich area of scholarship. Anyone familiar with the first edition will see immediately how undisciplined I have been about relying on its words. But whilst not many of the words survive, this book does have a similar ethos to the earlier book. It does not aspire to comprehensive coverage of EU environmental law, if such a thing were even possible. I hope that readers will forgive the inevitable omissions, and sympathise with the aim; I certainly do not claim to have covered everything that is interesting or important. In particular, the significant and important external dimension to EU environmental law and policy will not be explored in this book. This book seeks to provide a relatively concise examination of some key issues in EU environmental law and governance, through the mechanism of selected areas of substantive law. Whilst it is not formally so-structured, this has led essentially to four sections to the book. The first part explores core underlying principles, approaches and ideas, in chapters one

---

[1] AD Tarlock, 'Is There a There There in Environmental Law?' (2004) 19 *Journal of Land Use and Environmental Law* 213, 241, although note that Tarlock considers the ethical project to have failed.

to three. Second, significant techniques of regulation and themes of governance are explored in chapters four to six, which also explore some of the literature on 'governance', and the inevitable coexistence of hierarchical 'law' with more inclusive and flexible 'governance' in EU efforts to protect the environment. These chapters discuss industrial emissions and climate change in some detail, as well as other areas, including water protection, more briefly. Third, chapters seven and eight discuss the role of public participation in environmental decision-making, including detailed discussion in chapter seven of environmental assessment in the Member States. Finally, chapters nine and 10 focus on environmental protection in the internal market, examining first the regulation and authorisation of products (specifically chemicals) at EU level, and then the scope of national autonomy after EU-level regulation has taken place (specifically in respect of genetically modified organisms).

An examination of the ways in which law attempts to shape environmental decision-making is implicit in the approach taken in this book: what sort of information and which type of actor are most welcome within a process; who takes the final decision; what would constitute a good reason for that decision; and what form action might take. I have no wish to stake any claim for a particular definition of 'law' or 'governance', or indeed the 'environment' or 'decision-making', and this is not the place to discuss the large literatures on these topics. Chapter four returns explicitly to the considerable literature on 'EU governance'; and for current purposes, I am happy to take a conventional, even simplistic, approach to 'law', as the authority contained in EU legislation and judicial decisions. What is important, as I hope will become clear, is that 'law' and 'governance' co-exist in unavoidable and interesting ways in EU efforts to protect the environment.

I am grateful to a lot of people. All at Hart Publishing have made this process as easy as it possibly could be. I am grateful to those who offered support and friendly criticism of the first edition. Former students Fran Bodman, Ben du Feu and James Nierinck provided excellent research assistance. I count myself very fortunate to have the opportunity to talk my work through with talented taught and research students. I am also extremely grateful to Carolyn Abbot, Chiara Armeni, Carrie Bradshaw, Jane Holder, Joanne Scott and Elen Stokes for generosity with their time, energy and insight in reading drafts of parts of this book. Versions of some of the work here have been presented at the Centre for Law and the Environment at UCL and the Europa Institute at the University of Edinburgh, and I am grateful to all involved. I am, as always, especially grateful to Steve Fownes for his immeasurable help and support.

The intention has been to ensure that the law and policy in this book is up to date as at 1 September 2013, although some later developments have been included; all web links were also last accessed on that date.

Contents

Table of Cases

Table of Legislation

EU Treaties

International Treaties and Conventions

EU Secondary Legislation

Decisions

National Legislation

1

The Treaties and the Environment

INTRODUCTION

THE ORIGINAL EUROPEAN Economic Community (EEC) Treaty was silent on the environment. The new Communities faced immediate and urgent objectives of post-war economic recovery, and environmental protection was in any event virtually invisible as a policy concern in the 1950s. An awakening of public environmental consciousness in the 1960s, most potently symbolised by the first images of the Earth from space, led governments around the world to venture into environmental policy. The EEC took its first explicit and systematic steps into environmental policy in the early 1970s, on the basis of the European Council's generous, qualitative interpretation of the original objectives of the Treaty (including the 'continual improvement of living and working conditions' and 'a rapid increase in the standard of living'). Environmental protection was not explicitly introduced into the language of the Treaties until the Single European Act (SEA) in 1986.

The primary purpose of this chapter is to introduce the EU Treaties for environmental lawyers. It begins with a discussion of the Treaty on the Functioning of the European Union's (TFEU) environment Title, Title XX TFEU, Articles 191–193 (formerly 174–176), headed 'Environment'. This includes an exploration of the Treaty's environmental objectives and principles (with special attention to the precautionary principle and the polluter pays principle). Also contained in the environment Title is the legislative procedure by which environmental measures are agreed, and the remaining scope for national autonomy after the EU has legislated. It would obviously be premature to try to 'introduce' all relevant aspects of the Treaties in a single chapter; in particular, the Treaty provisions on sustainable development and environmental integration are discussed in chapter three.

The EU's competence on environmental matters is securely established by the TFEU. The middle section of this chapter briefly considers the role of subsidiarity in determining when EU competence should be exercised, that is when action on the environment should be taken at EU level. The economic and fiscal crisis that began in 2008 creates a sensitive context for ambitious EU environmental action, and it would be remiss not to pause very briefly to consider that. The final topic of this chapter is the role of 'rights' in environmental law, in particular the EU Charter on Fundamental Rights (CFR).

THE ENVIRONMENT TITLE

The development of EU environmental policy from inauspicious beginnings is a well-rehearsed story.[1] By the early 1970s, as mentioned above, environmental policy was firmly on the political agenda. Political agreement does not, however, provide legislative competence,[2] and until the SEA, there was no explicit Treaty base for environmental action. The Commission and Council nevertheless developed a body of environmental legislation through the predecessors to what are now Articles 115 and 352 TFEU. The first of these Articles provided for the 'approximation' of national provisions that 'directly affect the establishment or functioning of the common market'. The creation of the common (now internal) market, in which there was to be (inter alia) free movement of goods between Member States, has always been central to the EU. Environmental legislation developed under this Article as a policy dependent on, and supportive of, internal market thinking. The less frequently used predecessor to Article 352 provided for action 'necessary to attain, in the course of the operation of the common market, one of the objectives of the Community', in the absence of explicit powers, allowing an environmental policy to develop independently of the market. Internal market rationales continued (and continue) to dominate.

The expansion of EU action into the environmental sphere met with the agreement of Member States in Council, as well as Commission and European Parliament.[3] Environmental policy was thought to be politically popular, and the internal market framing of environmental policy helped reach less sympathetic actors. Equally, however, those agreeing early environmental measures may have failed to appreciate the significance of the legislation: there were few short-term costs since the early directives generally postponed implementation and compliance, and there are suggestions that the nature of the legal obligation to implement may not have been clear to all Member States.[4] Perhaps the key factor in the relative absence of controversy was that both Articles required unanimity in Council (in consultation with the European Parliament), so that Member States retained their sovereignty.[5]

Crucially, the political consensus was supported by the Court.[6] The Court confirmed early on that differences in national environmental regulation could distort competition, and so 'directly affect the establishment or functioning of the common market', as required by the predecessor to Article 115.[7] It also confirmed

---

[1] J Scott, *EC Environmental Law* (London, Longman, 1998).

[2] See now Art 5 TEU, the 'principle of conferral'.

[3] For the classic tale of how political and legal processes concurred in the expansion of competences (and not just in the environmental sphere), see JHH Weiler, 'The Transformation of Europe' (1991) 100 *Yale Law Journal* 2403.

[4] Eg R Macrory, 'The Enforcement of Community Environmental Laws: Some Critical Issues' (1992) 29 *Common Market Law Review* 347.

[5] And equally importantly, national governments secured power, rather than national parliaments, Weiler (n 3).

[6] Ibid.

[7] Case 92/79 *Commission v Italy* [1980] ECR 1115.

the adequacy of the predecessor to Article 352 as a legal basis for environmental legislation, since environmental protection is 'one of the Community's essential objectives',[8] sufficient to justify certain restrictions on the free movement of goods.

The SEA in 1986 provided an explicit legal base for environmental legislation, and began to set the framework for environmental decision-making discussed below. Environmental measures were subject to the same decision-making procedure as before: Council unanimity, in consultation with the European Parliament. So in that respect, the SEA appeared to be an unchallenging codification of the status quo. But, in order to speed up completion of the internal market, changes were also made to what is now Article 114 TFEU. Measures 'which have as their object the establishment and functioning of the Internal Market' could be enacted on the basis of qualified majority voting in Council, in cooperation (rather than mere consultation) with the European Parliament. Following inevitable disagreement over the choice of legal basis, the Court confirmed that Article 114 could be used for environmental measures.[9] Negotiating 'in the shadow of the vote' further transformed environmental law-making.[10] In turn, Treaty revision at Maastricht in 1992 introduced the same process, of qualified majority plus cooperation, to the environment Title.

Subsequent Treaty revision (at Nice, Amsterdam and Lisbon) made only small changes to the environment Title. The current Treaties were negotiated in Lisbon, following the abandonment of the Treaty Establishing a Constitution for Europe[11] after negative referenda in France and the Netherlands. The Lisbon Treaty, which entered into force in 2009, created two main Treaties: the Treaty on the European Union (TEU), which sets out general principles and institutional arrangements, and the TFEU.

Article 191: Environmental Objectives and Considerations

EU environmental policy is to contribute to the pursuit of a number of objectives: 'preserving, protecting and improving the quality of the environment; protecting human health; prudent and rational utilisation of natural resources; promoting measures at international level to deal with regional or worldwide environmental problems, and in particular combating climate change.'[12] These are relatively bland provisions, although we might note that reference to the internal market is, given the history, conspicuous by its absence. The explicit reference to climate change was added by the Lisbon Treaty (the only change made to the environment

---

[8] Case C-240/83 *Procureur de la République v Association de Défense des Brûleurs d'huiles Usagées* [1985] ECR 531 [13].
[9] Case C-300/89 *Commission v Council (Titanium Dioxide)* [1991] ECR 2867.
[10] Weiler (n 3) 2461.
[11] [2004] OJ C310/1.
[12] Art 191(1) TFEU.

Title). Climate change was always covered by the first three objectives of Article 191(1), and is obviously a 'worldwide environmental problem'. The EU has for some time presented itself as a leader on climate change.[13] The reluctance of the US to participate in key climate change agreements, however, has demonstrated the political contingency of commitment to multilateral negotiations, even of formerly enthusiastic multilateralists. Article 191 arguably makes it less likely that the issue will fall off the EU's agenda. Still, picking one environmental problem (however serious) does raise concerns about ongoing efforts to take a more holistic approach to environmental governance.

Article 191(3) requires the EU to 'take account' of four factors in 'preparing its policy on the environment'. These factors include 'environmental conditions in the various regions of the Union' and 'the economic and social development of the Union as a whole and the balanced development of its regions'. This points towards the possible need for different approaches to environmental problems in different parts of the EU. Article 191(2) similarly provides for a 'high level of protection taking into account the diversity of situations in the various regions of the Union'. The study of 'flexibility' or 'differentiation' in EU law can involve constitutional questions of differential participation in whole policy areas.[14] But Article 191 is probably more concerned with the routine variation in the responsibilities of Member States, often on a temporary basis, in EU environmental legislation, for example allowing particular Member States more time or more generous conditions for implementation. Flexible standards, allowing diverse national or local approaches, can also be built into legislation, as discussed in chapters four and five especially.

The other two considerations that should be taken into account in environmental policy are 'available scientific and technical data' and 'the potential benefits and costs of action or lack of action'. Both are clearly desirable and unobjectionable. The benign language of the Treaty, however, hints at more contested and complex, highly technical understandings of environmental problems and their resolution, to which we return in detail in chapter two.

Article 191(2): The Environmental Principles

Article 191(2) TFEU affirms the importance of a number of 'environmental principles':[15]

> Union policy on the environment shall aim at a high level of protection taking into account the diversity of situations in the various regions of the Union. It shall be based

---

[13] See eg S Oberthur, 'The European Union's Performance in the International Climate Change Regime' (2011) 33 *Journal of European Integration* 667.

[14] See eg N Walker, 'Sovereignty and Differentiated Integration in the European Union' (1998) 4 *European Law Journal* 355.

[15] For discussion of the evolution and role of the polluter pays, preventive and precautionary principles, see N de Sadeleer, *Environmental Principles: From Political Slogans to Legal Rules* (Oxford University Press, 2002).

on the precautionary principle and on the principles that preventive action should be taken, that environmental damage should as a priority be rectified at source and that the polluter should pay.

The High Level of Protection

The requirement for a high level of protection is a useful statement of principle. It is repeated in the Treaty's internal market provisions, so that measures based on Article 114 TFEU will also 'take as a base a high level of protection'; it is also found in the 'common provisions' in Article 3 TEU. The high level of protection provides a potentially important counterpoint to the centrality of economic objectives in the EU. It is not, however, particularly specific, and is likely to be reviewable only at the margins. Most famously, *Gianni Bettati v Safety Hi-Tech Srl* involved a challenge to the level of protection in a regulation on substances that deplete the ozone layer, and the Court concluded that 'a high level of protection' need not be the highest level of protection that is 'technically possible'.[16] Defining a high level of protection is part of the political task of determining acceptable levels of risk,[17] to which chapter two returns, leaving decision-makers considerable discretion.

The Precautionary Principle

The precautionary principle is subject to a wealth of scholarship, of case law and of policy elaboration. Chapter two returns to the role of science and risk assessment in EU environmental law, to scientific uncertainty, and so inevitably also to the precautionary principle. Most simply and importantly, the precautionary principle acknowledges the place of scientific uncertainties at the centre of environmental decision-making. On some interpretations, the precautionary principle simply allows protective action to be taken in the absence of scientific certainty that harm will otherwise result. This is no more than an acknowledgment of the inevitable, given that we never operate in conditions of full scientific certainty. This 'weak' approach is resisted by some on the basis that it adds nothing to good practice. And there is something in this: I would be surprised to learn of EU environmental measures that could not have been justified in the absence of the principle.[18] But that does not make the precautionary principle pointless. It has the potential to open up a space for the normative deliberation of the dilemmas sometimes posed by uncertainty, demanding attention to the process by

---

[16] Case C-341/95 *Gianni Bettati v Safety Hi-Tech Srl* [1998] ECR I-4355 [47].

[17] Of the high level of protection of human health, Case T-257/07 *France v Commission* (TSEs) [2011] ECR II-5827 [79]; and before the ECJ (Case C-601/11 P, not yet reported in the ECR) [136].

[18] V Heyvaert, 'Guidance without Constraint: Assessing the Impact of the Precautionary Principle on the European Community's Chemicals Policy' (2006) 6 *Yearbook of European Environmental Law* 27, of chemicals policy specifically.

which decisions are reached;[19] a subject to which we return in chapter two (and indeed throughout this book).

At the other extreme from this weak approach, a very strong version of the precautionary principle would be impossible to apply across the board. Such a strong approach would *require* precautionary regulatory action to be taken if there is any doubt about safety, so unless safety could be proved by the proponent of any activity or technology. Cass Sunstein criticises the precautionary principle, not because it 'leads in the wrong directions, but because it leads in no direction at all'.[20] It is 'paralysing', since it can only provide answers (of any description, right or wrong) because we fail to notice the risks associated with *not* taking the risks on which we focus:

> A decision to ban asbestos may cause manufacturers to use less safe substitutes. A decision to regulate nuclear power may increase the demand for coal-fired power plants, with harmful environmental consequences. Regulation of tropospheric ozone may control the health dangers of ozone, but ozone has various benefits as well, including protection against cataracts and skin cancer …[21]

This is an important observation, and the general point, that risks may be associated with regulation as well as its absence, is unlikely to be disputed. For current purposes, it demonstrates that the precautionary principle cannot provide easy answers to difficult questions. That may seem banal, but any assertion that 'the precautionary principle demands' any particular outcome should be treated with suspicion: this would be an attempt to provide a technical (in this case legal) answer to a political or normative question. Chapter two criticises similar efforts to provide technical answers to political questions through the disciplines of risk assessment or cost benefit analysis. Importantly, however, the very strong approach criticised by Sunstein bears little similarity to the version of the precautionary principle applied in EU law (or probably anywhere else). The precautionary principle as interpreted by the EU courts demands (at least) some level of scientific plausibility,[22] and prohibits 'disproportionate' measures.[23]

The Treaty does not attempt to define the precautionary principle. The closest we come to a legislative definition is found in Article 7 of the General Food

---

[19] E Fisher, 'Opening Pandora's Box: Contextualising the Precautionary Principle in the European Union' in E Vos and M Everson (eds), *Uncertain Risks Regulated* (Abingdon, Routledge-Cavendish, 2009).

[20] CR Sunstein, 'Beyond the Precautionary Principle' (2003) 151 *University of Pennsylvania Law Review* 1003, 1054.

[21] CR Sunstein, *Risk and Reason: Safety, Law and the Environment* (Cambridge, Cambridge University Press, 2002) 39.

[22] N de Sadeleer, 'The Precautionary Principle in EC Health and Environmental Law' (2006) 12 *European Law Journal* 139, eg 148.

[23] Case T-13/99 *Pfizer Animal Health SA v Council* [2002] ECR II-3305. In some cases, the precautionary principle applies via the principle of proportionality, see Case C-343/09 *Afton Chemical Ltd v Secretary of State for Transport* [2010] ECR I-7027 [54] (Kokott AG).

Law.[24] Under the heading 'precautionary principle', Article 7 provides that where 'following an assessment of available information, the possibility of harmful effects on health is identified but scientific uncertainty persists, provisional risk management measures' may be taken 'pending further scientific information for a more comprehensive risk assessment.' Measures 'shall be proportionate', 'no more restrictive of trade than is required' and regard must be had 'to technical and economic feasibility'. This definition shares certain features with the Commission's (earlier) *White Paper on the Precautionary Principle*:[25] the need for an initial assessment, the obligation to revisit a precautionary measure with further information, the precautionary principle as a tool of risk management (rather than risk assessment, a distinction discussed in chapter two), the obligation of proportionality, concerns about trade, and the need to consider economic issues. The 'litigious nature' of the precautionary principle means that our understanding of its limits and scope is now dominated by the approach of the EU Courts,[26] which is also broadly consistent with these criteria.

Many of the cases rehearse the basic proposition that 'where there is scientific uncertainty as to the existence or extent of risks ..., the Community institutions may ... take protective measures without having to wait until the reality and seriousness of those risks become fully apparent'.[27] Our understanding of the courts' decisions is in many cases dependent on their precise context.[28] Not only is the particular legislative framework important, but the implications of the precautionary principle may vary, depending on whether it is applied to EU level regulation, to national interruptions to the internal market, or to national implementation of EU law. Whilst the precautionary principle appears in the environment Title of the Treaty, its application has been described as a 'general principle' and an 'autonomous principle' of EU law, and is applied beyond environmental protection, especially to human health.[29]

Notwithstanding the diverse contexts, it is possible to draw some general conclusions from the case law. The most important cases are probably still the decisions in *Pfizer Animal Health SA v Council* and *Alpharma v Council*.[30] These

---

[24] Regulation 178/2002/EC laying down the general principles and requirements of food law, establishing the European Food Safety Authority and laying down procedures in matters of food safety ('General Food Law') [2002] OJ L31/1.

[25] European Commission, 'Communication on the Precautionary Principle' COM (2000) 1 final; all of these points can be found in the summary [2], [4], [5], [6].

[26] E Stokes, 'The EC Courts' Contribution to Refining the Parameters of Precaution' (2008) 11 *Journal of Risk Research* 491, 491.

[27] Eg *Pfizer* (n 23) [139]; similar terms were used in Case C-180/96 *UK v Commission (BSE)* [1998] ECR I-2265 (without referring expressly to the precautionary principle) [99].

[28] Fisher (n 19).

[29] Most explicitly in Cases T-74/00, T-76/00 and T141/00 *Artegodan v Commission* [2002] ECR II-4945 [184]. The ECJ upheld the General Court decision on grounds of lack of Commission competence to take the contested decision, and did not discuss the precautionary principle, Case C-39/03 P *Commission v Artegodan* [2003] ECR I-7885.

[30] *Pfizer* (n 23); Case T-70/99 *Alpharma v Council* [2002] ECR II-3495. I will cite *Pfizer* other than when there is a pertinent difference between the cases.

decisions, reached on almost identical facts on the same day, are about the use in animal feed of certain antibiotics as growth promoters, so that animals can be brought to slaughter in less time and with less feed. The development by bacteria of resistance to particular antibiotics, making the treatment of disease less effective, is a serious and well-recognised problem. Out of concern that the use of antibiotics in agriculture could contribute to antibiotic resistance in bacteria that cause illness in humans, the Council withdrew authorisation from the antibiotics manufactured by the applicants. It was common ground that neither the reality nor the seriousness of the risk to human health (particularly the link between antibiotics in agriculture and in humans) was scientifically proven, and that the precautionary principle applied. The parties disagreed, however, on the interpretation and application of the precautionary principle. We return to *Pfizer* in chapter two, especially in respect of the decision-making institutions' relationships with their scientific advisors. It is an extremely rich decision. For now, I want to dwell on four key points, each of which has been repeated in later cases.

First, the General Court held that regulation cannot lawfully be based on a 'purely hypothetical approach to the risk',[31] founded on a 'mere conjecture which has not been scientifically verified'.[32] Instead, in a distinction that 'fully expresses all the tension inherent in applying the precautionary principle',[33] the risk must be 'adequately backed up by the scientific data available at the time', even if 'the reality and extent thereof have not been "fully" demonstrated by conclusive scientific evidence'.[34] Identifying a single precise point at which there is enough scientific evidence for the precautionary principle to kick in is probably not possible, not least because this is context specific, depending on acceptability of risks (which in some cases may be driven by the legislative language) in particular cases.[35] But the cases do not seem to set a particularly high threshold for legitimate intervention with precautionary measures.[36] The language of 'plausible risk'[37] has been used, and in *Sweden v Commission (Paraquat)*, the General Court refers to 'the existence of solid evidence which, while not resolving scientific uncertainty, may reasonably raise doubts as to the safety of a substance'.[38] Certainly, there must be at least a basic level of scientific credibility to the problem addressed by the measure.[39]

---

[31] *Pfizer*, ibid [143]. Case C-41/02 *Commission v Netherlands (Fortified Foodstuffs)* [2004] ECR I-11375 applies the same formula to national measures [52].

[32] *Pfizer*, ibid [143].

[33] Case C-192/01 *Commission v Denmark* [2003] ECR I-9693 [101] (Mischo AG).

[34] *Pfizer* (n 23) [144].

[35] Eg Fisher (n 19).

[36] V Heyvaert, 'Facing the Consequences of the Precautionary Principle in European Community Law' (2006) 31 *European Law Review* 185. For a discussion of the case law, see Stokes (n 26); P Craig, *EU Administrative Law* (Oxford, Oxford University Press, 2012) Ch 21.

[37] *Denmark* (n 33) [102] (Mischo AG).

[38] Case T-229/04 *Sweden v Commission (Paraquat)* [2007] ECR II-2437 [161], [224]. See also *Artegodan*(n 29), which in a different legislative context requires 'solid and convincing evidence which … may reasonably raise doubts as to the safety and/or efficacy of the medicinal product' [192].

[39] De Sadeleer (n 22).

Secondly, a closely related point, the Court in *Pfizer* demands 'a scientific risk assessment ... before any preventive measures are taken'.[40] More recent decisions confirm this: the precautionary principle requires 'first, identification of the potential negative consequences for health ..., and, secondly, a comprehensive assessment of the risk to health based on the most reliable scientific data available and the most recent results of international research'.[41] Risk assessment is discussed in detail in chapter two below.[42] Thirdly, and again closely related to the other points, the Court clearly rejects any suggestion that a failure to establish positive proof of absolute safety might justify protective measures. There is no such thing as 'zero risk'.[43]

Fourthly, the precautionary principle is interpreted in *Pfizer* to require the prioritisation of 'public' objectives (in this case 'public health') over 'economic considerations'.[44] This provides important support for protective measures, but is not uncomplicated. It must depend to some degree on the legislative context.[45] And, recalling Sunstein,[46] it will not always be obvious what the most protective measure is. When the harms or benefits associated with a medicine are uncertain, for example, there may be trade-offs between the (perhaps uncertain) benefits of the drug and the (perhaps uncertain) hazard.[47] Nor is it likely that every case seeks the very highest level of protection, and the Court requires precautionary measures to comply with the principle of proportionality. Proportionality in EU law requires (at least) that a measure be both suitable and necessary: that the measure be effective at achieving its end, and that there be no less burdensome measure that could achieve the same end.[48] The precautionary principle affects the application of the principle of proportionality, since measures may have to be taken when it is not clear whether the measures are effective or necessary.[49] The Court also sometimes[50] applies a more contentious and invasive 'proportionality strictu sensu' test, which requires the burdens of the measure not to be disproportionate

---

[40] *Pfizer* (n 23) [155]. See Stokes (n 26) for discussion.

[41] Case C-77/09 *Gowan Comércio Internacional e Serviços Lda v Ministero della Salute* [2010] ECR I-13533 [75].

[42] For Member State measures, see *Netherlands* (n 31) [53]. Note that this requirement does not apply to legislator, see *Afton* (n 23) [32], although they must use 'available scientific and technical data', as discussed above.

[43] *Pfizer* (n 23) [145]. Also Commission, (n 25) 8. However, whilst regulation cannot lawfully be based on the applicant's inability to prove absolute safety, the 'acceptable' level of a specific risk can legitimately be zero, eg Case C-121/00 *Hahn* [2002] ECR I-9193.

[44] *Pfizer*, ibid [456]; also *Artegodan* (n 29), referring to 'public health, safety and the environment' [186]; *France (TSE)* (n 17): notwithstanding formal discretion for a judge hearing *interim* applications, the decision 'will almost inevitably lean in favour of protecting public health' [141] (General Court).

[45] Note eg the role of economic considerations in authorising 'substances of very high concern', ch 9 below.

[46] Above nn 20–21.

[47] *Artegodan* (n 29), concerned a medicine, and the difficulty of risk/benefit trade-offs pervades the decision.

[48] See Craig (n 36), chs 19 and 20; discussed further in ch 2 below.

[49] *Afton* (n 23) [62] Kokott AG.

[50] See Craig (n 36). *Gowan* (n 41), considers the first two conditions only.

to the benefits. However, the high value accorded to 'public' interests when the precautionary principle applies means that even highly burdensome measures are likely to survive, as in *Pfizer* itself.

Although expressed in mandatory language in some of the cases,[51] the precautionary principle has generally been used to provide a justification for protective regulatory action, rather than to condemn a failure to take action in the face of uncertainty. But the General Court did condemn measures for being inadequately protective of human health in a challenge brought by Sweden against the EU authorisation of paraquat as an active ingredient in pesticides.[52] One of the disputed issues was the link between paraquat and Parkinson's disease.[53] Failure to consider the literature containing 'indications of a link' between paraquat and Parkinson's constituted a relatively straightforward procedural irregularity.[54] The Court went further than this, however. The legislation provides that an active substance can only be included in the 'authorised' list at EU level if 'it may be expected' that there are (inter alia) 'no harmful effects on human or animal health'.[55] The General Court interpreted this very protective legislative language 'in the light of the precautionary principle', deciding that 'it must be established beyond a reasonable doubt' that the use of a substance will meet the requirements set out in the legislation.[56] The Court then concluded that certain studies pleaded by the applicants constituted precisely the 'solid evidence' that 'may reasonably raise doubts' about safety.[57] This decision is discussed further in chapter two.

The significance of legislative context for the application of the precautionary principle is clear in the *Sweden (Paraquat)* decision, but is even more obvious in the implementation of EU environmental law by the Member States. In *Waddenzee Cockle Fishers*[58] the Court interpreted the obligation in the Habitats Directive to carry out 'an appropriate assessment' of a plan or project that is 'likely' to have 'significant effects' on a protected site.[59] Applying the precautionary principle, the Court found that such an assessment is required if significant effects 'cannot be excluded on the basis of objective information'.[60] The Directive then (essentially) prohibits, subject to exceptions, projects that the assessment indicates would adversely affect the 'integrity' of the protected site. Again, the precautionary

---

[51] *Artegodan* (n 29).
[52] *Sweden (Paraquat)* (n 38); see C Anderson, 'Competing Models of EU Administration in Judicial Review of Risk Regulation' (2013) unpublished manuscript.
[53] Note also the complaint about effects on animals.
[54] *Sweden (Paraquat)* (n 38) [110].
[55] It is complicated, see ibid, especially [5], [8], [167].
[56] Ibid [170]; Anderson (n 52) is critical of the interpretation.
[57] *Sweden (Paraquat)* ibid [181], [185].
[58] Case C-127/02 *Landelijke Vereniging tot Behoud van de Waddenzee v Staatssecretaris van Landbouw, Natuurbeheer en Visserij* (*Waddenzee Cockle Fishers*) [2004] ECR I-7405.
[59] Directive 1992/43/EEC on the conservation of natural habitats and of wild fauna and flora ('Habitats Directive') [1992] OJ L206/7.
[60] *Waddenzee Cockle Fishers* (n 58) [44].

principle is applied and the Member State can authorise the activity (in this case mechanical cockle fishing) only if 'no reasonable scientific doubt remains as to the absence of such effects.'[61] Kokott AG in *Afton Chemical Ltd v Secretary of State for Transport* notes the legislative context: in *Waddenzee*, a risk assessment is not, as is usual, necessary before a protective measure may be taken, but before development may take place.[62] Furthermore, the Court's primary concern was to ensure the implementation of EU law. Still, the language ('cannot be excluded', 'no reasonable scientific doubt') does not include the caveats we might expect, although 'objective information' and 'reasonable scientific doubt' does leave room for manoeuvre with the national court. The Advocate General further refers to the need for proportionality.[63]

This case law on the precautionary principle is complex and often subtle. It is primarily procedural,[64] although the line between procedure and substance can be fuzzy. The broader academic and policy literature on the precautionary principle has moved well beyond any expectation that it can be seen as a 'bright line', demanding a particular outcome in a particular set of circumstances.[65] By taking uncertainty seriously, however, the precautionary principle suggests that 'the facts' alone cannot justify a decision, so that alternative forms of legitimacy must be required.[66] On this understanding, the precautionary principle points towards open, deliberative decision-making,[67] an area of EU environmental law discussed particularly in chapters seven and eight below. In order to hold decision-makers to account for the discretion inherent in the politics of precaution, however, the courts tend to emphasise the technique of risk assessment, as discussed in chapter two. This is an imperfect response, and scrutiny of the political quality of decisions, including obligations of transparency, participation and reason-giving, would be helpful.

The Preventive Principle

The principle that preventive action should be taken allows action to be taken to protect the environment before actual damage has occurred. Repairing damage after the event is environmentally, and often economically, less satisfactory than

---

[61] Ibid [59].

[62] *Afton* (n 23) [70] (Kokott AG).

[63] *Waddenzee Cockle Fishers* (n 58) [103] (Kokott AG).

[64] Although note *Sweden (Paraquat)* (n 38). See also J Corkin, 'Science, Legitimacy and the Law: Regulating Risk Regulation Judiciously in the European Community' (2008) *European Law Review* 359.

[65] E Fisher, 'Precaution, Precaution Everywhere: Developing a "Common Understanding" of the Precautionary Principle in the European Community' (2002) 9 *Maastricht Journal of European and Comparative Law* 7.

[66] Ibid.

[67] See also TK Naveen, *GMOs in Europe: Law, Technology and Public Contestations* (Cheltenham, Edward Elgar, 2014 forthcoming); de Sadeleer (n 15); T Christoforou, 'The Precautionary Principle and Democratizing Expertise: A European Legal Perspective' (2003) 30 *Science and Public Policy* 205.

preventing it in the first place, and much contemporary environmental regulation is designed to prevent rather than repair environmental harm.[68] The permitting schemes discussed in this book (for example in chapters five and seven) can be viewed as preventive measures, and the incentivising effects of economic instruments (discussed in chapters four and six) may also be viewed as 'preventive'. This is a very well-established and uncontroversial principle. However, given that the demand for prevention is not absolute or infinite, the level of prevention will always be open to discussion. Prevention demands prediction, the limits to which are discussed in chapter two, linking the preventive principle closely with the precautionary principle.

The Source Principle

The 'source' principle is closely related to the other principles.[69] Like the preventive principle, the source principle rests on the recognition that it should be more effective and efficient to deal with problems early (at source). The source principle also aims to ensure that communities bear all and only their own environmental costs, like the polluter pays principle. The applicants in *R v Secretary of State for the Environment, ex p Standley*, a preliminary reference from the English courts, were farmers of land designated under the Nitrates Directive, which requires Member States to designate as 'vulnerable zones' areas of land that drain into waters that have been identified as affected by nitrate pollution.[70] The amount of livestock manure that can be deposited on land in vulnerable zones is limited. The farmers argued that the UK had breached the source principle (and the polluter pays principle, discussed below) because the decision as to whether an area should be a nitrate vulnerable zone was assessed by reference to all nitrate pollution, not just pollution from agriculture, but only farmers were required to take action. The Court found that the arguments about the source principle 'are indissociable from ... arguments relating to breach of the principle of proportionality'.[71] The Court did not explore the relationship between the principles any further, but this implies that the restrictions imposed on the farmers had to be necessary and effective, and not disproportionate to their contribution to the problem.

---

[68] Note that as recently as European Commission, 'The Sixth Community Environment Action Programme: Final Assessment' COM (2011) 531 final, the 'key challenge' is identified as being 'to evolve from *remediation* to *prevention* of degradation', 11.

[69] De Sadeleer (n 15) 75, says that the prevention and source principles 'merge'.

[70] Case C-293/97 *R v Secretary of State for the Environment, ex p Standley* [1999] ECR I-2603; Directive 91/676/EEC concerning the protection of waters against pollution caused by nitrates from agricultural sources ('Nitrates Directive') [1991] OJ L375/1.

[71] Ibid [53].

The Polluter Pays Principle

The precise meaning and application of the polluter pays principle is also diffi-cult to pin down. Kokott AG sees the polluter pays principle as both an incentive to reduce environmental pollution, and as a principle for the fair allocation of costs.[72] Jacobs AG describes it as:

> conceived to deal with a market failure: pollution is perhaps the most important example of what economists call a negative externality, that is a loss (normally to society) which is not priced. In the absence of State intervention a producer of chemical products causing air pollution does not pay for that pollution. He can therefore ignore the costs to society in deciding how much to produce and at what price to sell his products.[73]

Dominated by an economic approach to environmental protection, the principle is often called in aid of economic instruments of regulation (such as environmen-tal taxation, discussed in chapter four below). However, the principle does not dictate any particular regulatory scheme, and often refers simply to the costs that any form of regulation may impose on polluters. For Léger AG, the polluter pays principle can embrace 'the costs of remedying pollution', the costs 'arising from the implementation of a policy of prevention', or the costs where, 'in return for the payment of a charge, the polluter is authorised to carry out a polluting activity'.[74] So what the polluter might be made to pay for is widely defined.

In *Futura Immobiliare v Comune di Casoria*, a group of Italian hotels challenged the way that their waste collection costs were calculated.[75] They argued that the approach taken, including a distinction drawn between hotels and residential property, amounted to calculating costs by revenue rather than the amount of waste produced, contrary to the polluter pays principle. Following Kokott AG, the Court of Justice recognised that the polluter pays principle should not place impossible hurdles in the way of regulation. Waste produced need not actually be measured for the purposes of the tax, but can be estimated;[76] 'precise cost accounting' is not necessary.[77] The Court emphasised the importance of pro-portionality, so that the key question is whether the costs are 'manifestly dispro-portionate to the volumes or nature of the waste' produced.[78] Kokott AG went further, stating that because revenue-earning capacity 'has no direct connection' with waste production, 'revenue-earning capacity cannot as a social factor justify higher contributions'.[79] Her insistence that the polluter pays principle applies to

---

[72] C-254/08 *Futura Immobiliare v Comune di Casoria* [2009] ECR I-6995 [31]–[32].
[73] C-126/01 *Ministère de l'Économie v GEMO SA* [2003] ECR I-13769 [66] (Jacobs AG). This was a case about state aids in the slaughter of animals not destined for human consumption.
[74] *Standley* (n 70) [93], [97] (Léger AG).
[75] *Futura Immobiliare* (n 72).
[76] Ibid [51].
[77] Ibid [54] (Kokott AG), citing Case C-188/07 *Commune de Mesquer v Total* [2008] ECR I-4501.
[78] Ibid [57]. See also *Standley* (n 70), which aligned the polluter pays principle, as well as the source principle with proportionality.
[79] Ibid [65]–[67].

'all social strata'[80] raises questions about the distributive impacts of economic instruments, to which chapter four returns. The suggestion that ability to pay cannot be taken into account in the design of measures is a matter of some concern,[81] since the acceptability and appropriateness of economic instruments depends in part on ensuring that they do not have regressive effects, and in particular do not affect the poor disproportionately.

Identifying the polluter who must pay has also been the subject of litigation. We are probably all polluters as individuals,[82] although the law is more likely to target industry or retailers. The decision in *Commune de Mesquer v Total* concerned the appalling pollution of the French coast following the wrecking of the oil tanker *Erika*. The spilled oil, when mixed with water and sediment, constituted 'waste', and so was subject to EU waste legislation. The Waste Framework Directive provided that 'In accordance with the polluter pays principle', the costs of waste disposal were to be borne by the current or previous holders of the waste, or by the 'producer of products from which the waste came'.[83] Identifying the 'polluter' was not straightforward, since numerous parties were involved in the process of producing, transporting and marketing the oil. Whilst the Court left the ultimate conclusion to the national court, it emphasised that the definition of polluter included anyone who had 'contributed to the risk that the pollution caused by the shipwreck would occur, in particular if he failed to take measures to prevent such an incident, such as measures concerning the choice of ship'.[84] This includes the producer of the oil. Moreover, if national law prevented that company from being liable, it would breach the polluter pays principle.[85]

The Environmental Liability Directive is 'based on the "polluter-pays" principle',[86] and requires the Member States to set up a scheme whereby operators have to prevent, or pay to remedy, particular types of environmental damage. *Raffinerie Mediterranee v Ministero dello sviluppo economico* involved high levels of historic pollution of a Sicilian bay; industries located close to the bay were required under Italian law to pay for its clean-up.[87] The Court held that national bodies need 'plausible evidence capable of justifying [any] presumption' that the defendants caused the harm in order to hold them liable for remediation under

---

[80] Ibid [66].

[81] Ibid [66]. She says that these questions may be taken into account separately, in 'social support' measures. The Court does not touch on distribution.

[82] In *Mesquer* (n 77), Kokott AG notes the public benefits from the transport of oil, and creates demand, and the state permits the regulatory activity [142].

[83] An earlier version was at stake in the case, see now Directive 2008/98/EC on waste and repealing certain Directives ('Waste Framework Directive') [2008] OJ L312/3, Art 14. The current version seems to grant greater discretion to the Member States in respect of producers of products.

[84] *Mesquer* (n 77) [78].

[85] Ibid [82].

[86] Directive 2004/35/EC on environmental liability with regard to the prevention and remedying of environmental damage ('Environmental Liability Directive') [2004] OJ L143/56, Art 1.

[87] Case C-378/08 *Raffinerie Mediterranee v Ministero dello sviluppo economico* [2010] ECR I-1919.

the Directive.[88] Otherwise, national law applies. Kokott AG also emphasised the causal link between damage and the 'polluter' who pays. The Directive explicitly requires causal links to be established, so we should perhaps not read too much into this. But we might note that Kokott AG accepted that 'it is not possible to derive from the "polluter pays principle" an absolute prohibition on imposing the costs of remedying environmental damage on parties other than polluters', since that would mean simply ignoring pollution when polluters cannot be identified, which would not be consistent with achieving a high level of environmental protection.[89]

Conclusions

It is difficult to draw general conclusions about the role of the environmental principles as a whole, since they pose diverse challenges and their significance varies. We can conclude that the courts are happy to engage with the environmental principles, which, as is apparent from the discussion here, are routinely used in the interpretation of EU environmental law. Their place in Article 191 TFEU makes them binding on the EU legislature, although review is limited: according to Kokott AG, a balance has to be struck between the different principles and objectives contained in the environment Title, and the criteria for the application of any one of them is in any event complex.[90] The precautionary principle at least has most commonly been used to defend regulatory action by the EU institutions.[91] The courts more generally leave a broad margin of discretion to the EU institutions, quashing a decision only when it is 'vitiated by a manifest error or a misuse of power or whether the Community institutions clearly exceeded the bounds of their discretion'.[92] We return to the nature and intensity of judicial review in chapter two. But it is clear that whilst the courts assert a high level of deference, EU decisions can in theory be struck down on the basis of the principles.[93] The principles are also binding on the Member States when they implement EU law.[94] Like the EU administration, the Member States use the principles in defence,[95] as well as having to defend their action against the principles.[96]

---

[88] Ibid [57].
[89] Ibid [112] (Kokott AG).
[90] *Mesquer* (n 77) [125], (Kokott AG).
[91] *Pfizer* (n 23).
[92] Ibid [166]; similar language is used in *Mesquer* (n 77) [25].
[93] *Sweden (Paraquat)* (n 38).
[94] On which see *Raffinerie* (n 87) [46].
[95] *Denmark* (n 33).
[96] *Waddenzee Cockle Fishers* (n 58).

Article 192: Decision-Making on the Environment

Environmental measures are subject to the 'ordinary legislative procedure', which requires the 'joint adoption' of legislation by the European Parliament and Council.[97] The Council acts by qualified majority. By way of exception, some areas are subject to the 'special legislative procedure', which requires unanimity in Council, subject to mere consultation with Parliament.[98] These areas are 'provisions primarily of a fiscal nature'; 'measures affecting: town and country planning, quantitative management of water resources …, land use, with the exception of waste management' and 'measures significantly affecting a Member State's choice between different energy sources and the general structure of its energy supply'. The line between measures subject to the ordinary and the special procedure is not always easily drawn,[99] and has rarely been challenged before the Court. The Court has however had the opportunity to interpret the 'quantitative management of water resources', which it approached both purposively and restrictively. When quantitative elements are only incidental, the measure does not fall under the exception.[100]

These areas are all sensitive to the Member States. Tax policy (measures of a fiscal nature) for example, goes to the heart of national sovereignty, and taxation and expenditure policies form central elements of national political debate. The requirement for unanimity makes the use of environmental taxation, discussed in chapter four, very difficult for the EU. The idea of an EU carbon tax was first proposed by the Commission in 1992, but in the face of severe opposition from some Member States, only a very weak Directive, which was full of exceptions, could eventually be agreed in 2003.[101] The most persistent resistance came from the UK and Spain, on sovereignty and development grounds respectively.[102] The EU emissions trading system, discussed in chapter six below, and now a centrepiece of EU climate change mitigation law, was adopted at least in part because of these institutional barriers to the adoption of a carbon tax. A new Directive was proposed by the Commission, at the request of the Council, in 2011. This proposal would set minimum tax levels to reflect both CO_2 levels and energy content.[103] The different interests of the Member States, and their reluctance to

---

[97] Art 289 TFEU.

[98] They can be moved to the 'ordinary procedure' by unanimity.

[99] See the discussion in JH Jans and HHB Vedder, *European Environmental Law: After Lisbon* (Groningen, Europa Law Publishing, 2012) 59–64.

[100] Case C-36/98 *Spain v Council* [2001] ECR I-779.

[101] Directive 2003/96/EC Restructuring the Community framework for the taxation of energy products and electricity [2003] OJ L283/51; European Commission, 'Proposal for a Council Directive Introducing a Tax on Carbon Dioxide Emissions and Energy' COM (1992) 226 final.

[102] A Jordan et al, 'European Governance and the Transfer of 'New' Environmental Policy Instruments (NEPIs) in the European Union' (2003) 81 *Public Administration* 555, 566.

[103] European Commission, 'Proposal for a Council Directive Amending Directive 2003/96/EC Restructuring the Community Framework for the Taxation of Energy Products and Electricity' COM (2011) 169.

disrupt significantly their own tax structure, makes unanimity on a challenging minimum rate problematic. The Commission's proposal that Member States respect the Directive's differential between the minimum rates for different forms of fuel is especially controversial with the Member States.[104]

Article 193: National Autonomy on the Environment

If the EU has not acted in an area, the Member States are able to pursue their own policy, subject to complying with basic internal market law, including the principle of free movement of goods contained in Article 34 TFEU. Environmental requirements can easily interfere with the free movement of goods. But as discussed in chapter 10 below, Member States are allowed to pursue particular public objectives, including environmental protection, under Article 36 TFEU or the 'mandatory requirements' doctrine, provided that their measures are proportionate. After EU level action has been taken, the Member States are no longer free to rely on Article 36 or the mandatory requirements doctrine to justify environmental protection measures. Safeguard clauses are included in legislation agreed under the environment Title 'where appropriate', and allow a Member State 'to take provisional measures, for non-economic environmental reasons'.[105] Further, EU action under the environment Title provides for only a minimum level of environmental protection common to the Member States, and 'shall not prevent any Member State from maintaining or introducing more stringent protective measures.' These 'more stringent measures' must be compatible with the rules of the Treaty, including the free movement rules.[106] The Treaty also requires the Member State to notify its more stringent measures to the Commission, although their validity is not conditional on this.[107]

In *Deponiezweckverband Eiterköpfe v Land Rheinland-Pfalz*, an operator of a landfill site challenged German measures on waste that were more stringent than the Landfill Directive:[108] for example, the Directive required Member States to reduce the amount of certain wastes going to landfill by a specified proportion, by particular dates; the German legislation required *lower* amounts by *earlier* dates. The ECJ confirmed that EU law does 'not seek to effect complete harmonisation in the area of the environment'.[109] To fall within Article 193, the 'more stringent' measures must 'follow the same policy of protecting the environment as the

---

[104] And has been rejected by the Council, see Press Release 3178th Council Meeting, Economic and Financial Affairs PRES/12/281. Many Member States currently provide favourable tax treatment for diesel. Friends of Europe, *Reforming Europe's Energy Taxation* (2012) provides a useful review of some of the different positions.

[105] Art 191(2) TFEU. Safeguard clauses are discussed in ch 10, see also Art 114(10) TFEU.

[106] Art 193 TFEU.

[107] Case C-2/10 *Azienda Agro-Zootecnica Franchini Sarl v Regione Puglia* [2011] ECR I-6561.

[108] Directive 1999/31/EC on the landfill of waste ('Landfill Directive') [1999] OJ L182/1.

[109] Case C-6/03 *Deponiezweckverband Eiterköpfe v Land Rheinland-Pfalz* [2005] ECR I-2753 [27].

Directive does'.[110] Generally, this will be obvious, but the potential difficulty is brought out by a challenge to Italian legislation that prohibited the building of wind farms within 200 metres of a site protected under the Habitats Directive.[111] The Habitats Directive provides a process for their assessment and evaluation of development, but does not impose a blanket ban on particular types of development. The Court found the Italian measure to be more protective than the Habitats Directive. It did not, however, consider the possibly competing environmental objective of climate change mitigation, other than finding there to be no breach of EU legislation on renewable energy.[112] The diverse values at stake in environmental protection means that the straightforward identification of 'more stringent' requirements cannot be taken for granted. Diverse governance approaches raise similar questions. For example, whether setting regulatory limits for carbon emissions is a 'more stringent' way of achieving climate change objectives than EU emissions trading, or actually undermines the EU legislation, is discussed briefly in chapter six.

Whether environmental measures should be based on internal market provisions or what is now Article 193 was controversial before the Maastricht Treaty because they relied on different decision-making processes, as discussed above. Both now use the ordinary legislative procedure, but disagreement remains.[113] Most importantly for current purposes,[114] the internal market and environment Titles apply different conditions to national freedom to regulate after the EU has taken action.[115] The conditions applied under Article 114 TFEU (to which chapter 10 returns), are stricter than those applied under Article 193. The identification of the correct legal base is legally and politically complex, and not always dealt with consistently.[116] The Court insists that choice of legal basis should be based on 'objective factors'.[117] If the legislation has a single 'main or predominant purpose', that should provide the legal base.[118] If, however, the Union's power is to be found in more than one Treaty provision, a dual legal basis may be required, and the procedures relating to both should be satisfied.[119] More than one legal base is

---

[110]   Ibid [41].

[111]   Habitats Directive (n 59).

[112]   Directive 2009/28/EC on the promotion of the use of energy from renewable sources [2009] OJ L140 52/16, discussed in ch 6.

[113]   N de Sadeleer, 'Environmental Governance and the Legal Bases Conundrum' [2012] *Yearbook of European Law* 1; K St Clair Bradley, 'Powers and Procedures in the EU Constitution: Legal Bases and the Court' in P Craig and G de Búrca (eds), *The Evolution of EU Law* (Oxford, Oxford University Press, 2011).

[114]   Institutional powers in the negotiation of international agreements also vary depending on choice of legal basis, de Sadeleer, ibid.

[115]   See eg J Scott, 'The Multi-Level Governance of Climate Change' in Craig and de Búrca (n 113) on the changed legal basis for Regulation 443/2009/EC setting emission performance standards for new passenger cars [2009] OJ L140/1.

[116]   St Clair Bradley (n 113).

[117]   Case 45/86 *Commission v Council* [1987] ECR 1493 [11].

[118]   Case C-178/03 *Commission v Parliament and Council* [2006] ECR I-107 [42].

[119]   St Clair Bradley (n 113).

sometimes used in the environmental arena. This creates obvious problems, but national autonomy can depend on whether the particular issue being tackled is related to the internal market or to environmental protection.[120]

THE CONTEXT FOR EU ACTION ON THE ENVIRONMENT

The language of crisis may be overused at the moment, and the EU was at the beginning of a constitutional crisis,[121] and had not long emerged from a corruption crisis,[122] when the first edition of this book was published in 2005. The economic and fiscal crisis beginning in 2008, however, cannot be ignored. It seemed, for a moment, as if the recession beginning in 2008 might be a crisis for 'business as usual' economic capitalism, allowing the reorientation of society in a more environmentally benign direction. The crisis might for example have prompted a reconsideration of materialistic values, an end to the search for perpetual economic growth, a re-tooling of the economy through 'green' stimulus measures, or even simply an end to constant de-regulatory pressure, recognising the importance of a strong public sector regulation to temper the self-interest of business. None of that has really happened. There may be opportunities for environmental measures that contribute to economic growth, and we return to the 'green economy' theme in chapter three. But times of economic hardship are commonly hard times for environmental protection, and the post-2008 recession is no exception. Arguing for policies that are perceived to be a cost to the economy (at least in the short term) is much more difficult when economic growth is at the top of a political agenda dominated by economic hardship. The potential negative effects of the economic crisis on environmental policy are probably compounded by a shift in electoral politics around the EU since the mid-2000s from the centre-left to the centre-right.[123] The centre-right tends to be less sympathetic to environmental measures (although sometimes the disagreement may be on how, rather than whether, to protect the environment).

Alongside its economic challenges, the EU faces simultaneous political challenges. The 'permissive consensus' that has allowed the EU to be pursued as an elite project far from public scrutiny for so many years has been replaced by a 'constraining dissensus'.[124] The crisis in the Eurozone has led for the first time to serious talk of the exit of a Member State. Low turnout at European Parliament

---

[120]   De Sadeleer (n 113); Jans and Vedder (n 99) 78.

[121]   Provoked by referenda rejecting the Constitutional Treaty in 2005.

[122]   Committee of Independent Experts, *Allegations Regarding Fraud, Mismanagement and Nepotism in the European Commission* (1999) led to the resignation of the entire Commission in 1999.

[123]   C Burns, N Carter and N Worsfold, 'Enlargement and the Environment: The Changing Behaviour of the European Parliament' (2012) 50 *Journal of Common Market Studies* 54.

[124]   L Hooghe and G Marks, 'A Post-Functionalist Theory of European Integration: From Permissive Consensus to Constraining Dissensus (2008) 39 *British Journal of Political Science* 1, dating the change from the early 1990s.

elections suggests a worrying lack of engagement with European integration.[125] In addition, Euro-sceptic views around Europe are significant,[126] whether due to the economic crisis or not.[127] Close to home, for me, we have the promise (or threat) from the UK Prime Minister to 'renegotiate' the treaties and hold a referendum on continued EU membership.[128] But equally, deeper integration (at least for Eurozone members) is a plausible outcome of the financial crisis, which has demonstrated the ever more profound interdependence between the Member States.

So these may be interesting times for EU environmental lawyers. Mainstream political rhetoric in the UK increasingly emphasises a 'trade-only' role for the EU.[129] But it is often argued that collective EU action on the environment contributes to the forging of connections between the EU and its citizens, arguably increasing its significance at times like this. EU environmental action is popular, enjoying consistently high levels of support from EU publics.[130]

Although EU *competence* on the environment is settled by the Treaty (at least for now), *when* the EU should act is not self-evident. 'Subsidiarity', first introduced into the new environment Title of the Treaty in the SEA, before being 'promoted' to a general principle by the Maastricht Treaty, is supposed to resolve this:

> Under the principle of subsidiarity, in areas which do not fall within its exclusive competence, the Union shall act only if and in so far as the objectives of the proposed action cannot be sufficiently achieved by the Member States, either at central level or at regional and local level, but can rather, by reason of the scale or effects of the proposed action, be better achieved at Union level.[131]

The principle of subsidiarity is not easy to apply.[132] The least problematic justification for EU action on the environment is probably the transboundary effects of pollution or environmental degradation. Environmental problems do not stop at national borders, and common action has an obvious rationale in this context. Economic rationales are equally important.[133] In particular, national measures to

---

[125] A Jordan and C Adelle, 'Preface' in A Jordan and C Adelle (eds), *Environmental Policy in the EU: Actors, Institutions and Processes* (Abingdon, Routledge, 2012).

[126] For a discussion of the variety of Euro-scepticism (and a discussion of the contentious line between criticism of the EU and Euro-scepticism), see the Special Issue (2013) 51(1) *Journal of Common Market Studies*.

[127] F Serrichio, M Tsakatika and L Quaglia, 'Euroscepticism and the Global Financial Crisis' (2013) 51 *Journal of Common Market Studies* 51 argue that the financial crisis is not a decisive factor. Certainly, Euro-scepticism is not a post-2008 phenomenon, see eg S Usherwood and N Startin, 'Euroscepticism as a Persistent Phenomenon' (2013) 51 *Journal of Common Market Studies* 1.

[128] On the 'balance of competences' review, see www.gov.uk/review-of-the-balance-of-competences.

[129] This is especially part of British Conservative Euro-scepticism, but Green Party Euro-scepticism, and some Euro-scepticism from the left, would point in the other direction, criticising the trade focus and urging a collective approach to environmental or social matters.

[130] See A Jordan, 'The Environmental Case for Europe: Britain's European Environmental Policy' CSERGE Working Paper EDM 06/11. A Lenschow and C Sprungk, 'The Myth of a Green Europe' (2010) 48 *Journal of Common Market Studies* 133 see 'Green Europe' as something like a foundational myth.

[131] Art 5 TFEU. Environmental competence is shared.

[132] P Craig, 'Subsidiarity: A Political and Legal Analysis' (2012) 50 *Journal of Common Market Studies* 72.

[133] N de Sadeleer, 'Principle of Subsidiarity and the EU Environmental Policy' (2012) 9 *Journal of European Environment and Planning Law* 63.

protect the environment may interfere with the free movement of goods, and so pose a challenge to the internal market. This is most obvious if the measures apply to goods (for example emissions standards for cars). But the argument that competition can be distorted by the higher costs of operating in a state that applies very stringent environmental standards to, for example, manufacturing, whilst controversial, is well-established in the EU, as discussed above.[134] An important related justification for EU level action is the 'race to the bottom' argument. This makes two assumptions: first, that industry migrates to areas with laxer environmental standards in order to gain a competitive advantage; secondly, that states compete for economic investment in part through environmental regulation, leading to a ratcheting down of environmental standards. The empirical work on regulatory competition between states does not provide clear evidence either that they compete on environmental protection, or whether any race is to the top or the bottom.[135] Nevertheless, avoiding a race to the bottom is a consistent rationale for EU environmental policy.[136]

But when environmental objectives can be 'better' achieved' at EU level, as per Article 5, is not susceptible to a straightforward technical answer. The relationship between the centre and the Member States (and local and regional authorities) is more complex than this suggestion that one level of regulation is 'better' than another, or indeed that they can possibly act in isolation.[137] The difficulty of separating national and EU authority will be seen at many points in this book. The Treaty *Protocol on the Application of the Principles of Subsidiarity and Proportionality* enhances political control of subsidiarity by providing procedures by which national parliamentarians can raise concerns with the EU institutions.[138] The Commission has withdrawn one of its proposals (although denying a breach of subsidiarity), following reasoned opinions from national parliaments.[139] The Protocol requires 'a detailed statement' on subsidiarity and proportionality to accompany draft legislation, substantiating the case for EU action 'by qualitative and, wherever possible, quantitative indicators'. This increasingly detailed information enhances opportunities for political scrutiny of subsidiarity, including by national parliaments.[140] It is possible that it will also enable enhanced judicial

---

[134] Above nn 6–9.

[135] See K Holzinger and T Sommerer, '"Race to the Bottom" or "Race to Brussels"? Environmental Competition in Europe' (2011) 49 *Journal of Common Market Studies* 315; V Heyvaert, 'Regulatory Competition—Accounting for the Transnational Dimension of Environmental Regulation' (2013) 25 *Journal of Environmental Law* 1 on continued competition after EU regulation.

[136] Eg Holzinger and Sommerer, ibid.

[137] De Sadeleer (n 133); on the role of how, as well as whether, to regulate, see R Schütze, 'Subsidiarity After Lisbon: Reinforcing the Safeguards of Federalism?' (2009) 68 *Cambridge Law Journal* 525.

[138] Protocol No 2 to the TFEU, *on the Application of the Principles of Subsidiarity and Proportionality*; Schütze, ibid.

[139] See the letters to parliaments, ec.europa.eu/dgs/secretariat_general/relations/relations_other/npo/letter_to_nal_parl_en.htm; discussed in European Commission, *Annual Report 2011 on Relations Between the European Commission and National Parliaments* COM (2012) 375 final.

[140] The impact assessment of Commission proposals is also expected to provide 'a proper justification of EU action on grounds of subsidiarity', European Commission, *Impact Assessment Guidelines* SEC (2009) 92, 8, discussed further in ch 2.

scrutiny.[141] There has so far been limited judicial intervention on subsidiarity. Craig calculates that there have only been 10 'real' subsidiarity challenges before the ECJ in 20 years, and whilst the Court has been willing to hear arguments on subsidiarity, it has taken an approach that is largely deferential to institutions' claims.[142]

THE EU CHARTER ON FUNDAMENTAL RIGHTS

There is a longstanding debate about whether human or fundamental rights 'help or hinder' environmental protection.[143] Necessarily anthropocentric and individualised, traditional approaches to *human* rights provide only contingent protection of collective interests in the environment, or of the environment itself. Human rights might even 'hinder' environmental protection, for example if the right to privacy limits our ability to scrutinise environmental decision-making.[144] There may also be concern that judicial involvement on a case by case basis, at the behest of those powerful individuals best able to use the courts, could interfere with rational priority setting.[145] However, the extreme nature of some of the facts brought, as a final resort, before the European Court of Human Rights (ECtHR) suggests that the protection of the environment through human rights can in some cases be important. And rights can have an important life beyond the courts,[146] adding a certain weight to environmental values, in a debate that frequently favours economic interests. The blatantly catastrophic threats of climate change have given a new impetus to the discussion of environmental rights.[147] And the adoption of the CFR in 2000 makes rights an important part of EU environmental law.

Environmental rights are conventionally divided into substantive rights to environmental quality, and procedural rights. Procedural rights dominate in EU

---

[141] A Alemanno, 'The Better Regulation Initiative at the Judicial Gate: A Trojan Horse within the Commission's Walls or the Way Forward?' (2009) 15 *European Law Journal* 382; K Lenaerts, 'The European Court of Justice and Process-Oriented Review' (2012) 31 *Yearbook of European Law* 3, especially the discussion of the use of the impact assessment in Case C-58/08 R *(on the application of Vodafone) v Secretary of State for Business, Enterprise and Regulatory Reform* [2010] ECR I-4999.

[142] Craig (n 132).

[143] C Gearty, 'Do Human Rights Help or Hinder Environmental Protection?' (2010) 1 *Journal of Human Rights and the Environment* 7.

[144] See ch 5. Property rights have been significant in the US, eg JL Sax, 'Takings, Private Property and Public Rights' (1971) 81 *Yale Law Journal* 149.

[145] This is enormously contentious, but see eg on rights to health, OL Motta Ferraz, 'Harming the Poor through Social Rights Litigation: Lessons from Brazil' (2010–11) 89 *Texas Law Review* 1643; M Gallanter, 'Why the "Haves" Come out Ahead: Speculations on the Limits of Legal Change' (1974) 9 *Law and Society Review* 95.

[146] Gearty (n 143); O Pedersen, 'European Environmental Human Rights and Environmental Rights: A Long Time Coming?' (2008) 21 *Georgetown International Environmental Law Review* 73.

[147] Eg S Caney, 'Cosmopolitan Justice, Rights and Global Climate Change' (2006) 19 *Canadian Journal of Law and Jurisprudence* 255; S Humphreys (ed), *Human Rights and Climate Change* (Cambridge, Cambridge University Press, 2010).

environmental law and globally.[148] Rights are often seen as central to citizenship, and procedural rights are often associated with environmental citizenship,[149] since an active, political participatory approach has been a common theme.[150] Environmental procedural rights (access to environmental information, rights to participate in environmental decision-making, and access to justice in environmental matters) are directly provided in many pieces of EU legislation, and are discussed in chapters seven and eight especially. Rights to information, to participate (and to protest) and to courts are fundamental underpinnings of any environmental right,[151] closely connected to substance. Bot AG, for example, describes the procedural rights of strategic environmental assessment as 'designed to guarantee everyone the right to live in an environment suitable for ensuring their health and well-being';[152] the procedural Aarhus Convention also 'recognises' in its recitals that 'every person has the right to live in an environment adequate to his or her health and well-being'.[153]

In the environmental sphere, there is a particular concern to match rights with duties.[154] The Preamble to the CFR provides that 'enjoyment of these rights entails responsibilities and duties with regard to other parties, the human community and to future generations'.[155] These duties might include the duty to take political action for environmental protection, 'the duty to protect and improve the quality of the environment by expressing concerns and by assisting the authorities responsible for preparing plans'.[156]

---

[148] A Boyle, 'Human Rights and the Environment: Where Next?' (2012) 23 *European Journal of International Law* 613. On the limits of procedure, see D Shelton, 'Developing Substantive Environmental Rights' (2010) 1 *Journal of Human Rights and the Environment* 89.

[149] A Dobson, *Citizenship and the Environment* (Oxford, Oxford University Press, 2003). On the place of republican, cosmopolitan or liberal citizenship, see respectively eg C Hilson, 'EU Environmental Solidarity and the Ecological Consumer: Towards a Republican Citizenship' in M Ross and Y Borgmann-Prebil (eds), *Promoting Solidarity in the European Union* (Oxford, Oxford University Press, 2010); Dobson, ibid; DR Bell, 'Liberal Environmental Citizenship' (2005) 14 *Environmental Politics* 179.

[150] G Smith, 'Green Citizenship and the Social Economy' (2005) 14 *Environmental Politics* 273. A less political and public form of citizenship focuses on 'virtue' in 'private' decision-making, for example in consumption choices. See all of Smith, Dobson and Hilson, ibid; Bell, ibid, disagrees.

[151] Gearty (n 143); also on the limited protection of environmental protest before the ECtHR. On the potential limits imposed on protest by law, see eg L Finchett-Maddock, 'Responding to the Private Regulation of Dissent: Climate Change Action, Popular Justice and the Right to Protest' (2013) 25 *Journal of Environmental Law* 293.

[152] Case C-474/10 *Department of the Environment for Northern Ireland v Seaport (NI) Ltd* not yet reported in the European Court Reports [27], citing the environment Title and the CFR.

[153] United Nations Economic Commission for Europe (UNECE) Convention on Access to Information, Public Participation in Decision-making and Access to Justice in Environmental Matters (1998) 38 ILM 517 (1999).

[154] Dobson (n 149).

[155] See also the Aarhus Convention recitals (n 153). On future generations and sustainable development, see ch 3.

[156] *Seaport* (n 152) [28] (Bot AG).

The CFR was accorded 'the same legal value as the Treaties' by the Lisbon Treaty in 2009,[157] and so binds the EU institutions, and the Member States when they implement EU law.[158] Article 37 CFR, entitled 'Environmental protection', provides that 'A high level of environmental protection and the improvement of the quality of the environment must be integrated into the policies of the Union and assured in accordance with the principle of sustainable development'.[159] The language is very similar to the environmental integration principle in Article 11 TFEU, and to the language of Article 3(3) TEU (the EU 'shall work for the sustainable development of Europe ... aiming at ... a high level of protection and improvement of the quality of the environment), both discussed in chapter three. Article 37 is not framed in terms of 'rights' at all, but is a 'principle',[160] so that according to the Charter is 'judicially cognisable' only in the interpretation of acts that implement it;[161] although this may not be limited to acts that deliberately and expressly implement Article 37.[162]

Given its similarity to existing language, and its status as a principle, it seems unlikely that Article 37 CFR will have a dramatic effect on environmental law. Its inclusion in the Charter is nevertheless important, given that other (including economic) interests enjoy any status gained by inclusion. Nor is Article 37 the limit of the Charter's environmental implications. The creation of justiciable rights to participate in environmental decision-making, mentioned above, directly 'greens' civil and political rights.[163] Other rights contained in the Charter may also be 'greened'. Although the European Convention for the Protection of Human Rights (ECHR) contains no right (or even reference) to environmental quality, the ECtHR has applied other rights, in particular the Article 8 right to respect for the home and private and family life, to environmental cases, requiring positive protective action from governments to control private sector pollution.[164] Rights 'which correspond to rights guaranteed' by the ECHR, shall be given the same 'meaning and scope' as in the ECHR (although EU law can provide 'more

---

[157] Art 6(1) TEU.

[158] Art 51(1) CFR. *Protocol on the Application of the Charter of Fundamental Rights of the European Union to Poland and to the United Kingdom* provides that the CFR does not create justiciable rights in Poland or the UK; see Craig (n 36) 487–90.

[159] Title IV, entitled 'Solidarity', and including, eg, fair and just working conditions, health care and consumer protection.

[160] G Marín Durán and E Morgera, 'Commentary on Article 37 of the EU Charter of Fundamental Rights—Environmental Protection' in S Peers et al (eds), *EU Charter of Fundamental Rights: A Commentary* (Oxford, Hart Publishing, 2013).

[161] Art 52(5) CFR.

[162] Craig (n 36) 470–71, envisages the principles being used in a similar way to the precautionary principle.

[163] In the language of A Boyle, *Human Rights and the Environment: A Reassessment* (United Nations Environment Programme (UNEP), 2010), (2008) 18 *Fordham Environmental Law Review* 471.

[164] Eg *Lopez Ostra v Spain* (1994) 20 EHRR 277; *Guerra v Italy* (1998) 26 EHRR 357; *Taskin v Turkey* (2006) 42 EHRR 50. On the environmental application of Art 6 ECHR (right to a court), see Pederson (n 146). On Art 2, the right to life, see eg *Oneryildiz v Turkey* (2005) 41 EHRR 20.

extensive protection').[165] A right to respect for the home and private and family life also appears in the CFR.[166]

Whilst the right to home and family life can be affected even without seriously endangering health under the ECHR, the level of pollution has to meet a minimum threshold, described in *Fadeyeva v Russia* as 'relative' and depending on 'all the circumstances of the case, such as the intensity and duration of the nuisance, its physical or mental effects'. There can be no claim if 'the detriment ... was negligible in comparison to the environmental hazards inherent to life in every modern city'.[167] The very severe pollution in *Fadayeva*, a case brought by residents living near the largest iron smelter in Russia, in an area excluded from human habitation under Russian law, did fall under Article 8. Attention to the environment is however contingent on the impact of the environmental harm on the home. In *Kyrtatos v Greece*, for example, the applicants were unable to establish that damage to the 'birds and other protected species' through development of a protected wetland, affected their private and family life.[168]

Article 8 ECHR is not absolute, but provides that any interference with the right must be 'in accordance with the law and ... necessary in a democratic society' to protect competing interests 'of national security, public safety or the economic well-being of the country, for the prevention of disorder or crime, for the protection of health or morals, or for the protection of the rights and freedoms of others'; the CFR also allows for such derogations.[169] The ECtHR asks whether the state has struck a fair balance between the individuals' rights and the competing, often economic, interests. Particular procedural steps may be required, including the provision of environmental information to those exposed to hazardous activities.[170] The ECtHR is concerned that processes be fair and pay adequate attention to the individual affected,[171] requiring in some cases a process of decision-making

---

[165] Art 52(3). Art 6 TEU provides for the EU to accede to the ECHR.

[166] Art 7, referred to in Case C-120/10 *European Air Transport SA v Collège d'environnement de la Région de Bruxelles-Capitale* [2011] ECR I-7865 (Cruz Villalón AG); on airport noise before the ECtHR see *Hatton v UK* (2003) 37 EHRR 28.

[167] *Fadeyeva v Russia* (2007) 45 EHRR 10 [69]. *Hardy v UK* (2012) 55 EHRR 28 applied the same approach to the risk of accidents associated with a development for the storage of liquid natural gas at Milford Haven [198].

[168] *Kyrtatos v Greece* (2005) 40 EHRR 16 [53]. Note the strange comment that 'it might have been otherwise' if the claim had been in respect of 'the destruction of a forest area in the vicinity of the applicants' house' [53], perhaps suggesting that some forms of natural environment (forests) are more closely connected to the home than others (swamps). There was a breach of Art 6 ECHR, since domestic rights and domestic court judgments had not been implemented.

[169] Art 52(1) CFR: 'any limitation on the exercise of the rights and freedoms recognised by this Charter must be provided for by law and respect the essence of those rights and freedoms. Subject to the principle of proportionality, limitations may be made only if they are necessary and genuinely meet objectives of general interest recognised by the Union or the need to protect the rights and freedoms of others.'

[170] Eg in *Guerra* (n 164). See C Hilson, 'Risk and the European Convention on Human Rights: Towards a New Approach' (2008–2009) 11 *Cambridge Yearbook of European Legal Studies* 353.

[171] Eg *Hardy v UK* (n 167) [219], *Taskin* (n 164) [118].

that sounds very like a form of environmental assessment.[172] It has said that the state must 'justify, using detailed and rigorous data, a situation in which certain individuals bear a heavy burden on behalf of the rest of the community'.[173] Failure to comply with domestic law, whilst not decisive, can be important.[174]

The ECtHR approach to environmental rights places a heavy emphasis on procedural protections.[175] One of the reasons for linking environmental rights with procedure is the controversy around appropriate levels of environmental quality.[176] In particular, the definition of environmental quality involves prioritisation between different environmental goods (such as local amenity or global climate), and between environmental protection and other public goods (including economic growth). The difficulty of defining appropriate levels of environmental quality also explains the frequent reliance on domestic law (and international norms such as World Health Organisation (WHO) or United Nations Environment Programme (UNEP) standards[177]) by the ECtHR. The ECJ is unlikely to be any more enthusiastic than the ECtHR for second-guessing levels of environmental protection set by the legislature.

Neither the Charter nor the ECHR have anything to say on the possibility of environmental rights that take the form of legal rights for 'forests, oceans, rivers', the environment generally,[178] applying independently of effects on human beings. In the classic article on the subject, Christopher Stone forcefully reminds us that 'each time there is a movement to confer rights onto some new "entity", the proposal is bound to sound odd or frightening or laughable'.[179] Without wanting to engage in this very big debate, which is less practically significant in the EU than the pursuit of procedural rights, the rights granted to environmental interest groups in the EU, discussed in chapters seven and eight, do begin to grant rights to nature in the way explored by Stone. But they are far from his proposed 'radical new conception of man's relationship to the rest of nature'.[180] EU environmental law is largely, if not overwhelmingly, anthropocentric.[181]

The Charter indicates the impossibility of ignoring the question of environmental rights, whilst its limits simultaneously also remind us how controversial explicit 'rights' to environmental quality remain. It is likely that the implementation

---

[172] *Taskin*, ibid [119].

[173] *Fadeyeva* (n 167) [128].

[174] *Fadeyeva*, ibid [99]; although this is not a requirement, the absence of 'domestic irregularity' was a feature in *Hatton* (n 166).

[175] On references to the Aarhus Convention by the ECtHR, see Hilson (n 170).

[176] Also Boyle (n 148).

[177] Shelton (n 148).

[178] CD Stone, 'Should Trees Have Standing? Toward Legal Rights for Natural Objects' (1972) 45 *Southern California Law Review* 450, 456.

[179] Ibid 455, having taken the reader through the 'unthinkability' of extending rights to, eg corporations, women, children, individuals from minority ethnic groups. See also Special Issue (2012) 3 *Journal of Human Rights and the Environment*.

[180] Stone, ibid 495.

[181] For an examination of the 'anthropocentrism' critique of environmental rights, see C Redgwell, 'Life, the Universe and Everything: A Critique of Anthropocentric Rights' in A Boyle and M Anderson (eds), *Human Rights Approaches to Environmental Protection* (Oxford, Oxford University Press, 1996).

of procedural rights through 'ordinary' EU legislation will be more important for environmental protection than Article 37 of the Charter.

CONCLUSIONS

The EU now possesses a vast and diverse body of environmental law. The slightly haphazard development of law and policy through the decades is not surprising, given the range of pressures and influences.[182] Environmental law addresses a vast range of issues, and has responded to unexpected crises, to diverse national priorities and to emerging environmental problems. Changes within the EU institutions, such as the election of Green Members of the European Parliament within an increasingly powerful European Parliament during the 1980s, have undoubtedly influenced the environmental agenda.[183] It is difficult to be sure whether enlargement of the EU dampened enthusiasm for environmental protection (as widely anticipated), given all the other changes that have taken place over the past decade.[184] It also remains to be seen how the current economic crisis will affect environmental law. The ebb and flow of both a de-regulatory economic agenda and public interest in environmental protection also have their effects.

Environmental protection finds its place among other public goods, and it would be surprising, and not necessarily desirable, to find legislation pursuing an ecological ethic, without any concern for other human (including economic) endeavours.[185] Environmental law must also live within more established sub-disciplines in EU law, including internal market and administrative law. Whilst environmental law influences those 'sub-disciplines', it also has to accommodate itself within them.

The objectives and principles contained in the Treaty should contribute to the coherence of EU environmental decision-making, and provide a firm constitutional basis for EU environmental law.[186] It seems unlikely that the CFR will add much to that, but the development of environmental law in the EU has been constantly surprising. There is however no avoiding diverse understandings of the environment, and what it means to protect it. These are questions that are rarely amenable to solution by improved understanding of the facts, but are essentially political. As such, the importance of questions of process in environmental law is not surprising, and that is where the next chapter turns.

---

[182] E Fisher et al, 'Maturity and Methodology: Starting a Debate about Environmental Law Scholarship' (2009) 21 *Journal of European Law* 213.

[183] D Chalmers, 'Inhabitants in the Field of EC Environmental Law' in Craig and de Búrca (eds), *The Evolution of EU Law* (Oxford, Oxford University Press, 1999).

[184] See the discussion in Burns, Carter and Worsfold (n 123).

[185] TS Aagaard, 'Environmental Law as a Legal Field: An Inquiry in Legal Taxonomy' (2010) 95 *Cornell Law Review* 221 argues that 'trade-offs' are inherent to, rather than a threat to, environmental law.

[186] The lack of which in the US is described as contributing to environmental law's 'legitimacy problems', AD Tarlock, 'Is There a There There in Environmental Law?' (2004) 19 *Journal of Land Use and Environmental Law* 213.

2

EU Environmental Decision-Making: Experts, Politics and Institutions

INTRODUCTION

THIS CHAPTER EXPLORES the approach to environmental administrative decision-making in the EU, with the aim of setting the scene for more detailed discussions in later chapters. I begin with an exploration of two forms of expertise which play a significant role in EU environmental law: risk assessment and cost benefit analysis (CBA). Without wishing to deny the potentially important contributions of these techniques to environmental governance, we must also explore their fragility. In particular, it is now very widely recognised that the 'facts' alone cannot provide an authoritative basis for decision-making, especially if (as will often be the case) either values are contested or the facts are unclear. In those circumstances, 'experts' have no monopoly on 'good judgment', and a good political process is necessary for a decision to be taken.

Although there is, as I hope will become clear, no crude bright line between expertise and politics,[1] the tension between these two modes of reasoning is a key issue in EU environmental law, and in this book. The EU's primary response to the importance of both facts and values to its decisions has been to institutionalise a separation between the provision of expertise and political responsibility for decisions. After introducing risk assessment and CBA, this chapter examines that division, before turning to the two sources of expertise and political legitimacy (respectively) that recur most frequently in this book: agencies, and 'comitology'. To pre-empt a little, comitology is the system by which Member States (in 'committee') are able to contribute to the Commission's implementation of administrative decisions in the EU. The final section of this chapter explores what might qualify as 'good' reasons for a decision; notwithstanding the acceptance that final decisions have political or normative aspects, they are still often explained on a largely, if not wholly, technical basis.

---

[1] Or science and democracy, E Fisher, *Risk Regulation and Administrative Constitutionalism* (Oxford, Hart Publishing, 2007).

RISK ASSESSMENT AND COST BENEFIT ANALYSIS

This section examines the complexities of two, closely related[2] techniques of decision-making: risk assessment and CBA. I provide only a simple outline here, and these techniques are not only complex, but are also much debated within the disciplines. Nor of course do these two techniques exhaust expert contributions to decision-making. The discussion here should be seen simply as indicative of the difficulties that can arise when technical expertise is privileged within a decision-making process.

Risk assessment and CBA in their various forms are called on at all stages of EU environmental law and governance. Although they are not mandatory, one or both technique is likely to play a part in 'impact assessment' (IA), a process described by the Commission as providing 'evidence for political decision-makers on the advantages and disadvantages of possible policy options by assessing their potential impacts'.[3] IA is carried out by the Commission on 'the most important Commission initiatives',[4] including primarily legislative proposals. Many of the routine administrative decisions discussed in this book (firming up vague legislative standards, authorising products, setting conditions in operating permits) also depend on CBA and risk assessment.

Whilst not mentioned in the Treaty, much environmental law and policy in the EU is underpinned by 'risk'. Most obviously in product regulation (chemicals, genetically modified organisms (GMOs)), the control of risk goes to the heart of the evolution of EU law: regulating risk at EU level seeks both to speak to the interests and concerns of EU publics, and to maintain and support the internal market through common standards. As well as being the *object* of regulation (the thing that is reduced through regulation), risk is also a technique of decision-making.[5] The Courts often demand 'scientific risk assessment' before the EU's administrative bodies can take a protective measure,[6] as does legislation.[7] The same constraints do not always apply to the legislature.[8] With perhaps less

---

[2] Eg L Heinzerling, 'Regulatory Costs of Mythic Proportions' (1998) 107 *Yale Law Journal* 1981. See also European Commission, 'Impact Assessment Guidelines' SEC (2009) 92, 26.

[3] Commission, ibid, 4.

[4] Ibid 6. The Commission itself decides annually which proposals are covered, see A Alemanno and A Meuwese, 'Impact Assessment of EU Non-Legislative Rulemaking: The Missing Link in "New Comitology"' (2013) 19 *European Law Journal* 76.

[5] Eg J Black, 'The Emergence of Risk Based Regulation and the New Public Risk Management in the United Kingdom' [2005] *Public Law* 512.

[6] Eg Case T-13/99 *Pfizer Animal Health SA v Council* [2002] ECR II-3305, and associated cases.

[7] Eg Directive 2001/18/EC on the deliberate release into the environment of genetically modified organisms [2001] OJ L106/1.

[8] Case C-343/09 *Afton Chemical Ltd v Secretary of State for Transport* [2010] ECR-I-7027 (Kokott AG). N de Sadeleer, 'The Precautionary Principle in EC Health and Environmental Law' (2006) 12 *European Law Journal* 139 is correct to insist, 151, that environmental legislation is often and properly not based on a formal risk assessment, although risk assessment is encouraged within IA. Much (not all) of the material discussed in this chapter refers to human health rather than the environment; the points are largely transferable, but the importance of context should be borne in mind (and is highlighted at different points below).

emphasis, non-product related environmental law is in many cases also driven by the logic of rendering risk acceptable, leaning to at least some degree on the technique of risk assessment.[9] Simplifying, the technique of risk assessment involves first the identification of a possible adverse effect, and then the calculation of the level of risk by reference to the severity of that adverse consequence, and its likelihood or probability.[10] Risk assessment need not be quantified, and a qualitative assessment of risks is possible. A vast amount of work lies behind risk assessment, which may depend for example on laboratory experiments, field work, or epidemiological studies. Risk assessment may involve complex modelling,[11] from computer simulations of the entire climate system,[12] to relatively simpler modelling of smaller systems, such as water quality in a particular river.[13]

CBA involves a comparison of the costs and benefits of a proposal, and is less pervasive in the EU than risk assessment, although, as mentioned in chapter one, the Treaty on the Functioning of the European Union (TFEU) contains an injunction to take account of 'the potential benefits and costs of action or lack of action'.[14] CBA emerged out of efforts to prioritise between publicly funded developments such as flood defences or roads, but is now applied more widely. As well as being an important aspect of IA, CBA is also sometimes required or encouraged as part of decision-making processes within an environmental legislative framework.[15] It should be noted that some of the (US) CBA scholarship discussed in this chapter takes issue with an extreme approach to CBA, in which virtually every regulatory measure must 'pass' a CBA, in the sense of establishing that the quantified benefits of an action are greater than its quantified costs. This extreme

---

[9] Environmental legislation does not always require risk assessment for administrative decisions, eg *Afton*, ibid (Kokott AG). Risk assessment is often required or encouraged, eg Directive 2010/75/EU on industrial emissions (integrated pollution prevention and control) ('Industrial Emissions Directive' (IED)) [2010] OJ L334/17.

[10] European Commission, 'Communication on the Precautionary Principle' COM (2000) 1 final, Annex III: 'hazard identification, hazard characterisation, appraisal of exposure, risk characterisation'.

[11] W Wagner, E Fisher and P Pascual, 'Misunderstanding Models in Environmental and Public Health Regulation' (2010) 18 *NYU Environmental Law Journal* 293 describes modelling as co-evolving with risk assessment.

[12] Eg DA Farber, 'Modelling Climate Change and Its Impacts: Law, Policy and Science' (2008) 86 *Texas Law Review* 1655.

[13] See generally N Oreskes, 'The Role of Quantitative Models in Science' in CD Canham, JJ Cole, WK Lauenroth (eds), *Models in Ecosystem Science* (Princeton University Press, 2003) for a brief history of modelling, which began with physical models, but now generally implies computer modelling; E Fisher, P Pascual and W Wagner, 'Understanding Environmental Models in their Legal and Regulatory Context' (2010) 22 *Journal of Environmental Law* 251. European Commission, 'Annexes to the Impact Assessment Guidelines' (2009) 11.4, outlines some of the models available in the EU.

[14] Art 191(3) TFEU.

[15] Eg Directive 2000/60/EC establishing a framework for the Community action in the field of water policy ('Water Framework Directive') [2000] OJ L327/1; Regulation 1907/2006/EC concerning the Registration, Evaluation, Authorisation and Restriction of Chemicals (REACH), establishing a European Chemicals Agency [2006] OJ L396/1; IED (n 9).

approach does not apply in the EU,[16] but the critique nevertheless provides important insights into CBA, and many of the concerns are relevant in the EU. As with risk assessment, CBA need not be quantitative. Relevant EU policy takes the trouble to recognise explicitly both that quantification (in money) will not always be possible or sensible, and that unquantified impacts may be important.[17] The Commission refers to this inclusion of unquantified effects as 'multi-criteria analysis', rather than CBA, applying 'cost benefit thinking to cases where there is a need to present impacts that are a mixture of qualitative, quantitative and monetary data'.[18] Although a CBA (or multi-criteria analysis) could be composed in whole or part of a narrative analysis of costs and benefits in the EU, quantification is certainly encouraged.[19] Advocates argue that quantifying the environmental benefits of a measure puts the environmental goods on an equal footing with other goods,[20] and provides arguments for regulatory action within the dominant political discourse of economic prosperity. Some of those concerned with environmental protection are, however, deeply uneasy about economic approaches to environmental regulation.

The somewhat stylised discussion of risk assessment and CBA in this section is designed to highlight two related points that are well established in the literature: the inevitability of value judgments within the technical assessment; and the need, ultimately, for legitimate political judgments on environmental protection.[21] First, the inevitable presence of uncertainty in the science behind risk assessment, which renders fragile any expectation that the 'facts' legitimise a decision, is closely related to both of these points. 'Risk' relies on establishing the probability of an identified hazard; when that is not possible, we are faced instead with uncertainty. Only in relatively trivial cases can science provide 'proof', rather than 'a robust consensus based on a process of inquiry that allows for continued scrutiny, re-examination, and revision'.[22] And in cases where there is an underlying

---

[16] Or even in quite this extreme form in the US, see eg C Sunstein, 'The Real World of Cost-Benefit Analysis: Thirty-Six Questions (and Almost as Many Answers)' (2013) *Harvard Law School Public Law and Legal Theory Working Paper Series, No 13-11.*

[17] Eg Commission (n 2) 38; European Chemicals Agency, *Guidance on the Preparation of Socio-Economic Analysis as Part of An Application for Authorisation* (Helsinki, ECHA, 2011) discussed in ch 9 below.

[18] Commission, ibid, 47; see also L Bergkamp and TT Smith Jr, 'Legal and Administrative Systems: Implications for Precautionary Regulation' in JB Wiener et al (eds), *The Reality of Precaution: Comparing Risk Regulation in the United States and Europe* (London, Earthscan, 2011).

[19] See eg the annual Impact Assessment Board reports, European Commission, 'Impact Assessment Board Report for 2012' (no number) 26. See also ch 3 on quantification in sustainable development indicators.

[20] D Pearce and EB Barbier, *Blueprint for a Sustainable Economy* (London, Earthscan, 2000).

[21] There are many methodological debates not raised here: eg RL Revesz and MA Livermore, *Retaking Rationality: How Cost-Benefit Analysis Can Better Protect the Environment and Our Health* (Oxford, Oxford University Press, 2008) identify 'eight fallacies'; Sunstein (n 16) poses 36 methodological questions.

[22] N Oreskes, 'Science and Public Policy: What's Proof Got to do with it?' (2004) 7 *Environmental Science and Policy* 369, 369–70.

value dispute, arriving at that robust consensus is likely to be slow.[23] Consensus is not demanded in EU law, which recognises the pervasiveness of disagreement, and indeed, the legitimacy of preferring minority over majority scientific views is fairly clear.[24]

'Uncertainty' might be due to data gaps and lack of information, which our legal frameworks acknowledge and attempt to address. One of the central objectives of chemicals regulation, for example, discussed in chapter nine, is to increase our understanding of chemicals. Research to fill gaps and improve our knowledge base is crucial. But equally, more information will never answer all of our questions. There will self-evidently always be new questions and new gaps. More profoundly, 'ignorance',[25] the 'we don't know what we don't know' question can be important: for decades nobody thought to investigate the impact of CFCs on stratospheric ozone, for example.[26] As discussed in chapter one, in EU law, 'hypothetical' risk is not a valid reason for a regulatory decision. The meaning of hypothetical risk is not clear, but if it includes a theoretical risk for which there is inadequate empirical evidence, it must also be the case that 'ignorance' can never be the basis for regulation. It is true that if we routinely demanded proof of safety, the world would be a different, probably poorer, place; and allowing administrators to demand proof of safety, without further constraints, would provide effectively limitless discretion. But to conclude as a consequence that ignorance is never a good reason for a decision is problematic. It forecloses the possibility of democratic discussion about the 'acceptability' of a hypothetical risk. For example, ignorance may be more salient if the contested activity raises ethical concerns, or has doubtful social benefits.[27]

A further category of uncertainty is 'indeterminacy', a situation in which not all of the parameters of systems and their interactions are known.[28] Veerle Heyvaert highlights the pervasive reductionism of risk assessment, applied 'substance-by-substance, technological application-by-application, product-by-product ... installation-by-installation and/or project-by-project'.[29] For current purposes, the

---

[23] Ibid.

[24] See eg the discussion in Case C-300/95 *Commission v United Kingdom* [1997] ECR I-2649 (especially Tesauro AG).

[25] I am following Wynne's typology, B Wynne, 'Uncertainty and Environmental Learning: Reconceiving Science and Policy in the Preventive Paradigm' (1992) 2 *Global Environmental Change* 111.

[26] Wynne, ibid, discusses the unexpectedly lengthy ban on consumption of sheep from the English Lake District after the Chernobyl nuclear accident. Scientists and policy makers did not know that they needed to know about the behaviour of radiocaesium in acid peaty soils, assuming that their knowledge about the behaviour of radiocaesium in alkaline chalky soils was universally applicable.

[27] B Wynne, 'Creating Public Alienation: Expert Cultures of Risk and Ethics on GMOs' (2001) 10 *Science as Culture* 445 argues that concern about ignorance or uncertainty is not necessarily a concern that the risk is too high, but may be about, eg, the unrealistic claims made for institutional knowledge.

[28] Wynne (n 25).

[29] V Heyvaert, 'Governing Climate Change: Towards a New Paradigm for Risk Regulation' (2011) 74 *Modern Law Review* 817, 825. Heyvaert explores the difference between what she labels 'conventional risk regulation' and the risks posed by climate change, providing an interesting analysis of the

literally unpredictable behaviour of ecological and social systems can be usefully emphasised. The high profile controversy over restrictions placed on three substances in the class of insecticides known as neonicotinoids, illustrates inevitable uncertainty about the behaviour of ecological systems.[30] The possible effects of these chemicals on pollinators (especially bees) have raised significant public concerns. But rather than the relatively well understood question of whether high doses of neonicotinoids kill bees, the concern is around the ways in which low environmental exposures affect the behaviour of bees in the environment, for example their foraging behaviour.[31] The EU institutions tried to expand risk assessment to embrace these broader questions, and models have also been developed in other areas to try to embrace some of the complexity of ecosystems. But no matter how sophisticated the model, it will only ever provide a representation of reality, and can never completely capture an open system. Things are left out because they are incorrectly thought to be irrelevant, or are not understood, or the necessary time, data or computer power are missing, or for a host of other reasons.[32] Uncertainty underlies our understanding of effects in ecosystems.

Alongside this 'ecosystem indeterminacy', 'social system indeterminacy' refers to the failure of human beings and human systems to behave consistently with the assumptions made in the risk assessment. In Germany in 2008, for example, bee keepers reported losses of 50–100 per cent of their hives when bees were exposed to neonicotinoids.[33] First, heavy rain had delayed the planting of corn, so that the neonicotinoid was applied to the seeds later than usual,[34] when bees were already foraging rapeseed in neighbouring fields; problems in the seed treatment process meant that dust was blown into the air by machinery; winds then blew the dust onto the bees. The behaviour of social systems (in this case farm workers, whose decisions were bound up with weather conditions) cannot be adequately

difficulties of applying risk assessment beyond what Wynne calls the 'relatively very well structured' problems alongside which it evolved (n 25, 113). The features of climate change that Heyvaert identifies as posing special challenges (risks are posed by business as usual rather than change, the systemic nature of the necessary response, and the need to avoid compartmentalisation) are problematic throughout environmental law.

[30] Active substances to be used in pesticides have to be approved at EU level under Regulation 1107/2009/EC concerning the placing of plant protection products on the market [2009] OJ L309/1. An active substance shall only be approved under this new Regulation 'if it may be expected' (inter alia) that it shall not have 'any harmful effects on human health', Art 4, further defined by reference to eg classification as a carcinogen. The approach is considered very stringent.

[31] European Food Safety Authority (EFSA), 'Conclusion on the Peer Review of the Pesticide Risk Assessment for Bees for the Active Substance Clothianidin' (2013) 11 *EFSA Journal* 3066; for the other two chemicals, see (2013) 11 *EFSA Journal* 3067 (thiamethoxam), and (2013) 11 *EFSA Journal* 3068 (imidacloprid).

[32] Oreskes (n 13), who doubts the value of long term modelling. See also DA Farber, 'Probabilities Behaving Badly: Complexity Theory and Environmental Uncertainty' (2003) 37 *University of California Davis Law Review* 145.

[33] A Alemanno, 'The Science, Law and Policy of Neonicotinoids and Bees: A New Test Case for the Precautionary Principle' (2013) 2 *European Journal of Risk Research* 191, at note 42.

[34] Neonicotinoids are applied to seeds rather than plants.

predicted in a risk assessment. Risk assessments are conditional on assumptions about the behaviour of both social and ecological systems.

Uncertainties, including for current purposes ignorance and indeterminacy, cannot be resolved by more or better science, but are an inevitable part of decision-making. Uncertainty around risk assessment in turn feeds into CBA, the outcomes of which can be highly variable and disputed.[35] The uncertainty may, however, often tend to underestimate the value of regulating. The costs of regulating are 'usually tangible, clearly allocated and often short term, whereas the costs of failing to act are less tangible, less clearly distributed and usually longer term'.[36] The benefits of a ban on neonicotinoids, for example, would be virtually impossible to quantify; but the immediate, direct costs to farmers from the loss of the pesticide are closer to hand. That is not to say that a careful qualitative assessment of the costs and benefits of acting may not be useful, and the unavailability of quantified benefits need not be fatal to regulatory action.[37] However, a one-sided CBA may mislead in some cases.[38]

But whilst difficult to predict and hard to price, the cost of physical effects, for example cleaning up polluted water, lost work through ill health, damage to crops, are relatively calculable. Non-physical values of environmental goods include aesthetic or spiritual value, 'bequest' value (knowing that the environment will be conserved for future generations), and 'existence' value (knowing that species or places with which we have no personal connection do indeed, exist).[39] Calculating these values compounds the uncertainties of CBA. 'Revealed preference' methods calculate what people actually pay for environmental resources, for example by reference to relative property values, or the pay differential in hazardous employment. But these exchanges do not necessarily provide justification for the profound social choices that might be at stake in the CBA: for example, it is not straightforward to assume that taking hazardous employment or living in a degraded environment involves a meaningful choice, on which we can base public policy. 'Hypothetical preference' methods are an alternative to 'revealed preference' methods. They are based on surveys of individuals' willingness to pay for the receipt of environmental

---

[35] See eg Revesz and Livermore (n 21). The CBA of REACH (n 15), was notoriously disputed, eg D Vogel, *The Politics of Precaution: Regulating Health, Safety, and Environmental Risks in Europe and the United States* (Princeton University Press, 2012) ch 5; European Commission, 'REACH: Extended Impact Assessment' SEC (2003) 1171/3.

[36] European Environmental Agency (EEA), *Late Lessons from Early Warnings: Science, Precaution, Innovation* (EEA Report No 1/2013) 565.

[37] Eg there was no quantitative assessment of benefits for REACH (n 15); Commission (n 35).

[38] This implies the need for some care about proposals to extend IA, to administrative, comitology decisions, if by implication that includes quantitative CBA. See Alemanno and Meuwese (n 4); Alemanno (n 33); E Chiti, 'European Agencies' Rulemaking: Powers, Procedures and Assessment' (2013) 19 *European Law Journal* 93 also seems to support this extension of IA.

[39] See eg the discussion in Revesz and Livermore (n 21), 'Fallacy 7: People Value Only What They Use', 119–29.

benefits[40] (or less frequently, willingness to accept payment for their loss).[41] They have their own limitations, for example, being partially dependent on the wealth of those participating in the hypothetical markets.[42]

This sort of distributive concern is a significant issue in CBA. In the absence of compensating mechanisms, placing the same weight on everyone's money, rich or poor, is likely to prioritise the environmental problems of the rich. Notoriously, 'discounting' future costs and benefits distributes goods between generations, and can mean that long term environmental effects have little practical impact on current decisions.[43] Discounting contributes to our understanding of trade-offs in respect of money: the promise of one Euro in the future is worth less than one Euro now. It may also be realistic in respect of injury to a current individual (I may be willing to pay more to avoid the loss of my arm, or life, now, than to avoid such a loss in 30 years[44]). But applying discounting between generations is much more problematic. The significance of discounting can be seen in the famous *Stern Review on the Economics of Climate Change*.[45] The Stern Review concluded that the economic costs of taking action to mitigate climate change now are outweighed by the benefits. It applied a low discount rate, to reflect the ethics of intergenerational distribution,[46] when a more conventional discount rate would have led to different conclusions. Stern demonstrates both that the choice of discount rate can be decisive for the answer provided by a CBA, and that criticisms of the discount rate have been heard in mainstream economics. But more profound concerns about CBA are not avoided by this methodological improvement. According to Helm, Stern provides 'a very conventional analysis, which points away from doing much about climate change now', but the low discount rate allows the Review 'to rescue its conclusion with a dose of highly debatable moral philosophy'.[47] Helm argues, to simplify, that we should take urgent action not because of Stern's CBA, but because the damaged climate is irreplaceable, and not capable of 'substitution' by human capital.[48] The more profound critique of CBA

---

[40] Which might be expressed eg as a tax per household (Revsez and Livermore, ibid, 124–25 on the valuation of the Exxon Valdez oil spill), or entrance fees to a national park, or higher prices for consumer goods.

[41] There is a vast literature on valuation methodologies. For current purposes, see Commission (n 13) [9.1].

[42] Eg G Smith, *Deliberative Democracy and the Environment* (London, Routledge, 2003) 36.

[43] RL Revesz, 'Environmental Regulation, Cost-Benefit Analysis, and the Discounting of Human Lives' (1999) 99 *Columbia Law Review* 941.

[44] Even this is not self-evident, see Revsz and Livermore (n 21) 103. Nor does this imply that willingness to pay to avoid loss of life or limb decreases with age.

[45] HM Treasury, *The Stern Review on the Economics of Climate Change* (UK Treasury, 2006). There are dozens of reviews, critical and supportive.

[46] 1.4%; by way of comparison, the Commission uses a discount rate of 4% in its IA, see Commission (n 13) [11.6], although note the acknowledgement that a lower discount rate may be appropriate for long-term effects.

[47] D Helm, 'Climate-Change Policy: Why has So Little Been Achieved?' (2008) 24 *Oxford Review of Economic Policy* 211, 230.

[48] See also ch 3 below.

is that the real trade-off is not between money now and more money later, but between a variety of social resources now, and environmental devastation later.

More generally, the absence or presence of environmental regulation distributes risk, benefits, harm and costs, raising ethically significant questions that are not susceptible to numerical manipulation, and are best addressed through political discussion. Who benefits from the running of a risk, and who bears that risk, is a question for political rather than technical assessment. Critics of agricultural bio-technology for example, are concerned that its high capital costs and intellectual property protection may systematically disadvantage small and organic farmers in the EU, and enhance corporate control of food and agriculture; advocates and critics of GMOs argue about whether impacts on poor farmers and consumers in developing countries will be positive or negative.[49] CBA and risk assessment have very little to contribute to these discussions. They also deal very badly with unlikely, but catastrophic, or even simply very large, harms. Without the intervention of normative judgment, a very high likelihood of one death is numerically similar to a low likelihood of 10,000 deaths; their social and ethical impacts are however very different.[50]

Risk assessment and CBA do not provide a single, inevitable result. Value judgments and assumptions, the accuracy or appropriateness of which is likely to be debated, are made at every stage.[51] One obvious choice in CBA is selecting the discount rate. Deciding between a survey of 'willingness to pay' or 'willingness to accept', or between 'revealed preference' and 'hypothetical preference' also produces consistently different figures. The scope of the 'community of concern', that is whose costs and values count, is another inevitably value-based decision. Even taking human wants as the ultimate frame of reference is an important judgment, and the assumption that efficiency is a good in itself is enormously contentious.[52]

Similarly in risk assessment, choices are made. The disagreement over neo-nicotinoids demonstrates the diverse ways in which we might characterise our risk: acute or chronic exposure, different exposure pathways, lethal or sub-lethal effects. Estimates of the effect of a low, but perhaps lengthy, human exposure to a particular pollutant may be made on the basis of high exposure of laboratory animals, so that predictions rely on modelling, extrapolations, averaging, and numerous other techniques, all of which require the exercise of professional judgment. Assumptions embedded in technical assessment also dictate, for example, the role of the precautionary principle. US scholars often present CBA and the

---

[49] See M Lee, *EU Regulation of GMOs: Law and Decision Making for a New Technology* (Cheltenham, Edward Elgar, 2008) ch 2.

[50] A number could be allocated to those effects.

[51] Heinzerling (n 2) provides more examples. See also Revesz and Livermore (n 21) 77–84, regarding 'life years saved' or 'lives saved'.

[52] M Sagoff, *The Economy of the Earth: Philosophy, Law and the Environment* (Cambridge, Cambridge University Press, 1988).

precautionary principle as implacably opposed and competing philosophies,[53] and the EU institutions apply the precautionary principle at the political, risk management stage of decision-making, rather than to technical risk assessment.[54] But as Driesen points out, CBA requires practitioners to engage with uncertainty, and they can choose to do so in a precautionary way.[55] Similarly, a precautionary set of assumptions is perfectly possible in a risk assessment.[56]

The assumptions applied during technical assessments are often not consciously adopted as such, and so are rarely externally questioned.[57] Professional judgments are legitimate, and necessary, and standardised professional practices reduce the 'politics' of any individual decision. The point is not that those involved pervert the exercise deliberately. The point is that neither CBA nor risk assessment provides a single neutral assessment, which stands above politics and values.[58]

One appeal of both CBA and risk assessment is in the promise of a common metric by which competing social goods (harm to bees and increased crop productivity, for example) can be compared in an apparently simple and objective way. But even leaving aside the diversity of human values, it is not possible to assess environmental protection along a single dimension. For example, the potential tension between climate change mitigation and other environmental values is apparent when burning biofuels (such as wood) in cities adds to urban air pollution, with effects on health, or when renewable energy infrastructure, such as wind farms, affects local ecosystems. Political choices must be made about the distribution of harms and benefits, and about what shall be valued most highly.

Risk assessment and CBA share many features, and are often linked in regulatory policy.[59] There are, however, some important differences between them. First, the impossibility of determining how much risk is acceptable, how safe is safe enough, through technical risk assessment, is accepted even by those most wedded to risk assessment. At the extreme, science might occasionally speak for itself: for example, both the immediate and complete cessation of the burning of fossil fuels, and the unconstrained addition of carbon to the atmosphere, would be disastrous. But in between, our choices cannot be determined by science alone, although science informs them. On the other hand, whilst few would argue that quantitative CBA always and inevitably dictates regulatory action, one of its

---

[53] Eg C Sunstein, *Risk and Reason: Safety, Law and the Environment* (Cambridge, Cambridge University Press, 2002); DA Kysar, 'It Might Have Been: Risk, Precaution, and Opportunity Costs' (2006) 22 *Journal of Land Use and Environmental Law* 1. CBA is not out of the question in the EU approach to the precautionary principle, *Pfizer* (n 6).

[54] *Pfizer*, ibid; Commission (n 10).

[55] DM Driesen, 'Cost-Benefit Analysis and the Precautionary Principle: Can They Be Reconciled?' (2013) available at www.works.bepress.com/david_driesen/8/.

[56] Driesen, ibid; de Sadeleer (n 8).

[57] Expert Group on Science and Governance, *Taking European Knowledge Society Seriously* (European Commission, 2007) ch 6.

[58] Eg A Stirling et al, 'Empowering Designs: Towards More Progressive Appraisal of Sustainability' (2007) *STEPs Working Paper* 3.

[59] Commission (n 2).

purposes is precisely to contribute to, and sometimes to answer, that political 'acceptable risk' question. CBA purports to tell us whether or not regulation is worthwhile. Secondly, environmental protection self-evidently cannot do without the science behind risk assessment, even if particular elements of methodology are problematic. It is only through various scientific disciplines that we recognise many environmental problems: that climate change is a global and anthropogenic phenomenon, for example, is not intuitively observable, even for people who are sure that something odd is happening to the weather; the effects of lead on cognitive development cannot be observed by the senses. By contrast, whilst the methodologies of CBA are also disputed, and those concerned that CBA under-values the environment may need to engage in the methodological debate,[60] some advocate the abandonment of the technique as a policy tool.[61]

For current purposes, whether we are concerned with risk assessment, CBA, or another technique entirely, and even if, as seems likely, CBA becomes more important in the EU, deciding environmental priorities, deciding between environmental and other priorities, and distributing goods and bads, are all fundamentally political tasks, which require a politically legitimate decision.

EXPERTISE AND POLITICS IN EU RISK REGULATION

Dispute over the role of highly technical methodologies in environmental decision-making reflects a perennial debate, which echoes throughout this book, about the nature of environmental problems. There is no crude binary competition between facts and values, science and politics. But 'the facts' are less self-evident than they sometimes appear, and values are not an illegitimate intruder in 'objective' decision-making, but properly the subject of debate. Similarly, uncertainty is nothing special. The inevitability of uncertainty means that it should never be used as a rhetorical device to stymy action (either regulatory action or innovative activity). But nor should uncertainty be denied by a technical presentation of probabilities, or an assumption that an unknown likelihood is the same as a low likelihood.[62] In terms of practical decision-making, uncertainty is always important, since it emphasises the need for flexible, adaptive approaches to governance. Its centrality to a decision depends on precisely what is at stake, the 'social commitments' associated with the evidence;[63] so the salience of an absence

---

[60]   This is the basic thesis of Revesz and Livermore (n 21).

[61]   F Ackerman and L Heinzerling, *Priceless: On Knowing the Price of Everything and the Value of Nothing* (New York, The New Press, 2004).

[62]   See DA Kysar, *Regulating from Nowhere: Environmental Law and the Search for Objectivity* (New Haven, Yale University Press, 2010) on Nordhaus' implicit assumption in his CBA of climate change mitigation that an event that is uncertain in the sense that probability is unknown, is actually unlikely, 94–95.

[63]   Wynne (n 25). See S Jasanoff, 'Transparency in Public Science: Purposes, Reasons, Limits' (2006) 69 *Law and Contemporary Problems* 21 on 'manufacturing uncertainty' to avoid regulation.

of 'proof' depends on whether values and interests are divided, or more or less consensual. As Sheila Jasanoff puts it, 'stopping rules' will 'block sceptical inquiry' at some point that 'society' deems 'reasonable';[64] what society deems 'reasonable' is likely to vary according to the sensitivity of the topic. The constant challenging of climate change science provides a good example, explicable at least in part by the challenges climate change presents to some of our deepest values and beliefs about the physical and social world.[65]

Whilst technical assessments are straightforwardly relied on without dispute in many routine decisions, few, if any, decisions really are purely technical. Daniel Sarewitz uses the 2000 US Presidential Election to make the point. The very close result in this election depended on which candidate had won in Florida. This sounds like a simply and easily established fact—how many votes were cast for each of Gore and Bush? 'On its face, it is hard to imagine a problem more suited to a technical approach'.[66] And yet it raised all sorts of questions as to when a vote 'counts'. Most notoriously, do we dismiss a vote when the voting intention is clear, but the voter did not push the vote-punch machine hard enough to separate the 'chad' from the card? The disagreement was ultimately resolved, not by looking for the technical truth of votes cast, but by political and judicial process. This was accepted as providing a legitimate outcome (a president basically accepted as such even by those who did not vote for him), says Sarewitz, because the political and judicial process was broadly accepted as legitimate.[67] So as well as demonstrating the elusiveness of simple technical resolution to debates, this example also illustrates our ability to carry on in the absence of facts, provided we have a politically legitimate arbiter. The political legitimacy of administrative decision-makers, in the EU and elsewhere, is, however, relatively weak, raising additional challenges.

The main institutional response to the imperative of integrating the political and the technical in the EU, shared with many other jurisdictions, has been to introduce a clear division between the decision-making responsibility of political institutions, and the purely advisory role of expert advisors (alongside an emphasis on transparency, discussed below). The EU institutions (Courts,[68] legislators,[69] Commission[70]) expressly recognise the political nature of the final decision. The division between 'risk assessment', a technical process for experts, and risk

---

[64] Jasanoff, ibid, 37.

[65] M Hulme, *Why We Disagree about Climate Change: Understanding Controversy, Inaction and Opportunity* (Cambridge, Cambridge University Press, 2009) ch 3; Oreskes (n 22), for a comparison with the less politically sensitive science of plate tectonics.

[66] D Sarewitz, 'How Science Makes Environmental Controversy Worse' (2004) 7 *Environmental Science and Policy* 385, 387.

[67] Some would disagree, and I would suggest that a final determination by a court may sometimes be a way of asserting the technical (in this case legal) *facts* over values. The point, however, remains.

[68] Eg *Pfizer* (n 6).

[69] Eg Regulation 178/2002/EC laying down the general principles and requirements of food law, establishing the European Food Safety Authority and laying down procedures in matters of food safety ('General Food Law') [2002] OJ L31/1.

[70] Commission (n 2); above n 10.

'management', a political process for political institutions, is well-developed.[71] Nor do EU regulations have to 'pass' a CBA, establishing that the benefits 'justify' the costs. IA is explicitly 'an aid to political decision-making, not a substitute for it',[72] and the different institutions involved in legislation may draw 'different conclusions from the available information'.[73]

But the EU simultaneously continues to emphasise technical assessment. The emphasis on quantification in IA, for example, seems to be increasing,[74] as does the framing of environmental values in economic terms through sustainable development indicators, discussed in chapter three. Recent legislation like the Water Framework Directive and chemicals regulation also creates an important space for CBA, albeit leaving decisions to regulatory judgment.[75] Even more clearly, as discussed in chapter one, the Courts generally consider a risk assessment to be a mandatory starting point for administrative decisions. Whilst the institutions are categorically not bound by experts, if the political institution does not follow the opinion of its expert advisor, it must provide 'specific reasons for its findings', and those reasons 'must be of a scientific level at least commensurate with that of the opinion in question'.[76] Similarly, when EU institutions are required to assess complex technical or scientific issues, they may only adopt a regulatory measure without consulting the relevant EU level scientific committee in 'exceptional circumstances', and where there are 'otherwise adequate guarantees of scientific objectivity'.[77] The decision in *Gowan Comércio Internacional e Serviços Lda v Ministero della Salute*[78] has been criticised for failing to follow up its assertion that this risk assessment did not bind the final decision-makers, with the requirement for 'commensurate' scientific expertise.[79] However, the Court did require 'a comprehensive assessment of the risk to health based on the most reliable scientific data available and the most recent results of international research',[80] and noted various sources relied on by the Commission.[81] It said that this information verified the existence of 'some scientific uncertainty' (rather than 'hypothetical risk'), which justified precautionary action.[82] And again, the legislative context matters, and in some cases will preclude a demand for risk

---

[71] See eg Commission (n 10).

[72] Commission (n 2) 4.

[73] *Afton* (n 8) [85] (Kokott AG), see also the Court's judgment [30] and [58].

[74] Commission (n 19); O Fritsch et al, 'Regulatory Quality in the European Commission and the UK: Old Questions and New Findings' *CEPS Working Document* 2012–362.

[75] See n 15; see chs 4 and 9.

[76] *Pfizer* (n 6) [199].

[77] Case T-70/99 *Alpharma v Council* [2002] ECR II-3495 [213].

[78] Case C-77/09 *Gowan Comércio Internacional e Serviços Lda v Ministero della Salute* [2010] ECR I-13533, a case about a fungicide suspected of having endocrine disrupting properties.

[79] A Alemanno, 'C-77/09 *Gowan Comércio Internacional e Serviços Lda v Ministero della Salute*' (2011) 48 *Common Market Law Review* 1329, highlighting in particular the absence of explanation for the change of position between the Commission's initial proposal, and the final decision.

[80] *Gowan* (n 78) [75].

[81] Ibid [78].

[82] Ibid [79].

assessment to justify action: Kokott AG in *Afton Chemical Ltd v Secretary of State for Transport*, for example, points out that EU chemicals legislation effectively bans some substances *pending* risk assessment.[83]

Judicial review in this area is predominantly procedural, and substantive review has traditionally been undertaken with a high degree of deference,[84] the courts intervening only when a decision is 'vitiated by a manifest error or a misuse of power or whether the Community institutions clearly exceeded the bounds of their discretion'.[85] But there is a close relationship between process and substantive review.[86] The development of a procedural duty to show due care or diligence in decision-making has allowed the courts to engage in detailed scrutiny of the scientific basis for a decision, even whilst maintaining the deferential language.[87] The language used in *Gowan* is typical; whilst emphasising institutional discretion, 'the exercise of that discretion is not ... excluded from review by the Court', which 'must verify whether the relevant procedural rules have been complied with, whether the facts admitted by the Commission have been accurately stated and whether there has been a manifest error of appraisal or a misuse of power'; in the process, the Court 'must verify whether that institution has examined, carefully and impartially, all the relevant facts of the individual case, facts which support the conclusions reached.'[88] Whilst this language allows detailed review of the evidence relied upon by the political decision-maker, the Court has been criticised for failing to follow its own instructions and scrutinise in adequate detail the sufficiency of the scientific information on which the institutions claim to rely.[89] Predicting the intensity of review is not easy. *France v Commission (TSE)* and *Sweden v Commission (Paraquat)* are suggestive of the extremes. In *France*, the General Court was only prepared to annul if the evidence produced by the applicant was 'sufficient to make the factual assessments used in the act

---

[83] *Afton* (n 8): 'no data, no market', ch 9 below.

[84] This is not straightforward, P Craig, *EU Administrative Law* (Oxford, Oxford University Press, 2012), especially ch 15. See also K Lenaerts, 'The European Court of Justice and Process-Oriented Review' (2012) 31 *Yearbook of European Law* 3.

[85] This is a well-used formula, *Pfizer* (n 6) [166].

[86] Craig (n 84), especially 353; E Vos, 'The European Court of Justice in the Face of Scientific Uncertainty and Complexity' in M Dawson, B de Witte and E Muir (eds), *Judicial Activism at the European Court of Justice* (Cheltenham, Edward Elgar, 2013).

[87] Craig, ibid, 333. Case C-269/90 *Technische Universität München v Hauptzollamt München-Mitte* [1991] ECR I-5469 is often seen as a pivotal case, Craig, ibid; E Stokes, 'The EC Courts' Contribution to Refining the Parameters of Precaution' (2008) 11 *Journal of Risk Research* 491.

[88] *Gowan* (n 78) [56], [57]. Similar language applies even to the EU legislator, who, although not constrained by risk assessment in the same way (*Afton* (n 8) [34]), 'is obliged to base its choice on objective criteria appropriate to the aim pursued by the legislation in question ... taking into account all the facts and the technical and scientific data available at the time', eg Case C-127/07 *Société Arcelor Atlantique v Ministre de l'Ecologie et du Développement Durable* [2008] ECR I-9895 [58].

[89] Eg Alemanno (n 79); K-H Ladeur, 'The Introduction of the Precautionary Principle into EU Law: A Pyrrhic Victory for Environmental and Public Health Law? Decision-Making under Conditions of Complexity in Multi-Level Political Systems' (2003) 40 *Common Market Law Review* 1455.

implausible'.[90] In *Sweden*, as discussed in chapter one, the General Court found that the institutions had responded inadequately to one particular scientific study.[91] It is difficult to support a routine intervention into the choice between scientific claims, even if that is framed in terms of the *adequacy* of those scientific claims and the *adequacy* of the institutions' engagement with those claims.[92] Not only does the Court lack expertise in these matters, but as discussed above, these sorts of choices may not be amenable to expertise at all.

The Courts have had far less to say on CBA than on risk assessment. The increasing role of CBA in EU environmental law and governance, as discussed above, may bring it before the courts more often. The General Court in *Pfizer* made the somewhat alarming suggestion that it would assess the proportionality of precautionary measures 'in the framework of a cost/benefit analysis'.[93] But the Court seemed not to contemplate an obligation for a precautionary measure to 'pass' a CBA, in the sense of requiring monetised benefits to outweigh the costs, and seemed to maintain proportionality as a space for broader judgment of the pros and cons of action, rather than a narrow quantitative calculation.[94] Similarly, the Commission views the examination of costs and benefits of precautionary action as 'not simply an economic cost-benefit analysis'.[95] Later cases have not returned to CBA, and so we might cautiously conclude that proportionality remains a matter of broad evaluation, rather than quantification. The Courts have had more cause to consider 'complex economic assessments' in other areas, especially state aids and competition law. This is the main area in which the duty on decision-makers to show due care or diligence was developed, using similar language to that used in the cases on the assessment of scientific evidence.[96] So if CBA does indeed become a more central element of environmental regulation, debate may ensue, for example, as to the intensity of judicial review of the quality of the economic evidence. The fact that all the key institutional actors have recognised that final decisions require a politically legitimate decision-making process suggests that a more decisive role for CBA, in which the economic 'facts' would answer political questions, is not on the horizon.

---

[90] Case T-257/07 *France v Commission (TSE)* [2011] ECR II-05827 [86]. This language was not repeated by the Court of Justice of the European Union (CJEU), Case C-601/11 P, although the two courts took similarly deferential approaches.

[91] Case T-229/04 *Sweden v Commission (Paraquat)* [2007] ECR II-2437.

[92] Also J Corkin, 'Science, Legitimacy and the Law: Regulating Risk Regulation Judiciously in the European Community' (2008) 33 *European Law Review* 359. Remember also that the General Court in *Sweden*, ibid, had a much more straightforward procedural decision in hand, see ch 1. Note that I am not suggesting that the authors cited in n 89 are calling for a naive substantive review by the Court; eg Alemanno is explicitly calling for the Court to carry out the review of process that it claims to be doing.

[93] *Pfizer* (n 6) [413].

[94] Ibid [464]–[475].

[95] Commission (n 10) 5.

[96] Eg M Jaeger, 'The Standard of Review in Competition Cases Involving Complex Economic Assessments: Towards the Marginalisation of the Marginal Review?' (2011) 2 *Journal of European Competition Law and Practice* 295. See n 88.

The somewhat unhelpful conclusion is that expert input is crucial, but the final decision is political. Quite where the emphasis lies in the EU, between expertise and politics, is a matter of some disagreement, complicated perhaps by a number of difficulties. First, the distinction between the technical and the political is not as clear-cut as the EU dichotomy might suggest. Positively, the independence of the technical assessment from the decision-maker's political judgment means that the decision-maker's political choices are ultimately transparent,[97] but it is simply not possible to draw clear lines between the technical and the political elements of the decision. Secondly, as discussed in the final section below, some decisions may be presented in scientific form, even if they are (also) based on political concerns.

Thirdly, the cases suggest that the answer varies. Again, *Sweden (Paraquat)* and *France (TSE)* bear comparison. Whilst the outcome points in a more 'precautionary' direction, the reduced scope for political judgment in *Sweden* should not be overlooked: science (combined with a very demanding interpretation of the legislation) was decisive.[98] *France (TSE)*, by contrast, emphasises the importance of political judgment in areas of uncertainty. TSEs are neurodegenerative diseases, affecting humans and animals, and which include BSE (mad cow disease). The Commission (with comitology) relaxed bans that had been imposed on the human consumption of sheep- and goat-meat from a herd in which one animal had been found to have a TSE. This relaxation was in response (basically) to new testing methods allowing improved identification of BSE specifically, and increased confidence that other TSEs are not transmissible to humans. The decision suggests that the dispute was less about what the science says, with broad (not complete) agreement between the parties on relevant gaps and uncertainties,[99] than about what should be done about that evidence, a political risk acceptability decision. The Commission decision that the level of risk (or probably better, 'uncertainty') was acceptable was not disturbed by the General Court; and the ECJ confirms that 'given the Commission's broad discretion for the purposes of determining the level of risk deemed unacceptable for society, the General Court was right to confine its review to manifest errors of assessment'.[100] The 'no harm' standard in the relevant legislation on paraquat, discussed in chapter one, may well have influenced the strong judicial intervention in *Sweden*. However, the relevant legislation on TSEs contained a similarly hard-edged bar on any reduction in the level of protection of human health,[101] but in this case the Court emphasised the institutions' political discretion with respect to the acceptability of risk to society. Whilst the language of the background legislation is clearly very important, the Court exercises a certain freedom of interpretation.

---

[97] C Anderson, 'Competing Models of EU Administration in Judicial Review of Risk Regulation' (unpublished manuscript, 2013).

[98] Ibid; *Sweden (Paraquat)* (n 91).

[99] *France (TSE)* (n 90), eg [56] (ECJ judgment).

[100] Ibid [143] (ECJ judgment).

[101] See ibid [5] (ECJ judgment).

The Courts' recognition of the politics of regulation is welcome and significant. It does however raise difficult questions about the political legitimacy of the EU's administrative decision-making process. This legitimacy is (unsurprisingly) taken for granted by the Court, but actually not self-evident, as discussed in the next section, and indeed throughout this book.[102] Further, the barriers (judicial and political) to any routine consideration of the values behind regulatory action or inaction remain significant and unacknowledged; the final section below returns to this.

THE INSTITUTIONS OF EXPERTISE AND POLITICS IN EU ADMINISTRATION

This Chapter is not primarily concerned with the making of legislation, but with administrative decisions, such as the setting of detailed rules and standards, or the authorisation of products and activities. All jurisdictions need to be able to do this, and creating a legitimate process is always challenging. The EU institutions get their scientific advice from a range of sources, including the private sector and international agencies. Much scientific advice, however, now comes via EU agencies. Similarly, the final 'political' decision can come from various institutional combinations. But most commonly, the decision is taken by the Commission with comitology. So, acknowledging that the position can be more complicated, the institutionalisation of the purported risk assessment/risk management, technical/political, facts/values paradigm, will be explored through a discussion of agencies and comitology.

Agencies

The number of EU agencies has increased dramatically over recent years.[103] In many jurisdictions, agencies play a central regulatory role, for example setting regulatory standards, authorising products and activities, and enforcing regulation. The role and power of EU agencies is enormously varied, and some have something close to this regulatory power.[104] Most, however, do not have decision-making powers, but provide for the complex institutionalisation of expertise.

---

[102] See also V Heyvaert, 'Facing the Consequences of the Precautionary Principle in European Community Law' (2006) 31 *European Law Review* 185. Heyvaert raises the question of trust in decision-makers, K Lenaerts, '"In the Union We Trust": Trust-Enhancing Principles of Community Law' (2004) 41 *Common Market Law Review* 317. Note that even in *Gowan* (n 78), where there was no explicit insistence on 'commensurate' scientific evidence, there was no focus on political process.

[103] For a history, see Craig (n 84).

[104] See M Shapiro, 'Independent Agencies' in P Craig and G de Búrca (eds), *The Evolution of EU Law* (Oxford, Oxford University Press, 2011).

The European Environment Agency (EEA) has an information gathering and reporting role.[105] It is to provide 'objective, reliable and comparable information at European level'.[106] It produces reports on many issues, as well as a 'state of the environment' report every four years.[107] The EEA does not have a legislatively defined role in regulatory processes, such as permitting or standard setting. Other agencies are perhaps more relevant for environmental lawyers. The European Chemicals Agency (ECHA), discussed in chapter nine, administers the chemicals registration scheme,[108] which is central to the EU's efforts to generate adequate information on all chemicals. It also provides 'technical opinions' that feed into final Commission (comitology) decisions on crucial issues, such as the authorisation of chemicals identified as being of very high concern. The European Food Safety Authority (EFSA) similarly feeds information into some important environmental decisions, notably for current purposes decisions to authorise GMOs and active substances in pesticides. Both ECHA and EFSA also interpret complex legislation, for example issuing guidance on how to carry out socio-economic analysis for the authorisation or restriction of chemicals (ECHA), and on how to carry out a risk assessment for the authorisation of GMOs (EFSA). Agency guidance is not strictly legally binding, but it is capable of considerable legal and practical effects.[109]

The Commission may have the final word, but agency opinions can be highly influential, and legally, the Commission will need good (scientific) reasons for disagreeing.[110] The Commission invariably follows the EFSA Opinion on GMOs, for example.[111] Even the EEA could be a powerful source of information, identifying and framing EU 'problems' and creating demands for EU 'solutions', since policy-makers seek to justify their actions in the light of scientific knowledge provided. Having said that, however, it is quite unusual to see the EEA driving policy, and its influence seems not to be very great.[112]

---

[105] Regulation 401/2009/EC on the European Environment Agency and the European Environment Information and Observation Network [2009] OJ L126/13 (codified version). See R Dilling, 'Improving Implementation by Networking: The Role of The European Environment Agency' in C Knill and A Lenschow (eds), *Implementing EU Environmental Policy* (Manchester, Manchester University Press, 2000).

[106] Regulation 401/2009, ibid, Art 1(2).

[107] Regulation 1367/2006/EC on the application of the provisions of the Aarhus Convention on Access to Information, Public Participation in Decision-making and Access to Justice in Environmental Matters to Community institutions and bodies [2006] OJ L264/13, Art 4(4).

[108] REACH (n 15).

[109] See ch 4 below.

[110] *Pfizer* (n 6).

[111] Not just in respect of GMOs, E Vos, 'Responding to Catastrophe: Towards a New Architecture for EU Food Safety Regulation?' in CF Sabel and J Zeitlin (eds), *Experimentalist Governance in the European Union: Towards a New Architecture* (Oxford, Oxford University Press, 2010). In some of the cases discussed above, the Commission patently did not follow the scientific advice it received.

[112] Although see AR Zito, 'European Agencies as Agents of Governance and EU Learning' (2009) 16 *Journal of European Public Policy* 1224, on links with the Commission and European Parliament.

Whilst the processes by which EU agencies exercise their powers are (problematically[113]) diverse, there are common issues in the governance of the ECHA and EFSA. Both contain scientific committees for the provision of scientific information, often on the receipt of initial opinions or information from industry or a Member State. The centralisation inherent in the creation of an EU agency is mediated by the strong involvement of the Member States at different points, especially in respect of the ECHA, as discussed in chapter nine. Member State involvement is, however, also heavily institutionalised within the EFSA.[114] Independence, from Member States, the EU institutions and the relevant industry, is another key governance requirement called on throughout the relevant regulations.[115] There is an obvious tension between independence and the emphasis on the need for openness to contacts with stakeholders, including industry, and with the Member States and institutions.[116] The agencies do not have the resources to carry out all necessary research themselves, and need the resources of industry and the Member States.

The agencies' constitutions also give transparency a high value. EFSA is required to 'ensure that it carries out its activities with a high level of transparency'.[117] References to transparency also litter REACH.[118] Both agencies are subject to various requirements to publish documents, and to accept comments during the production of advice and guidance. Whilst certainly imperfect, there is at least recognition that scientific processes benefit from scrutiny. Transparency around scientific uncertainty specifically is also emphasised. EFSA is required to 'exercise vigilance' in respect of 'any potential source of divergence' between its scientific opinions and those of other bodies. Having shared scientific information, either the divergence should be resolved, or a joint document published 'clarifying the contentious scientific issues and identifying the relevant uncertainties in the data'.[119] Similar provisions apply to the ECHA, which must 'take care to ensure early identification of potential sources of conflict between its opinions and those of other bodies' working at EU level (only).[120] The bodies are to work together to identify potentially contentious points and, in the case of a 'fundamental conflict', are either to resolve the conflict or produce a joint document for submission to the Commission 'clarifying the scientific and/or technical points of conflict'.[121] By contrast with EFSA, there is no explicit requirement that this document be made public.

---

[113] Chiti (n 38); European Commission, 'Roadmap on the Follow-Up to the Common Approach on EU Decentralised Agencies' (2012).

[114] For discussion, see Vos (n 111) 155; Lee (n 49).

[115] General Food Law (n 69); REACH (n 15).

[116] Worryingly, EU Court of Auditors, *Management of Conflict of Interest in Selected EU Agencies* (Court of Auditors, Special Report No 15/2012) found that neither the ECHA (especially) nor the EFSA had 'adequately managed conflict of interest situations' [89].

[117] General Food Law (n 69) Art 38; Art 10 on risk communication.

[118] REACH (n 15).

[119] General Food Law (n 69) Art 30.

[120] REACH (n 15) Art 95(1). Although note the role of the Member State Committee in resolving divergences between the Member States, Art 76(1)(e), Ch 9.

[121] Ibid Art 95(3).

The proliferation and power of EU agencies is somewhat paradoxical, given the political reluctance of existing institutions to cede power.[122] An early ECJ decision, *Meroni*, has been interpreted to prohibit the delegation of wide discretionary powers to agencies.[123] It may not in fact really restrict the evolution of agencies in the way claimed,[124] but the more recent case law, discussed above, emphasising the need for final decisions to be taken by a politically legitimate body, tends to reinforce it. The survival of *Meroni* may also however reveal a reluctance to acknowledge openly the inevitably political nature of the 'technical' tasks that are delegated to the agency.

Agencies are not the only forum for the provision of technical expertise in the EU. A perusal of this book indicates that a range of ad hoc committees perform key governance roles in EU environmental law. Scientific committees (within or outside agencies) are not supposed to be political, and even if they consist of Member State experts, they are not supposed to 'represent' the Member States.[125] The lines between political and technical decision-making are, however, as easily confused in committees as anywhere else. More participatory groups, for example those developing the vague norms contained in the Industrial Emissions Directive (IED),[126] are discussed in chapters four and five.

Comitology

EU administration involves a bewildering variety of committees, at every stage from the preparation of policy to the implementation of legislation. Committees proliferated outside formal Treaty provisions, as an attempt to provide the institutions with technical and scientific information, as well as to allow for Member States to 'supervise' Commission intervention in legislative frameworks.[127] In many cases, rather than, or as well as, 'supervision', committees provide an institution for cooperation between different actors.[128] 'Comitology' is a term strictly applicable only to the committees, composed of Member State representatives, that

---

[122] The sensitivity of the Commission's own influence can be seen in Commission (n 115). See also Craig (n 84); Vos (n 111) on the possibility of national relationships with EFSA coming at the expense of the Commission.

[123] In Case 9/56 *Meroni v High Authority* [1957/8] ECR 133. For discussion, see M Chamon, 'EU Agencies between *Meroni* and *Romano* or the Devil and the Deep Blue Sea' (2011) 48 *Common Market Law Review* 1055.

[124] And if it did, existing agencies would fall foul of its requirements, Chamon ibid.

[125] Eg there is no sense of national 'representation' on EFSA's 19 member (four of whom are British) GMO panel, see www.efsa.europa.eu/en/gmo/gmomembers.htm.

[126] IED (n 9).

[127] For discussion, see eg E Vos, '50 Years of European Integration, 45 Years of Comitology' *Maastricht Faculty of Law Working Papers* 2009-3.

[128] Ibid. Regulation 182/2011/EU laying down the rules and general principles concerning mechanisms for control by Member States of the Commission's exercise of implementing powers ('Comitology Regulation') [2011] OJ L55/13 has built in additional opportunities for cooperation, especially Arts 3 and 6, below. Craig (n 84) 120, on competing rationales for comitology.

supervise powers of implementation that have been granted to the Commission by legislation.[129] The Lisbon Treaty introduced a division of Commission acts into 'delegated' and 'implementing' acts; comitology used to apply across the board, but now only applies to 'implementing' acts.[130] The distinction between delegated and implementing acts is not clear,[131] and will be subject to litigation.[132]

The use of comitology is widespread in environmental law, and examples come up in virtually every chapter of this book.[133] Article 291 TFEU confirms that the implementation of EU law is a national responsibility. However, sometimes 'uniform conditions for implementing legally binding Union acts are needed', in which case legislation can confer implementing powers on the Commission. The 2011 Comitology Regulation establishes the detailed procedure for the adoption of implementing acts by the Commission.[134] The 'examination procedure' applies, inter alia, to decisions relating to 'the environment, security and safety, or protection of the health or safety, of humans, animals or plants', and so most decisions that concern us.[135]

The Commission puts a draft implementing act to the examination committee, made up of 'representatives of the Member States' and chaired by a (non-voting) member of the Commission.[136] 'Any committee member' may 'suggest amendments', and the Commission can present amended drafts at any point. Opportunities for negotiation, collaboration and consensus are emphasised.[137] The Commission must 'inform' the committee of the way in which 'discussions and suggestions have been taken into account', especially 'those suggestions which have been largely supported within the committee'. Together with the requirement that the Commission should 'endeavour to find solutions which command the widest possible support within the committee', this provides an emphasis on

---

[129] There is an enormous literature on this topic. Post-Lisbon, see P Craig, 'Delegated Acts, Implementing Acts and the New Comitology Regulation' (2011) 36 *Environmental Law Review* 671; S Peers and M Costa, 'Accountability for Delegated and Implementing Acts after the Treaty of Lisbon' (2012) *European Law Journal* 427; R Schütze, '"Delegated Legislation" in the (New) European Union: A Constitutional Analysis' (2011) 74 *Modern Law Review* 661.

[130] What would now be delegated acts, but were made subject to 'regulatory procedure with scrutiny' under the old system of comitology remain subject to that procedure pending legislation, Comitology Regulation (n 128) Art 12.

[131] Craig (n 129); Peers and Costa (n 129).

[132] In Case C-427/12 *Commission v Parliament*, the Commission will argue that the implementing powers conferred upon it for the purposes of setting fees payable to the ECHA should in fact have been delegated powers.

[133] In 2010 there were 32 comitology committees in the environmental area, 30 in 2011, more than in any other single area (although holding fewer meetings and providing fewer opinions), European Commission, 'Report from the Commission on the Working of Committees During 2011' COM (2012) 685 final [2.1], [2.2].

[134] Comitology Regulation (n 128).

[135] Ibid Art 2(2). The 'advisory procedure' applies when the examination procedure does not apply, Art 4(2), or if 'duly justified', Art 2(3).

[136] Ibid Art 5.

[137] By contrast, the written procedure (used in undefined 'duly justified cases') allows a measure to be passed in the absence of disagreement by a deadline; any committee member can terminate the written procedure.

moving towards consensus, suggesting that the Commission will not simply make the fewest concessions to national interests that are necessary to reach a qualified majority. The committee can provide a positive or negative opinion on the Commission's draft, by qualified majority voting. In the vast majority of cases, comitology committees simply agree with the Commission, and the measure is adopted.[138] If the examination committee rejects the draft, the Commission cannot adopt it; but if a rejected act is 'necessary', the Commission can either submit an amended draft to the committee, or submit the original draft to the appeal committee.[139]

If the examination committee does not reach an opinion in either direction, then in most environmental cases, the draft must be referred to the appeal committee.[140] Reference to the appeal committee has replaced the escalation to the Council under the old system.[141] The involvement of the Council ensured that if the committee did not agree with the Commission, decisions were exposed to high level political scrutiny. Whilst institutionally, the appeal committee is separate from the Council, high level political intervention remains possible,[142] allowing for national political supervision, and with that the potential reflection of national political (and democratic) concerns. As with the examination committee, amendments can be proposed by members or presented by the Commission, and the Commission has to seek wide support and explain its response to suggestions. The appeal committee can adopt or reject a draft by a qualified majority. If there is a positive opinion, the Commission 'shall' adopt its draft; if there is a negative opinion, it 'shall not' adopt it. If there is no opinion, the Commission 'may adopt' its draft.

It is only in the most contentious areas, where there is really no decision that everyone is willing to live with (even if they do not strictly 'agree'), that the committees are unable to reach a qualified majority in either direction. The decision on neonicotinoids, discussed above, is one of those unusual decisions taken by the Commission following a stalemate in both examination and appeal committee;[143] some Member States, including the UK, think that the role of neonicotinoids in agriculture is too important to lose. The Commission has also acted alone in

---

[138] Vos (n 127) 25. See also Commission (n 133).

[139] The immediate adoption of an implementing act is exceptionally possible, Comitology Regulation (n 128) Arts 7 and 8.

[140] The Commission 'may' simply adopt its draft immediately, unless (inter alia) the measure relates to 'the protection of the health or safety of humans, animals or plants', ibid, Art 5(4).

[141] Ibid Art 6.

[142] Rules of procedure for the appeal committee (Regulation (EU) No 182/2011)—Adopted by the appeal committee on 29 March 2011 [2011] OJ C183/13 provide that 'the level of representation ... should be of a sufficiently high and horizontal nature, including at Ministerial level ...'.

[143] Commission Implementing Regulation 485/2013/EU amending Implementing Regulation 540/2011/EU as regards the conditions of approval of the active substances clothianidin, thiamethoxam and imidacloprid and prohibiting the use and sale of seeds treated with plant protection products containing those active substances (2013) OJ L139/12, Recital 20. The *Gowan* fungicide decision (n 78) also met with stalemate in comitology.

authorising GMOs. The deliberate release into the environment or placing on the market of a GMO must be authorised through comitology following an initial risk assessment by EFSA. Profound concerns about the implications of the technology led to what amounted to a de facto moratorium on new authorisations of GMOs in 1998, broken by a new authorisation in 2004.[144] Insurmountable divides between the Member States, however, meant that between the first authorisation in 2004 and the introduction of 'new' comitology in 2011, the Member States were unable to reach a qualified majority either for or against the Commission's proposal. Things are no simpler post-Lisbon, notwithstanding increased emphasis on collaboration, and decisions continue to be taken by the Commission in the absence of a decision in either examination or appeal committee.[145]

That good, legitimate decisions demand good, legitimate fora for political decision-making is an important theme of this chapter. The cases of GMOs and neonicotinoids, whilst unusual, illustrate the political significance of decisions taken through comitology. The ability of the Commission to take action avoids regulatory impasse. But it also means that even accountability towards the Member States (the most basic of the accountability mechanisms provided by comitology[146]) is missing. Furthermore, those cases where qualified majorities cannot be reached are precisely the cases in which the political stakes are high and concerns very sensitive. And yet these are the cases in which the Commission, the institution arguably most removed from European publics, exercises its authority alone. On the other hand, however, the failure of comitology in these two aberrational cases[147] highlights the strengths of effective comitology in other cases. Comitology has the potential to connect Commission decisions with national (and potentially democratic) concerns. In this vein, whilst the legitimacy of comitology has always been controversial, some argue that comitology *provides* legitimacy by creating mechanisms for 'deliberative supranationalism'.[148] 'Deliberative supranationalism' argues that comitology rests on 'good arguments', formulated in terms of the (EU-wide) public interest, rather than negotiation around positions of (national) self-interest. This important line of thought takes us beyond the 'supervisory' role of comitology, emphasising a more cooperative way of working, although whether committees actually do deliberate (rather than bargain from self-interested positions) is

---

[144] For discussion, see Lee (n 49).

[145] Authorisation decisions can be found on the GMO register, ec.europa.eu/food/dyna/gm_register/index_en.cfm. Most recently, see Commission Implementing Decision 2013/327/EU authorising the placing on the market of food containing or consisting of genetically modified oilseed rape Ms8, Rf3 and Ms8 × Rf3, or food and feed produced from those genetically modified organisms [2013] OJ L175/57.

[146] Peers and Costa (n 129).

[147] Vos (n 111), suggests that positions are more entrenched for foodstuffs generally.

[148] C Joerges and J Neyer, 'From Intergovernmental Bargaining to Deliberative Process: The Constitutionalisation of Comitology' (1997) 3 *European Law Journal* 273; C Joerges, '"Good Governance" Through Comitology?' in C Joerges and E Vos (eds), *EU Committees: Social Regulation, Law and Politics* (Oxford, Hart Publishing, 1999).

contested.[149] More importantly, deliberation by comitology elites does not in itself respond to certain pressing concerns about comitology as a political institution. The examination committees are composed of national experts who share a common professional understanding of the problem, and these sorts of expert groups have well-observed tendencies to remain ignorant of external perspectives on a problem. Even national 'representation' can be an illusion in these communities.[150] Further, comitology committees are largely sheltered from the gaze of the public, including the media and those affected by the decision,[151] and in most cases (not neonicotinoids or GMOs) also from high level political attention.

The enhancement of transparency is generally seen as a minimum concession to the political reality of the decisions taken by comitology. But whilst progress has been made, and a certain amount of information is available on the Commission's comitology register, even specialists find it difficult to identify consistently who is making decisions, and on what basis.[152] Opportunities for European Parliament participation are also important. At the moment, whilst neither Council nor Parliament have a direct role in the comitology committee, each has a 'right of scrutiny', a power to 'at any time indicate to the Commission' that they are of the view that a draft exceeds the implementing powers. This is a relatively weak power, since the Commission is obliged merely to 'review' the draft 'taking account of the positions expressed', and then inform the institutions 'whether it intends to maintain, amend or withdraw the draft implementing act'.[153] However, it does allow the Parliament in particular to draw attention to controversial acts in cases of political disagreement.

The Court quite properly insists that final decisions are taken by a political body, making conventional calls on the role of Parliament and Council in legitimising Commission action.[154] Parliament and Council are of course important, and the challenges faced by the Commission may not be so different from those faced by administrative bodies in national jurisdictions. But the Commission-plus-comitology process raises acutely the sort of questions discussed elsewhere in this book about opportunities for external scrutiny and public involvement in decision-making.

For the sake of completeness, Article 290 TFEU provides that legislators may 'delegate' to the Commission 'the power to adopt non-legislative acts of general application to supplement or amend certain non-essential elements of the legislative act'. The IED, for example, empowers the Commission to adapt parts of the Directive (in particular on monitoring, and compliance with emission limit

---

[149] See discussion of the scholarly reception of 'deliberative supranationalism' and evidence for deliberation in Vos (n 127) 21–24.

[150] Eg JHH Weiler, 'Epilogue: "Comitology" as Revolution—Infranationalism, Constitutionalism and Democracy' in Joerges and Vos (n 148).

[151] See generally (n 130); the contributions to Joerges and Vos, ibid.

[152] For criticism, see Craig (n 129).

[153] Comitology Regulation (n 128) Art 11.

[154] *Pfizer* (n 6).

values), in line with 'scientific and technical progress'.[155] This sort of provision is very common in environmental directives; the legislative system would be overwhelmed by every technical detail of every piece of legislation. But given what we have already said about the complexity of scientific and technical knowledge, it is clear that keeping up to date is not a wholly neutral task, and important choices for the quality of the environment and the health of industry are implicit in detailed rules. The Treaty limits delegation to 'non-essential' areas, so that significant issues need to go back to the legislative process, but the boundary is fraught.[156]

The Lisbon Treaty effectively removed the Member State input into delegated acts that was previously imposed on the Commission by comitology.[157] The European Parliament gained, since Parliament or Council may revoke a delegation, or prevent the entry into force of individual delegated acts by objection.[158] But this is very different from the early, informed and potentially detailed input provided by the examination committee. To avoid the loss of expertise implicit in the loss of comitology committees, the intention seems to be to set up advisory committees.[159] The Commission has set up an ad hoc expert committee for advice on delegation under the IED.[160] These groups are not subject to the constraints of comitology, and although (unlike comitology committees) they are advisory only, enough has been said to appreciate their potential significance. The Commission has had a register of expert groups since 2009. It is however incomplete and in some respects inaccurate, and information on the experts' affiliation is not routinely supplied.[161] In the absence of rules of procedure and accountability, the operation of these groups is likely to be even more obscure than 'comitology'.[162]

GOOD REASONS IN EU ENVIRONMENTAL LAW

A right to reasons is guaranteed in Article 296 TFEU, and has been developed by the Court in a number of cases.[163] Reason-giving is a basic requirement of fair

---

[155] IED (n 9) Art 74.

[156] Schütze (n 129), for discussion and analysis of the case law.

[157] The Treaty requires the 'objectives, content, scope and duration of the delegation of power' to be set out in the legislative act. A Common Understanding agreed by Commission, Council and Parliament (Council of the European Union, 8753/11) builds on this, providing (non-mandatory) 'standard clauses' to be used in legislation providing for delegation. IED (n 9), was passed before the Common Understanding, but shares some of its features, Arts 76 and 77.

[158] By simple majority and qualified majority respectively.

[159] Common Understanding (n 157), provides that the Commission will consult with the Member States when preparing a delegated act, 'including at expert level' [4].

[160] The Industrial Emissions Expert Group (IEEG), ec.europa.eu/environment/air/pollutants/stationary/ied/implementation.htm. The members are from public authorities according to the Register of Expert Groups, ec.europa.eu/transparency/regexpert/.

[161] Peers and Costa (n 129).

[162] See the discussion of Art 298 TFEU in ch 8.

[163] Craig (n 84) 340 onwards.

regulatory processes, and the purposes of reason-giving are well-rehearsed (see also chapter seven). Reasons provide some assurance that the decision-maker has reflected on its decision. They allow affected parties to know why a decision has been taken, and allow for judicial and public scrutiny. For current purposes, what is permitted as a legitimate reason for a decision is crucial for the way in which decisions are constructed and explained in the EU.[164]

The judicial preference seems to be for a technical explanation of a decision. Whilst the ultimate authority is political, as discussed above, the decision has to be explained by reference to scientific information, and risk assessment. Even if it is true that in most cases, the Courts apply their conditions on the adequacy of expert advice with little 'real bite',[165] the requirement for adequate scientific information structures the presentation of the justification for the decision. There would be two, opposite, dangers of *requiring* a technical explanation of a decision. First, the full range of values at stake may never be properly considered by a politically legitimate body. Or alternatively, and perhaps even more likely, decisions reached on the basis of political commitments may be presented and justified as if they were based on technical evidence. Minority science is, quite rightly, a legitimate basis for a decision at all levels. But light judicial scrutiny of the quality or nature of the science relied on creates a real possibility that decision-makers will select the evidence that meets the needs of their decision,[166] or will wittingly or unwittingly over-emphasise the role of scientific information in a political decision.[167] This leaves us without a proper account of the real (political) reasons for a decision, which cannot therefore be challenged, either politically or judicially. The premature closure of *political* debate may in turn encourage the sometimes sterile debate on competing science.

So it is important that, as discussed above, EU law at least strives to leave space for politics. Further, it is sometimes, predominantly in respect of food-related risks (including GMOs and pesticides), explicitly provided in the legislation that a risk management decision can be based, not only on the risk assessment, but also on 'other legitimate factors relevant to the matter under consideration'.[168] 'Other factors' include 'societal, economic, traditional, ethical and environmental factors and the feasibility of controls';[169] politics and values are clearly not systematically ignored as irrelevant. But 'other legitimate factors' operate within a particular legal context. Administrative powers must be exercised exclusively or primarily

---

[164] M Lee, 'Beyond Safety? The Broadening Scope of Risk Regulation' (2009) 62 *Current Legal Problems* 242.

[165] V Heyvaert, 'Guidance without Constraint: Assessing the Impact of the Precautionary Principle on the European Community's Chemicals Policy' (2006) 6 *Yearbook of European Environmental Law* 27; also n 89.

[166] C Hilson, 'Beyond Rationality? Judicial Review and Public Concern in the EU and the WTO' (2005) 56 *Northern Ireland Legal Quarterly* 320; Heyvaert, ibid.

[167] W Wagner, 'The Science Charade in Toxic Risk Regulation' (1995) 95 *Columbia Law Review* 1613.

[168] Regulation 1829/2003 on genetically modified food and feed [2003] OJ L268/1, Art 7.

[169] General Food Law (n 69) Recital 19.

for purposes for which they were granted,[170] and in the case of both GMOs and pesticides, the grounds for refusing authorisation are drawn largely (not entirely[171]) around environmental protection and safety for humans. So whilst the acceptable level of risk to human health and the environment is a clearly legitimate reason for a decision, broader concerns (such as the distributive or ethical impacts of a technology), whilst legitimate, are more difficult to incorporate. Furthermore, the case law discussed above, with its preference for technical explanations,[172] also suggests that 'other legitimate factors' will be relied on very rarely; I am not aware of any decision that depends explicitly on 'other legitimate factors'. Chapter 10 returns, in a slightly different context, to one of the neglected facets of this story: the need for political decision-makers to become more adept and more accustomed to explaining and justifying (including providing evidence for) 'good reasons' (including public opinion) that are not associated with technical processes.

There are also non-legal, political, incentives for a technical framing of decisions. Porter explains numbers (and graphs and formulae) as 'strategies of communication',[173] which appear to speak to diverse audiences: the language of numbers allows different levels of governance to *appear* to speak across their different cultural contexts. The diversity of the fora demanding justification (local, national, EU and global, lay public and expert) enhances political pressure to explain through the apparently neutral language of technical assessment; an assertion of the 'facts' as a universal justification of action.[174] It may be that the contested legitimacy of the EU political institutions, the Commission in particular, enhances the appeal of 'the facts'. And it may, in any event, be difficult to exercise independent judgment, and articulate an autonomous decision, if a technical assessment, perhaps a complex and sophisticated model, appears to point in a particular direction. The inscrutability of CBA and risk assessment is a real concern if we value political debate on what should properly be done to protect the environment. Arcane and complex technical processes may also function to exclude broader publics from decision-making processes. One way of enhancing the autonomy of political decision-makers is thought to be an insistence on transparency about the uncertainties and the choices that are implicit in the assessments. An emphasis on transparency of the technical decision-making process, especially with regard to uncertainty and disagreement, has become a conventional element of the 'governance' of expertise. The risk assessment of neonicotinoids, for

---

[170] See eg Case C-84/94 *United Kingdom v Council* [1996] ECR I-5755 [69]; Case 331/88 *R v MAFF ex p Fedesa* [1990] ECR I-4023.

[171] Eg consumer protection is a relevant concern under Regulation 1829/2003 (n 168).

[172] For detailed discussion, see Lee (n 164), including the discussion of Case C-66/04 *United Kingdom v Parliament (Smoke Flavourings)* [2005] ECR I-10553 in which the UK unsuccessfully challenged the 'other legitimate factors' formula on the basis that it allowed too much discretion, and the Court tied that discussion to the legal context.

[173] TM Porter, *Trust in Numbers: The Pursuit of Objectivity in Science and Public Life* (Princeton University Press, 1995) viii.

[174] Lee (n 164).

example, drew specific attention to data gaps, for example with respect to long term risks to honey bees.[175] A range of figures is often included in CBA in order to avoid the illusion of precision, and uncertainties are often expressed;[176] writing on models is replete with warnings that models are not truths, and Wagner et al advocate 'a comprehensive explication of uncertainties, assumptions and model framing'.[177] It is also plausible that increased disagreement over CBAs and risk assessment enhances our capacity to look behind them. Indeed, I recognise the paradox in this chapter, which criticises the closing down of political debate precisely through the examination of cases that provoke high profile political and legal disagreement. However, it is unlikely that all important problems will gain the sort of expert attention and translation that open up these questions. Transparency, in the sense of providing a good indication to non-specialists of what is important about an assessment, and what has been measured and how, is neither straightforward nor a complete solution.[178] The still-incomplete assessment looks even more comprehensive and compelling than before, and 'there is no evidence that this problem will be solved by surrounding the numbers with more words'.[179] No matter how carefully technical advisors caveat their opinions and narrate uncertainty, the advice can become hardened as fact.[180] Nevertheless, a clear setting out of assumptions and uncertainties is a minimum requirement if there is to be a legitimate political decision.

It is unfortunate, as mentioned in the Preface, that there is no space for a detailed discussion of the external dimension.[181] In particular, the World Trade Organisation (WTO) is an important feature of EU decision-making. As in the EU, at a global level, environmental or health and safety measures can interrupt trade in goods, and so in the interests of trade liberalisation and for the avoidance of protectionism, the WTO demands that regulation be supported by evidence. Simplistically, we might to some degree see the EU emphasis on risk assessment as a response to the demands of the WTO, as well as an effort to control the discretion of EU and national decision-makers.[182] As in the EU, the WTO in principle recognises that science does not provide all the answers, and there is space for debate and disagreement over the conclusions that might be drawn from scientific evidence.

---

[175] Commission (n 143).

[176] Sunstein (n 16).

[177] Wagner et al (n 11) 353.

[178] Ibid, advocate advisory panels and the subsidy of under-represented stakeholders; Driesen (n 55) advocates a summary not of numbers, but of the most important effects with a note of whether those effects are quantified or not.

[179] Heinzerling (n 2) 2065.

[180] Oreskes (n 13) on flood warnings; Fisher (n 1) ch 2 on BSE. Note Fisher's focus on administrative context (rather than relations between science and politics).

[181] Of a vast literature, see eg J Peel, *Science and Risk Regulation in International Law* (Cambridge, Cambridge University Press, 2010).

[182] See eg Stokes (n 87); J Scott and E Vos, 'The Juridification of Uncertainty: Observations on the Ambivalence of the Precautionary Principle within the EU and the WTO' in C Joerges and R Dehousse, *Good Governance in Europe's Integrated Market* (Oxford, Oxford University Press, 2002).

CONCLUSIONS

The political and ethical significance of environmental decision-making is unavoidable. That is not to say that technical modes of evaluation should be rejected, and few would advocate a wholly closed, expert-determined form of decision-making, certainly in the EU. Douglas A Kysar encapsulates the reductionism of technical decision-making, specifically the authoritative role of CBA in US regulation:

> once we talked of environmental rights rather than of optimal risk trade-offs; of the grave challenges posed by uncertainty regarding potentially disastrous or irreversible consequences of human action, rather than of risk aversion and the option value of delay; of the stewardship obligations we incur on behalf of future generations, rather than of discounted welfare maximisation ...[183]

Precisely one of the attractions of technical tools of assessment is to avoid talking this more politically contentious and difficult ethical language, and the political perspective on environmental governance does still need defending. However, the EU institutions do make an imperfect, but somewhat admirable, attempt to ensure space for the consideration of values, and for reaching a political decision. Given the difficulties of ensuring a good forum for politically legitimate decision-making, the transparency, scrutiny and varying forms of participation emphasised in this book, are, whilst not easy or complete responses, important.

---

[183] Kysar (n 62) 2.

3

Sustainable Development

INTRODUCTION

USTAINABILITY HAS BEEN described as 'one of the most contested words in the political vocabulary'.[1] And yet, perhaps paradoxically, sustainable development is also a virtually uncontested central reference point in all manner of policy debates, and is a pervasive term in environmental debate. The World Commission on Environment and Development published the seminal work on sustainable development in 1987, the 'Brundtland Report'.[2] This report provides an influential and widely adopted (including by the EU[3]) 'definition' of sustainable development as development that 'meets the needs of the present without compromising the ability of future generations to meet their own needs'.[4] Sustainable development was initially a child of international law and policy, and arguably its strength still lies in the international development arena.

This chapter begins by discussing some key issues in sustainable development, as it evolved in international law. After this brief introduction, I turn to sustainable development in EU law and policy, including the role of the 'environmental integration' principle. The 'green economy' was a major theme of the latest international conference on sustainable development and is increasingly central in the EU; that will be explored in the following section. The danger that the environmentally protective core of sustainable development will be overwhelmed by the pursuit of economic growth is real, in the EU and elsewhere. This chapter then turns to EU governance of sustainable development, in particular examining the use of 'indicators', and the disappointingly weak mechanisms for reporting and review. Sustainable development continues to have a potentially important role to play, but this examination of the governance framework suggests that its value as a policy concept in the EU, notwithstanding its place in the Treaties and legislation, is rather fragile. It is central to this chapter that sustainable development is ultimately a political question, based on values that are properly the subject of public debate. Sustainable development demands, and at its best provides,

---

[1] A Dobson, *Green Political Thought* (London, Routledge, 2000) 62.

[2] Named for its Chair, Gro Harlem Brundtland, *World Commission on Environment and Development, Our Common Future* (Oxford, Oxford University Press, 1987).

[3] Eg European Commission, 'A Sustainable Europe for a Better World: A European Union Strategy for Sustainable Development' COM (2001) 264 final (the Sustainable Development Strategy).

[4] Brundtland Report (n 2) 8 and 43.

consensual space for that debate about how we pursue some social objectives, without compromising others.

THE INTERNATIONAL EVOLUTION
OF SUSTAINABLE DEVELOPMENT

'Sustainable development' emerged at the international level out of an attempt to reconcile the agendas of rich and poor countries, especially the economic development concerns of the poor, and the environmental concerns of the wealthy.[5] It was first acknowledged that human development and environmental protection must be brought together at the Stockholm Conference on Environment and Development in 1972.[6] The developing/developed country, economic/environmental division is of course overly polarised.[7] In particular, the coupling of economic growth with environmental protection is equally attractive for the wealthy world, with a similar power to bring together potentially competing economic and environmental actors inside and outside government. Sustainable development provides common language and common objectives, which are a starting point (rather than a conclusion) for debate.[8]

The UN Convention on Environment and Development (the famous Rio Earth Conference) took place in 1992. For our purposes, the *Rio Declaration on Environment and Development* (the Rio Declaration) is most significant for its elaboration of environmental principles, such as the precautionary principle and the polluter pays principle discussed in chapter one, which whilst well-established now, were hard-fought.[9] In 2002, the *Johannesburg Declaration on Sustainable Development* (the Johannesburg Declaration)[10] provided what has become a competitor to the Brundtland 'definition' of sustainable development, asserting 'the interdependent and mutually reinforcing pillars of sustainable development—economic development, social development and environmental protection'.[11] This lacks the elegance of the Brundtland approach, but reflects

---

[5] For discussion of persistent tensions between developing and developed countries, see L Rajamani, 'From Stockholm to Johannesburg: The Anatomy of Dissonance in the International Environmental Dialogue' (2003) 12 *Review of European Community and International Environmental Law* 23; P Kohona, 'The Future We Wanted—The Future We Will Get' (2012) 42 *Environmental Policy and Law* 137.

[6] UN Doc A/CONF.48/14.

[7] On tensions between developing countries, see K Morrow, 'Rio+20, the Green Economy and Re-orienting Sustainable Development' (2012) 14 *Environmental Law Review* 279.

[8] See especially M Jacobs, 'Sustainable Development as a Contested Concept' in A Dobson (ed), *Fairness and Futurity: Essays on Environmental Sustainability and Social Justice* (Oxford, Oxford University Press, 1999).

[9] Principles 15 and 16.

[10] UN Doc A/CONF.199/20. For critical discussion, see M Pallemaerts, 'International Law and Sustainable Development: Any Progress in Johannesburg?' (2003) 12 *Review of European Community and International Environmental Law* 1.

[11] Johannesburg Declaration ibid [5].

dominant understandings of sustainable development, appealing to a number of different 'good things'. Both the Brundtland and Johannesburg approaches were picked up in the agreement reached at the 'Rio+20' conference in 2012, *The Future We Want*,[12] which commits to '[ensuring] the promotion of an economically, socially and environmentally sustainable future for our planet and for present and future generations'.[13] Rio+20 conceptualises the three pillars as three 'dimensions', which may place greater emphasis on the *integration* of economic, social and environmental concerns. That the pursuit of 'economic development, social development and environmental protection' should attract widespread consensus is unsurprising. The consensus can reveal itself to be something of an illusion when one attempts to identify the precise meaning of sustainable development in particular cases.

As a definition, the Brundtland soundbite (development that 'meets the needs of the present without compromising the ability of future generations to meet their own needs'[14]) is not particularly helpful. A single phrase selected from a report that runs to almost 400 pages, it cannot do justice even to the report itself, let alone the huge academic and political literature on sustainable development. It highlights, however, the centrality of justice to future generations, which is perhaps the most distinctive element of sustainable development. Notwithstanding the desirability of other, including economic,[15] bequests to the future, depleting environmental resources is the clearest way in which we prejudice future generations: 'the results of present profligacy are rapidly closing the options for future generations'.[16] There is a complex debate around the desirability and feasibility of formulating duties and rights in respect of future generations.[17] But even accepting that intuitive notions of justice extend to at least some future generations, this impulse of responsibility does not tell us what to do: how to prioritise current and future generations, or how future generations are likely to value environmental, economic and social bequests. Sustainable development is often seen as an injunction to leave open the greatest possible range of options, but this is not straightforward either.[18] Specific development paths or decisions cannot be determined by acknowledging the importance of future generations, although a debate may be sparked. The significance of 'future generations' in academic and policy

---

[12] *The Future We Want* UN Doc A/Res/66/288. Proposals are often made for a fourth pillar, on topics including culture, health, peace and security.

[13] Ibid [1]. The themes of Rio+20 were the green economy and institutions for sustainable development, ibid [12]. On the latter, see R Clémençon, 'Welcome to the Anthropocene: Rio+20 and the Meaning of Sustainable Development' (2012) 21 *Journal of Environment and Development* 311.

[14] Brundtland Report (n 2) 8 and 43.

[15] Eg, the disagreement about the speed with which national debt should be reduced is often framed in terms of inter-generational justice in the UK.

[16] Brundtland Report (n 2) 8.

[17] Eg E Brown Weiss, 'Intergenerational Equity: A Legal Framework for Global Environmental Change in E Brown Weiss (ed), *Environmental Change and International Law: New Challenges and Dimensions* (Tokyo, United Nations University Press, 1992); contributions to Dobson (n 8).

[18] A Dobson, *Citizenship and the Environment* (Oxford, Oxford University Press, 2003) ch 4.

analysis of sustainable development is constantly reinforced by repetition of the Brundtland 'definition'. Even the Brundtland Report itself, however, pays relatively little attention to future generations, compared to justice within the current generation. After an appearance in the Rio Declaration,[19] the very long-term future was decidedly neglected in the Johannesburg Declaration. Vague references to the future continue to pepper *The Future We Want*,[20] although the main focus is on the present generation. Given the importance of the long term to environmental protection, this may be of some concern.[21]

Justice within the current generation, specifically the links between 'poverty, inequality and environmental degradation', rather than inter-generational justice for future generations, was the major theme of the Brundtland Report.[22] It confirmed the legitimacy and necessity of continued economic development, even in the face of environmental problems, and the imperative of environmental protection in the face of poverty. The connections between environmental protection and poverty eradication are drawn from the observation that the global poor bear the brunt of environmental degradation, being more likely to live in environmentally degraded areas;[23] more likely to rely directly on environmental resources (forests, soil, climate) for food, shelter and warmth; and less able to protect themselves from the effects of environmental degradation such as climate change. And just as the poor suffer from environmental degradation, the poor may degrade the environment in search of survival. It is often agreed that a certain level of prosperity is necessary before environmental protection becomes either desirable or technically feasible.[24] None of this should distract attention from the contribution of rich developed economies (and individuals in them) to environmental damage. But importantly, sustainable development attempts to side step the perception that environmental protection is a hobby of the rich. The ways in which the different dimensions of sustainable development feature in actual decisions are not dictated by the concept itself.

---

[19] 'The right to development must be fulfilled so as to equitably meet developmental and environmental needs of present and future generations', principle 3.

[20] Above (n 12). As well as the title, see eg [1], [31], [39], [50], [86], [158], [191], [197].

[21] M Jacobs, *Environmental Modernisation: The New Labour Agenda* (London, Fabian Society, 1999) argues that the severity of current environmental degradation means that references to the future are no longer necessary.

[22] Brundtland Report (n 2) xii. This pervades the Report, but see eg 2–3; 28–30; chs 5 and 9. This also pervades European Commission, 'A Decent Life for All: Ending Poverty and Giving the World a Sustainable Future' COM (2013) 92 final, eg 3.

[23] This resonates also with the environmental justice movement within developed countries, touched on below.

[24] This is in part a broad political argument, but sometimes refers to the 'environmental Kuznets curve', which posits that certain forms of environmental degradation can be seen first to increase, but then to decline, with an increase in per capita income. The conclusion should not be drawn that economic growth will necessarily take care of all environmental degradation. See DA Kysar, *Regulating from Nowhere: Environmental Law and the Search for Objectivity* (New Haven, Yale University Press, 2010) 128–30.

One of the major outcomes of Rio+20 was the commitment to begin a process for the agreement of 'sustainable development goals' (SDGs), which will spell out some more content for sustainable development.[25] *The Future We Want* places SDGs in the context of the UN Millennium Development Goals (MDGs).[26] The MDGs were agreed at the turn of the millennium in eight areas: poverty and hunger; universal education; gender equality; child health; maternal health; HIV/AIDS; environmental sustainability; and global partnership.[27] The MDGs are supplemented by targets and official indicators: for example, the goal of poverty eradication is supplemented by a target to 'halve between 1990 and 2015 the proportion of people whose income is less than $1 a day'.[28] The target date for the MDGs is 2015, when they expire. Whilst the MDGs focus on poverty, and on the developing world,[29] the SDGs have to be 'global in nature',[30] and include 'all three dimensions of sustainable development and their interlinkages'.[31] The MDGs were simply stated, and although not without their critics, they captured the development agenda and contributed to broad agreement around the pursuit of particular focused development objectives. This is a considerable achievement. Learning from this, SDGs are to be 'action oriented, concise and easy to communicate, limited in number, aspirational'.[32] Whilst simplicity is a great political strength of 'goals' like this, it has its drawbacks. Conspicuous absences are inevitable (for example climate change does not feature in the MDGs, nor do reproductive rights), and the appropriate degree of ambition will always be controversial.[33] Averages can disguise national inequalities, or lead to an emphasis on quantity over quality,[34] and causal links are not clear. There is also a risk of over-prioritising the things that can be easily measured.

---

[25] Information on process for the agreement of SDGs can be found at sustainabledevelopment.un.org/index.php?menu=1300. The UN Secretary General's High Level Panel of Eminent Persons reported in 2013, *A New Global Partnership: Eradicate Poverty and Transform Economies through Sustainable Development* (New York, United Nations, 2013), identifying five 'transformative shifts', and 12 (indicative) goals.

[26] *The Future We Want* (n 12) [18], [245]. Millennium Declaration UN Doc A/RES/55/2, see www.un.org/millenniumgoals/.

[27] Relationships between developing/developed countries, and developing countries and the private sector.

[28] See United Nations, *Millennium Development Goals Report 2013* (New York, UN, 2013). Now $1.25, ibid.

[29] Including the four targets within the 'sustainability' MDG: 'integrating sustainable development into country policies and programmes and reverse the loss of environmental resources', reducing biodiversity loss, halving the proportion of the population without access to safe drinking water and basic sanitation, and achieving (by 2020) 'a significant improvement in the lives of at least 100 million slum dwellers'.

[30] *The Future We Want* (n 12) [247].

[31] Ibid [246].

[32] Ibid [247].

[33] Eg, whilst the 100 million people target for slums has been met, the number of people living in slums has increased, United Nations (n 28) 50.

[34] Eg, the primary education target is measured by numbers in primary education, and not the quality of that education.

Although the SDGs are to cover all three 'dimensions' of sustainable development, poverty eradication is still at its heart, described in *The Future We Want* as the 'greatest global challenge facing the world today'.[35] The centrality of poverty is often seen as a manifestation of the growing strength of developing countries in international negotiations, from the time of the first Rio conference.[36] The emphasis on poverty should remind us that economic growth can be an ethically serious concern to stand alongside environmental protection, straddling the economic and social elements of sustainable development. The 'social development' dimension of sustainable development also addresses a wide range of social justice and equality issues *within* nations and regions, including for example in *The Future We Want* 'gender equality and women's empowerment', 'universal health coverage', 'decent work for all', 'equal access to education'.[37]

Andrea Ross expressed concern some years ago that the environment could get 'squeezed out' of sustainable development, given all the good things being promised, and that the dominance of sustainable development could actually lead to the neglect of environmental protection.[38] The danger of 'squeezing out' environmental protection is particularly acute when social development merges into the pursuit of economic growth. Growth is a core aspect of poverty eradication as understood in all of these international agreements, and in the EU, as discussed below. *The Future We Want* reasserts commitment to a list of earlier environmental agreements, including the three treaties agreed at the first Rio conference in 1992,[39] and discusses various environmental issues, including oceans, climate change and biodiversity.[40] It does not, however, contain any specific and novel environmental commitments.[41] Both the SDGs and the 'green economy' (another important outcome of Rio+20, discussed below) have the potential to become challenging environmental commitments, putting paid to concerns about sustainable development squeezing out the environment at the international level. But in neither case can environmental commitments go without saying, and the danger of consensus around (economic) growth at virtually any (environmental) cost is also real.

---

[35] *The Future We Want* (n 12) [2]. Ending poverty is the first 'transformative shift' identified by the Eminent Persons (n 25), expressed as a need to 'leave no one behind'. Poverty was also a major focus in Johannesburg, although with little in the way of fresh commitments, see L Kimball, FX Perrez and J Werksman, 'The Results of the World Summit on Sustainable Development: Targets, Institutions and Trade Implications' (2002) 13 *Yearbook of International Environmental Law* 3.

[36] Clémençon (n 13).

[37] *The Future We Want* (n 12) [8], [139], [147], [229].

[38] A Ross, 'Is the Environment Getting Squeezed Out of Sustainable Development?' [2003] *Public Law* 249, discussing the UK.

[39] United Nations Framework Convention on Climate Change (1992) 31 ILM 851, the Convention on Biological Diversity (1992) 31 ILM 818, and the Convention to Combat Desertification 1992 (1994) 33 ILM 1328.

[40] *The Future We Want* (n 12) [158], [190], [197]. On the UN Environment Programme's role in the preparation of Rio+20, see Morrow (n 7).

[41] For a critical review, see Clémençon (n 13).

SUSTAINABLE DEVELOPMENT IN EU LAW AND POLICY

Article 3(3) of the Treaty on European Union (TEU) provides:

> The Union shall establish an internal market. It shall work for the sustainable development of Europe based on balanced economic growth and price stability, a highly competitive social market economy, aiming at full employment and social progress, and a high level of protection and improvement of the quality of the environment. It shall promote scientific and technological advance.

Environmental protection is clearly part of Article 3, but the emphasis is, arguably, on the economic side, in particular in the reference to economic *growth* (albeit balanced). Sustainable development has an important place in the treaties, also featuring in the recitals to the TEU and in the provisions on external action.[42] I focus here on the internal dimension, but as suggested in the Preface, not because the external dimension is unimportant.

Sustainable development as an attempt to minimise the trade-off between economic growth and environmental protection has been implicit and explicit in a number of EU environmental action programmes.[43] A broader approach, with more focus on the social dimension, emerged in the 2001 Sustainable Development Strategy,[44] and a Renewed Strategy was adopted by the European Council in 2006.[45] The Renewed Strategy, like its predecessor, adopts the classic approach: 'the needs of the present generation should be met without compromising the ability of future generations to meet their own needs', and including the three pillars of 'environmental protection', 'social equity and cohesion' and 'economic prosperity' in its four 'key objectives' (together with 'meeting our international responsibilities').

The EU Sustainable Development Strategy was, however, rather overshadowed by the economically-oriented 'Lisbon Agenda',[46] which aimed to make the EU 'the most competitive and dynamic knowledge-based economy in the world, capable of sustainable economic growth with more and better jobs and greater social cohesion'.[47] Improving economic performance was at the heart of the Lisbon

---

[42] Art 3(5) TEU; Art 21 TEU.

[43] Eg 5th Environmental Action Programme, *Towards Sustainability: A European Community Programme of Policy and Action in Relation to the Environment and Sustainable Development* [1993] OJ C138/5. The proposed 7th Environmental Action Programme (7th EAP) is also full of references to sustainability, European Commission, *Proposal for a Decision of the European Parliament and of the Council on a General Union Environment Action Programme to 2020, 'Living Well, Within the Limits of Our Planet'* COM (2012) 710 final. See M Pallemaerts, 'Developing More Sustainability?' in A Jordan and C Adelle (eds), *Environmental Policy in the EU: Actors, Institutions and Processes* (Abingdon, Routledge, 2013) on the evolution of sustainable development in the EU.

[44] Commission (n 3).

[45] *Renewed Sustainable Development Strategy* (2006), European Council Document 10917/06.

[46] Eg R Steurer and G Berger, 'The EU's Double-Track Pursuit of Sustainable Development in the 2000s: How Lisbon and Sustainable Development Strategies Ran Past Each Other' (2011) 18 *International Journal of Sustainable Development and World Ecology* 99; Pallemaerts (n 43).

[47] Lisbon European Council Conclusions, 23 and 24 March 2000.

Agenda, although it also contained some important social objectives, on issues including training, employment, social exclusion and poverty. The addition of an environmental perspective by the Sustainable Development Strategy, whilst important, always seemed like something of an afterthought.[48] The successor to Lisbon, 'Europe 2020: A Strategy for Smart, Sustainable and Inclusive Growth',[49] is now said by the Commission to be the main instrument for the pursuit of sustainable development.[50] It does have a more significant sustainable development agenda than Lisbon, including 'resource efficiency, low carbon economy, research and innovation, employment, social inclusion and youth',[51] as well as the 'green economy' theme discussed further below. But the focus of *Europe 2020* is very much on responding to the economic crisis, and economic growth is the priority. Employment is the main social concern; climate change the main environmental concern. This shallow approach to the social and environmental dimensions of sustainable development is not surprising given the severity of the economic shock. It is at least something that the economy should be 'smart' ('based on knowledge and innovation'), 'sustainable' ('more resource efficient, greener and more competitive') and 'inclusive' ('high employment'; 'delivering economic, social and territorial cohesion').[52] But if environmental values are cast aside when things get difficult, there is little hope of progress.

Although *Europe 2020* is not completely bereft of environmental concerns, its dominance of the sustainable development agenda does not bode well for the 'squeezing out' of environmental protection.[53] The Commission's proposed 7th Environmental Action Programme (7th EAP) adds an independent, overarching environmental strategy to mediate the pursuit of growth.[54] That the 7th EAP is being prepared at all (and it is still to be agreed through the ordinary legislative process) was not a foregone conclusion.[55] Given the weak embedding of environmental objectives (other than climate change) in *Europe 2020*, an independent

---

[48] The Gothenburg European Council in 2001 brought the sustainable development strategy within the Lisbon process.

[49] European Commission, 'Europe 2020: A Strategy for Smart, Sustainable and Inclusive Growth' COM (2010) 2020 final.

[50] The Commission says it will implement its Rio+20 commitments 'in particular' through *Europe 2020*, see Commission (n 22) 6; also European Commission, 'Rio+20: Towards the Green Economy and Better Governance' COM (2011) 363 final. There seems to be some disagreement between Council and Commission, see the Commission's 'statement' appended to Council Conclusions, *Rio+20: Outcome and Follow Up to the UNCSD 2012 Summit*, 25 October 2012. See also the discussion in European Sustainable Development Network (ESDN) Quarterly Report No 28, *The Future of the EU SDS in Light of the Rio+20 Outcomes* (ESDN, 2013).

[51] Highlighted by Commission (n 22).

[52] Commission (n 49) 10.

[53] ESDN Quarterly Report, *Sustainable Development Governance and Policies in the Light of Major EU Policy Strategies and International Developments* (ESDN, 2011) analyses the limited coverage in *Europe 2020*.

[54] Above (n 43).

[55] European Commission, 'Impact Assessment of Proposal for a Decision on a General Union Environment Action Programme to 2020, "Living Well, Within the Limits of Our Planet"' SWD (2012) 398 final, 43.

environmental planning and review process is important. The 7th EAP may also help to 'underpin and legitimise the environmental agenda'.[56]

EU environmental legislation often, although by no means invariably,[57] refers to sustainable development, generally presenting environmental legislation as the mechanism by which its environmental dimension is implemented.[58] Non-environmental legislation only rarely mentions sustainable development,[59] and explicit duties of sustainable development (subject to the obligation contained in Article 3(3) TEU) are rare.[60] As well as legitimising the incorporation of environmental considerations into other areas,[61] sustainable development also brings economic considerations into the pursuit of environmental values. *R v Secretary of State for Environment, Transport and the Regions, ex p First Corporate Shipping*[62] concerned a challenge by a property owner against the UK Government's notification of a site to the Commission for designation under the Habitats Directive.[63] In his discussion of the relevance of economic considerations in the designation of sites for nature conservation purposes under the Directive, Léger AG observes that:

> sustainable development does not mean that the interests of the environment must necessarily and systematically prevail over the interests defended in the context of the other policies pursued by the Community ... On the contrary, it emphasises the necessary balance between various interests which sometimes clash, but which must be reconciled.[64]

---

[56] Ibid [6.2.1]. However, environmental action programmes have so far had relatively limited policy impact, I von Homeyer, 'Emerging Experimentalism in EU Environmental Governance' in CF Sabel and J Zeitlin (eds), *Experimentalist Governance in the European Union: Towards a New Architecture* (Oxford, Oxford University Press, 2010).

[57] Eg there is no reference to sustainable development in Directive 2010/75/EU on Industrial Emissions (Integrated Pollution Prevention and Control) [2010] OJ L334/17, although there was in its predecessor, Directive 2008/1/EC Concerning Integrated Pollution Prevention and Control [2008] OJ L24/8, Recital 10. Art 3 TEU nevertheless applies.

[58] Eg Regulation 1907/2006/EC concerning the Registration, Evaluation, Authorisation and Restriction of Chemicals (REACH) [2006] OJ L396/1 provides that 'A high level of human health and environmental protection should be ensured ... with the goal of achieving sustainable development', Recital 3.

[59] Legislation relating to external trade agreements frequently refers to sustainable development. In terms similar to environmental legislation, Directive 2011/24/EU on the application of patients' rights in cross-border healthcare [2011] OJ L88/45, refers to the contribution of health systems to sustainable development, Recital 3.

[60] By contrast with the UK, see A Ross, 'Why Legislate for Sustainable Development? An Examination of Sustainable Development Provisions in UK and Scottish Statutes' (2008) 20 *Journal of Environmental Law* 35. Eg the Greater London Authority Act 1999, provides for the exercise of certain powers 'in the way which it considers best calculated ... to contribute towards the achievement of sustainable development in the United Kingdom', s 30(5).

[61] Mainly through the integration principle, see below.

[62] Case C-371/98 *R v Secretary of State for Environment, Transport and the Regions, ex p First Corporate Shipping* [2000] ECR-I 9235. See D McGillivray, 'Valuing Nature: Economic Value, Conservation Values and Sustainable Development' (2002) 14 *Journal of Environmental Law* 85.

[63] Directive 1992/43/EEC on the conservation of natural habitats and of wild fauna and flora ('Habitats Directive') [1992] OJ L206/7.

[64] *First Corporate Shipping* (n 62) [54] (Léger AG). The Court did not refer to this part of the Opinion.

Whilst the idea that there are difficult decisions to be made is unobjectionable, this approach is a demonstration of sustainable development enhancing the status of economic concerns in environmental decisions. On the particular facts of the case, it allows economic concerns to creep into a decision that, arguably, should be taken on ecological grounds alone.[65]

To take a different example, undefined ideas of sustainability ('sustainable water policy', 'sustainable use', encouragingly also 'environmental sustainability') pervade the Water Framework Directive.[66] The 'purposes' of the Directive include the promotion of 'sustainable water use based on a long-term protection of available water resources'.[67] As discussed in chapter four, the Water Framework Directive sets an overarching ambitious environmental target of 'good water status', but alongside extensive opportunities to meet alternative, less onerous standards. An initial reading of the Directive would suggest that 'sustainable development' constrains the use of alternatives to this primary environmental objective; but equally, it may allow those exceptions to be shaped around economic arguments. For example, 'new modifications' (such as reservoirs or canalisation) to water bodies, or 'alterations to the level of bodies of groundwater' (for example by abstraction) may mean that a body of water fails to achieve good water status. One of the ways in which the Member State can nevertheless avoid a breach of the Directive is if the benefits 'to the environment and to society' of meeting the Directive's ecological objectives are 'outweighed by the benefits of the new modifications or alterations to human health, to the maintenance of human safety or to *sustainable development*'.[68] Further conditions apply, but essentially sustainable development is balanced *against* water status. We might see in the Water Framework Directive the (mis)use of the philosophy of sustainable development to undermine ecological objectives. Or alternatively, perhaps the ambitious ecological objectives are only possible because they can be compromised in necessary cases. In that case, the philosophy of sustainable development would be doing precisely what it is supposed to, given the intimate connection between the use of water and human and economic wellbeing. Either way, at best sustainable development opens up the space for these debates to take place during implementation. It is unlikely that the word 'sustainable' alone imposes significant *legal* constraints on decisions.[69]

---

[65] McGillivray (n 62).

[66] Directive 2000/60/EC establishing a framework for community action in the field of water policy ('Water Framework Directive') [2000] OJ L327/1, Recitals 5, 13, 18, 23, 41. Note also eg the mediation of health and environmental concerns by economic (or socio-economic) concerns under REACH (n 58), ch 9 below.

[67] Ibid Art 1.

[68] Ibid Art 4(7), italics added. See also Art 4(3).

[69] In the context of a controversial river diversion in Greece, Kokott AG held that 'despite its detrimental effects on the environment, water power is a typical example of sustainable power generation'; 'irrigation of agricultural land is to be regarded as an overriding public interest or—perhaps—as a sustainable development measure', Case C-43/10 *Nomarchiaki Aftodioikisi Aitoloakarnanias* not yet reported in the ECR, [84]–[91]. Common Implementation Strategy, *Guidance Document No 1 Economics and the Environment—The Implementation Challenge of the Water Framework Directive*

Sustainable development could raise serious questions about the EU's social and economic order. A radical approach to sustainable development would need to put the very real tension between economic development, social development and environmental protection at the forefront of the debate. Whilst in the long term, and in the aggregate, environmental protection may indeed be compatible with, and necessary for, economic and social benefits, short-term conflicts are real. The basic insistence in the EU that our current lifestyle is consistent with environmental protection (and social justice, etc) brings out the central optimism of sustainable development as a concept. Positively, it at least enables debate and modest steps in a society embedded, as the EU is, in the market economy. Nevertheless, the further marginalisation of the more challenging aspects of sustainable development within economic strategy is worrying, and confirms the importance of maintaining a strong environmental strategy that is independent of sustainable development.

ENVIRONMENTAL INTEGRATION

A core aspect of the implementation of sustainable development in the EU is the 'integration principle', contained in Article 11 of the Treaty on the Functioning of the European Union (TFEU):[70] 'Environmental protection requirements must be integrated into the definition and implementation of the Union policies and activities, in particular with a view to promoting sustainable development'. Improving 'environmental integration and policy coherence' remains one of the nine 'priority objectives' of the proposed 7th EAP.[71] At its simplest, environmental policy integration attempts to act on the recognition that more can be achieved by incorporating environmental concerns within other policy areas (such as agriculture, transport, industry, tourism) than by leaving them to explicitly 'environmental' policy.[72] Like sustainable development, environmental integration is in part an effort to 'shift from a traditional antagonistic model' of the relationship between different policy objectives and policy actors, 'to a new co-operative model'.[73]

Notwithstanding long standing political and legal support, introduced in the new environment Title of the Single European Act 1986, and 'promoted' to a

(2003) does little more than rehearse the difficulties and competing approaches to sustainable development, see Box D2a.2 and 216.

[70] On the development of environmental policy integration, see A Jordan, A Schout and M Unfried, 'Policy Coordination' in Jordan and Adelle (n 43).

[71] 7th EAP (n 43).

[72] European Commission, 'A Blueprint to Safeguard Europe's Water Resources' COM (2012) 673 final is a good example.

[73] J Hertin and F Berkhout, 'Analysing Institutional Strategies for Environmental Policy Integration: The Case of EU Enterprise Policy' (2003) 5 *Journal of Environmental Policy and Planning* 39, 44. See also Mazák AG: 'the objectives of the common agricultural policy and those of environmental protection are not mutually exclusive; rather they should be considered to be complementary', Case C-61/09 *Landkreis Bad Dürkheim v Aufsichts-und Dienstleistungsdirektion* [2010] ECR I-9763 [20].

general principle in the Amsterdam Treaty of 1997, the consensus seems to be that environmental integration is poorly understood and poorly implemented.[74] Integration is difficult to institutionalise, demanding the involvement of and cooperation between many actors in different parts of the decision-making process,[75] and is especially difficult in the EU's fragmented decision-making context.[76] Procedural approaches to integration have dominated.[77] Environmental assessment, discussed in chapter seven, can make an important contribution; impact assessment of major policy initiatives, discussed in chapter two, is the dominant mechanism for integration at EU level.[78] The outcome of a policy of integration on the ground is poorly understood,[79] although it is easy to identify anecdotally areas of any policy where environmental concerns have blatantly not been integrated.

Jordan and Lenschow compare strong approaches to integration, in which priority is given to environmental objectives,[80] with weaker approaches, which emphasise the search for win-win options and weigh the different objectives more evenly.[81] The latter seems to be the approach taken in the EU. Geelhoeld AG, for example, has rejected the proposition that Article 11 requires environmental protection to 'always be taken to be the prevalent interest', confirming instead its procedural ('take due account') dimension.[82] In this respect, the integration principle at least legitimises the relevance of environmental considerations to other areas of policy, and the Treaty's mandatory language[83] should create an obligation on decision-makers. Environmental protection may 'form part of'[84] or even be 'regarded as an objective' of other areas of policy.[85] But save an egregious failure to

[74] A Jordan and A Lenschow, 'Environmental Policy Integration: A State of the Art Review' (2010) 20 *Environmental Policy and Governance* 147.

[75] For a sense of the challenges, see also European Environment Agency (EEA), *Environmental Policy Integration in Europe: Administrative Culture and Practices* (EEA Technical Report No 5/2005).

[76] Jordan, Schout and Unfried (n 70).

[77] Hertin and Berkhout (n 73).

[78] The role of impact assessment is reaffirmed by the 7th EAP (n 43). The 'Cardiff process', which placed responsibility for integration on the different Council formations, 'quietly expired' during the mid-2000s, Jordan and Lenschow (n 74) 154; Cardiff is not mentioned in the proposed 7th EAP, ibid. The website survives, although there has been no obvious activity since the mid-2000s, europa.eu/legislation_summaries/environment/sustainable_development/l28075_en.htm. EEA (n 75), dismisses Cardiff as 'little more than the development of a roadmap', 29.

[79] Jordan and Lenschow, ibid.

[80] Ibid; see also W Lafferty and E Hovden, 'Environmental Policy Integration: Towards an Analytical Framework' (2003) 12 *Environmental Policy* 1.

[81] Ambiguously, the EEA (n 75) interprets environmental policy integration as requiring environmental issues to be 'reflected' in policy-making, as well as part of a general effort to coordinate policy, Executive Summary.

[82] Case C-161/04 *Austria v European Parliament and Council* [2006] ECR I-7183 [59] (Geelhoed AG).

[83] By contrast with the language of the other 'integration' principles, discussed below, text at nn 87–88. Case C-379/98 *PreussenElektra AG v Schleswag AG* [2001] ECR I-2099: 'Article 6 is not merely programmatic; it imposes legal obligations' [231] (Jacobs AG).

[84] Eg Case C-428/07 *R (on the application of Horvath) v Secretary of State for Environment, Food and Rural Affairs* [2009] ECR I-6355 [29].

[85] Eg Case C-440/05 *Commission v Council* [2007] ECR I-9097 [60].

consider relevant information, it is difficult to imagine a successful judicial review based on a failure to integrate.[86]

Environmental policy was the only beneficiary of 'integration' before Lisbon. Now, environmental integration sits alongside other similar provisions, on 'the promotion of a high level of employment, the guarantee of adequate social protection, the fight against social exclusion, and a high level of education, training and protection of human health', consumer protection, animal welfare and discrimination,[87] as well as a general requirement on the EU to 'ensure consistency between its policies and activities, taking all of its objectives into account'.[88] Whilst the range of integration principles may reduce the visibility and status of environmental integration, it is more in line with the breadth of sustainable development.[89] It also puts paid to any lingering hope that environmental policy integration might be about the *prioritisation*, rather than the simple consideration, of environmental values. Integration seems to be a tool to enhance 'policy coherence' generally, ensuring that all relevant issues are understood and considered as fully as possible, rather than a tool of environmental protection.[90] Whilst this may be a conceptually limited approach to integration,[91] and should be part of any policy process, it is at least an important minimum.[92]

THE GREEN ECONOMY

One of the real achievements of sustainable development has been to make the case that, at least in principle, environmental protection need not be a challenge to economic growth. This perspective on sustainable development has now been strongly asserted as the 'green economy'[93] theme in Rio+20.[94] Michael Jacobs identifies two versions of the 'green economy' thesis: first that regulating for

---

[86] G Marín Durán and E Morgera, 'Commentary on Article 37 of the EU Charter on Fundamental Rights—Environmental Protection' in S Peers et al (eds), *The EU Charter of Fundamental Rights: A Commentary* (Oxford, Hart Publishing, 2014).

[87] Arts 8–13 TFEU.

[88] Art 7 TFEU.

[89] Integration, of economic, social *and* environmental issues, is a Policy Guiding Principle found in the *Renewed Strategy* (n 45).

[90] A Persson, *Environmental Policy Integration: An Introduction* (Stockholm, Stockholm Environmental Institute, 2004) distinguishes between 'normative' and 'organisational' approaches to environmental policy integration, 19–20, citing LJ Lundqvist, *Sweden and Ecological Governance: Straddling the Fence* (Manchester, Manchester University Press, 2004).

[91] Lafferty and Hovden (n 80).

[92] And procedure and substance cannot be separated, see eg chs 2 and 7.

[93] See M Jacobs, 'Green Growth: Economic Theory and Political Discourse', *Grantham Research Institute on Climate Change and the Environment Working Paper* No 92 (2012) for a very useful discussion of the economic theory behind 'green growth', which he describes as a 'sister term' of 'green economy'. On the institutional development of the green economy, see Jacobs, ibid; E Morgera and A Savaresi, 'A Conceptual and Legal Perspective on the Green Economy' (2013) 22 *Review of European Community and International Environmental Law* 14. For sceptical discussion, see Morrow (n 7).

[94] *The Future We Want* (n 12) contains a full section on the 'green economy'.

environmental protection is less economically costly than doing nothing;[95] and secondly, that environmental protection is not simply compatible with good economic performance, but can actually improve economic performance, even in the relatively short term. The proposed 7th EAP claims 'important socio-economic benefits' from environmental protection, including employment and the exploitation of the global market for 'eco-industries',[96] as well as cost savings from resource efficiency.[97] The theoretical and empirical claims for the green economy are, of course, disputed,[98] and it is 'quite plausible that *some* environmental policies will be growth-enhancing, but others will act as a constraint'.[99] Given that some of the time, and especially in the short term, economic and environmental (and social) objectives will conflict, the role of values and politics in making choices, as discussed below, remains crucial.

The green economy, undefined in *The Future We Want*, appears to narrow sustainable development to the economy/environment linkage. For some, this enhanced focus is a great advantage, but that does depend on what one wants from sustainable development. Michael Jacobs argued in an earlier paper that approaches to sustainable development differ along four main fault lines: the degree of environmental protection required; the importance of equity; the role of public participation; and the scope of the subject matter. Jacobs suggested that a radical, challenging approach to sustainable development will tend to argue for higher levels of environmental protection, a central role for equity and public participation, and a broad scope to the subject matter covered by sustainable development. Whilst the level of environmental protection remains open, the green economy otherwise, at first glance, focuses on a narrow set of economy/environment concerns. However, for better (ambition) or worse (lack of focus), the approach to the green economy at Rio+20 is set 'in the context of sustainable development and poverty eradication'. Rather than superseding sustainable development, it is 'one of the important tools available for achieving sustainable development', and 'should contribute to eradicating poverty as well as sustained economic growth, enhancing social inclusion, improving human welfare and creating opportunities for employment and decent work for all, while maintaining the healthy functioning of the Earth's ecosystems'.[100]

The green economy is one aspect of *Europe 2020*, and 'a resource-efficient, green and competitive low-carbon economy' is one of the nine priority objectives of the proposed 7th EAP. *Europe 2020* frames the 'green' part of the green economy primarily in terms of climate change, which is the only one of the five 'headline

---

[95] See Jacobs (n 93).

[96] Commission (n 43) [29].

[97] Commission, ibid. See also Commission (n 55), Annex V, which adds discussion of environmental taxes and environmentally harmful subsidies, the internalisation of environmental externalities, see ch 4.

[98] Jacobs (n 93).

[99] Ibid 16.

[100] *The Future We Want* (n 12) [56]. Jacobs (n 8).

targets' that could be described as environmental. Environmental relevance is slightly extended by concern with resource efficiency, and a *Resource Efficient Europe* is one of the seven 'flagship initiatives' set in motion by *Europe 2020*,[101] as well as an important feature of the proposed 7th EAP. Resource (including carbon) efficiency is important, but has well known limitations. In particular, efficiency does not necessarily reduce resource consumption overall, for example if cars are more fuel efficient, but we drive further.[102] The Commission acknowledges that 'overall, consumption is increasing over time and generally faster than improvements in resource efficiency',[103] and the European Environment Agency (EEA) observes that the EU is better at resource efficiency than ecosystem resilience, describing the relationship between resource efficiency, decreased environmental pressures and ecosystem resilience as 'ill-defined'.[104]

Jacobs attributes the rise of the 'green growth' discourse to the 'decreasing traction' of sustainable development, as well as (and probably related to) continued environmental degradation after years of sustainable development policy.[105] We might also note the coincidence of this discourse with economic recession,[106] when resurrecting economic growth is perceived to be of absolutely central importance, and arguing against growth, even for the slowing down of growth, is politically very difficult.[107] Green growth has emerged from a 'mainstream and pragmatic community of environment-economic policymakers', whilst sustainable development was, at least in part, a conscious response to the 'limits to growth' debate of the 1970s.[108] For current purposes, the central thesis of 'limits to growth' is that because the resources of the earth are finite, human ingenuity will not allow us to design our way out of trouble: technological fixes to environmental problems will at best postpone, rather than prevent, environmental collapse.[109] Limits to growth envision absolute incompatibility between economic growth and environmental protection, making the pursuit of pragmatic environmental protection measures very difficult. Although the debate about environmental limits did not simply go away with

---

[101] European Commission, 'A Resource-Efficient Europe—Flagship Initiative under the Europe 2020 Strategy' COM (2011) 21. Note also the industrial policy flagship initiative (European Commission, 'An Integrated Industrial Policy for the Globalisation Era: Putting Competitiveness and Sustainability at Centre Stage' COM (2010) 614), which discusses the green economy, focussing on competitiveness.

[102] Commission (n 43). Resource efficiency is relatively wide ranging, including a concern for biodiversity.

[103] Commission (n 55) 33.

[104] EEA, *Environmental Indicator Report 2012: Ecosystem Resilience and Resource Efficiency in a Green Economy in Europe* (EEA, 2012), Part 3; [124].

[105] See n 93. The proposed 7th EAP paints a grim picture of current environmental trends (n 43) 7.

[106] Also Morgera and Savaresi (n 93).

[107] There is of course much to say on this, and important voices argue against the assumption that growth is a necessary part of the good life, see eg T Jackson, *Prosperity without Growth: Economics for a Finite Planet* (London, Earthscan, 2009).

[108] Jacobs (n 93) 6.

[109] DH Meadows et al, *The Limits to Growth: A Report for the Club of Rome's Project on the Predicament of Mankind* (New York, Universe Books, 1972). See the discussion in Dobson (n 1).

the rise of sustainable development,[110] sustainable development is a concept that denies absolute limits. It asserts that whilst, for example, some resources are non-renewable, limits are equally determined by technological and social organisation; and 'technological and social organisation can be both managed and improved to make way for a new era of economic growth'.[111] The serious disruption to ways of life and human values implied by an acceptance of limits was deliberately absent from sustainable development, even before the rise of the 'green economy'.

If the green economy is just one part of sustainable development, it is also a rhetorically powerful sharpening of an existing environment/economy debate. Its potential to narrow the scope of sustainable development in the EU is seen in the dominance of economic growth, mediated by a shallow greening through climate change and resource efficiency, over other objectives in *Europe 2020,* and the dominance of *Europe 2020* in policy-making. Like sustainable development itself, the green economy may be a Trojan horse for business as usual, or a minor technical tweak to business as usual. If we place the emphasis on the 'green', however, it could be a (missed) opportunity to '[place] environmental management at the centre of economic development'.[112] All depends on its implementation; as Jacobs puts it, political economy is as important as economic theory.[113]

IMPLEMENTATION AND GOVERNANCE OF SUSTAINABLE DEVELOPMENT

Sustainable development has not so far featured heavily in judicial review, and it is difficult to imagine a court condemning a particular decision as substantively unsustainable. Sustainable development can also be difficult to challenge politically. A decision might be deemed sustainable because of its impact on poverty, or because it provides employment, whilst others might place greater emphasis on the environmental impact. Critics who say that sustainable development can justify any decision are not quite correct though. Sustainable development provides language for the political censure of a decision, and we might ask whether calling *Europe 2020* a sustainable development strategy is simply an abuse of language.[114] But the tractability of sustainable development means that additional criteria are necessary if we are to hold decision-makers to account for the quality of implementation.

---

[110] G Mace, 'The Limits to Sustainability Science: Ecological Constraints or Endless Innovation?' (2012) 10 *PLOS Biology,* available at www.plosbiology.org/article/info:doi/10.1371/journal.pbio.1001343.

[111] Brundtland Report (n 2) 8.

[112] Morgera and Savaresi (n 93) 23.

[113] Jacobs (n 93) 18.

[114] The furore in the UK over the justification of a crudely pro-development draft national planning policy framework in terms of 'sustainable development' is another example. Some sense of the debate can be seen in Department of Communities and Local Government (DCLG), *National Planning Policy Framework: Summary of Consultation Responses* (DCLG, 2012).

The promotion of indicators to measure progress in sustainable development dates back to the first Rio conference. Like SDGs, sustainable development indicators (SDIs) attempt to simplify and render measurable a complex idea, increasing transparency by providing something specific for which decision-makers can be held to account.[115] Whilst the language is sometimes used interchangeably, goals or targets specify a desired end point, and indicators simply provide information on the direction of travel, without necessarily telling us when we have 'arrived'. Goals are often designed to drive progress and/or to hold actors to account. Some indicators might simply provide a snapshot of a situation for which no one can easily be held to account, but which might help policy-making. In the EU, common indicators also allow comparison and spread of good practice between Member States.

The usual approach to measuring the 'success' of a country, and the most widely adopted indicator of all, is gross domestic product (GDP). GDP per capita is the first SDI in the EU, the headline indicator of the 'socio-economic development' theme.[116] GDP measures in money the goods and services produced in a country, and its limitations are well-rehearsed.[117] For example, undesirable activities, including pertinently the cost of cleaning up pollution, add to GDP. Nor does GDP have anything to say about distribution, so that GDP can rise alongside rising poverty. There are many reasons for GDP's success, but one is 'the powerful attraction of a single headline figure allowing simple comparisons of socio-economic performance over time or across countries'.[118] 'Composite indicators', of which one of the better known is perhaps the 'ecological footprint' method, attempt to provide a similarly clear ranking of a country's overall environmental performance.[119] What is included in composite indicators, and how the different criteria should be weighed, are highly contested matters. Composite indicators might be 'better regarded as invitations to look more closely at the various components that underlie them'.[120]

The Future We Want added to already persistent calls to judge performance on measures beyond GDP.[121] There are various possible approaches, one of which is the simple reference to a wider range of indicators that has long been implicit in SDIs. The EU has a 'beyond GDP' project to develop 'indicators that are as clear

---

[115] A Ross, *Sustainable Development Law in the UK: From Rhetoric to Reality* (Abingdon, Earthscan, 2012) ch 9 discusses in detail the roles of different types of indicators; also EEA (n 75), ch 3.

[116] Eurostat, *Sustainable Development in the European Union: 2011 Monitoring Report of the EU Sustainable Development Strategy* (Luxembourg, European Union, 2011).

[117] See JE Stiglitz, A Sen, J-P Fitoussi, *Report by the Commission on the Measurement of Economic Performance and Social Progress* (2009) (the 'Stiglitz-Sen-Fitoussi Report').

[118] Stiglitz-Sen-Fitoussi ibid [135] (Narrative Report).

[119] See the discussion in ibid and European Commission, 'GDP and Beyond: Measuring Progress in a Changing World' COM (2009) 433 final.

[120] Stiglitz-Sen-Fitoussi, ibid [140]. We might say the same about GDP.

[121] *The Future We Want* (n 12) [38]. Stiglitz-Sen-Fitoussi, ibid, provides an extremely useful review of the issues.

and appealing as GDP, but more inclusive of environmental and social aspects of progress'.[122] An emerging consensus around the value of measuring 'wellbeing' has also received a lot of attention. The Stiglitz-Sen-Fitoussi Commission, reporting to the French President, identified eight dimensions of wellbeing, each of which should in principle be reported on simultaneously: material living standards; health; education; personal activities including work; political voice and governance; social connections and relationships; environment (present and future); insecurity (economic as well as physical).[123] This approach to wellbeing would not be out of place in a conventional set of SDIs. Both objective and subjective (perceived wellbeing, for example self-reported levels of 'overall life satisfaction' or happiness[124]) measurements can be taken into account. Importantly, these dimensions of wellbeing cannot be taken to indicate adequate levels of environmental quality over time; high levels of wellbeing may be compatible with environmental degradation. The Stiglitz-Sen-Fitoussi Report places heavy emphasis on the importance of separate environmental evaluation,[125] and this warning should apply to the use of any set of SDIs. The 7th EAP should provide for an independent review of environmental indicators in the EU.[126]

Economic analysis, including the expression of environmental resources in monetary terms, can also be a significant element of SDIs. The EU is developing an approach that measures 'capital' to assess sustainable development,[127] and it is striking that the proposed 7th EAP frames one of its priority objectives in terms of protecting, conserving and enhancing 'natural capital', rather than biodiversity or resilient ecosystems, for example. Framing natural resources as capital is not a new notion, and has been very influential in attempts to 'measure' sustainable development. Total capital stock is comprised of natural capital, physical capital and human capital, including for example technology, works of art and factories, as well as forest, fossil fuels and an intact ozone layer. What has become known as 'weak' sustainability (although just as 'sustainable development' has no fixed and stable meaning, nor does 'weak' or 'strong' sustainability[128]) requires the bequest of at least equal amounts of 'total capital stock' to future generations: natural, human and physical capital are essentially substitutable. 'Strong' sustainability on the other hand denies the fungibility of human or physical capital with natural

---

[122] www.beyond-gdp.eu; Commission (n 119).

[123] Stiglitz-Sen-Fitoussi (n 117) 14.

[124] Eurofound, *Third European Quality of Life Survey: Quality of life in Europe: Impacts of the crisis* (Luxembourg, European Union, 2012); the former is said to be 'cognitive', the latter 'emotional'. Measuring subjective wellbeing can be controversial, since it tends not to change a great deal, but can also change arbitrarily and be influenced by, for example, the last question asked.

[125] Stiglitz-Sen-Fitoussi (n 117) [36] (Narrative Report).

[126] 7th EAP (n 43).

[127] European Commission, 'Our Life Insurance, Our Natural Capital: an EU Biodiversity Strategy to 2020' COM (2011) 244 final.

[128] Or indeed 'very weak' and 'absurdly strong' sustainability, see A Holland, 'Substitutability: Or, Why Strong Sustainability is Weak and Absurdly Strong Sustainability is not Absurd' in J Foster (ed), *Valuing Nature? Economics, Ethics and the Environment* (London, Routledge, 1997).

capital, and requires natural capital to be maintained. The dispute between strong and weak sustainability lies in disagreement over whether 'natural capital has a unique or essential role in sustaining human welfare',[129] and the degree of permissible substitution. Neither weak nor strong sustainability argues for either infinite or zero substitutability: weak sustainability would not argue that everything (climate for example) is capable of substitution; and strong sustainability does not deny absolutely the possibility of depleting natural capital.[130] An inability to predict which natural resources are 'critical' to human wellbeing mean that this is as much a political as a technical or economic argument.[131]

On the one hand (in common with the longstanding language of 'natural resources', or the more recent turn to 'ecosystem services') the framing of the debate in terms of 'capital' emphasises economic dependence on ecosystems: 'the EU's economic prosperity and well-being is underpinned by its natural capital, which includes ecosystems that provide essential goods and services, from fertile soil and multi-functional forests to productive land and seas ...'.[132] But it is also a 'loaded' term,[133] which emphasises the commodification of nature, and may ultimately support measuring the 'environment' in wholly monetary terms. The Stiglitz-Sen-Fitoussi Report emphasises the importance of physical environmental indicators for the evaluation of sustainable development.[134] The EEA does gather data and report on physical indicators, including on biodiversity, where the 'natural capital' approach is most developed.[135]

The EU maintains data on a range of indicators from a range of sources, including *Europe 2020*, the *Renewed Strategy*, environmental action programmes, as well as disparate areas of law and policy. The proposed 7th EAP lists targets and indicators from existing law and policy, and promises the development of further indicators in conjunction with the 'flagship initiative', *A Resource Efficient Europe*.[136] The miscellany of indicators in the EU makes the tracking of performance more difficult than it should be. Broadly, the five headline targets and seven flagship initiatives of *Europe 2020* are monitored through EU and national reporting

---

[129] D Pearce and EB Barbier, *Blueprint for a Sustainable Economy* (London, Earthscan, 2000) 23. See also the discussion in ch 2 of the criticism of HM Treasury, *The Stern Review on the Economics of Climate Change* (UK Treasury, 2006) by D Helm, 'Climate Change Policy: Why has So Little Been Achieved?' (2008) 24 *Oxford Review of Economic Policy* 211.

[130] H Daly, 'On Wilfred Beckerman's Critique of Sustainable Development' (1995) 4 *Environmental Values* 49.

[131] M Arias-Moldonado, 'Rethinking Sustainability in the Anthropocene' (2013) 22 *Environmental Politics* 428. This is resonant of the discussion of 'limits', below.

[132] Commission (n 43) [16].

[133] Dobson (n 18) 155.

[134] Stiglitz-Sen-Fitoussi (n 117) [39] (Narrative Report).

[135] Commission (n 127), has a headline target of 'Halting the loss of biodiversity and the degradation of ecosystem services in the EU by 2020', and emphasises the importance of data gathering and monitoring.

[136] Commission (n 43); see also (n 101).

cycles.[137] The EEA keeps data on over 200 environmental indicators, and reports every four years on the state of the environment.[138] SDIs are reported on by Eurostat every two years.[139] The Eurostat reports do not aim to assess 'success', 'as there is no political or scientific consensus on what this state of sustainability would be, or on the optimal levels for many of the indicators'; reporting instead 'provides a relative assessment of whether the EU is moving in the right direction' on the SDIs.[140] Sunshine and cloud symbols are used to indicate 'favourable', 'moderately favourable', 'moderately unfavourable' and 'clearly unfavourable' change. This is clear, and potentially resonant with a broad public, but obviously simplistic.[141]

There is no shortage of reporting. But reporting should not be the end of the matter. The 2011 Eurostat report concludes that since 'nearly half of the headline indicators are moving in a moderately unfavourable direction, it cannot yet be concluded that the European Union is on a pathway to sustainable development',[142] an appropriately modest response that leaves it to political actors to draw stronger inferences. There seems, however, to be no obligation on EU actors to respond to data on SDIs. The Commission seems not to have reported properly on sustainable development since 2009.[143] By contrast, the *Europe 2020* targets and flagship initiatives are subject to high profile review: the *Annual Growth Survey* sets out the priorities for national and EU level reporting;[144] Member States submit their 'National Reform Programmes'; and the Commission makes 'country specific recommendations', which need to be discussed by Council and endorsed by European Council.[145] There is an explicit comparison of national performance.[146] Almost by accident, monitoring and review of the environmental and the economic seem to have been separated, with all of the emphasis on the economic.

---

[137] The Lisbon Agenda was famously subject to the 'open method of coordination', an archetype of the move to 'new governance' discussed in ch 4 below, with an elaborate set of guidelines, indicators and benchmarks, and for the use of publicity and peer review. There is an enormous literature, see P Craig and G de Búrca, *EU Law: Text, Cases and Materials* (Oxford, Oxford University Press, 2011) ch 6.

[138] EEA, *The European Environment: State and Outlook 2010* (EEA, 2010).

[139] The latest report at the time of writing is Eurostat (n 116). The 2013 monitoring report was released in December 2013.

[140] Ibid 11.

[141] Eg, the report recognises that improvement in climate change indicators is attributable to economic downturn rather than long-term innovation (on which see ch 6 below), ibid 24, but that cannot be reflected in the pictoral representation.

[142] Ibid, 13.

[143] European Commission, 'Mainstreaming Sustainable Development into EU Policies: 2009 Review of the European Union Strategy for Sustainable Development' COM (2009) 400 final. Oddly, this review came before the 2009 Eurostat report, ibid 3. The Commission was supposed to report every second year, 'Renewed Strategy' (n 45). See EESC, *Opinion on the 2011 Monitoring Report on the EU's Sustainable Development Strategy (own initiative opinion)* (Brussels, EESC, 2012). This is, however, little more than a summary, highlighting some of the negative trends, and emphasising the importance of political debate. It did criticise the Commission for failing to report on progress [1.2]. By 2012, however, the Commission had turned to *Europe 2020* for sustainable development strategy (n 50).

[144] The 2013 survey barely mentions the environment (or even climate change), COM (2012) 750 final.

[145] ec.europa.eu/europe2020/index_en.htm.

[146] ec.europa.eu/europe2020/making-it-happen/key-areas/index_en.htm.

An open-ended objective like sustainable development resists familiar legal mechanisms of accountability. Chapter four discusses the merits of broadly framed objectives, and sustainable development might usefully be considered in that context. Governance mechanisms that ensure the generation of knowledge and adaptation of norms in response to lessons learned are important. The data gathering and initial reporting on SDIs provides opportunities for learning, although currently without significant additional incentives to adapt policies in response. Obligations on the Commission to respond to performance exist in specific pieces of environmental legislation, but not currently in respect of overall performance. An obligation on political actors, most obviously the Commission and Member States, but also Council and Parliament, to respond to performance on broader environmental (and social) indicators, as they do on *Europe 2020*, is sorely needed. The relative absence of the Parliament in official sustainable development discourse is especially striking. Open and public reporting would allow for public (including environmental interest group), as well as peer (Member State and EU institutions), review and political debate. That is possible for *Europe 2020*, and there is some potential for environmental indicators in the promise that the proposed 7th EAP is to be monitored 'in the context of the *Europe 2020* Strategy's regular monitoring process'.[147] A re-energising of something like the network of Member State sustainable development coordinators[148] would heighten the opportunities for peer review and challenge.

A wealth of technical expertise is being applied to sustainable development, especially through the use of indicators. As discussed in the previous two chapters, technical expertise alone cannot provide everything we need to pursue sustainable development. First, inevitable uncertainty about the short and long-term effects of human activity precludes clear technical answers to questions about sustainable development. Even retrospectively, the availability and quality of data on SDIs,[149] together with their simplistic representation (sunshine and clouds), raise questions about knowledge. And uncertainty is magnified if composite indicators are used, and all values are expressed in the same (possibly monetary) currency.[150] Secondly, identifying indicators implies some commitment on what contributes to 'sustainability',[151] as well as prioritisation and balancing between the different aspects of sustainable development (environmental against economic, but also,

---

[147] 7th EAP (n 43) [101].

[148] They have had little influence, and were not invited to contribute to the development of the *2020 Strategy*, Steurer and Berger (n 46) 104.

[149] L Ledoux, R Mertens and P Wolff, 'EU Sustainable Development Indicators: An Overview' (2005) 29 *Natural Resources Forum* 392 discuss the quality of the data for the EU SDIs.

[150] A Stirling, 'The Appraisal of Sustainability: Some Problems and Possible Responses' (1999) 4 *Local Environment* 111.

[151] On a smaller scale, see the discussion of the choice of indicators to represent the quality of a water ecosystem, H Josefsson and L Baaner, 'The Water Framework Directive—A Directive for the Twenty-First Century?' (2011) 23 *Journal of Environmental Law* 463, 470.

for example, local air pollution against climate change).[152] This makes sustainable development an unavoidably political matter, based on values that might properly be subjected to debate. Assessing 'success' or 'failure' when a range of indicators move in different directions for different reasons, is similarly politically complex.[153] Thirdly, whilst information and expertise on physical environments is crucial, even if clear and certain it cannot provide an answer to the 'big' questions about how we should prioritise different social, economic and environmental goods. There is no 'analytical fix' to sustainable development; it is a 'social process' rather than an analytical exercise.[154]

We might also note the potential of environmental impact assessment, strategic environmental assessment and regulatory impact assessment, discussed in chapters seven and two, to contribute to sustainable development.[155] As with SDIs, there is some tension between the technical and the political aspects of environmental assessment. For now, as procedural tools, the requirement to assess the likely environmental (and social) impacts of a proposed development, activity or policy, provides a tool for integrating environmental issues into decision-making. Impact assessments are often subject to at least some consultation opportunities. An open, participatory process of decision-making allows the values involved in difficult decisions to be explicitly discussed, potentially capturing the multi-dimensionality of sustainable development.[156] If done with a 'democratising' intent, public participation can also contribute to the 'social development' aspect of sustainable development.

Nor can technical assessments easily tell us about 'justice', a recurring notion in sustainable development, in particular the relationship between inter- and intra-generational justice.[157] Whatever its intuitive core, 'justice' is subject to many competing, contentious and complex definitions and approaches. The environmental justice movement as it developed in the US examined collective discrimination, highlighting the relationship between the environment and poverty or race, in particular the exposure of those belonging to minority groups to greater environmental risks and worse environmental conditions than other citizens.[158] The way in which environmental goods and bads are distributed, in space (globally) and over time, is a significant issue in sustainable development. There has been relatively little research into environmental justice in the EU, and

---

[152] Eg E Rametsteiner et al, 'Sustainability Indicator Development—Science or Political Negotiation?' (2011) 11 *Ecological Indicators* 61.

[153] Ibid.

[154] Stirling (n 150) 121 and 131.

[155] Commission, 7th EAP (n 43); *The Future We Want* (n 12) [63].

[156] Stirling (n 150) 119. See chs 7 and 8.

[157] M Stallworthy, 'Environmental Justice Imperatives for an Era of Climate Change' (2009) 36 *Journal of Law and Society* 55 argues for greater reliance on environmental justice, in part because of the failure of sustainable development, 56.

[158] OW Pedersen, 'Environmental Justice in the UK: Uncertainty, Ambiguity and the Law' (2011) 31 *Legal Studies* 279 provides a useful brief overview of the emergence of environmental justice in a number of jurisdictions.

we do not have a detailed understanding of how environmental goods (such as access to green spaces) and bads (such as pollution) are distributed.[159] As with the approach to environmental rights discussed in chapter one, environmental justice in the EU is dominated by a procedural approach, in the sense that a 'just' process of decision-making makes for a 'just' decision, focusing on the sorts of participatory rights discussed in chapters seven and eight. A more substantive approach, aiming for the just distribution of environmental goods and bads may be especially difficult to square with the free-market liberal direction of the EU.[160] But justice is an important factor in sustainable development, challenging technocratic approaches to decision-making, and with the potential to pose a radical challenge to our ways of life.[161]

CONCLUSIONS

The position of sustainable development in the EU is a little more fragile now than when I wrote the first edition of this book. Dissatisfaction with sustainable development's vagueness grows, as does the critique that its assertion of the compatibility between conflicting objectives is empty rhetoric that fails to adequately protect the environment.[162] The strength of sustainable development holds the clue to its weakness. That sustainable development is vague in its aspirations and content cannot really be denied,[163] but that is not necessarily environmentally disadvantageous.[164] In its vagueness, sustainable development provides space for the environmental case to be made.[165] Many, however, now reject sustainable development's ability to provide space for the 'green' argument in the day to day battles over environmental regulation.[166] Andrea Ross, an important observer of sustainable development, for example, argues that 'early interpretations of sustainable development as a vague, malleable policy tool based on weak sustainability' have failed.[167] She argues for a turn to 'ecological sustainability' or 'respecting

[159] But see J Holder, 'Building Spatial Europe: An Environmental Justice Perspective' in J Scott (ed), *Environmental Protection: European Law and Governance* (Oxford, Oxford University Press, 2009); A Layard and J Holder, 'Seeking Spatial and Environmental Justice for People and Places within the European Union' in A Philippopoulos-Mihalopoulos (ed), *Law and Ecology: New Environmental Foundations* (Abingdon, Routledge, 2011).

[160] Holder, ibid.

[161] On the ways in which 'environmental justice' pushes boundaries, see D Schlosberg, 'Theorising Environmental Justice: The Expanding Sphere of a Discourse' (2013) 22 *Environmental Politics* 37.

[162] Eg Morrow (n 7); Stallworthy (n 157).

[163] A requirement for a supplier to demonstrate 'sustainable purchasing' and how it contributes to 'improving the sustainability of the coffee market' is not clear enough to comply with the 'obligation of transparency' in public procurement, Case C-368/10 *Commission v Netherlands* not yet reported in the ECR.

[164] See Jacobs (n 8), for a discussion of the benefits of vagueness.

[165] Ibid.

[166] Jacobs (n 93).

[167] A Ross, 'Modern Interpretations of Sustainable Development' (2009) 36 *Journal of Law and Society* 32, 33.

the Earth's environmental limits' as a separate normative principle.[168] It is, as discussed, important that environmental protection continues to be addressed ambitiously and independently, and this greater emphasis on the environment would be desirable. But these terms are unlikely to be any more self-executing or purely technically determinable than 'sustainable development'. Limits, for example, is an argument about values as much as physical states. There are certainly physical limits at which particular species, ecosystems or human activities will cease (although fine predictions are probably impossible), and technological fixes will not always be available; profound change is necessary. But limits vary depending on whether we apply them to species, ecosystems, or human activities, and the political question is still how much we want to protect those species, ecosystems or human activities.[169] Even the identification of relatively clear limits beyond which human life is impossible is of only limited policy assistance, since presumably our ambition is far greater than survival. I doubt that there is any overarching language that can shortcut the need to argue in detail for environmental prioritisation in decision-making. Whenever the complexity of a problem demands something other than straightforward quantitative or qualitative rules, we face these difficulties.

It is unwise to make predictions, but it seems unlikely that 'sustainable development', well embedded as it is in law and policy, will cease to be a core term in EU environmental law and policy. Arguing for its removal without a convincing successor would be politically difficult—the promise that genuinely positive social objectives can be reconciled is simply irresistible (who would want to do away with development that 'meets the needs of the present without compromising the ability of future generations to meet their own needs'?). Several decades of intellectual investment have even given sustainable development a certain moral and conceptual heft, albeit one that cuts both ways, and can be appropriated by powerful interests. The 'green economy' is certainly an attractive flag around which to gather political momentum, as is 'wellbeing'. Equally, however, both fit very neatly into existing approaches to sustainable development and this seems to be a casting around for fresh language, rather than new ideas or new approaches to implementation. By contrast, a turn to 'ecological sustainability', may be a more meaningful shift, prioritising environmental protection in such a way as to demand a real change to our ways of carrying on. But it would still demand a political exercise that assesses environmental, economic and social effects in any particular case. It is quite proper that there is a continuous debate about the meaning of sustainable development. It is dynamic and open, allowing for the prioritisation of different social objectives.

---

[168] A Ross (n 115) ch 12, and ibid. Ross makes a good case for plausibility, with climate change at the centre. Note the reference to 'environmental sustainability' in the Water Framework Directive (n 66).

[169] Dobson (n 18) 146, referring to 'thresholds' rather than 'limits'. See also Royal Commission on Environmental Pollution, *Demographic Change and the Environment* (2011) Cm 8001, 60.

4

Instruments and Governance I: Setting the Scene

INTRODUCTION

EU GOVERNANCE IS a complex and inclusive notion, and the subject of a simply enormous theoretical and empirical literature. The purpose here is not, for fear of intensifying the frustrating 'contestation over naming rights',[1] to defend a fresh definition of governance, or to draw clear lines between the different members of the governance 'family', such as 'new', 'experimentalist' or 'networked' governance.[2] Instead, working broadly within the 'new' governance scholarship, I explore and highlight three different themes of contemporary EU environmental protection.[3] First, new governance emphasises flexibility over fixed hierarchical commands, and the use of softer rather than harder legal measures. Secondly, new governance tends to emphasise the inclusion of a range of public and private actors in collaborative decision-making. Deliberation in the public interest, and a willingness to change position, are thought to be important.[4] Thirdly, a strong emphasis is placed on the generation of information and knowledge, which implies a need to adapt in response to lessons learned.

There are strong resonances between these three themes of new governance and regulatory scholarship. Some (especially political scientists) see 'regulation' as a narrower, more legalistic, concept than 'governance', referring to the hard legal

---

[1] B Karkkainen, '"New Governance" in Legal Thought and in the World: Some Splitting as Antidote to Overzealous Lumping' (2004–05) 89 *Minnesota Law Review* 471, 478.

[2] G de Búrca and J Scott (eds), *Law and New Governance in the EU and the US* (Oxford, Hart Publishing, 2006); CF Sabel and J Zeitlin (eds), *Experimentalist Governance in the European Union: Towards a New Architecture* (Oxford, Oxford University Press, 2010); G de Búrca, 'New Governance and Experimentalism: An Introduction' [2010] *Wisconsin Law Review* 227.

[3] Others divide their analysis differently, although there are similarities in substance: eg P Craig and G de Búrca, *EU Law: Text, Cases and Materials* (Oxford, Oxford University Press, 2011), emphasise 'the shift away from hierarchical governance', 159; G de Búrca and J Scott, 'New Governance, Law and Constitutionalism' in de Búrca and Scott (n 2) emphasise approaches that are 'less rigid, less prescriptive, less committed to uniform outcomes, and less hierarchical in nature', 2; J Scott and D Trubek, 'Mind the Gap: Law and New Approaches to Governance in the European Union' (2002) 8 *European Law Journal* 1 discuss participation and power sharing; multi-level integration; diversity and decentralisation; deliberation; flexibility and revisability; experimentation and knowledge-creation, 5–6.

[4] CF Sabel and J Zeitlin, 'Learning from Difference: The New Architecture of Experimentalist Governance in the EU' in Sabel and Zeitlin (n 2).

rules within a broader governance context. But both 'governance' and 'regulation' are subject to bewildering definitional proliferation and contestation,[5] and both are capable of very expansive interpretation; for current purposes, 'regulation' is perfectly able to cover the ground addressed by new governance, certainly our three themes.[6] Both regulation and governance scholars try to address the limitations of 'traditional' legal approaches to environmental protection, in purposeful activity designed to influence behaviour.[7] I am not suggesting that the two notions are always precisely the same, and the choice of language may well tell us something about the commitments of those involved. This chapter, however, will simply explore the different approaches taken in EU environmental protection, regardless of labels.

The purpose of this chapter is to set the scene for issues that recur throughout this book. It begins with a brief discussion of the 'command and control' approach to regulation, which is not only crucial in the practice of environmental protection, but is also the approach against which much of the new governance and regulation literature defines itself. After examining in turn the three overlapping themes of new governance outlined above, I turn to some of the perennial legitimacy challenges associated with new governance. I then turn to three key 'alternative' instruments of regulation, examining economic instruments, voluntary instruments (especially corporate social responsibility) and the regulatory role of information in EU environmental law. The line between the 'themes' of governance and the 'tools' of regulation is not a bright one, as I hope will be clear.

DIRECT REGULATION

Elaborate administrative systems for environmental protection have gradually been put in place in many jurisdictions, requiring public regulators to set, monitor and enforce appropriate standards. Not surprisingly, EU environmental policy initially turned confidently to this form of public direction, commonly and loosely labelled 'command and control' regulation: 'the term "command and control" refers to the prescriptive nature of the regulation, the command, supported by the imposition of some negative sanction, the control'.[8] Command and control is often the norm against which 'alternative' approaches to regulation define

---

[5] On 'governance', see K Armstrong, 'The Character of EU Law and Governance: From "Community Method" to New Modes of Governance' (2011) 64 *Current Legal Problems* 179; on 'regulation', J Black, 'Decentring Regulation: Understanding the Role of Regulation and Self-Regulation in a Post-Regulatory World' (2001) 54 *Current Legal Problems* 103.

[6] Eg R Baldwin, C Scott and C Hood (eds), *A Reader on Regulation* (Oxford, Oxford University Press, 1998). J Black, 'Paradoxes and Failures: "New Governance" Techniques and the Financial Crisis' (2012) 75 *Modern Law Review* 1037, describes 'principles-based regulation' and 'de-centred regulation' as 'new governance'.

[7] Not all approaches assume intentionality on the part of governor/regulator.

[8] C Abbot, 'Environmental Command Regulation' in B Richardson and S Wood (eds), *Environmental Law for Sustainability* (Oxford, Hart Publishing, 2006) 61.

themselves; 'new' governance is often defined against something rather similar, for example 'top-down control using fixed statutes, detailed rules and judicial enforcement'.[9] Whilst (again) the match is not perfect, sufficiently similar questions are raised to see the approaches to governance and regulation discussed in this chapter as responses to the limitations of 'command-and-control-type legal institutions'.[10]

Through 'a combination of prohibitions, licences and standards', commands are issued, controlled by monitoring, reporting and inspection regimes, and threats of criminal or other forms of liability.[11] Examples abound in EU environmental law. Permits are at the heart of the control of industrial emissions, and environmental assessment, discussed in chapters five and seven. The Water Framework Directive (WFD), notable for the ambitious and innovative approach discussed later in this chapter, nevertheless relies on the traditional method of prior authorisation of emissions into and abstractions from water.[12] In each of these cases, EU legislation requires the national authorities to exercise their own command capacity over activities in the Member State. In other cases, including the regulation of chemicals and of genetically modified organisms, discussed in chapters nine and 10, the authorisation takes place at EU level.

'Command and control' was a phrase coined with derogatory intent, with connotations of soviet-style interference in private life. The derogatory overtones may have lessened over time, and when the phrase is used here it is for the virtue of familiarity, with no derogatory intent. In most cases, however, I use the term 'direct regulation'.[13] Direct regulation is subject to severe criticism. In some cases, the criticism is of a caricature, in which a public authority dictates uniform environmental standards, across a large area, and applies prescribed methods of meeting those standards to every installation. This extreme approach would be surprising, but there are nevertheless some real concerns about direct regulation.[14]

First, direct regulation is said to make impossible demands of the regulator. The notion that one single institution (or even group of institutions) has all the knowledge, information, and indeed power, to address environmental problems seems far-fetched.[15] This leads to a constant reliance on outsiders (the regulated

---

[9] DM Trubek and LG Trubek, 'New Governance and Legal Regulation: Complementarity, Rivalry and Transformation' (2007) 13 *Columbia Journal of European Law* 539, 543. New governance is often seen as 'not law', DM Trubek and LG Trubek, 'The World Turned Upside Down: Reflections on New Governance and the Transformation of Law' [2010] *Wisconsin Law Review* 719.

[10] A phrase used with little ado by G de Búrca and J Scott, 'Introduction' (2007) 13 *Columbia Journal of European Law* 513, eg 514. Scott and Trubek (n 3), describe new governance as any significant departure from the 'classic community method', essentially the legislative process.

[11] Abbot (n 8) 63.

[12] Directive 2000/60/EC establishing a framework for Community action in the field of water policy ('Water Framework Directive' (WFD)) [2000] OJ L327/1.

[13] See also Abbot (n 8); M Gunningham and P Grabosky with D Sinclair, *Smart Regulation: Designing Environmental Policy* (Oxford, Clarendon Press, 1998).

[14] Black (n 5) 106.

[15] Ibid.

industry and third parties) to enhance regulatory capacity. For example, the involvement of a range of public and private actors in problem-solving is part of the collaborative 'theme' of new governance, discussed below. Economic instruments of regulation attempt to make use of the knowledge and expertise of the regulated, as do voluntary instruments. Enhancing public access to information is thought to harness the knowledge and experience of third parties such as environmental interest groups or concerned citizens. A scrutinising role for third parties is also called on to address other forms of regulatory failure. Outsiders provide a partial response to concerns about 'regulatory capture',[16] according to which regulators come to share the interests of the regulated to the detriment of the public interest. Capture theory comes in various guises: the 'revolving door', for example, is concerned about the extent to which key personnel move between industry and the regulator, and 'life cycle' theory claims that an ambitious new regulator is dominated by the industry over time, as public attention to the problem being regulated diminishes.[17] The existence and extent of capture is controversial, but it is clearly a possibility.[18] Third party monitoring can also enhance scrutiny for failures that fall short of capture, which becomes even more important if collaborative governance between regulator and industry exacerbates the risk of excessive industry influence over its own regulation.

Secondly, direct regulation is said to be less cost effective than other approaches, in the sense of demanding more resources from both regulator and regulated than is necessary. The discussion in this chapter and subsequent chapters suggests that neither new governance nor alternative instruments are undemanding in this sense. Whatever approach is taken to governance, there is no escaping the need for regulatory resources (money, information, expertise).[19]

A further set of concerns revolves around the allegedly static nature of direct regulation. Fixed environmental standards in direct regulation are continually outpaced, both by more effective technology, and by increasingly complex environmental problems. The regulated parties have no regulatory incentive to implement new technology, or to respond to new problems, as long as they are in compliance with the (outdated) legislation.[20] Inflexible rules are also open to 'gaming' or 'creative compliance': 'using the law to escape legal control without actually violating legal rules', especially likely with 'clearly defined, highly administrable rules, an emphasis on uniformity, consistency and predictability'.[21]

---

[16] Classically, see the role of public interest groups in I Ayres and J Braithwaite, *Responsive Regulation: Transcending the Deregulation Debate* (Oxford, Oxford University Press, 1995).

[17] C Abbot, 'Bridging the Gap—Non-state Actors and the Challenges of Regulating New Technology' (2012) 39 *Journal of Law and Society* 329.

[18] Ibid.

[19] The global financial crisis is a timely reminder, eg C Ford, 'New Governance in the Teeth of Human Frailty: Lessons from Financial Regulation' (2010) *Wisconsin Law Review* 441.

[20] Gunningham and Grabosky (n 13).

[21] D McBarnet and C Whelan, 'The Elusive Spirit of the Law: Formalism and the Struggle for Legal Control' (1991) 54 *Modern Law Review* 848, 849; C Hood, 'Gaming in Targetworld: The Targets Approach to Managing British Public Services' (2006) 66 *Public Administration Review* 515.

Direct regulation need not be static, and the efforts to build adaptability into the Industrial Emissions Directive (IED) are discussed in chapter five.[22] Another, related, criticism of direct regulation is its alleged inability to stimulate technological innovation in the regulated industry. This is probably too simplistic, since direct regulation can in the right circumstances stimulate innovation, whilst alternative (for example economic) approaches do not automatically do so,[23] but the overall criticism remains.

Finally, whatever its achievements thus far, some argue that direct regulation has reached its limits, and is inadequate for new or persistent environmental challenges. The traditional licensing mechanism, with public sector monitoring and enforcement, is best suited to point source pollution, and to obvious harm. Tackling diffuse harms or heterogeneous activities through direct regulation is more difficult.[24] It is not surprising that the governance of climate change has been particularly innovative, given the complex and deep roots of carbon emissions in economic and social life, as well as its entry on to the regulatory agenda at a time of most enthusiasm for economic instruments of regulation.

Two things should be noted before proceeding. First, direct regulation (command of industry by regulators, and of the Member State authorities by EU legislation) and traditional hierarchical forms of law remain powerful and effective. Even for climate change, direct regulation is crucial.[25] Secondly, 'new' or 'alternative' approaches do not by any means resolve the challenges of environmental protection. But governing is complex, and a range of approaches is taken in EU environmental law.

THEMES OF NEW GOVERNANCE

The language of 'newness' can sometimes raise hackles, and there really is little new under the sun. There has certainly not been a complete rejection of 'old' hierarchies in favour of 'new' governance approaches. Hard-edged, enforceable legal rules, sometimes in substantive environmental standards, frequently in procedural requirements, remain fundamental features of EU environmental law and

---

[22] Directive 2010/75/EU on industrial emissions (integrated pollution prevention and control) ('Industrial Emissions Directive' (IED)) [2010] OJ L334/17.

[23] ME Porter and C van der Linde, 'Toward a New Conception of the Environment-Competitiveness Relationship' (1995) 9 *Journal of Economic Perspectives* 97 explore the potential for well-designed environmental regulation to stimulate innovation leading to competitive benefits for industry. D Driesen, 'Economic Instruments for Sustainable Development' in Richardson and Wood (n 8), argues that direct regulation can indeed stimulate innovation, and criticises the capacity of emissions trading to stimulate adequate innovation, see ch 6.

[24] Abbot (n 8).

[25] I von Homeyer, 'The Evolution of EU Environmental Governance' in J Scott (ed), *Environmental Protection: European Law and Governance* (Oxford, Oxford University Press, 2009) sees the evolving EU regulation of climate change as a return to command and control.

governance, often sitting alongside newer, more flexible approaches.[26] New governance, for current purposes, simply provides a way of conceptualising, describing and analysing regulatory phenomena, as well as identifying a new emphasis on the part of those seeking to govern. The Commission, for example, does support and encourage many of the themes identified here. It is often ambitious about seeking out innovative ways of achieving environmental objectives, even if ambivalent about those elements of new governance that might escape the control of the EU institutions.[27]

In this section, I focus primarily on the relationship between EU legislation and national regulators (and sometimes national regulated parties), along the themes identified in the introduction: flexibility, collaboration and learning. In this context, 'new governance' responds to the limitations of EU 'command' of the Member States. It should not be thought however that (new) governance has nothing to say about the relationship between regulators and regulated parties: it does, and has been an important and controversial aspect of national regulation.[28]

Flexibility

The flexibility found in 'differentiated' participation by some Member States in some areas of EU integration is a longstanding and recurrent constitutional debate in the EU.[29] In addition, environmental legislation has often contained some temporary or permanent variation of the obligations undertaken by the Member States.[30] For current purposes, the inherent flexibility found in the use of vaguely defined, open-ended environmental norms in EU legislation, is of greater interest.

The 'best available techniques' (BAT) standard at the heart of the (IED)[31] is a classic example of such a flexible, open-ended standard. BAT, as discussed in chapter five, is defined at length in the legislation, but not precisely. The legislation sets out a range of factors that should be considered in deciding what constitutes BAT, but without dictating any particular approach. Another important example can be found in the central norm of 'good water status' in the WFD.[32] 'Good water

[26] On 'hybridity' and interdependence between law and governance, see Scott and de Búrca (n 3). See also the discussion on industrial emissions in ch 5.

[27] See eg ch 5 for a discussion on the Commission's response to inconsistent use of 'BAT reference documents'; European Commission, 'White Paper on European Governance' COM (2001) 428 final.

[28] See eg Black (n 5); N Gunningham, 'Environmental Law, Regulation and Governance: Shifting Architectures' (2009) 21 *Journal of Environmental Law* 179.

[29] See eg N Walker, 'Sovereignty and Differentiated Integration in the European Union' (1998) 4 *European Law Journal* 355; more recently, J-C Piris, *The Future of Europe: Towards a Two-Speed EU?* (Cambridge, Cambridge University Press, 2012).

[30] See eg the different targets discussed in ch 6 below.

[31] IED (n 22).

[32] WFD (n 12). For detailed discussion, see M Lee, 'Law and Governance of Water Protection Policy' in Scott (n 25).

status' is subject to complex, lengthy, but open description in the Directive itself, which again sets out a range of relevant considerations. BAT and good water status allow different responses in different circumstances, and might be contrasted with a bright line rule, such as an obligation to enforce fixed quantitative limits on pollution, whether emitted from an installation, or present in the environment.[33] Uncertain language may sometimes be a result of difficult negotiation, and amount simply to a postponement of decisions. But equally, ambitious objectives may just not find a home in bright line rules, and 'good water status', for example, is indeed ambitious: it embraces all impacts on water, including construction and abstraction, as well as pollution; and the 'ecological' element of the definition, whilst extremely complicated, is basically assessed by reference to 'naturalness'.[34]

The fact that a norm is flexible or open-ended in its definition does not *in itself* prevent it from constituting 'hard' law, in the sense of being formally legally binding.[35] So 'good water status' can be binding—but whether or not it is met in any particular case is open to interpretation. A second form of flexibility can, however, be built into legislation by blurring the line between compliance and breach. For example, in some cases, Member States are required to 'protect, enhance and restore' all bodies of water, with the *'aim'* of achieving good water status. The meaning of this part of the legislation is not entirely clear,[36] but prima facie, an obligation to 'aim' to meet a particular standard, whilst potentially onerous for the Member States,[37] is not the same as an obligation to meet it. To the extent that legislation, like the WFD, creates an obligation of best efforts rather than of result,[38] flexibility in implementation is increased. Furthermore, even in those cases where the relevant obligations 'shall' be met,[39] the breach/compliance division is not always entirely straightforward: in both the WFD and the IED, 'escape

---

[33] See Black (n 6) on 'principles based regulation' as compared with 'rules based regulation'. Note that both Directives also include these sorts of standard: see ch 5 on the IED; 'good water status' under the WFD does include some quantitative limits on pollution.

[34] Waters with good ecological status are subject to 'low levels of distortion resulting from human activity', deviating 'only slightly from those normally associated with the surface water body type under undisturbed conditions', WFD (n 12) Annex V. W Howarth, 'The Progression Towards Ecological Quality Standards' (2006) 18 *Journal of Environmental Law* 3 and H Josefsson and L Baaner, 'The Water Framework Directive—A Directive for the Twenty-First Century?' (2011) 23 *Journal of Environmental Law* 463 criticise the static nature of the standard.

[35] Eg Case C-32/05 *Commission v Luxembourg* [2006] ECR I-11323: Member States are obliged to ensure that 'objectives formulated in general and unquantifiable terms' are 'attained', but have flexibility in how to achieve that [39], [43].

[36] JJH van Kempen, 'Countering the Obscurity of Obligations in European Environmental Law: An Analysis of Article 4 of the European Water Framework Directive' (2012) 24 *Journal of Environmental Law* 499 argues that Art 4 imposes obligations of result, and that 'aim' does not appear in all language versions, 531–32.

[37] Van Kempen, ibid.

[38] For discussion of these different types of obligation, see ibid.

[39] WFD (n 12) Art 4 contains a range of obligations, some of which do not include the language of 'aim' (although again, see n 36).

clauses'[40] provide significant opportunities for the Member States to derogate from the core obligations.[41]

Open-ended terms, including BAT and good water status, are often subject to more detailed and precise articulation beyond the legislation, in such a way that at least some of their uncertainty and open-endedness disappears. In the case of BAT and good water status, this articulation takes place through elaborate collaborative governance mechanisms, discussed in the next section. The detail of legislation may also be pinned down through more routine approaches, such as Commission Guidance documents.[42] The detailed norms, whether issued by the Commission alone or through a collaborative mechanism, might be described as 'soft', in the sense that they are not formally legally binding. The line between 'binding' and 'not-binding', however, is blurred. Even in the absence of legally binding force, 'soft' measures can have manifold and significant practical and legal effects.[43] For example, soft measures may (or even must) be taken into account by national decision-makers, and the institution that issues soft law cannot depart from it without good reason.[44] These sorts of measures may also enjoy considerable authority because they embody respected expertise, or because they have been agreed through processes considered legitimate. They may in such circumstances be complied with *as if* they were mandatory. Non-binding measures may also be understood by national regulators or regulated parties as a short-cut to compliance, especially if they have the support of the Commission,[45] and especially if ensuring compliance would otherwise be onerous. If the national regulator is treating Commission guidance as if it were mandatory, as far as the regulated party is concerned, it effectively *is* mandatory.[46] Incentives for compliance with soft measures can also be designed into regulation: with product standardisation, for example, certification with (non-binding) standards set by European standardisation bodies provides a presumption of compliance with EU law.

The line between hard and soft law is not as sharp as we might expect,[47] in three respects. First, as above, 'soft' measures might have hard impacts. Secondly, 'soft' law can make the transition to a hard, mandatory status. But just as soft law is not

---

[40] KW Abbott et al, 'The Concept of Legalization' (2000) 54 *International Organisation* 401 (of international law).

[41] WFD (n 12) Art 4(3)–(7). The IED derogations are discussed in detail in ch 5.

[42] F Snyder, 'The Effectiveness of European Community Law: Institutions, Processes, Tools and Techniques' (1993) 56 *Modern Law Review* 19; L Senden, 'Soft Post-Legislative Rulemaking: A Time for More Stringent Control' (2013) 19 *European Law Journal* 57.

[43] See Senden, ibid; J Scott, 'In Legal Limbo: Post-Legislative Guidance as a Challenge for European Administrative Law' (2011) 48 *Common Market Law Review* 329; T Hervey, '"Adjudicating in the Shadow of the Informal Settlement?": The Court of Justice of the European Union, "New Governance" and Social Welfare' (2010) 63 *Current Legal Problems* 92.

[44] Senden, ibid.

[45] Ibid.

[46] O Stefan, 'European Union Soft Law: New Developments Concerning the Divide between Legally Binding Force and Legal Effects' (2012) 75 *Modern Law Review* 879.

[47] Probably the most cited approach is Abbott et al (n 40), which discusses a spectrum of soft/hard law, by reference to criteria of 'obligation', 'precision' and 'delegation'.

without effect, hard law often leaves considerable space for regulatory judgment. This transition from soft to hard law may be less transformative than it seems. Finally, soft law and hard law (including for example procedural obligations as to what to take into account, who to consult, as well as quantitative emission limits and environmental quality standards) exist side by side in the same legal instrument.[48] All three of these boundary blurrings are apparent in the IED, discussed in detail in chapter five.

We return to some of the challenges associated with more flexible measures below. Benefits include the possibility of different solutions in different conditions, potentially leading to improved environmental protection and reduced cost. The diverse (environmental, social and economic) needs of the Member States might be accommodated better than if spelled out in detailed legislation. Flexible approaches may also be more dynamic, in the sense that their interpretation may be more swiftly adapted to learning from experience and to changing conditions.[49]

Collaborative Governance

Wide participation in decision-making speaks to a range of anxieties about EU environmental law, and we return to public participation in later chapters, especially chapters seven and eight. One notable manifestation of participation in the EU has been the evolution of fora in which a range of public and private stakeholders, potentially including industry, national regulators and environmental interest groups, collaborate to specify in more detail the content of open-ended legislative norms. Without wishing to add further complexity of definition,[50] by 'collaborative governance', I mean the provision of a forum in which a range of public and private actors, from different levels of governance (local, regional, national, EU) are able to work closely and intensively on solving, or even identifying, a common problem. Collaborative governance implies something more than consultation, in the potential for deliberation and interaction; and less than public participation, given that there will be restrictions on who can take part.[51]

---

[48] See (n 26).

[49] The 'soft law' elaboration of flexible norms is not always easy to change. For example, industry estimates the cost of participating in the production of a single 'Seville' document at around one million Euros, C Koutalakis, A Buzogany and TA Borzel, 'When Soft Regulation is Not Enough: the Integrated Pollution Prevantion and Control Directive of the European Union' (2010) 4 *Regulation and Governance* 329, fn 10; each document is expected to take 31–39 months to complete, Commission Implementing Decision 2012/119/EU laying down rules concerning guidance on the collection of data and on the drawing up of BAT reference documents and on their quality assurance [2012] OJ L63/1 [1.2.4].

[50] Karkkainen (n 1).

[51] J Freeman, 'Collaborative Governance in the Administrative State' (1997–98) 45 *University of California, Los Angeles Law Review* 1 sees collaborative governance as an escape from an adversarial model of interest representation, in a specifically US context that is very different from the discussion here.

We find collaborative governance mechanisms throughout EU law. In some cases, it shares some features with what the Commission calls 'co-regulation', that is 'the mechanism whereby a Community legislative act entrusts the attainment of the objectives defined by the legislative authority to parties which are recognised in the field (such as economic operators, the social partners, non-governmental organisations, or associations)'.[52] Co-regulation is epitomised by the well-known and widespread 'new approach' to product standardisation, which dates from the mid-1980s. Legislation sets out the 'essential requirements' for a product, which are elaborated in voluntary standards developed by European standardisation bodies, composed of largely private sector national standard-setting organisations. As mentioned above, compliance with these voluntary standards leads to a presumption of compliance with EU law.

The 'Seville process' for the collaborative amplification of 'BAT' is discussed in detail in chapter five. The Common Implementation Strategy (CIS) under the WFD is another notable example of collaborative governance.[53] It provides for a joint approach to implementation of the WFD, with networks of experts, including national and EU level regulators and civil servants, as well as private actors, working together. The CIS exchanges and manages information and data, and tests and validates different approaches to the Directive. It enables Member States to share the significant technical and human resources required for implementation. One of the CIS's more important tasks has been to develop non-binding guidance documents, on subjects including the analysis of pressures and impacts on water, monitoring, economic analysis and public participation. These are very detailed, highly technical and lengthy documents, setting out agreed positions that imply the distribution of costs, risks and benefits, as well as having a major role in determining the environmental outcomes of the WFD.

Information and Learning

The EU 'has sought to put in place frameworks which encourage the generation of rich, up-to-date, information about environmental quality' and environmental hazards.[54] As mentioned above, one of the concerns about direct regulation is that it cannot easily account for the fragmentation between different social actors of information and knowledge. Opportunities or obligations for diverse actors to generate and share knowledge are legion in EU environmental governance. Principles like the 'no data, no market' approach to chemicals regulation create

[52] European Parliament, Council and Commission, Interinstitutional Agreement on Better Law-Making [2003] OJ C321/1 [18]; P Verbruggen, 'Does Co-Regulation Strengthen EU Legitimacy?' (2009) 15 *European Law Journal* 425.
[53] ec.europa.eu/environment/water/water-framework/objectives/implementation_en.htm.
[54] J Scott, 'Preface' in Scott (n 25) v.

a high incentive for industry to generate and share information.[55] Fora such as the WFD's CIS, or the IED's Seville process provide important opportunities for the generation and sharing of information and knowledge, and for collaborative learning about environmental problems and their governance. Whilst not always quite as elaborate as CIS or Seville, the ubiquity of networks and committees for the sharing of knowledge and information suggests the high priority placed on knowledge and information in the EU.

Planning obligations, commonly imposed on the Member States by environmental directives, also demand the generation of information. The River Basin Management Plan drawn up by national authorities under the WFD every six years, for example, requires the generation and collection of information on every river basin district.[56] As part of their planning, the Member States must identify water bodies at risk of failing the environmental quality objectives, and the main human pressures on those water bodies.[57] Information is rarely neutral, and these national planning obligations have the potential to shape national responses to environmental legislation. Moreover, because the information is publicly available, public scrutiny has the potential to create external pressure to respond to problems. Information can also shape EU responses, with the River Basin Management Plans most obviously resonating in the CIS. Periodic reporting by the Member States to the Commission on the implementation of a directive is generally matched by an obligation on the Commission to respond,[58] and in some cases an express obligation to consider whether to put forward a legislative proposal.[59] Joanne Scott and Jane Holder trace the evolution of environmental assessment legislation alongside reporting obligations, noting the contribution of national and Commission reporting to the 'iterative evaluation and adaptation of Directives'.[60]

Continued ignorance on the quality of water bodies in the EU,[61] however, indicates the difficulties of using law to enhance knowledge in difficult areas. The quality of reports, and of the learning and reflection, may not match the theory. Reports from both Member States and the Commission (often via consultants) may seem superficial and hurried, sometimes descriptive rather than evaluative, sometimes self-serving.[62] But the potential exists for genuine learning. And

---

[55] See ch 9 below.

[56] WFD (n 12) Art 13.

[57] Ibid Annex II, Annex VII.

[58] European Commission, 'Report on the Implementation of the Water Framework Directive: River Basin Management Plans' COM (2012) 670 final.

[59] Eg IED (n 22) Art 73.

[60] J Scott and J Holder, 'Law and New Environmental Governance in the European Union' in de Búrca and Scott (n 2).

[61] Commission (n 58); European Environment Bureau (EEB), *10 Years of the Water Framework Directive: A Toothless Tiger?* (EEB, 2010).

[62] See the criticism of the integrated pollution prevention and control (IPPC) review process in E Bohne, 'The Implementation of the IPPC Directive from a Comparative Perspective and Lessons for its Recast' (2008) 5 *Journal of European Environmental and Planning Law* 1.

pragmatically, this illustrates the need to monitor and enforce these learning obligations just as carefully as substantive obligations; information is not a less demanding option.

If a governance regime is to learn from experience, hard-won knowledge and understanding must be capable of diffusion into practice and legislation, and of use and re-use over the longer term. Whilst the data collected nationally under the WFD is often inadequately stored and inaccessible,[63] there is the potential for spaces like the CIS and Seville to improve matters by organising information. An ambition for learning also requires there to be opportunities and incentives for practice actually to be modified in the light of experience. The availability of information on the need for improvement may create a political demand for the revision of standards. Legislative obligations periodically to consider standards afresh provide a stronger incentive.[64]

PERENNIAL CONCERNS

There is some (sometimes angry) discussion of whether 'new' governance is a real or interesting phenomenon at all.[65] It seems, however, relatively clear *both* that the attributes of new governance are common features of EU environmental protection, in some cases self-consciously exploited as a useful technique, *and* that 'old' approaches of hierarchical standard setting, including hard-edged substantive and procedural legislative standards, are still important. The complexity and diversity of EU environmental law defies easy categorisation into particular varieties of law and governance, and any polarised contest between different approaches is rather sterile: new and old, hard and soft, law and governance, sit side by side. Whilst we might confidently decline to enter this particular debate, it is important to be alert to some of the more substantive concerns about new environmental governance. These tend to coalesce around enforcement, and accountability and legitimacy. As highly predictable criticisms, responses should be provided within the future 'architecture'[66] of governance.

Regulators generally find narrowly framed rules easier to enforce through formal mechanisms.[67] This is apparent in the Commission's frustration over the implementation of the open-ended demands of BAT, discussed in chapter five. Introducing more easily enforced, hard-edged, bright line rules would, however,

---

[63] F Hering et al, 'The European Water Framework Directive at the Age of 10: A Critical Review of the Achievements with Recommendations for the Future' (2010) 408 *Science of the Total Environment* 4007.

[64] IED (n 22) Recital 13; Guidance Documents under CIS frequently state their revisability, and as discussed below, the River Basin Management Plans are revised every six years.

[65] See D Kelemen, *Eurolegalism: The Transformation of Law and Regulation in the European Union* (Cambridge MA, Harvard University Press, 2011); K Holzinger, C Knill and A Schafer, 'Rhetoric or Reality? "New Governance" in EU Environmental Policy' (2006) 12 *European Law Journal* 403.

[66] Ford (n 19).

[67] R Baldwin, 'Why Rules Don't Work' (1990) 53 *Modern Law Review* 321.

compromise the comprehensiveness and ambition of standards like 'BAT' and 'good water status', which are inevitably case-specific and evaluative. Whilst there are limits to the formal enforcement of these norms, however, legislation can be designed to increase the possibility for scrutiny and monitoring capacity.[68] For example, although 'good water status' is simply an 'aim' in the WFD, when a body of water does not achieve or is at risk of failing to achieve good water status, a public explanation has to be provided, both of the failure and of the necessary extra monitoring and remedial obligations.[69] In addition to scrutiny by the lay public, for example local people, CIS provides a forum for peer review (Member State to Member State, plus Commission) of progress, and for review by other experts. Expert, 'effective and informed monitoring'[70] is important: real scrutiny is made possible not by 'the *availability* of information in a strictly technical sense' but by 'the human capital and other endowments necessary to *process* it in any meaningful way'.[71] The more technical and complex the topic, the greater are the demands on the party doing the holding to account.[72] As well as being expert enough to engage, however, real scrutiny demands participants who are also detached enough to 'want to query the objectives and methods'.[73] There is a danger that expert groups might 'degenerate into a complacent "old boy network", their accountability function blunted by mutual interest'.[74] This leads us neatly into questions of legitimacy and accountability that are also a recurring concern in new governance.

'Legitimacy' and 'accountability' are closely connected and complex terms, subjects of a vast literature, and often used to signal different sources of unease. They are not quite empty vessels, but may imply very general criticism that is filled in by the audience.[75] The 'obligation to explain and justify conduct'[76] is the heart of accountability, which describes a 'tool for citizens to force those vested with public power to speak the truth'.[77] On most analyses, accountability requires some form

---

[68] CF Sabel and WH Simon, 'Epilogue: Accountability without Sovereignty' in de Búrca and Scott (n 2).

[69] WFD (n 12) Art 11(5); see the similar 'comply or explain' approach in the IED, ch 5.

[70] de Búrca (n 2) 235.

[71] D Awrey, W Blair and D Kershaw, 'Between Law and Markets: Is There a Role for Culture and Ethics in Financial Regulation?' *LSE Law, Society and Economy Working Papers* 14/2012, 8.

[72] J Black, 'Calling Regulators to Account: Challenges, Capacities and Prospects' *LSE: Law, Society and Economy Working Papers* 15/2012.

[73] S Jasanoff, 'Transparency in Public Science: Purposes, Reasons, Limits' (2006) 69 *Law and Contemporary Problems* 21, 37 and 34.

[74] C Harlow and R Rawlings, 'Promoting Accountability in Multilevel Governance: A Network Approach' (2007) 13 *European Law Journal* 542, 545. The emphasis of new governance on expertise could also reduce the ability to contest outcomes, ch 2; M Dawson, 'Transforming into What? New Governance in the EU and the "Managerial Sensibility" in Modern Law' [2010] *Wisconsin Law Review* 389.

[75] E Fisher, 'The European Union in the Age of Accountability' (2004) 24 *Oxford Journal of Legal Studies* 495.

[76] M Bovens, 'Analysing and Assessing Accountability: A Conceptual Framework' (2007) 13 *European Law Journal* 447, 450.

[77] M Bovens, T Schillemans and P Hart, 'Does Public Accountability Work? An Assessment Tool' (2008) 86 *Public Administration* 225, 225.

of external scrutiny, and sometimes, associated consequences.[78] Accountability is assessed along the dimensions of who is held accountable, to whom, for what and when. Lawyers are accustomed to looking to courts for legal accountability, but soft measures and less formal institutional arrangements are not always amenable to judicial review. Nor do familiar political forms of (democratic) accountability easily capture new governance actors. The rich and expanding literature on accountability in part reflects the complexity and fragmentation of the exercise of authority.

By legitimacy, we are crudely concerned with the acceptability of decisions to those affected by them, as well as the acceptability of the political processes by which they were reached. The EU literature often divides legitimacy into 'output' legitimacy and 'input' legitimacy.[79] Input legitimacy is concerned with the (generally democratic) quality of the 'inputs' to decision-making. Output legitimacy emphasises the quality of the outputs of decision-making processes (peace and prosperity at the grandest generality, highly appropriate environmental standards for our purposes). Some of those most concerned about output legitimacy even go so far as to argue that areas of (EU) regulation like environmental law can and must be sheltered from democratic pressures, because they have a technical, non-political focus, and so can be judged purely in output terms.[80] But as discussed in chapter two, environmental decision-making depends on values as well as facts, and politics as well as technical expertise. Input and output legitimacy cannot be cleanly separated.[81]

Outright rejection of new governance techniques because of concerns about accountability and legitimacy implicitly assumes that environmental norms will otherwise be agreed by the high politics of democratically familiar institutional arrangements. In fact, it is probably unrealistic to expect EU legislation to command and control the detail of environmental protection (of 'good water status', for example). Some form of extra-legislative process is present in most jurisdictions, and the dilemmas associated with expertise and elite participation are ubiquitous in the day to day activities of the EU. Whilst bearing in mind the possible trade-offs with 'output', some form of oversight by representative bodies should be possible in new governance. The Commission has undertaken to give Parliament 'the opportunity to express its views' before it makes use of 'soft law' in areas in

---

[78] A Benz, C Harlow and Y Papadopoulos, 'Introduction' (2007) 13 *European Law Journal* 44. Sanctions have pros and cons, see Harlow and Rawlings (n 74).

[79] See further the discussion in chs 7 and 8; JHH Weiler, 'In the Face of Crisis: Input Legitimacy, Output Legitimacy and the Political Messianism of European Integration' (2012) 34 *European Integration* 825.

[80] G Majone, 'The Regulatory State and its Legitimacy Problems' (1999) 22 *West European Politics* 1. For discussion of the impact of moving beyond 'technical' issues, see G Majone, 'Rethinking European Integration after the Debt Crisis' *European University Institute, Working Paper No 3/2012*.

[81] R Bellamy, 'Democracy Without Democracy? Can the EU's Democratic "Outputs" be Separated from the Democratic "Inputs" Provided by Competitive Parties and Majority Rule?' [2010] 17 *Journal of European Public Policy* 2.

which Parliament 'is usually involved in the legislative process'.[82] This is a small step, but a positive one. Its effectiveness depends not only on the Commission's commitment, but also on the development of appropriate procedures (for example via specialist committees) in Parliament. Beyond Parliament, we look to the transparency of decision-making processes and 'the broadest possible degree of stakeholder participation compatible with effective decision-making'.[83]

If there are limits to the contribution of traditional democratic mechanisms to the legitimacy of new governance, the complexity of governance also demands a certain modesty in respect of law's contribution to legitimacy and accountability. Even when self-conscious efforts are made to use a 'hard', hierarchical legal response to enhance accountability, ambiguity remains. This is explored further in respect of the legislative changes introduced by the IED in chapter five.[84] But whilst law has much to be modest about, both courts and legislators have a fundamental role in ensuring transparency, inclusion and opportunities for political and legal contestation. Minimum procedural standards for administrative decision-making are a possibility,[85] but, in any event, individual pieces of legislation could usefully be structured to ensure, for example, the publication of drafts of key documents (together with obligations to respond to comments on those drafts), and the mandatory inclusion of environmental interest groups in those fora where industry participates.

New environmental governance frameworks, such as those in the WFD and the IED, are patchy in the attention they pay to guaranteeing transparency and inclusion. A call for transparency can seem banal, and transparency can have its own pathologies.[86] But it is a crucial starting point for any form of legal accountability, or equally importantly here, for political debate. Nor does the meaning of 'wide' participation speak for itself. The IED requires environmental interest groups to be represented within the Seville process, and there are policy commitments to their inclusion at certain stages of the CIS.[87] Draft documents are made public (in English only) during the IED Seville process, although without providing any process for external comments to be fed into the decision; some CIS documents are published in draft form, although there appears to be no systematic approach.

---

[82] European Parliament and European Commission, Framework Agreement on Relations between the European Parliament and the European Commission (no number) [2010] OJ L304/47 [43].

[83] De Búrca (n 2) 235.

[84] This is examined more explicitly in M Lee, 'The Ambiguity of Multi-Level Governance and (De-)harmonisation in EU Environmental Law' (2013–2014) *Cambridge Yearbook of European Legal Studies* forthcoming.

[85] Art 298 of the Treaty on the Functioning of the European Union (TFEU); D Curtin, H Hofmann and J Mendes, 'Constitutionalising EU Executive Rule-Making Procedures: A Research Agenda' (2013) 19 *European Law Journal* 1. See ch 8.

[86] See E Fisher, 'Transparency and Administrative Law: A Critical Evaluation' (2010) 63 *Current Legal Problems* 272; Jasanoff (n 73).

[87] IED (n 22) Art 13; Strategic Document, *Common Implementation Strategy for the Water Framework Directive* (2001), ec.europa.eu/environment/water/water-framework/objectives/pdf/strategy.pdf. The CIS does not have a legislative basis.

The question of language is tricky, given the resources required for translation, but the need to be able to work in English to participate fully in Seville or CIS has an obvious potential to exclude concerned actors.[88]

Transparency should also apply to information on who takes decisions, and how. There is certainly no easy access to information as to who participates in the CIS, and the website containing documents is extremely difficult to navigate. The members of drafting and oversight groups are listed in at least some of the CIS guidance documents, although their affiliations, if given, are opaque, since they are untranslated or limited to acronyms; and no detail is provided on broader consultation processes.[89] Law could demand this sort of information. Instead, data protection law has developed into a potentially damaging limitation on the availability of information about who participates in a collaborative decision-making process. Information on membership of the working groups in Seville, for example, is no longer made routinely available (although information is made available on request), as discussed in chapter five.

We return to the imperfect but crucial responses to concerns raised by new governance mechanisms at numerous points in the chapters that follow. Traditional forms of law (as elaborated in legislation and by the Court), should allow for the widest participation possible, and expose governance frameworks to scrutiny, rather than shelter them. The courts could play a crucial role,[90] but there are major and recurrent concerns about the Court of Justice's restrictive approach to both standing and to the acts that it is prepared to review.[91]

INSTRUMENTS OF REGULATION

Direct regulation is just one tool, or instrument, or mechanism of regulation (or governance) of many. Much regulatory theory (which is blessed with even more flavours than governance) emphasises the importance of a range of tools. The Commission is certainly preoccupied with the use of a range of diverse regulatory instruments at EU and national level.[92] Analysis in terms of 'instruments' of regulation is useful, but equally, we should note that the choice of regulatory

---

[88] Case C-410/09 *Polska Telefonia v Prezes Urzedu Komunikacji Elektronicznej* [2011] ECR I-3853 holds that, even if the relevant measure shapes the behaviour of national regulators, there is no need for instruments without binding effects on individuals to be published in all official languages. See Stefan (n 46).

[89] See eg CIS, *Guidance Document no 24, River Basin Management in a Changing Climate* (2009), Annex IX and 4.

[90] J Scott and S Sturm, 'Courts as Catalysts: Re-Thinking the Judicial Role in New Governance' (2007) 13 *Columbia Journal of European Law* 565; Dawson (n 74), in addition considers the combined legal and political role of the European Ombudsman; Harlow and Rawlings (n 74) also see the Ombudsman as an important source of accountability.

[91] Scott (n 43); Senden (n 42).

[92] See most recently European Commission, 'Proposal for a Decision of the European Parliament and of the Council on a General Union Environment Action Programme to 2020, "Living Well, within the Limits of our Planet"' COM (2012) 710 final.

instrument may be more than a technical question, and may contribute to the shaping of the values being pursued. A focus on means should not distract from the importance of the ends being pursued, nor from the question of how those decisions as to ends are taken. This section explores briefly three regulatory instruments, which recur in other chapters: economic or market instruments, voluntary instruments and information.

Economic Instruments

At least rhetorically, economic instruments[93] have been enthusiastically embraced by the European institutions. As discussed in chapter one, environmental taxes require the unanimous agreement of the Member States in Council, and so are difficult to achieve, and there is still relatively limited experience at EU level of economic instruments more generally. The EU Emissions Trading Scheme (EU ETS), discussed in chapter six below, is a prominent exception.[94] More modest interventions, like the Environmental Liability Directive, can also be described as an economic instrument, since requiring polluters to remedy, or pay the costs of remedying, environmental damage, forces them to bear some of the costs of breaching environmental legislation.[95] The Commission is also exploring the potential of economic instruments in conservation law, including the possibility of 'biodiversity banking', which envisages the creation of a market in which credits awarded for activities with positive outcomes for biodiversity could be purchased to offset damage to biodiversity.[96] This could feed into the provision in the Habitats Directive that only allows certain harmful developments to go ahead if the Member State takes appropriate 'compensatory measures'.[97]

---

[93] DM Driesen, *The Economic Dynamics of Environmental Law* (London, MIT Press, 2003) and RL Revesz, P Sands and RB Stewart (eds), *Environmental Law, The Economy and Sustainable Development* (Cambridge, Cambridge University Press, 2000) are useful sources.

[94] The EU ETS was introduced by Directive 2003/87/EC establishing a scheme for greenhouse gas emission allowance trading within the Community ('Emissions Trading Directive') [2003] OJ L275/32, as amended.

[95] Directive 2004/35/EC on environmental liability with regard to the prevention and remedying of environmental damage ('Environmental Liability Directive') [2004] OJ L143/56.

[96] See eg ICF GHK, *Exploring Potential Demand for and Supply of Habitat Banking in the EU and Appropriate Design Elements for a Habitat Banking Scheme* (2013, document prepared for the European Commission); see also the Commission website, ec.europa.eu/environment/enveco/biodiversity/.

[97] Directive 1992/43/EC on the conservation of natural habitats and of wild fauna and flora ('Habitats Directive') [1992] OJ L206/7, Art 6 allows a project that will 'adversely affect the integrity' of a protected site to go ahead only if there are 'imperative reasons of overriding public interest', *and* there are no alternative solutions, *and* compensation is provided. See D McGillivray, 'Compensating Biodiversity Loss: The EU Commission's Approach to Compensation under Article 6 of the Habitats Directive' (2012) 24 *Journal of Environmental Law* 417.

There is more experience of economic instruments in the Member States,[98] and EU legislation sometimes encourages the Member States to impose economic instruments. For example, whilst the 'programme of measures' that Member States are required to put in place for the implementation of the WFD must include command measures, 'economic or fiscal instruments' of regulation are explicitly mentioned as a 'supplementary' measure of implementation, which 'shall' be included in the programme of measures 'where necessary'.[99]

Perhaps the classic economic instrument (just as the permit is the classic command and control instrument) is a tax. A tax is a 'price-based' mechanism, in which the regulator sets the price, in order to get the 'right' level of pollution.[100] One way of identifying the 'right' price is to internalise the polluter's externalities (for example the cost of dead crops, of cleaning up drinking water, of ill health, or of ecological damage). The operator of a factory has to purchase machinery, raw materials and labour, but in an unregulated market does not have to purchase the use of the environment, reducing the cost of production. Not only is this intuitively unfair, but economically, artificially low prices lead to an inefficient level of production (too much production). Another way to identify the 'right' price is to find the level at which an adequate incentive is provided to change behaviour. This level must be higher than marginal abatement costs; that is the cost of abating each additional unit of pollution, which generally gets higher as we get closer to the elimination of pollution.

Getting the price 'right' is, however, virtually impossible. Calculating externalities depends on profoundly uncertain and controversial economic valuations of particular predicted or actual environmental impacts, which are in turn uncertain. Only a rough approximation of some of the relevant externalities is likely.[101] And the ability of a tax to change behaviour is determined by a number of uncertain and uncontrollable factors, such as the elasticity of demand, the availability of substitutes and the profits or economic efficiency of particular firms. Furthermore, creating effective incentives or adequate cost internalisation may be unpopular: in the UK, the rising cost of household energy has been widely blamed on 'green' economic instruments, for example.

As well as internalising externalities, and influencing behaviour, economic instruments can also raise revenue for government. This is most obvious for taxes, but as we see in chapter six, auctioning allowances for emissions trading

---

[98] Eg Case C-254/08 *Futura Immobiliare srl v Comune di Casonia* [2009] ECR I-6995, ch 1 above. The subsidisation of environmentally beneficial activities (including by their exclusion from tax) also raises internal market issues, eg Case C-379/98 *PreussenElektra AG v Schhleswag AG* [2001] ECR I-2099.

[99] WFD (n 12) Art 11(4) and Annex VI, part B (iii).

[100] This can be contrasted with emissions trading, which is prima facie a 'quantity-based' instrument in which the regulator sets the overall amount of pollution, and the price is set by the operation of the market. Driesen (n 23).

[101] A Ogus, 'Nudging and Rectifying: The Use of Fiscal Instruments for Regulatory Purposes' (1999) 19 *Legal Studies* 245. See ch 2.

also generates income. The environmental objective of changing behaviour might conflict with the objective of raising revenue, since as behaviour changes in an environmentally beneficial direction, revenue might fall.[102] Nevertheless, the possibility of generating income for government is sometimes considered a major advantage of economic instruments. 'Hypothecation', that is reserving certain government revenue for particular (in this case environmental) purposes, has obvious attractions, but any such instructions at EU level may be resisted by national governments,[103] and hypothecation is often resisted by finance ministries at a national level. Moreover, the opportunity to reduce tax on social 'goods' such as employment, is a major attraction of taxing 'bads' such as pollution, in which case hypothecation is not possible, since the funds must go to the general purposes previously served by taxing employment.

The distributive impact of economic instruments can be important. Progressive taxation is, simply put, taxation that redistributes wealth from the richer to the poorer; regressive taxation is its opposite. Broadly, taxing consumption, rather than income, tends to be regressive, and adding to the cost of essentials (such as domestic fuel) is likely to have a greater effect on poorer households that spend a greater proportion of their income on necessities.[104] Whether an economic instrument is regressive, however, depends on who pays and who receives precisely what. If revenue from environmental measures is used to reduce the costs of employment, then the socially progressive nature of reducing unemployment should be included in the assessment of the tax. Moreover, if the poor suffer most from environmental degradation, doing nothing may turn out to be regressive. Direct regulation also has distributive effects, depending on who bears the cost and reaps the benefit of environmental regulation. This is obviously controversial, but it seems to be the case that unless care is taken, increasing the cost of essentials through economic instruments may be regressive; if compensatory measures are taken, it need not be.[105]

One of the main arguments in favour of economic instruments is that they are said to be more cost-effective than direct regulation. Marginal abatement costs vary, and some firms (or sectors, or countries) may be able to reduce pollution very cheaply; others may find it much more costly, depending on factors including the age, location or scale of the plant. Requiring the same level of abatement from all operators may not be the most cost effective way of reducing pollution (although of course direct regulation can be much more subtle than that). Establishing a price for a unit of pollution (or some other criterion

---

[102] Although when allowances are auctioned in an ETS, the price may increase as availability is restricted.

[103] See the hortatory language in the EU ETS (n 94) Art 10(3), ch 6 below.

[104] See S Tindale and C Hewett, 'Must the Poor Pay More? Sustainable Development, Social Justice and Environmental Taxation' in A Dobson (ed), *Fairness and Futurity: Essays on Environmental Sustainability and Social Justice* (Oxford, Oxford University Press, 1999) for an engaging analysis.

[105] Ibid; I Preston et al, *Designing Carbon Taxation to Protect Low-Income Households* (York, Joseph Rowntree Foundation, 2013). See ch 1 on Kokott AG's resistance to taking social effects into account when designing environmental regulation; *Futura* (n 98).

of environmental harm) leaves polluters to decide for themselves how much pollution they generate. Rational polluters will reduce pollution for as long as polluting (including the economic instrument) costs more than abatement. Economic instruments also partially respond to the argument that direct regulation makes impossible demands of the regulator, by leaving the final decision to the regulated industry, and its decisional resources.

Market instruments are subject to a range of criticisms. They do not allow the public sector to escape difficult or costly procedures. Tax, for example, is rarely noted as a model of bureaucratic ease and simplicity, and as will be apparent in chapter six, emissions trading depends on extremely complex and demanding administrative arrangements. Notwithstanding a mistrust of government by some advocates of economic instruments, a market approach to environmental regulation requires a sophisticated government apparatus, operated by highly (economically) qualified individuals in the public interest.[106] Further, the assumption behind economic instruments is that everybody behaves like a rational economic calculator; when they do not, other approaches to regulation may have greater potential. And if all regulated parties do indeed behave like rational economic calculators, we should expect gaming and non-compliance, so that significant public resources will have to be devoted to monitoring and enforcement.[107] More generally, there are questions around the ability of economic instruments to deliver in practice on their theoretical promise. The impact on environmental quality may be unpredictable, depending on uncertain economic calculations and on polluters behaving in economically rational ways. Emissions trading schemes are supposed to be more predictable than taxes, given that a 'cap' is set on pollution.

Applying economic instruments to biodiversity or habitats conservation (rather than pollution) raises particularly acute difficulties. McGillivray summarises the challenges as 'profound questions about commensurability and fungibility; of valuation; and of regulatory flexibility, discretion, monitoring, enforcement and follow-through'.[108] In particular, whilst a ton of carbon is more or less the same in whatever circumstances it is emitted,[109] we might note the difficulty of ensuring that any replacement habitat or biodiversity is of the same or better quality than what has been lost, and indeed whether a valued habitat can ever be truly recreated or replaced. Furthermore, replacing a damaged urban green space somewhere far away may provide ecological benefits, but its social role will be very different.[110]

---

[106] J Dryzek, *The Politics of the Earth: Environmental Discourses* (Oxford, Oxford University Press, 1997).

[107] A Dobson, *Citizenship and the Environment* (Oxford, Oxford University Press, 2003) Introduction, discusses the taxation of household waste.

[108] McGillivray (n 97) 419; C Reid, 'The Privatisation of Biodiversity? Possible New Approaches to Nature Conservation Law in the UK' (2011) 23 *Journal of Environmental Law* 203.

[109] Of course, other pollutants may have significant local effects, but the point remains.

[110] C Reid and W Nsoh, 'The Privatisation of Biodiversity' *Paper Presented at the Society of Legal Scholars Annual Conference 2013* (Edinburgh).

Michael Sandel spells out two further key criticisms (he is also concerned with effectiveness) of the expansion of market norms into areas where they may not (and at least never used to) belong.[111] One is equality and fairness. So a tax on petrol consumption (for example) means that the rich can continue in their normal polluting ways, the poor cannot. We touched on these distributive issues earlier, and return briefly to a global distributive perspective in chapter six. Sandel's other criticism is 'corruption': that 'market values crowd out nonmarket norms worth caring about'.[112] Dobson also criticises the way in which the use of economic instruments 'encourages the idea that sustainability makes no moral or ethical demands on us'.[113] This critique is also relevant to effectiveness: price signals are likely to lead to superficial changes in behaviour, and when it no longer makes economic sense to protect the environment, so be it.[114]

A final concern, reminiscent of the discussion in chapter two, is the limited public control over the market instrument. The prioritisation of highly technical economic expertise can obscure the inevitable value judgments being made. Chapter six touches again on the possible inscrutability and rigidity of economic instruments. Even if the overall objectives of environmental policy are set by public debate, and economic instruments are effective, once the market system is in place, political control of that process becomes very difficult.

Voluntary Instruments and Corporate Social Responsibility

The use of 'softer' measures in new governance was discussed above. Equally, soft measures are tools through which a regulator might manage its relationship with the regulated. At the extreme, soft law constitutes wholly voluntary undertakings by industry, and hard law an EU (or national) legislative standard, wholly external to the industry, imposed and enforced. These two extremes are unusual, with voluntary measures generally being subject to some external pressure, and hard law to some negotiation.

'Self-regulation' is a complex and contested notion. The Commission defines self-regulation as:

the possibility for economic operators, the social partners, non-governmental organisations or associations to adopt amongst themselves and for themselves common guidelines at European level (particularly codes of practice or sectoral agreements).[115]

---

[111] M Sandel, *What Money Can't Buy: The Moral Limits of Markets* (London, Allen Lane, 2012); M Sagoff, *The Economy of the Earth: Philosophy, Law and the Environment* (Cambridge, Cambridge University Press, 1988).
[112] Sandel, ibid 8 and 113.
[113] A Dobson, *Sustainability Citizenship* (London, Greenhouse, 2011) 5.
[114] Dobson (n 107).
[115] Interinstitutional Agreement (n 52) [22].

Self-regulation also commonly applies to commitments at the single firm level, or sectorally at the international, national or local level. One useful way to think about the role of 'voluntary' approaches to environmental protection is to consider environmental protection as an aspect of 'corporate social responsibility' (CSR), defined by the Commission as 'the responsibility of enterprises for their impacts on society'.[116] CSR seeks to reorient corporate responsibility from a unique focus on profit maximisation for shareholders, to a broader set of public-oriented objectives. Most advocacy of CSR, within and beyond the corporate community, focuses on the 'business case' for CSR;[117] that responsibility is good for profits. Profit might accrue from the cost savings associated with reduced resource consumption,[118] or from the new market opportunities associated with ethical products (fair trade or organic for example), or the attractiveness of a 'green' reputation to some consumers. Risk avoidance, including the risk of being targeted by civil society protest against particular brands or products, is another profit maximising possibility.[119] The business case has been very important in overcoming resistance to CSR,[120] but has serious limits. Empirically, the link between CSR and business success is uncertain;[121] and the good will not always prosper.[122] The business case may in part depend on the strength of the consumer in the particular sector, and CSR probably has most impact on large consumer-oriented firms and brands. The business case also assumes away conflict between profit and environmental protection, which are not only real, but arguably fundamental to the extent that consumer-driven CSR campaigns rely on encouraging consumption.[123] Moreover, valuing environmental protection purely in terms of economic benefit is problematic, as discussed in chapter two.

Concerns about environmental effectiveness include questions around the lack of incentive to go beyond business as usual, and around monitoring and implementation of 'voluntary' commitments. Industry-wide approaches create the risk of free riders, individual companies that get the advantage of improved

---

[116] European Commission, 'A Renewed EU Strategy 2011–14 for Corporate Social Responsibility' COM (2011) 681 final [3.1].

[117] See for discussion C Bradshaw, 'The Environmental Business Case and Unenlightened Shareholder Value' (2013) 33 *Legal Studies* 141.

[118] These win-win opportunities are often missed, Porter and van der Linde (n 23); see also ch 6.

[119] D McBarnet, 'Corporate Social Responsibility beyond Law, Through Law, for Law: The New Corporate Accountability' in D McBarnet, A Voiculescu and T Campbell (eds), *The New Corporate Accountability: Corporate Social Responsibility and the Law* (Cambridge, Cambridge University Press, 2007) cites the association of Nike with child labour and of Shell with the Nigerian Government's persecution of the Ogoni people. More recently, we might consider the campaigns against corporate tax arrangements in the UK, www.ukuncut.org.uk/targets/.

[120] In particular the argument (see classically M Friedman, 'The Social Responsibility of Business is to Increase its Profits' *The New York Times Magazine*, 13 September 1970) that it is illegitimate and even unlawful to manage the company in any way other than in the interests of shareholders. See McBarnet, ibid, for discussion.

[121] Bradshaw (n 117).

[122] McBarnet (n 119).

[123] C Bradshaw, *Corporations, Responsibility and the Environment* (University College London, PhD thesis, 2013).

sectoral reputation and reduced attention from regulators, without committing themselves. There are also concerns about CSR being used as a marketing tool, with misleading claims and 'green washing',[124] or more broadly as a discourse to legitimise the power of large corporations.[125] CSR may be used as a technique to undermine formal binding regulatory standards.[126] Furthermore, the 'right' thing to do is not always self-evident. Environmental protection is often a contested concept, and difficult choices have to be made between different environmental goods. A plurality of non-environmental values might also be at stake, with tensions between, for example, environmental protection and the provision of cheap food to the poor, or between environmental protection and trade with a developing country. The 'privatisation' of these choices is bound to be controversial.

These are very real concerns. Those supporting CSR would point to its greater responsiveness and flexibility, its capacity to create a more self-critical, self-reflexive, environmentally focused organisation, in response to the limitations of direct regulation outlined above.[127] The possibility of non- or creative compliance with hard legal rules reminds us that turning to law is not a simple answer.[128] Moreover, the line between voluntary and imposed measures is not a bright one. The relationship between 'law' and 'CSR' raises similar complex questions similar to the relationship between 'hard' and 'soft' law, and 'law' and 'governance'. The work of Neil Gunningham and colleagues on the 'licence to operate' is helpful.[129] Gunningham et al's 'licence to operate' is made up of not only the 'legal licence', but also the 'economic licence', the 'social licence', and the 'collective social licence'. The legal licence is literally the obligation to comply with the law, including the regulatory permit. The economic licence refers to the firm's economic viability, and requires the support of shareholders, banks and customers. The social licence is about the broad acceptability of operations to third parties, including local communities and environmental interest groups. Informal sanctions for breach of the social licence may include reputational damage, with possible effects in the market via consumers, investors and employees, and political demands for more stringent regulation. The collective social licence, resonating with the Commission's focus on EU wide sectoral self-regulatory undertakings, emphasises the interest of all

---

[124] See eg www.greenwashgold.org/.

[125] SB Banerjee, 'Corporate Social Responsibility: The Good, The Bad and the Ugly' (2008) 34 *Critical Sociology* 51.

[126] McBarnet (n 119). On CSR as a 'neutralisation' technique in the tobacco industry, see G Fooks et al, 'The Limits of Corporate Social Responsibility: Techniques of Neutralization, Stakeholder Management and Political CSR' (2013) 112 *Journal of Business Ethics* 283.

[127] Eg Bradshaw (n 123), citing C Parker, *The Open Corporation: Effective Self-regulation and Democracy* (Cambridge, Cambridge University Press, 2010).

[128] McBarnet (n 119) argues that one of the most important potential contributions of CSR is to address 'creative compliance'; this resonates with the tone of the campaign against corporate tax avoidance (n 119).

[129] N Gunningham, RA Kagan, D Thornton, *Shades of Green: Business, Regulation, and Environment* (Stanford University Press, 2003); N Gunningham, 'Corporate Environmental Responsibility: Law and the Limits of Voluntarism' in McBarnet, Voiculescu and Campbell (n 119).

operators in a particular sector to ensure responsible behaviour by others in the sector.[130] For example, all deep water oil extraction was the subject of additional scrutiny and popular concern following the BP Gulf of Mexico disaster in 2010. Importantly, the different strands of licence interact. Social pressure can reverberate into the legal and the economic licences. Mandatory and voluntary measures are closely connected, and the legal licence can empower social stakeholders, and make the 'social licence' more robust.[131] 'Complementary regulation' identified by the Commission, for example, includes measures 'to promote transparency, create market incentives for responsible business conduct, and ensure corporate accountability.[132] Mechanisms including enhanced obligations of information disclosure,[133] enhanced rights of public participation in decision-making by the company (or regulator) and access to the courts have a potentially important role to play in CSR.

Information as a Tool of Regulation

Information plays many different roles in environmental policy;[134] we have already considered some of its characteristics, and discuss it further in later chapters. One basic challenge for environmental regulators is their ability to gather adequate information and knowledge on environmental problems. EU environmental regulation attempts to create a framework within which diverse information is generated, shared and subject to external scrutiny, to enrich the regulator's understanding of the environment, and improve the substantive quality of regulatory decisions. Due to the fact that, in many cases, the regulated industry enjoys the best information resources, regulated parties are often required to provide the information on which regulation is based. This essential role for regulated parties raises some challenges, discussed at various points in this book, especially in respect of industrial emissions (chapter five) and chemicals (chapter nine).

One role for information, in addition to providing the basis for regulators to act, is to try to stimulate behaviour change by individuals or organisations. Environmental harm might be in part due to ignorance, so that improved knowledge will in itself improve performance. Behaviour change is very complicated,[135] and there is a long history of disappointment at the failure of education to lead

---

[130] On other operators in a sector as 'surrogate' regulators, see Abbot (n 17).

[131] Gunningham (n 129). McBarnet (n 119) reviews other legal tactics, including private law actions.

[132] Commission (n 116) [3.4].

[133] On the introduction of environmental measures into corporate annual reports, see Fourth Council Directive 1978/660/EEC on the annual accounts of certain types of companies [1978] OJ L222/11; on the UK Companies Act 2006 s 172, see Bradshaw (n 117).

[134] See K Yeung, 'Government by Publicity Management: Sunshine or Spin?' [2005] *Public Law* 360.

[135] Eg E Shove, 'Beyond the ABC: Climate Change Policy and Theories of Social Change' (2010) 42 *Environment and Planning A* 1273; Yeung, ibid.

to action.[136] But knowledge may be one starting point. More ambitiously, it is possible that obligations to gather (and reflect on) environmental information may support the evolution of a self-critical, environmentally self-aware, organisation; chapter seven returns to this. Experimental evidence tentatively suggests that forcing people to confront directly the ethical (environmental) implications of their decisions may enhance the consideration and influence of those ethical issues.[137]

Access to information may serve regulatory purposes by enabling third parties (those living near an installation, environmental interest groups, consumers) to exert pressure on polluters, enforcing the 'social licence'.[138] In some cases, information is provided directly to consumers, allowing markets to operate in part around a product's environmental characteristics.[139] Save with respect to the energy use of products, mandatory labelling is relatively unusual in the EU,[140] and voluntary labelling of green credentials is much more common.[141] The broader public release of information is often mandatory, however. For example applications for authorisation, and opinions and draft decisions, as well as final decisions, may have to be published in accordance with a particular legislative scheme.[142] The European Pollutant Release and Transfer Register (PRTR) is a register of environmental data searchable by area, industrial facility, activity or pollutant,[143] covering a range of sources and pollutants, including diffuse pollution and waste transfers. Further legal rights of access to environmental information on request are discussed in chapters seven and eight.

These mechanisms do have their limitations. Publication in the PRTR is slow, with information on 2011 only added in May 2013. Comparability can be difficult, since methodologies vary across the EU, and the raw data does not always reveal the relative performance of installations, for example their emissions per unit of production.[144] A right to information on request requires the requestor to know what she is looking for. Furthermore, if information is to play a regulatory

---

[136] Eg A Dobson, *Green Political Thought* (London, Routledge, 2000) 115–16.

[137] Bradshaw (n 123); Awrey, Blair and Kershaw (n 71).

[138] See n 129.

[139] See generally eg C Hilson, 'EU Ecological Solidarity and the Ecological Consumer: Towards a Republican Citizenship' in M Ross and Y Borgmann-Prebil (eds), *Promoting Solidarity in the European Union* (Oxford, Oxford University Press, 2010).

[140] Directive 2010/30/EU on the indication by labeling and standard product information of the consumption of energy and other resources by energy-related products [2010] OJ L153/1. Information for consumers is conspicuous by its relative absence in chemicals regulation, see ch 9, but on other occasions labelling is at the heart of the regulatory debate. Food seems to raise particular issues: on mandatory labelling of genetically modified organisms (GMOs), see M Lee, *EU Regulation of GMOs: Law and Decision Making for a New Technology* (London, Edward Elgar, 2008); for nanotechnology, see E Stokes, 'You Are What You Eat: Market Citizens and the Right to Know About Nano Foods' (2011) 2 *Journal of Human Rights and the Environment* 178.

[141] See eg Regulation 66/2010/EC on the EU ecolabel [2010] OJ L27/1.

[142] See eg chs 5 and 9.

[143] Regulation 166/2006/EC concerning the establishment of a European Pollutant Release and Transfer Register [2006] OJ L33/1, prtr.ec.europa.eu/.

[144] prtr.ec.europa.eu/pgFAQ.aspx.

role, then as has already been mentioned, there may be a need for 'translation' for lay audiences.[145] Legislation rarely takes this into consideration, although in some cases, an obligation to provide a non-technical summary of information is placed on the industry.[146] But environmental interest groups are often expected to play this interpretive role, translating data into terms that are useful for the lay public (eg consumers, or those living near an industrial facility), and are politically tractable.[147] Whilst far from perfect, however, the EU provides relatively broad rights of access to information, which can enable public and peer, political and legal, pressure, and may provide incentives for improved performance.

CONCLUSIONS

Neo-liberal advocacy of de-regulation in the 1980s was generally framed in opposition to a very narrowly conceptualised form of command and control 'regulation'. Non-command and control instruments were seen as 'less' regulatory, and linked with the ascendancy of market-oriented thinking generally, and with mistrust of government.[148] 'New governance' is also sometimes associated by its critics with a neo-liberal agenda that would undermine and under-value the role of government. True advocates of de-regulation, however, expect governments to leave markets alone, and neither 'alternative' instruments of regulation nor 'new' governance leaves markets to themselves. Trying to insist upon sharp distinctions between 'new' and 'old' governance, or 'traditional' and 'alternative' regulation is a game of diminishing returns; it is easy to identify strands of both opposing pairs in EU environmental law. Both BAT and good water status, for example, sit within a direct regulatory scheme, in the sense that the EU legislation 'commands' the Member States to achieve these environmental objectives, and in the sense that the Member States must rely at least in part on permitting systems to do so. Bright lines between 'new' and 'old' governance are elusive.

Some of the heat of the deregulation debate seems to have dissipated, but the critique and renewal of direct regulation has not just been an academic exercise. The Commission also proclaims its turn to 'better' or 'smarter' regulation.[149] At its crudest, the 'better regulation' agenda in the EU is simply a euphemism for

---

[145] Jasanoff (n 73) 27, of pollution inventories specifically.

[146] In respect of environmental impact assessment, see ch 7 below. An applicant for a permit under the IED is also required to provide a non-technical summary, (n 22) Art 12(1).

[147] This has happened to some extent with information on chemicals, see ch 9 below.

[148] Dryzek (n 106).

[149] See CM Radaelli, 'Whither Better Regulation for the Lisbon Agenda' (2007) 14 *Journal of European Public Policy* 190. The Commission's approach to 'smart regulation' (European Commission, 'Smart Regulation in the European Union' COM (2010) 543 final) is different from Gunningham and Grabosky's approach (n 13), which advocates 'the use of multiple rather than single policy instruments and a broader range of regulatory actors', and 'harnessing institutions and resources residing "outside" the public sector' (Gunningham (n 28) 200–01).

de-regulation, and reducing burdens for industry is a key theme.[150] It can also be more than that, however. Whilst pervaded by a rhetoric of reducing regulatory 'burdens', the Commission's *Smart Regulation* communication explicitly asserts that 'Regulation has a positive and necessary role to play',[151] emphasising transparency, accountability and evidence, and a more holistic approach to the policy cycle. And rather than focusing on regulatory burdens, the Commission's 2000 'White Paper on European Governance', which responded more or less explicitly to the popular mistrust of the European Union at the time, placed participation at the (rhetorical if not actual) centre of European governance.[152]

Some of the criticisms of direct regulation have been overdrawn, and some of the responses bring with them challenges of their own. Efforts can and should be made to respond to these fresh challenges; the legitimacy, accountability and effectiveness of environmental governance cannot be taken for granted. The post mortems on the global financial crisis suggest a pervasive under-appreciation of industry self-interest, and over-estimation of industry capacity to manage risk.[153] The potential for similar pitfalls in the environmental arena is clear. Whatever approach we take to EU environmental governance and regulation, a prodigious level of energy is required for effective environmental governance, and there is no escape from the need for public resources, in terms of money, expertise and information.

---

[150] For a striking example, see European Commission, 'Smart Regulation: Responding to the Needs of Small and Medium-Sized Enterprises' COM (2013) 122 final.

[151] Commission (n 149) 2; also European Commission, *Better Regulation—Simply Explained* (Luxembourg, European Commission, 2006) 3.

[152] Commission (n 27); ch 8 below.

[153] Black (n 6); Ford (n 19).

5

Instruments and Governance II: The Direct Regulation of Industrial Pollution

INTRODUCTION

THE INDUSTRIAL EMISSIONS Directive (IED)[1] revolves around command and control or direct regulation, discussed in the previous chapter: all installations or activities covered by the Directive need a permit from the regulator. As well as illustrating the specifically EU context of direct regulation, the IED allows us to explore three important issues. First, we see an example of what in chapter four I referred to (loosely) as 'collaborative governance'. Substantively flexible legislative standards are coupled with a framework within which more detailed environmental norms are generated beyond the legislation. Secondly, legislative changes to the status of standards set in this collaborative forum suggest that there is no straightforward line to be drawn between harmonisation and decentralisation in EU environmental law.[2] Thirdly, the IED allows us to examine the ways in which opportunities for institutional environmental learning are encouraged in EU environmental legislation.

After an introduction to the IED, this chapter discusses these three issues in turn. Further, some of the legal changes introduced by the IED seem to have been prompted, at least in part, by concerns about implementation, and this chapter outlines some of the responses to the well-known difficulties of ensuring adequate implementation of EU environmental law. Perhaps the most important role of the Member States in EU environmental law lies in their obligation to implement EU environmental law on the ground.

---

[1] Directive 2010/75/EU on industrial emissions (integrated pollution prevention and control) ('Industrial Emissions Directive' (IED)) [2010] OJ L334/17.

[2] Explored explicitly in M Lee, 'The Ambiguity of Multi-Level Governance and (De-harmonisation in EU Environmental Law' (2014) *Cambridge Yearbook of European Legal Studies* forthcoming.

INTRODUCING THE IED

The IED was agreed in 2010 and replaces the Integrated Pollution Prevention and Control (IPPC) Directive,[3] as well as a number of Directives applying to specific sectors (large combustion plants, waste incineration and co-incineration plants, installations and activities using organic solvents, and installations producing titanium dioxide). It is the central piece of legislation dealing with the environmental effects of industrial installations. This chapter focuses on Chapter II of the IED, which contains the overarching provisions on IPPC, and applies to activities listed in Annex I of the Directive. Fairly conventionally, these are primarily major industrial activities, such as chemical and energy industries, as well as certain intensive farming operations.[4]

At the heart of IPPC is the aim to deal with the environmental media of soil, water and air in an 'integrated' manner, in order 'to achieve a high level of protection of the environment taken as a whole'.[5] It involves 'an integrated, overall look at the polluting and consuming potential of the installation'.[6] IPPC attempts to overcome a tendency for traditional media-specific approaches to regulation to transfer pollution from one environmental medium to another, for example because the stringency of regulation or its enforcement is uneven. Trying to identify what is best for the environment as a whole compounds the difficult value judgments involved in environmental decision-making. For example, a comparison between a very small risk to human health and a more dramatic impact on river ecology cannot be made by technical information alone.[7]

'Integration' in the IED is limited in certain respects. In particular, it is narrower than the integration principle found in Article 11 of the Treaty on the Functioning of the European Union (TFEU) and discussed in chapter three, where the concern is to integrate environmental considerations into other areas, from farming to transport to the economy (although of course, the IED integrates environmental concerns into the activities that it regulates).[8] The opportunity to embed broader environmental standards in the permitting process was not taken by the Court

---

[3] References will be to Directive 2008/1/EC concerning integrated pollution prevention and control [2008] OJ L24/8; see also the original Directive 1996/61/EC on integrated pollution prevention and control [1996] OJ L257/26.

[4] The ECJ takes a purposive (environmental) approach to the interpretation of the Annex. See eg Case C-585/10 *Møller v Haderslev Kommune*, not yet published in the ECR, on the meaning of 'sow'.

[5] IED (n 1) Art 1.

[6] European Commission, 'BREF on Economics and Cross-Media Effects' (July 2006) v, which is 'a document to be taken into account where there are significant cross-media effects', see Commission Implementing Decision 2012/119/EU laying down rules concerning guidance on the collection of data and on the drawing up of BAT reference documents and on their quality assurance [2012] OJ L63/1 [2.3.7.2.5], [2.6.2].

[7] A sense of the complexity can be seen in Commission, ibid [2.5], [2.6].

[8] K Kulovesi, E Morgera, M Muñoz, 'Environmental Integration and Multi-Faceted International Dimensions of EU Law: Unpacking the EU's 2009 Climate and Energy Package' (2011) 48 *Common Market Law Review* 829 describe a more holistic approach to environmental protection as 'internal integration'.

of Justice in a challenge brought by an environmental interest group to permits granted by the Dutch Government to three power stations. The claimants argued that the permits would lead to the breach of 'national emissions ceilings' set in EU legislation for nitrogen oxides and sulphur dioxide.[9] The ECJ rejected any obligation even to *take account* of the national emissions ceilings.[10] Nor does the Directive require the Member States to integrate their institutional permitting arrangements, although IPPC may be more difficult to embed into administrative systems that address the environmental media separately.[11] Notwithstanding these limitations, however, the effort to integrate is important.

The Directive sets out in some detail what must be contained in any permit. It makes use of some of the key types of environmental standard in EU environmental law.[12] First, 'emission limit values' (ELVs) restrict the amount of a particular pollutant that can be emitted by a polluter.[13] The Annexes to the IED contain some minimum EU-wide ELVs. Other ELVs are worked out by reference to what could be achieved by use of 'best available techniques' (BAT). Compliance with standards associated with BAT is, as discussed below, generally mandatory. The permit must require an operator to meet 'ELVs associated with the BAT',[14] but 'without prescribing the use of any technique or specific technology'.[15] This flexibility as to how to meet a standard is valued because it provides operators with an incentive (even if they do not all use it) to discover cheaper or better ways of achieving regulatory objectives,[16] and operators are assumed to have better understanding of these issues than regulators. Secondly, 'environmental quality standards' (EQSs) restrict the amount of a pollutant in the receiving environment, air or a body of water, for example.[17] They control emissions only to the extent 'necessary' to protect the environment, and so are sometimes claimed to be more flexible than ELVs. The main drawback of quality standards is the incentive to export pollution. As Gertrude Lubbe-Wolf points out, quality standards are not

---

[9] Set by Directive 2001/81/EC on national emission ceilings for certain atmospheric pollutants [2001] OJ L309/22; Case C-165/09 *Stichting Natuur en Milieu v College van Gedeputeerde Staten van Groningen* [2011] ECR I-4599.

[10] Disagreeing with Kokott AG, who would have gone further than a 'take into account' obligation, concluding that new emissions from a new power station are not to be permitted if national emissions ceilings are breached, barring 'absolutely overriding reasons in the public interest', ibid [112]–[115] (Kokott AG).

[11] B Lange, 'The EU Directive on Industrial Emissions: Squaring the Circle of Integrated, Harmonised and Ambitious Technology Standards?' (2011) 13 *Environmental Law Review* 199.

[12] For discussion of standards, see C Abbot, 'Environmental Command Regulation' in B Richardson and S Wood (eds), *Environmental Law for Sustainability* (Oxford, Hart Publishing, 2006). Terminology varies.

[13] Defined by IED (n 1) Art 3(5).

[14] Ibid Art 3(13).

[15] Ibid Art 15(2). Note that 'emission limit values may be supplemented or replaced by equivalent parameters or technical measures ensuring an equivalent level of environmental protection', Art 14(2).

[16] D Driesen, 'Economic Instruments for Sustainable Development' in Richardson and Wood (n 12) 281–82.

[17] Defined by IED (n 1) Art 3(6).

likely to require a comprehensive assessment: of soil acidification in Sweden and the ozone layer above the North Pole, for example.[18] Thirdly, a 'technology' or 'specification' standard demands a particular type of technology or process, providing less flexibility than either ELVs or EQSs. In some cases, BAT may be defined in such a way as to amount to this sort of standard; but as discussed below, that is not its main purpose.

Substantively, Article 11 IED requires the Member States to ensure that activities are carried out in accordance with certain 'general principles'. The eight general principles include the application of BAT, as well as the need to take 'all the appropriate preventive measures … against pollution' and to ensure that 'no significant pollution is caused'.[19] Article 14(1) provides that the permit must, inter alia, include conditions to ensure compliance with those general principles. It must also set ELVs for the polluting substances listed in the Directive and polluting substances 'likely to be emitted from the installation in significant quantities'.[20] ELVs are, as mentioned above, either set in the legislation, or, as discussed in more detail below, set by reference to BAT. Permit conditions must also ensure compliance with EQSs.[21] This means that in some cases, the permit may need to set ELVs stricter than those associated with BAT; and even in those cases in which ELVs are allowed to drop below BAT, EQSs must still be met.

It should already be evident that BAT plays a key role in the IED. BAT is defined in the Directive as:

> the most effective and advanced stage in the development of activities and their methods of operation which indicates the practical suitability of particular techniques for providing the basis for emission limit values and other permit conditions designed to prevent and, where that is not practicable, to reduce emissions and the impact on the environment as a whole.[22]

Working out what amounts to BAT in any particular case will require considerable effort. 'Techniques' is further defined to include 'both the technology used, and the way in which the installation is designed, built, maintained, operated and decommissioned'. Best is 'the most effective in achieving a high general level of protection of the environment as a whole', which looks like a single mindedly environmental concern, and reinforces the holistic (whole environment) aspirations of BAT. 'Availability' introduces cost and practicality concerns: 'available techniques' are 'those developed on a scale which allows implementation in the relevant industrial sector, under economically and technically viable conditions,

---

[18] G Lübbe-Wolff, 'Efficient Environmental Legislation—On Different Philosophies of Pollution Control in Europe' (2001) 13 *Journal of Environmental Law* 79.

[19] IED (n 1) Art 11.

[20] Ibid Art 14(1)(a); Annex II contains the list of pollutants.

[21] Ibid Arts 14(1) and 18. The definition of EQS in Art 3(6) refers to EQSs 'set out in Union law'. This includes eg Directive 2000/60/EC establishing a framework for the Community action in the field of water policy [2000] OJ L327/1; Directive 2008/50/EC on ambient air quality and cleaner air for Europe [2008] OJ L152/1.

[22] IED, ibid, Art 3(10).

taking into consideration the costs and advantages'. The technique must be 'reasonably accessible to the operator', but whether it is 'used or produced inside the Member State in question' is irrelevant, preventing them favouring a national approach to pollution abatement.[23]

The role of costs in defining BAT is, not surprisingly, controversial.[24] Costs and advantages are clearly to be taken into account, but there is no further detail in the legislation on which costs and advantages might be relevant, the appropriate response to those costs and advantages, or when costs are too high. Detailed guidance has been produced on economic methodologies, but without providing decisive criteria for decisions.[25] In practice, costs are used in different ways during the negotiation of BAT, from general and vague comments about costs, to detailed costings of particular interventions.[26] A formal cost benefit analysis (CBA) is suggested by the statement that identifying 'which technique offers the most value (environmental benefits) for money (costs)' is 'crucial', although there is no obligation to monetise environmental benefits.[27]

Annex III provides 12 additional 'criteria for determining best available techniques', including the use of low-waste technology, technological advances, the consumption and nature of raw materials (including water) used in the process, and 'the need to prevent or reduce to a minimum the overall impact of the emissions on the environment and the risks to it'.

The IED provides that the 'public concerned' (explicitly including environmental interest groups) must be given 'early and effective opportunities to participate' in permitting procedures.[28] There are also provisions requiring cross-border consultation, if a Member State is aware that an installation 'is likely to have significant negative effects' on the environment of another Member State, or if the other Member State so requests.[29] The language on participation is very similar to that found in environmental assessment legislation, discussed in chapter seven. The detail of public participation is in the hands of the Member States. Relatively shallow consultation mechanisms would suffice, although richer, more deliberative approaches are possible. The obligation to provide information on the results of consultation, and an explanation of how those results were taken into account, provides a relatively sharp form of accountability to participants.[30] A good deal of the detail on the reaching of the authorisation decision is also made public, including the use of the derogations discussed below.

---

[23] All ibid Art 3(10).
[24] Generally, B Lange, *Implementing EU Pollution Control: Law and Integration* (Cambridge, Cambridge University Press, 2008).
[25] Commission (2006) (n 6) Ch 5.
[26] Lange (n 24) ch 7.
[27] Commission (2006) (n 6) 51, 52. Note the discussion of CBA in ch 2 above.
[28] IED (n 1) Art 24 (1); Annex IV.
[29] Ibid Art 26.
[30] Ibid Art 24(2)(c).

COLLABORATIVE GOVERNANCE IN SEVILLE

The European IPPC Bureau, based in Seville, plays a crucial role in the implementation of the IED.[31] The Bureau administers what has become known as the Seville process, by which 'BAT reference documents' (BREFs) are drafted. BREFs set out BAT in more detail for particular issues or sectors.[32] Whilst the Seville process initially evolved outside the framework of the original IPPC Directive, it is now formalised by Article 13 of the IED. The Commission (with comitology, discussed in chapter two) has also published a detailed implementation Decision addressing the BREF drafting process.[33]

The Commission decides when to draft or review a BREF.[34] The initial 'exchange of information' on BAT takes place in a Technical Working Group (TWG). The TWG must include 'Member States, the industries concerned, non-governmental organisations promoting environmental protection and the Commission',[35] and is composed of 40 to 100 experts for each BREF.[36] The European IPPC Bureau 'coordinates', 'leads' and 'steers' the work carried out by the TWGs.[37] It seeks information from members of the TWG, and presents formal and informal drafts to the TWG for comment.[38] 'Consensus ... is sought' in the TWG, but 'it is not a prerequisite' for a decision.[39] A BREF can record 'split views', provided that the dissenting view is based on information available to the Bureau at the time of drafting, and supported by a 'valid' rationale ('appropriate technical, cross-media or economic data or information relevant to the definition of BAT').[40]

There was an effort under the IPPC Directive to separate the 'technical' TWG from the 'political' stage of decision-making.[41] But the technical discussion was never simply 'technical', in the sense of being subject to straightforwardly right and wrong answers, free from choices with political consequences. Bettina Lange's study of the BREF decision-making process suggests that interest representation (and hence negotiation and compromise, rather than simple fact finding) can be expected in the BREF committees.[42] Given the discussion in chapter two, it is not at all surprising that BAT turns out to be a mixture of the technical and the political, the evaluative and the factual, private interest bargaining and public interest deliberation. The Commission explicitly acknowledges that identifying the 'best'

---

[31] See eippcb.jrc.ec.europa.eu/.

[32] Defined by IED (n 1) Art 3(11).

[33] Decision 2012/119/EU (n 6).

[34] IED (n 1) Art 13; taking into account the view of the forum (the forum is discussed below).

[35] Ibid Art 13.

[36] eippcb.jrc.ec.europa.eu/about/who_is_who.html.

[37] Decision 2012/119/EU (n 6) [4.5].

[38] Ibid Table 1 [1.2.4].

[39] Ibid [4.4.2].

[40] Ibid [4.6.2.3.2].

[41] For a detailed discussion, see Lange (n 24).

[42] Ibid ch 5. See also European Environmental Bureau (EEB), *New Features under the Industrial Emissions Directive* (EEB, 2011) which is critical of 'political' negotiations in TWGs.

technique is a matter of expert judgment, and there is no pretence that this can be a purely technical exercise.[43]

In addition to the 'exchange of information' that takes place in the TWG, the Commission must 'establish and regularly convene' a forum. This is composed of 'representatives of Member States, the industries concerned, non-governmental organisations promoting environmental protection', but not (by contrast with the TWG) the Commission.[44] The Commission Decision establishing the forum limits membership to '*international* organisations representing industries concerned', and the environmental interest groups 'shall have an acceptable degree of European representation'.[45] Members of the forum are responsible for nominating members ('their representatives') to the TWGs,[46] and one of the forum's tasks is to 'remove or modify' a split view expressed by 'their own' TWG representative.[47]

The most important role for the forum is to provide an 'opinion' on the content of the BREF proposed by the TWG.[48] The opinion is made public, and is taken into account by the Commission when it draws up draft 'BAT conclusions'. BAT Conclusions are the part of the BREF setting out conclusions on BAT,[49] which must then be agreed through a comitology process. The most important change to the Seville process by the IED is this formal adoption of BAT conclusions through comitology. Formerly, BREFs were simply published by the Commission under the IPPC Directive. The more formal procedure reflects the more formal status of the BAT conclusions under the IED, discussed in the next section below.

As discussed in chapter four, collaborative governance processes such as the one found in Seville provide crucial information and knowledge from a range of sources, and open up the possibility of shared problem-solving. Seville is, in some senses, a participatory and inclusive process, extending formal participation in norm generation beyond the EU institutions. But there are real concerns about who participates in the Seville process, especially the potential for industry to dominate. There may also be concerns that Seville is dominated by larger and wealthier Member States. Membership of TWGs has always included environmental interest groups as a counterbalance to industry (in fact, often just the European Environment Bureau),[50] and this became a formal requirement under the IED.[51]

---

[43] Commission (2006) (n 6).

[44] IED (n 1) Art 13(3).

[45] Commission Decision establishing a forum for the exchange of information pursuant to Article 13 of the Directive 2010/75/EU on industrial emissions [2011] OJ C146/3 Art 4 (emphasis added). The Commission's preference to deal with pan-European interests is clear, and returns as an issue in ch 8 below.

[46] Decision 2012/119/EU (n 6) [4.3].

[47] Ibid [1.3].

[48] IED (n 1) Art 13(4).

[49] Defined by IED, ibid Art 3(12). BREFs have a common format, and ch 5 contains the 'BAT Conclusions'.

[50] C Koutalakis, 'Regulatory Effects of Participatory Environmental Networks: The Case of the "Seville Process"' (2005), eu-newgov.org/datalists/deliverables_detail.asp?Project_ID=14.

[51] IED (n 1) Art 13.

Research into membership of the TWGs suggest that participation rates have been reasonably balanced between the Member States, that about half of the participants in the TWGs are Member States and the Commission, companies and industry associations make up most of the rest, and research institutes and environmental interest groups around 11 per cent.[52] This data is quite old now.[53] Worryingly, the European IPPC Bureau no longer proactively makes available information on who participates in TWGs, due to 'new database protection rules'.[54]

The potential for data protection to damage the legitimacy of collaborative governance fora was mentioned in chapter four. Article 8 of the EU Charter on Fundamental Rights (CFR) provides that 'Everyone has the right to the protection of personal data concerning him or her';[55] and personal data 'must be processed fairly for specified purposes and on the basis of the consent of the person concerned or some other legitimate basis laid down by law';[56] data protection also features in the Treaties, and more detailed rules are provided in secondary legislation.[57] Chapter eight discusses the EU rules on access to documents, which seek to enhance transparency, another highly valued constitutional principle.[58] Both transparency and data protection are subject to complex rules and a range of exceptions. Without wishing to go into enormous detail, two cases are especially important for the transparency of collaborative governance. *European Commission v Bavarian Lager* involved an investigation by the Commission into UK laws that allowed publicans to be 'tied' into an exclusive purchasing agreement with breweries.[59] Bavarian Lager challenged the removal from a document of the names of those participating in a relevant meeting. Sharpston AG emphasised 'the context (an official meeting involving representatives of an industrial group acting as spokesmen for their employers, and thus purely in a professional capacity)' and the 'principle of transparency' to justify release of the information.[60] This powerful argument was not accepted by the Court, which held that participants' names constituted personal information that should be protected. The affiliations rather than the names of participants are of greatest interest (indeed names alone tell us very little). Simply removing the names and providing affiliations instead may in some cases still run into data protection issues, since the rules apply to 'any

---

[52] Koutalakis (n 50).

[53] Dating from 2004; the EEB (n 42), without citing examples or statistics, suggests that industry participation has increased, 9.

[54] Email communication, 26 June 2012.

[55] Said to be 'closely connected' with the right to protection of private life in Art 7 CFR, Joined Cases C-92/09 and C-93/09 *Schecke v Land Hessen* not yet reported in the ECR .

[56] Art 8(2) CFR.

[57] Art 16 TFEU; Art 39 of the Treaty on European Union (TEU); Directive 1995/46/EC on the protection of individuals with regard to the processing of personal data and on the free movement of such data [1995] OJ L281/31.

[58] Art 11 TEU; Regulation 1049/2001/EC regarding public access to European Parliament, Council and Commission documents [2001] OJ L145/43.

[59] C-28/08 P *European Commission v Bavarian Lager* [2010] ECR I-6055.

[60] Ibid [192] (Kokott AG).

information' relating to an 'identified or *identifiable* individual'.[61] *Schecke v Land Hessen*, a preliminary reference regarding the compatibility of an obligation to disclose information on the recipients of agricultural subsidies with data protection obligations, may be more promising.[62] *Schecke* emphasised the need to strike a balance between public interests in transparency and the protection of personal data, which are not subject to any fixed hierarchy:[63] 'The right to the protection of personal data is not, however, an absolute right, but must be considered in relation to its function in society'.[64]

The removal of all information on participants in TWGs from the Seville website may be going further than is necessary; the European IPPC Bureau (and the Commission) could justify an approach that allows scrutiny of the interests represented in decision-making and balances the values of transparency and data protection.[65] This is also reflected in the Commission's proposed amendments to the data protection regulations, which provide that 'Names, titles and functions of public office holders, civil servants and interest representatives in relation with their professional activities shall be disclosed unless, given the particular circumstances, disclosure would adversely affect the person concerned.'[66] However, and importantly, on specific request, the European IPPC Bureau has made available information on which organisations participate in TWGs.[67]

The information provided by the Bureau on request reveals that seven organisations classified as an 'environmental NGO' (non-governmental organisation) take part in TWGs, compared to over 200 classified as an 'industrial NGO'. This sort of information is difficult to interpret. For example, it is clear that one environmental NGO, the European Environment Bureau (EEB), attends most if not all TWGs, whilst industry representation is much more fragmented. Of 44 participant organisations in the TWG for the BREF for iron and steel production, it appears that two were environmental interest groups (the EEB and ÖKOPOL), 14 were from industry, and the rest represented the Member States.[68] Whilst pure

[61] *Schecke* (n 54) [52]; Directive 95/06 (n 56) Art 2(a).

[62] Ibid.

[63] M Bobek, 'Case Note' (2011) 48 *Common Market Law Review* 2005.

[64] *Schecke* (n 54) [48]; since cited in Case C-543/09 *Deutsche Telecom v Germany* [2011] ECR I-3441 [51].

[65] More generally, see Bobek (n 63). In *Schecke*, ibid, the institutions had not properly balanced the different values at stake [86]. The requirement for limitations to be provided for by law (n 56), does not necessarily demand a legislative process involving the European Parliament, K Lenaerts, 'Exploring the Limits of the EU Charter of Fundamental Rights' [2012] *European Constitutional Law Review* 375. The European IPPC Bureau could also seek early permission to release information from the participants, as encouraged by the European Ombudsman, F O'Regan, 'Access to Documents Containing Personal Data' [2011] *Competition Law International* 67.

[66] European Commission, 'Proposal for a Regulation Regarding Public Access to European Parliament, Council and Commission Documents' COM (2008) 229 final, Art 4(5). This proposal does not seem likely to make progress, see ch 8 below.

[67] Email communication with European IPPC Bureau, 25 July 2012.

[68] Ibid. The data is not particularly easy to interpret, but it seems that of the Member States: Denmark, Finland, Germany, Greece, Hungary, Ireland, Luxemburg, Poland, Slovenia, Spain, Sweden

numbers are a crude measure of legitimacy, the information on participation in TWGs is sufficient to raise some concern about the role of industry. Information on the forum is available on the Commission's Register of Expert Groups. No names are provided, but information on affiliations and groups confirms that industry is heavily represented.[69]

Even if we know who participates, identifying which 'interests' are represented is not straightforward. A large number of Member State representatives participate in the TWGs. Sometimes Member States might have a distinct 'regulatory' interest (eg using BREF drafting to contribute to the achievement of their own environmental objectives), at other times their interests overlap with a powerful industry.[70] The EEB points to industry experts increasingly taking on the role of Member State representative.[71] This is borne out by a perusal of the list of UK representatives in TWGs, which as well as the Environment Agency, the Department of the Environment, Food and Rural Affairs, and the Scottish Environmental Protection Agency, includes a number of industry groups.[72] Industry interests may also be heterogeneous. In some cases, industrial representatives will wish to reduce their own regulatory burdens. If, on the other hand, one representative is subject to high standards, perhaps because it is exposed to consumer pressure, it may want to export those standards to competitors.[73]

Furthermore, what the different participants are actually able to contribute is as important as presence in the room, a subject to which chapter eight returns. At the crudest level of exclusion, discussions in TWGs take place in English, without translation services,[74] although there is now an obligation to translate the BAT conclusions into all official languages.[75] Participating in the Seville process is enormously resource intensive,[76] which may limit the capacity of environmental interest groups (and other affected parties, such as small business) to participate as fully as the best resourced industry groups. The Commission seems to acknowledge that industry's access to resources of expertise and information gives it considerable influence. In particular, the 'most comprehensive information'[77] on

and the UK were each represented by one organisation; Belgium and France two; Portugal three; Italy four; and the Netherlands five.

[69] ec.europa.eu/transparency/regexpert/index.cfm. Three are classified as 'NGO' (and seem to be environmental interest groups), 55 as 'international organization' (and seem to be industry groups).

[70] Lange (n 24) ch 5.

[71] EEB (n 42) 9; Lange (n 24) 110.

[72] See n 67.

[73] Or may profit from regulation in other ways, see classically B Yandle, 'Bootlegger and Baptists— The Education of a Regulatory Economist' [1983] *Regulation* 13.

[74] Lange (n 24) 105; see also Decision 2012/119/EU (n 6) [4.6.2.1].

[75] IED (n 1) Art 13(6).

[76] Koutalakis (n 50), cites an industry association estimate of €1 million for effective participation, fn 10. A new BREF is expected to take 31–39 months to get through the TWG process, Decision 2012/119/EU (n 6) [1.2.4].

[77] European Commission, 'On the Road to Sustainable Production: Progress in Implementing Council Directive 96/61/EC Concerning Integrated Pollution Prevention and Control' COM (2003) 354 final, 17.

BAT comes from industry. And whilst various sources of data on costs have been identified,[78] industry seems to play a key role.[79]

Transparency is, as mentioned in chapter four, a common response to close involvement of private actors in governance mechanisms. The availability of information on who participates in the TWGs was discussed above. References to transparency pervade both the Commission Implementing Decision on drawing up BREFs, and the BREF on economics and cross-media effects.[80] These documents are primarily concerned with transparency about the way in which BREFs are decided, 'so that any part of the process can be validated or audited'.[81] For example, the source of data on costs should be recorded, as should uncertainty around that data.[82] As discussed in chapter two, openness on the assumptions embedded in technical assessments, and the scope of uncertainty, could enhance the ability of political decision-makers (and outsiders) to exercise judgment. Transparency in this sense is directed not towards the public, but towards those drawing up BAT conclusions: the members of the TWG and the forum, the comitology committee and national regulators. There are some opportunities for broader scrutiny of the BREF process. Draft BREFs are published, although this is not required by the Directive. As mentioned above, the Opinion of the forum is published. But there is no general right for any particular environmental interest group (for example) to contribute to the drafting process,[83] and there is no mechanism by which the comments of those not included in the TWG might be fed into the process.[84]

Given that much of the best information is often held by industry, their 'enrolment' or 'surrogacy' in the regulatory process can make a crucial positive contribution to the regulatory process.[85] BREF drafting is an effort to overcome information asymmetry, to learn from and to use the information resources of industry. Various 'good faith' type obligations are imposed on TWG members.[86] But any industry dominance is also due precisely to their superior resources, including resources of information. Formalising through legislation the inclusion of environmental interest groups is a positive step, but the problem is less their right to participate than their capacity to match the contributions of industry.

---

[78] Eg industry, suppliers, consultants, published information, Commission (2006) (n 6), outlines a number of sources of cost data, but emphasises the need to 'think critically about the validity of the data' [3.2.1].

[79] Commission (n 77) 17.

[80] See n 6.

[81] Commission (2006) (n 6) iii.

[82] Ibid [3.2.1], [3.2.2].

[83] Environmental interest groups and industry have to be nominated to the TWG. Nor is there any protected role for organised groups such as trade unions.

[84] By contrast, see the process for feeding in comments of TWG members, Decision 2012/119/EU (n 6) [4.6.6].

[85] C Abbot, 'Bridging the Gap—Non-state Actors and the Challenges of Regulating New Technology' (2012) 39 *Journal of Law and Society* 329; J Black, 'Enrolling Actors in Regulatory Systems: Examples from UK Financial Services Regulation' [2003] *Public Law* 63.

[86] Decision 2012/119/EU (n 6) [4.4.2].

The adoption of BAT conclusions by a comitology process is supposed to provide a politically legitimate process for the final decision, but as discussed in chapter two, comitology is not without its own legitimacy issues, in part precisely because of the isolation of the process from public scrutiny.

HARMONISATION: THE ROLE OF BREFS

Under the IPPC Directive, BREFs were not formally binding on Member State permitting authorities. The application of BAT was, and remains, a principle with which the permit must ensure compliance. But BREFs were simply one factor to take into account when determining BAT in the Member States. The IED enhances their status. Article 14(3) now provides that 'BAT conclusions' (contained in the BREF[87]) are '*the* reference' for setting permit conditions, rather than one factor amongst many.[88] Article 15(3) provides that ELVs must be at least as strict as those associated with the BAT 'laid down in the BAT conclusions'.[89] If there are no relevant BAT conclusions (because a BREF has not been agreed), the regulator determines BAT, after consulting the operator.[90]

There is clearly a link between the formal adoption of BAT conclusions through comitology, and their enhanced status. Article 15(3) on ELVs refers to the decision on BAT Conclusions adopted through comitology,[91] so Article 15(3) does not apply to unadopted conclusions. Neither Article 14(4), nor the Article 3 definition of 'BAT conclusions', refers to comitology, suggesting that even if not formally adopted, the conclusions in the BREF are still 'the' reference point for BAT. Similarly, BREFs adopted by the Commission before the IED applied (without comitology, and on the assumption that they would not be binding) 'shall apply as BAT conclusions', but not for the purposes of Article 15(3).[92] A case challenging the legality of the application parts of the BREF on cement, lime and magnesium oxide manufacturing industries is pending before the General Court, and although BAT Conclusions have since been formally adopted, we may gain some further insights into the BREF process.[93]

On the face of it, the relationship between national regulators and the BREF under the IED is very different from the situation under the IPPC Directive, when

---

[87] See n 49.

[88] IED (n 1) Art 14(3) (emphasis added); see n 49.

[89] Ibid Art 15(3).

[90] Ibid Art 14(6).

[91] By reference to IED, ibid, Art 13(5).

[92] Ibid Art 13(7).

[93] Case T-158/11 *Magnesitas de Rubián SA v Parliament and Council*. The challenged BREF is published in [2010] OJ C166/5; Commission Implementing Decision 2013/163/EU establishing the best available techniques (BAT) conclusions under Directive 2010/75/EU of the European Parliament and of the Council on industrial emissions for the production of cement, lime and magnesium oxide [2013] OJ L56/1. Complaints include inadequate inclusion of the applicants in the TWG, and failure to record the split views expressed by the applicants.

the BREF was simply one factor in the assessment of BAT in any particular case. And there are some absolutely crucial legal differences. The position is however more subtle than appearances suggest. The introduction of firmer harmonisation in the IED raises questions about the degree of flexibility really left to Member States under the IPPC Directive. The fuzzy line between soft and hard law was discussed in chapter four. To say that BREFs were not binding under the IPPC Directive does not mean that they were without effect. The BREFs carried considerable scientific, if not legal, authority, with the potential for significant practical effects.[94] Most importantly, whilst BREFs were not mandatory, BAT was. Assessing BAT locally requires 'significant cognitive, material and political capacities of both state regulators and industry',[95] particularly in Member States with fewer resources to devote to environmental regulation.[96] So if enforcement of BAT had been a realistic possibility, BREFs would have provided a tempting refuge for Member States.

Notwithstanding the potential authority of BREFs under the IPPC Directive, an apparently important motivation for the harder status of the BAT Conclusions under the IED was Commission concern that 'permits issued for implementing the IPPC Directive often include conditions that are not based on BAT as described in the BREFs with little, if any, justification for such deviation'.[97] The IPPC Directive, however, was not designed to provide uniform substantive environmental standards. It acknowledged the principle that varied local conditions require varied local environmental regulation, even if the precise scale of the 'local' (especially between national and local flexibility) was never entirely clear.[98] Some might disagree with that principle, or mistrust those required to implement it. But mere variation from BREFs did not imply failure of the IPPC Directive

---

[94] See ch 4 above. BREFs have been used by the Court and Advocate Generals as an aid to interpretation, see C-188/07 *Commune de Mesquer v Total* [2008] ECR I-4501 [47] (Kokott AG) and Case C-235/02 *Saetti and Frediani* [2004] ECR I-1005 [42], both on the definition of 'waste'. Case C-473/07 *Association Nationale pour la Protection des Eaux et Rivières-TOS v Ministère de l'Écologie, du Développement et de l'Aménagement Durables* [2009] ECR I-319 illustrates the limits of the BREF [29]–[31].

[95] C Koutalakis, A Buzogany and TA Börzel, 'When Soft Regulation is Not Enough: The Integrated Pollution Prevention and Control Directive of the European Union' (2010) 4 *Regulation and Governance* 329, 332.

[96] Ibid, indeed find that in both Romania and Greece, for example, BREFs were simply 'validated' through command and control style government orders, rather than used as a guide. The study also included Hungary and Poland.

[97] European Commission, 'Proposal for a Directive on Industrial Emissions (Integrated Pollution Prevention and Control) (Recast)' COM (2007) 844 final, 9; also European Commission, 'Report on the Implementation of Directive 2008/1/EC Concerning Integrated Pollution Prevention and Control and Directive 1999/13/EC on the Limitation of Emissions of Volatile Organic Compounds due to the Use of Organic Solvents in Certain Activities and Installations' COM (2010) 593 final, 4.

[98] J Scott, 'Flexibility, "Proceduralization", and Environmental Governance in the EU' in G de Búrca and J Scott (eds), *Constitutional Change in the EU: From Uniformity to Flexibility* (Oxford, Hart Publishing, 2000). Who enjoys flexibility will depend in part on national constitutional arrangements. 'General Binding Rules' can be set nationally for ('at least') a sector, and then incorporated directly into permit conditions, IED (n 1) Art 3(8).

in its own terms. It was even, arguably, an indicator of success. Of course, the reference to 'justification' in this quotation from the Commission is important. We would indeed have expected deviations from BREFs to be *explicable* in terms of BAT, even if there was no legislative requirement for an actual explanation.[99] And the reason-giving required in the IED, discussed below, picks up on the importance of justification.

Although 'soft', the BREFs were not without effect under the old IPPC Directive. Nor is the status of the BAT Conclusions quite as 'hard' as it might seem at first sight under the IED. First, Article 15(4) provides for a derogation from the BAT ELV, if applying the BAT conclusions:

> would lead to disproportionately higher costs compared to the environmental benefits, due to either
> (a)   the geographical location or the local environmental conditions of the installation concerned; or
> (b)   the technical characteristics of the installation concerned.

The local discretion described in this provision, relating to the nature of the plant as well as the local environment, is potentially highly individualised. The EEB 'strongly regretted' the Article 15(4) derogation, seeing it as a 'loophole'.[100] But equally, Article 15(4) is all that remains of the attention to local conditions under the IPPC Directive,[101] and of the ethos that divergent conditions may legitimately require divergent responses.[102] The Article 15(4) derogation is subject to both substantive and procedural constraints. There are two very clear substantive, environmental, provisos. First, EQSs set in legislation must in any event be met, so that harmonised minimum standards take priority. Secondly, ELVs set in the Annexes to the Directive may not be breached. So for example, large combustion plants, subject in most cases to both BAT and the narrower specific provisions of Chapter III of the IED must, irrespective of local conditions, comply with minimum ELVs set out in Annex V.[103] In addition, Article 15(4) demands that there be 'no significant pollution', and 'a high level of protection of the environment as a whole'. Being more open-ended, these conditions will be more difficult to enforce. The primary condition for operation of the derogation is that costs be 'disproportionate' as above; this may also be open to a variety of interpretations from a general evaluation of pros and cons to a full blown CBA. The Commission has to consider whether to issue guidance to 'further clarify ... the criteria to be

---

[99] The Court may however have required reasons, see eg Case C-75/08 *R (on the application of Mellor) v Secretary of State for Communities and Local Government* [2009] ECR I-3799, in the context of environmental assessment.

[100] EEB (n 42) 7.

[101] Directive 2008/1/EC (n 3) Art 9 on permitting.

[102] Although the IED (n 1) should take into account, 'when necessary, the economic situation and specific local characteristics of the place in which the industrial activity is taking place', Recital 2.

[103] Note that there has been some debate about whether BAT applies, or whether Chapter III is *lex specialis* for large combustion plants, see EEB (n 42), Ch 3. Art 15(4) seems reasonably clear.

taken into account'.[104] This might pin down the substantive criteria in more detail, but in the meantime, the procedural constraints are an important control on the national use of Article 15(4). Member States must report to the Commission on the use of Article 15(4), and the assessment and justification of the use of Article 15(4) must be documented by the regulator in an annex to the permit. These two obligations of reason-giving and publicity mean that the derogation is applied in the knowledge that its application will be subject to scrutiny. The reason-giving obligation responds to the Commission's concern that there may, in the past, have been no (good) reasons for not using BREFs.

So the possibility for local derogation is one way in which the 'harder' status of the BREFs is nuanced. Secondly, the nature of these harmonised norms is not entirely straightforward. Whilst they close down discretion in some areas, they are still open-ended in many respects.[105] This means that there is not always a simple read-across from BAT conclusions to permit conditions.[106] Their mandatory legal status does not remove the need for context specific regulatory judgment. One of the first set of BAT conclusions agreed through committee, for iron and steel production, confirms the continued importance of local or national regulatory judgment.[107] The document is complex and lengthy, and refers to seven other potentially relevant BREFs.[108] Some of the BAT conclusions' qualitative management demands could simply be directly incorporated into a permit. This might be the case, for example, with the detailed obligation in the BAT Conclusions in respect of implementing an Environmental Management System (EMS).[109] Even if easily incorporated into the permit, it would not necessarily be straightforward to comply, or to monitor compliance. The BAT Conclusions also provide some clear, quantitative ELVs associated with BAT, potentially providing a simple, hard-edged standard for inclusion in permits. But these are often expressed as ranges, and these ranges 'may reflect the differences within a given type of installation (eg difference in the grade/purity and quality of the final product, differences in design, construction, size and capacity of the installation)'.[110] The same applies to other parts of the BAT conclusions, for example on appropriate energy efficiency techniques. What amounts to BAT explicitly 'depends on the scope of the process, the product quality and the types of installation...'.[111] This requires regulators to exercise judgment, rather than just mechanically apply the BAT Conclusions.

[104] IED (n 1) Art 15(4).

[105] See Lange (n 24), on 'open' and 'closed' norms, ch 6.

[106] The EEB criticises the BREFs on the basis that it is 'difficult to derive ELVs for permit writers' (n 42) 10.

[107] Commission Implementing Decision 2012/135/EU establishing the best available techniques (BAT) conclusions under Directive 2010/75/EU of the European Parliament and of the Council on industrial emissions for iron and steel production [2012] OJ L70/63.

[108] Ibid 66–67.

[109] This seems to be common to BAT Conclusions.

[110] Decision 2012/135/EU (n 107) 67.

[111] Eg '[t]he existing configuration of the water circuits may limit applicability of BAT for water management', Decision 2012/135/EU, ibid 75.

Furthermore, the BREF on economic and cross-media effects makes it clear that some methodologies used in Seville are not appropriate for application at the local level. For example, 'average acidification potential' might be used in a BREF, but is explicitly not appropriate 'when the location of the proposal is known':[112] so any BAT Conclusions using average acidification potential cannot be simply applied, but need to be adapted to local circumstances. Finally, as expressly required by the Commission Implementing Decision,[113] BAT conclusions confirm that 'The techniques listed and described in these BAT conclusions are neither prescriptive nor exhaustive. Other techniques may be used that ensure at least an equivalent level of environmental protection'.[114]

In short, the environmental standards applied at the local or national level continue to depend on regulatory judgment. Monitoring compliance with the complex and sometimes open-ended demands of the BAT Conclusions is in any case likely to be challenging, both for the Commission and national regulators.

None of this should be very surprising, given the complexity of the regulatory exercise, but it demonstrates that setting BAT at EU level by no means renders the national implementation a mechanical exercise of transposition. Even when BAT Conclusions are a mandatory reference point, national regulators still have a crucial and difficult evaluative role, and accountability is not straightforward. In fact, if the intention of the IED was to create a common European implementation of BAT, it is likely that it will need to be supplemented by further efforts at collaborative governance, alongside this hard law intervention. But this time, collaboration will be needed not just within the Seville groups, but also between Seville and local regulators and industry.

The remaining flexibility for national or local regulation leaves some space for the operation of public participation at the local level. In any decision-making process, the legal and policy background to a decision shapes the ways in which public participation might affect a decision. Local participation is most meaningful in a context of local decision-making, and prior commitment to BAT conclusions necessarily restricts the scope of the public participation. The ability to provide for stricter obligations,[115] the opportunity for derogation, as well as the often open nature of the BAT conclusions, leaves some space for local interests at the permitting stage. There is however likely to be some disconnection between the expression of public concern and the technical priorities of the Directive, which the Directive does nothing to address. The IED takes an instrumental approach to public participation, more about monitoring the application of EU norms than about allowing citizens a democratic stake in the decisions that shape their world.

---

[112] Commission (2006) (n 6) [2.5.4]; see also [2.6.4] on general 'screening local environmental effects'.

[113] Decision 2012/119/EU (n 6) [3.1].

[114] Decision 2012/135/EU (n 107) 67.

[115] IED (n 1) Art 14(4).

INSTITUTIONAL LEARNING

The role of learning in new governance was discussed in the previous chapter. One of the IED's important characteristics is its attempt to stimulate thought and learning by those involved in regulation. The most obvious forum for learning is the Seville process, discussed above. But more generally, decisions are based on a significant amount of data and information, gathered from diverse sources, and potentially subject to contestation. So in addition to Seville, individual operators are required to include a wide range of information in applications, including on use of raw materials and on emissions and waste. The obligation, for example, to produce a 'baseline report' on soil and water quality if certain hazardous substances are produced or released,[116] has the potential to enhance our understanding of these subjects. In the absence of this obligation, operators have every incentive to remain ignorant. The operator's information obligations are not limited to applications for a permit. Monitoring provisions are included in permits,[117] and can also be found in BAT conclusions. The operator has to supply information to the regulator during the operation of the permit 'at least annually'.[118] This information allows the regulator to monitor compliance, and to compare emissions levels and BAT.

The dynamic nature of BAT also implies learning. BAT changes with time: 'new measures and techniques may emerge, science and technologies are continuously developing, and new or emerging processes are being successfully introduced into the industry'.[119] Recital 13 to the Directive provides that the Commission should 'aim' to update BREFs 'not later than 8 years after the publication of the previous version', although this is not repeated in the legally binding part of the Directive.[120] BREFs have to consider 'emerging' as well as 'best available' techniques. An 'emerging technique' is a novel technique that, if commercially developed, could provide either a higher level of environmental protection or cost savings.[121] There needs to be a 'good chance that they may become BAT in the (near) future'.[122] Regulators can grant a 'temporary derogation' from BAT obligations of up to nine months for the 'testing and use' of 'emerging techniques'.[123]

Certain aspects of the IED enhance incentives for operator reflection on environmental performance. As well as information gathering for the permit application and for monitoring, the ability of the operator to use any technique to meet its ELVs allows for innovation within the regulated installation.[124] The IED also

---

[116] Ibid Art 22(2).
[117] Ibid Art 16(1).
[118] Ibid Art 14(1)(d).
[119] Decision 2012/119/EU (n 6) [1.2.2].
[120] Recital 13 is referred to in Decision 2012/119/EU, ibid, [1.2.2].
[121] IED (n 1) Art 3(14).
[122] Decision 2012/119/EU (n 6) [2.3.9].
[123] IED (n 1) Art 15(5).
[124] See (n 15) on ELVs.

attempts to encourage participation in the EU's Eco-Management and Audit Scheme,[125] which provides a system whereby organisations voluntarily commit themselves to internal environmental management and independent verification of that management. This process is intended to encourage self-critical reflection on environmental performance, and active engagement with environmental impacts. The IED takes an innovative approach to national inspection and enforcement, resolving a lengthy debate on the role of an eco-management and audit scheme (EMAS) in enforcement. The frequency of site visits 'shall be based on a systematic appraisal of the environmental risks of the installations concerned', one factor in which is whether the operator participates in EMAS.[126]

Regulators also have learning obligations. They are required to follow or be informed of developments in BAT, and that information has to be made available to the public.[127] Article 21 of the IED requires regulators to 'periodically reconsider', and if necessary update, permit conditions. In addition, there is an obligation for reconsideration of a permit within four years of the adoption of BAT Conclusions relating to the 'main activity' of an installation.

The IED requires Member States to report to the Commission every three years, providing information including representative data on emissions and pollution, on ELVs and the application of BAT, as well as specifically on the use of the Article 15(4) derogation and on emerging techniques.[128] In response, the Commission has to review and report on the operation of the Directive, and put forward a legislative proposal 'where appropriate',[129] expressly keeping EU harmonisation in the background of the Directive.[130] This sort of public information and justification exercise is potentially a powerful tool to encourage learning and adaptation.[131] The rethinking of the role of BREFs in itself reflects learning about BAT. Autonomous assessment of BAT, at national or local level, was proving arduous (and arguably, easily avoided), and the Commission felt that the BREFs were not relied on as they should have been.

In short, the Directive demands the generation of diverse information, first to form the context for decision-making within the regulatory framework and secondly to reflect upon the regulatory framework itself. A range of actors participate

---

[125] Regulation 1221/2009/EC on the voluntary participation by organisations in a Community eco-management and audit scheme (EMAS) [2009] OJ L342/1.

[126] IED (n 1) Art 23(4)(c). Also: '(a) the potential and actual impacts of the installations concerned on human health and the environment taking into account the levels and types of emissions, the sensitivity of the local environment and the risk of accidents; (b) the record of compliance with permit conditions'. The Commission can issue guidance.

[127] IED, ibid, Art 19.

[128] Ibid Art 72.

[129] Ibid Art 73.

[130] Ibid Art 75(1). Certain specific issues must be considered for action, including an assessment of the need for new EU-wide minimum ELVs, or for rules on monitoring and compliance of activities.

[131] See the discussion in ch 4; CF Sabel and J Zeitlin, 'Learning from Difference: The New Architecture of Experimentalist Governance in the EU' in CF Sabel and J Zeitlin (eds), *Experimentalist Governance in the European Union: Towards a New Architecture* (Oxford, Oxford University Press, 2010).

in that process, and an expectation of adaptation to new information is at least implicit. On other occasions, however, the 'learning' aspect may be no more than a delaying tactic. For example, there was some debate during the drafting of the IED of systematically extending fixed quantitative ELVs. Requiring the Commission to revisit the need for ELVs on a three yearly basis is a compromise. It might be that additional information will make it clear whether BAT is working or we need harmonised ELVs. More likely, this is a disagreement based on a value judgment about the type of harmonisation we really want, rather than a disagreement amenable to data.

IMPLEMENTATION AND ENFORCEMENT

Concern about implementation has clearly driven the legal framework for the control of industrial pollution, influencing the 'hardening' of the BAT standard, as well as other aspects of the IED. But the notorious and persistent 'implementation deficit' in EU environmental law is far from limited to industrial pollution, or to BAT-style open-ended standards. A 2012 Commission Communication on the subject starts from the EEA's 'State of the Environment Report', which concludes that 'the EU appears to be locked in a number of status-quo and downward trends which are moving away from, rather than towards sustainability'.[132] The Commission couples this with an acknowledgement that environmental matters are already subject to legislation, and concludes that 'the main challenge now is one of effective implementation'.[133] In an indication of the obsession with quantification in the EU, the costs of failing to implement EU environmental law have been estimated at around fifty billion euros.[134]

The Commission's role as 'guardian of the treaty', and its powers under Article 258 TFEU to bring a Member State before the ECJ, need little rehearsal here.[135] The limitations of the centralised enforcement of environmental law under Article 258 can be considerable.[136] First, it is indirect: obligations are formally owed by central government, whilst central government may not control the implementation of environmental law. The actual breach of EU environmental law, for example failure to comply with a permit, or failure to meet quality standards, may have

---

[132] European Commission, 'Improving the Delivery of Benefits from EU Environmental Measures: Building Confidence through Better Knowledge and Responsiveness' COM (2012) 95 final, 2.

[133] Ibid 2. Implementation is 'Priority objective 4' in European Commission, 'Proposal for a Decision of the European Parliament and of the Council on a General Union Environment Action Programme to 2020, "Living Well, within the Limits of our Planet"' COM (2012) 710 final. This emphasis is far from new, and has been on the agenda for many years: eg European Commission, 'Implementing Community Environmental Law' COM (1996) 500 final.

[134] Commission (n 132) 3.

[135] See P Wennerås, *The Enforcement of EC Environmental Law* (Oxford, Oxford University Press, 2007), ch 6.

[136] Eg ibid; R Macrory, 'The Enforcement of Community Environmental Laws: Some Critical Issues' (1992) 29 *Common Market Law Review* 347.

been committed by a private sector polluter, perhaps authorised or tolerated by a decentralised regulator. In formal terms, there is no enforcement gap, since the Commission takes action against central government. But this indirect approach relies, even after enforcement action, on the capacity of the central government to ensure compliance.

Second, identifying breaches of EU environmental law can be difficult. The Commission's ability to monitor the formal implementation of directives is supported by obligations on the Member States to report to the Commission on the transposition of directives. Failure to report is considered a serious breach, and uniquely, the Court is able to impose a penalty payment when it finds a failure to report under Article 258.[137] Assessing whether purported implementation is actually consistent with the EU obligations may be more challenging, requiring a sophisticated knowledge of national law. And monitoring *practical* implementation, actual standards of environmental quality, is even more difficult. It is clear that the Commission found enforcement of the obligation under the IPPC Directive to include BAT in permits very challenging. It would have required sophisticated analysis of the Member State's actual process for applying BAT to installations. Moreover, because implementation is inevitably a moving target in the environmental sphere (environmental conditions change, knowledge and regulation evolve), it is unrealistic to anticipate a moment at which compliance is 'complete', once and for all.

In the past, the purely declaratory nature of an Article 258 judgment was an obvious limitation on its effectiveness. Article 260 TFEU allows the Commission to bring a further action seeking financial penalties against Member States that fail to comply.[138] Not surprisingly, given the implementation problem, a disproportionate number of environmental cases appear in the Article 260 docket.[139] Article 260 is a powerful resource. However, in the case of real Member State defiance, where the Member State understands its vital national interest to be at stake, there is no way to force a Member State to comply with a decision under Article 258 or 260.[140] The limits of formal enforcement of EU law under Articles 258–60 may be to some extent inherent in the nature of EU law: 'poor implementation ... remains very much a "safety valve" ... "postdecisional" politics are an integral and, we suspect, never-ending part of the wider struggle between actors at different governance levels to shape the European integration process'.[141] This is really to restate the problem, but it is not a counsel of despair; simply a reminder that in most cases implementation ultimately relies on mutual cooperation, rather than

---

[137] Art 260(3) TFEU. Rather than having to bring a second action.

[138] For detail on calculation, see B Jack, 'Article 260(2) TFEU: An Effective Judicial Procedure for the Enforcement of Judgments?' (2013) 19 *European Law Journal* 404.

[139] B Jack, 'Enforcing Member State Compliance with EU Environmental Law: A Critical evaluation of the Use of financial Penalties' (2011) 23 *Journal of Environmental Law* 73.

[140] See Jack's discussion of Case C-109/08 *Commission v Greece* [2009] ECR I-4657 (n 138).

[141] A Jordan and J Tosun, 'Policy Implementation' in A Jordan and C Adelle (eds), *Environmental Policy in the EU: Actors, Institutions and Processes* (Abingdon, Routledge, 2013), 262.

a top-down process. Attention needs to be paid to national capabilities, as well as to national cynicism.

Various ways of approaching the implementation deficit are being pursued. Some do indeed focus on formal Commission enforcement. For example, the possibility of a fine under Article 260 TFEU was introduced by the Maastricht Treaty, and refined further in Lisbon. In addition, the Commission has attempted to rationalise its processes by focussing on particular categories of infringement, such as a failure to report. But formal enforcement cannot necessarily respond to the diverse and sometimes complex reasons for breach of EU environmental law.[142] For example, Member States may encounter political difficulties,[143] especially if responsibility for environmental regulation cuts across national distributions of power and responsibility. In some cases, compliance with EU environmental law requires considerable resources. This is clearest when major infrastructure investment, for example sewerage system upgrades to comply with water quality standards, is necessary. But it may also be the case in more mundane situations, such as the need to upgrade industrial facilities, and resource availability may be a significant constraint on monitoring and enforcement capacity. The IED, for example, is a technically difficult piece of legislation, legally and scientifically, and setting permit conditions that are consistent with its terms demands considerable resources from the national regulators.

Whilst the Court has insisted on many occasions that a state cannot rely on internal administrative, political or practical difficulties to justify a failure to implement,[144] it is clear that simple punishment or exhortation may leave genuine difficulties unaddressed. Most of the efforts to improve implementation do not focus on the formal Treaty enforcement process. The IED, for example, contains a number of provisions that are concerned specifically with the improvement of implementation, such as the obligation to include monitoring and reporting responsibilities in permits, and other provisions mentioned below. The hardening legal status of BREFs in the IED was also at least in part a response to the challenging enforcement dynamics of flexible standards.

The empowerment of individuals and environmental interest groups may also assist in implementation. Routine reporting obligations, together with the provision of information and opportunities to participate, both found in the IED as discussed above,[145] enhance opportunities for political scrutiny. This is coupled with the obligation in the IED to ensure that environmental interest groups have standing before the national courts.[146] This watchdog role for third

---

[142] Macrory (n 136).

[143] Eg Case 79/72 *Commission v Italy* [1973] ECR 667.

[144] Ibid.

[145] There is a striking emphasis on information in Commission (n 132), in particular the usability of that information in checking implementation.

[146] IED (n 1) Art 25. This is discussed in ch 7 below, along with similar provisions in Directive 2011/92/EU on the assessment of the effects of certain public and private projects on the environment (codification) [2012] OJ L26/2.

parties before the national courts is possible in part because of the doctrine of direct effect, which allows private parties to use unimplemented EU law in the national courts.[147] Early limitations on the use of direct effect in the environmental sphere, whilst they have not disappeared, are much reduced.[148] First, direct effect was initially focused on the protection of individual rights. Environmental law, protecting common interests in the environment, was generally not readily conceptualised in terms of rights, although rights to the protection of human health were sometimes called on,[149] and procedural rights, such as the rights to information and participation in the IED, may be relatively straightforward. The Court has increasingly emphasised direct effect's role in ensuring the effectiveness of EU law, and the ability of national courts to use EU law to review the legality of a Member State's actions.[150] Deciding whether a particular provision of EU law is capable of direct effect is now close to a simple question of justiciability.[151] The second major limitation on the role of direct effect in ensuring the implementation of environmental law is the proviso that directives (the most common form of environmental law) have no horizontal direct effect, so that unimplemented directives only apply against public authorities. The case law in this area is difficult to rationalise, but whilst the Court continues to insist upon the bar on horizontal direct effect, it does allow for 'mere adverse repercussions on the rights of third parties'.[152] Directives are no longer systematically ineffective when their application would have implications for private polluters or developers.[153]

Another category of responses to poor implementation has been to try to enhance the capacity of national regulators. The EU 'Network for the Implementation and Enforcement of Environmental Law' (IMPEL) is an informal network of national environmental inspectorates that examines and reports on various enforcement concerns, and aims to encourage learning and exchange of best practice between Member States and between sectors.[154] Something similar has been provided specifically for the regulation of chemicals, in the shape of a Forum for Member State Exchange of Information on Enforcement, whose role includes the exchange of best practice, identifying joint inspections and harmonised enforcement strategies, and liaising with industry.[155] The Forum seems

---

[147] Coupled with primacy, which means that EU law takes priority over conflicting national provisions.

[148] On the broadening scope of direct effect, see B de Witte, 'Direct Effect, Primacy, and the Nature of the Legal Order' in in P Craig and G de Búrca (eds), *The Evolution of EU Law* (Oxford, Oxford University Press, 2011). See also Wennerås (n 135).

[149] Recently, see Case C-237/07 *Janecek v Freistaat Bayern* [2008] ECR I-6221.

[150] See the line of cases coming out of Case C-72/95 *Aannemersebedrijf PK Kraaijeveld BV v Gedeputeerde Staten van Zuid-Holland (Dutch Dykes)*[1996] ECR I-5403.

[151] De Witte (n 148) 331.

[152] Case C-201/02 *R (on the application of Wells) v Secretary of State for Transport, Local Government and the Regions* [2004] ECR I-723 [57].

[153] De Witte (n 148).

[154] See impel.eu/

[155] Regulation 1907/2006/EC concerning the Registration, Evaluation, Authorisation and Restriction of Chemicals (REACH), establishing a European Chemicals Agency [2006] OJL396/1, Arts 76–77.

currently to be most valued by Member States with little experience of chemicals legislation enforcement.[156]

Article 23 of the IED imposes unusually detailed inspection obligations on the Member States.[157] Member States have to produce an 'environmental inspection plan', which includes 'procedures for drawing up programmes' for routine and non-routine environmental inspections. Following 'serious environmental complaints, serious environmental accidents, incidents and occurrences of non-compliance' there 'shall' be a non-routine inspection. The frequency of routine site visits is to be based on the environmental risk posed by the installations, not falling below once a year for installations 'posing the highest risk', and three yearly for the lowest. An 'important case of non-compliance' shall provoke an additional visit within six months. The report of a site visit must be made available to the public, and the regulator must ensure that 'all necessary actions identified in the report' are taken 'within a reasonable period'.

The Member States generally enjoy discretion as to the penalties they impose on wrongdoers, provided that they are 'effective, proportionate and dissuasive'.[158] The EU emissions trading scheme, discussed in the next chapter, most unusually sets a fixed penalty for breach.[159] The Environmental Liability Directive is slightly different, in that it attempts to ensure that different enforcement tools are available to national regulators.[160] The Environmental Liability Directive requires the Member States to put in place an administrative scheme under which polluters pay for the restoration of environmental damage, providing funds for the restoration of environmental harm, and potentially also incentives for compliance.[161] Whilst environmental liability was initially proposed on the basis of a range of rationales, the objective of improving implementation moved centre-stage during its development.[162] This can be detected in the close relationship between environmental liability and existing, substantive environmental legislation: both environmental damage and the parties subject to strict environmental liability are defined by reference to other legislation.[163] In addition, although the scheme is prima facie strict liability, Member States are able to provide a defence for

---

[156] European Commission, 'Staff Working Document Accompanying General Report on REACH' SWD (2013) 25, 101.

[157] 'Environmental inspection' is defined in IED (n 1) Art 3(22).

[158] IED, ibid, Art 79; this is standard language.

[159] Directive 2003/87/EC establishing a scheme for greenhouse gas emission allowance trading within the Community (as amended) [2003] OJ L275/32, Art 16(3).

[160] Directive 2004/35/EC on environmental liability with regard to the prevention and remedying of environmental damage ('Environmental Liability Directive') [2004] OJ L143/56.

[161] See eg ibid Recital 2.

[162] M Lee, 'The Changing Aims of Environmental Liability' (2002) 14 *Environmental Law and Management* 185.

[163] Environmental Liability Directive (n 160) Art 2 provides for three categories of environmental damage: damage to protected species and habitats, defined by reference to EU nature conservation legislation; water damage, defined by reference to EU water legislation; and land damage, defined by reference to risk to human health (in the absence of EU level legislation on the subject). Annex III lists the relevant occupational activities, which are those governed by EU environmental law. Fault based

polluters who cause damage notwithstanding compliance with regulation, such as an IED permit.[164] Along similar lines to the Environmental Liability Directive, the Criminal Law Directive requires the Member States to ensure the availability of criminal prosecution in response to a breach of EU environmental law. Criminal penalties must be available for the breach of some environmental legislation if 'committed intentionally or with at least serious negligence'.[165]

The longstanding and wide-ranging concerns about the implementation of EU environmental law are reflected in some of the provisions of the IED. More generally, a range of approaches is being taken to respond to poor implementation, far from limited to formal top-down judicial enforcement.

CONCLUSIONS

The open and loosely defined nature of BAT meant that the original IPPC Directive became representative of the focus on procedure (rather than clearly defined, explicit standards of environmental quality or performance) in EU environmental legislation.[166] As such, it was highly innovative. However, the IPPC Directive and its successor, the IED, also turn around what is in principle a very simple permitting regime. It is 'command and control', although far from the inflexible rigid standards caricatured in some of the literature. The IED demonstrates the complexity and diversity of environmental norms in the EU, of their generation and of their application. Seen from within a paradigm of 'new governance', discussed in chapter four, we might focus on the substantive flexibility on the face of the Directive (the open-ended, even vague environmental norm of BAT), the collaborative fora for generating more detailed norms, and the emphasis on information and learning.

The Seville process has been formalised in the journey from IPPC to IED, and the final decision placed firmly within the familiar political process of comitology. The IED has a far greater emphasis on centralisation than the IPPC Directive did. But, the progress from IPPC Directive to IED also illustrates that the lines between hard and soft law, and EU harmonisation and national autonomy, are less clear or stable than might be expected. The scope for local intervention is in legal terms less dramatically different from what was *intended* in the IPPC Directive than it appears at first sight.

---

liability applies to 'occupational activities' not listed, in respect of damage to protected species and habitats only, Art 3(1)(b).

[164] Ibid Art 8(4). This applies only in the absence of fault.

[165] Directive 2008/99/EC on the protection of the environment through criminal law [2008] OJ L328/28. Using the environment title as legal basis for this measure was controversial, but confirmed in Case C-176/03 *Commission v Council* [2005] ECR I-7879.

[166] Scott (n 98).

6

Instruments and Governance III: Climate Change

INTRODUCTION

CLIMATE CHANGE, WHICH has implications on an unimaginable scale, reaching every part of our social, political and economic life,[1] is far more than an 'environmental' problem. It is often, aptly, characterised as the archetypal 'wicked problem'. Tame problems 'appear to be definable, understandable and consensual'; wicked problems are problems where 'theory is inadequate for decent forecasting' and 'our intelligence is insufficient to our tasks'. Wicked problems have no obvious solution: 'at best they are only re-solved—over and over again'.[2] The wickedness of climate change can be seen in the way it cuts across sectors and borders, resists technological fixes, and challenges entrenched social norms and practices that rely on high carbon consumption.[3]

The 'greenhouse gas' potential of carbon dioxide and some other gases has been understood scientifically for many decades.[4] These gases prevent the escape of energy from the earth's atmosphere and raise global temperatures, disrupting the climate. The Intergovernmental Panel on Climate Change (IPCC) was established in 1988 to assess the scientific basis and risks of climate change.[5] Calling on the collective expertise of many scientists, the IPCC has now been through four influential reporting cycles, with the fifth expected in 2014. Its confidence about both the impacts of climate change and its anthropogenic nature has increased through each cycle. The 'physical science' contribution to the fifth assessment report was published in September 2013. It found that 'warming of the climate system is unequivocal', and 'it is extremely likely that human influence has been

---

[1] M Hulme, *Why We Disagree About Climate Change: Understanding Controversy, Inaction and Opportunity* (Cambridge, Cambridge University Press, 2009).

[2] H Rittel and M Webber, 'Dilemmas in a General Theory of Planning' (1973) 4 *Policy Sciences* 155, 160.

[3] A Jordan, D Huitema and H van Asselt, 'Climate Change Policy in the European Union: An Introduction' in A Jordan et al (eds), *Climate Change Policy in the European Union: Confronting the Dilemmas of Mitigation and Adaptation* (Cambridge, Cambridge University Press, 2012).

[4] See SR Weart, *The Discovery of Global Warming* (London, Harvard University Press, 2003).

[5] On the politics behind the IPCC's evolution and early development, S Agrawala, 'Context and Early Origins of the International Panel on Climate Change' (1998) 39 *Climate Change* 605.

the dominant cause of the observed warming since the mid-20th century'.[6] Although the IPCC has been subject to intense critical scrutiny from those who deny the existence or significance of anthropogenic climate change, it is likely that its consensus methodology makes IPCC predictions, if anything, conservative.[7] More acutely than any other area, however, climate change demonstrates that simply understanding the devastating consequences of our collective and individual behaviour does not lead to action.

In the face of this challenge, the core of the EU's policy on climate change can be found in the 'package' of measures contained in '20 20 by 2020: Europe's Climate Change Opportunity'.[8] The EU sets itself a number of suspiciously symmetrical obligations: by 2020, a 20 per cent reduction in carbon emissions from 1990 levels; 20 per cent of final energy consumed to be from renewable sources; and 20 per cent energy efficiency compared to projections. The EU has undertaken to increase the overall reduction commitment to 30 per cent by 2020 if there is an international agreement committing other developed countries to 'comparable emission reductions', and 'economically more advanced developing countries' to 'adequate' contribution 'according to their responsibilities and respective capabilities'.[9] The 'relentless optimism' of target setting plays a central role in climate change governance.[10] There is a danger that climate change targets satisfy a political wish to be seen to do something, especially when pledges are made by politicians who have long moved on by the final reckoning. They can, however, also provide a form of legal and/or political accountability, by identifying a relatively simple metric of success,[11] and their high political visibility may make backsliding more difficult.[12]

There is now a vast patchwork of legislation on climate change at EU level. This chapter, taking the opportunity to explore the use of different regulatory instruments in EU environmental law, will look at just three topics: the EU emissions trading scheme; renewable energy; and energy efficiency in buildings. Two things not examined here, for reasons of space not importance, should be mentioned. First, carbon capture and storage, a controversial technology that it is hoped will allow us to capture carbon emitted by large installations, and store it in geological

---

[6] IPCC, 'Climate Change 2013: The Physical Science Basis' (2013), ipcc.ch/report/ar5/wg1/. See *Summary for Policy Makers*, B and D.3. 'Extremely likely' constitutes a greater than 95% confidence, ff 2.

[7] B Wynne 'Strange Weather, Again: Climate Science as Political Art' (2010) 27 *Theory, Culture & Society* 289 on the understatement of impacts.

[8] European Commission, '20 20 by 2020: Europe's Climate Change Opportunity' COM (2008) 30 final. K Kulovesi, E Morgera, M Muñoz, 'Environmental Integration and Multi-Faceted International Dimensions of EU Law: Unpacking the EU's 2009 Climate and Energy Package' (2011) 48 *Common Market Law Rev* 829.

[9] Commission, ibid, 2–3.

[10] G Prins and S Rayner, *The Wrong Trousers: Radically Rethinking Climate Policy* (2007) eureka. bodleian.ox.ac.uk/66/1/TheWrongTrousers.pdf, 4.

[11] See also the discussion of indicators in ch 3 above.

[12] Contributing to the 'stickiness' of climate change law, see n 42.

formations, is an important element of the EU's *2020* package.[13] And second, even if mitigation efforts are successful, we are committed to a level of anthropogenic climate change that makes adaptation to a changed climate necessary.[14]

INTERNATIONAL CONTEXT

All EU environmental law sits in a multi-level framework that includes international norms, negotiations and agreements. This international context is especially visible here, however, partly because the EU has presented itself as a leader on climate change,[15] and partly because of the inevitably global dimensions of the problem. EU climate change legislation is explicitly connected to the international regime for climate change mitigation, for example in the possible 30 per cent target mentioned above, by allowing other 'adjustments' to reflect international agreement, and by encouraging multilateral action through preferential treatment of those subject to such agreement.[16]

The United Nations Framework Convention on Climate Change (UNFCCC), agreed at the Rio conference in 1992, was the first international agreement on climate change. It set the 'ultimate objective' of the 'stabilization of greenhouse gas concentrations in the atmosphere at a level that would prevent dangerous anthropogenic interference with the climate system'.[17] The interpretation of this objective is not straightforward.[18] It is not simply binary: 'dangerous' or 'not dangerous'.[19] There will be costs and benefits, unevenly distributed, wherever the line is drawn, making a purely scientific interpretation of 'danger' impossible. Notwithstanding the challenges, the 'ultimate objective' has been interpreted, at EU and international level, as a 2°C change in global temperature from pre-industrial levels.[20] International agreements keep the temperature target open to review, specifically with the possibility of strengthening it to 1.5°C;[21] the fear of small island states that they will disappear beneath rising seas at 2° brings the

---

[13] Commission (n 8); Directive 2009/31/EC on the geological storage of carbon dioxide [2009] OJ L140/114.

[14] Of a growing literature, see the contributions to Jordan et al (n 3).

[15] For a discussion of the evolution of EU leadership, see for example S Oberthur, 'The European Union's Performance in the International Climate Change Regime' (2011) 33 *Journal of European Integration* 667.

[16] Kulovesi, Morgera and Muñoz (n 8).

[17] United Nations Framework Convention on Climate Change (1992) 31 ILM 851, Art 2.

[18] See MT Boykoff, D Frame, and S Randalls, 'Discursive Stability Meets Climate Instability: A Critical Exploration of the Concept of "Climate Stablization" in Contemporary Climate Policy' (2010) 20 *Global Environmental Change* 53.

[19] 'Limits' are rarely binary, see also ch 3.

[20] Eg Decision 406/2009/EC on the effort of Member States to reduce their greenhouse gas emissions to meet the community's greenhouse gas emission reduction commitments up to 2020 ('Effort Sharing Decision') [2009] OJ L140/136, Recital 2; Copenhagen Accord 2010 [1].

[21] Eg Decision 1/CP.16 *The Cancun Agreements: Outcome of the work of the Ad Hoc Working Group on Long-term Cooperative Action under the Convention* [2], [4], [139].

value judgments starkly into view. Unfortunately, not only is the adequacy of the temperature target contentious, but so is its feasibility.[22] The temperature target has been re-framed as a concentration target, the maximum amount of carbon dioxide in the atmosphere, which is generally but contentiously set at 450 parts per million (ppm), compared to around 273 ppm before the industrial revolution. This concentration target is in turn represented as reductions in emissions by particular target dates (for example, a 20 per cent reduction by 2020), and these targets arguably receive most of the legal and political attention.[23] Even this very brief outline should make it clear that the objectives of climate change law are complex and socially constructed.[24] Although there is a high level of scientific consensus, there are multiple uncertainties at each stage.[25] Uncertainty should not be an incentive to inaction, but a warning against inflexibility or complacency.

The Kyoto Protocol to the UNFCCC set binding greenhouse gas emission reduction targets for Annex I countries, which are essentially developed countries.[26] The US, notoriously, did not ratify the Kyoto Protocol, and so was not made subject to a binding target. The reduction targets added up to a total five per cent reduction in greenhouse gas emissions by 2012, relative to 1990, divided unevenly between the members of Annex I. Because non-Annex I countries had no binding targets, global carbon emissions can continue to rise even if Kyoto is complied with. The Member States of the EU were allowed to meet their obligations jointly, as the 'EU bubble'. The overall EU-15's eight per cent target is likely to be easily achieved.[27] The Kyoto Protocol introduced three 'flexibility mechanisms': the Clean Development Mechanism (CDM), which provides credits for the funding of carbon reduction activities in developing countries; Joint Implementation (JI), which provides for the funding of projects by Annex I countries in other Annex I countries; and international emissions trading, which allows countries to buy and sell their allowances. The most significant trading, to which we return below, is the CDM.[28]

---

[22] Eg K Anderson and A Bows, 'Beyond "Dangerous" Climate Change: Emission Scenarios for a New World' (2011) 309 *Philosophical Transactions of the Royal Society A* 20.

[23] Boykoff et al (n 18).

[24] Wynne (n 7) on 'socially constructed understatement', 295.

[25] N Oreskes, 'Science and Public Policy: What's Proof Got to Do With It?' (2004) 7 *Environmental Science & Policy* 369. Nor does increased knowledge reduce uncertainty, M Maslin, 'Cascading Uncertainty in Climate Change Models and its Implications for Policy' (2013) *The Geographical Journal* 1.

[26] Kyoto Protocol to the United Nations Framework Convention on Climate Change United Nations 37 (1997) ILM 22.

[27] European Environment Agency (EEA), 'Greenhouse Gas Emission Trends and Projections in Europe 2012' (EEA Report No 6/2012). The EEA will publish 'approximated' emissions data for 2012 in Autumn 2013, and official figures will be available and submitted to the UN in 2014, EEA, 'Why Did Greenhouse Gas Emissions Decrease in the EU in 2011?' (EEA Analysis, 2013) 24. The EU-15 are the 15 Member States before enlargement into Central and Eastern Europe in 2004.

[28] Sandbag, 'Help or Hindrance: Offsetting in the EU ETS' (2012) sandbag.org.uk/reports/; MW Wara, 'Measuring the Clean Development Mechanism's Performance and Potential' (2008) 55 *University of California, Los Angeles Law Review* 1759.

Developing (non-Annex I) countries, did not take on any binding emissions reduction commitments at Kyoto. The precise meaning of the international legal principle of 'common but differentiated responsibility'[29] is much debated, but it requires differential obligations that reflect (variously) the historical and/or ongoing contribution to the problem, and/or the ability to respond.[30] According to the UNFCCC, developed countries should 'take the lead'.[31] But the persistence of a crude division between developed and developing countries is contested.[32] The treatment of all developing countries as a homogenous group, given both global economic competition between developed and some developing countries, and increasing emissions from major industrialising countries such as China and India, have contributed to the difficulties of reaching agreement on climate change governance after the expiry of Kyoto in 2012.[33] Post-Kyoto commitments were initially to have been agreed at the Copenhagen Conference of the Parties (COP) in 2009, a notoriously disappointing meeting. The UN negotiations more or less fell apart, but following agreement of the *Copenhagen Accord* outside the framework of the UN, states volunteered mitigation targets on a 'bottom up' basis. Much of the *Copenhagen Accord* was subsequently incorporated into the UN system by COP 16 in Cancún in 2010,[34] which also noted the mitigation pledges made by states following Copenhagen. In itself, the volunteering of commitments is not problematic; the difficulty is in ensuring adequate international monitoring and adequately ambitious targets. Current pledges to 2020 are thought to fall well short of the 2° target.[35]

At the Doha COP in 2012,[36] agreement was reached to extend the Kyoto Protocol to 2020, although with depleted developed country membership (no Canada, Japan, New Zealand, or Russia, and still no US), and with inadequate targets.[37] There is still no cap on carbon from major industrialising economies, other than their voluntary Cancún commitments; developing countries have generally only offered to reduce carbon intensity, that is carbon emissions per unit of gross

---

[29] Rio Declaration on Environment and Development (1992) A/CONF.151/26, principle 7; UNFCCC (n 17) Art 3.1, 'common but differentiated responsibilities and respective capabilities'.

[30] L Rajamani, *Differential Treatment in International Environmental Law* (Oxford, Oxford University Press, 2006).

[31] UNFCCC (n 17) Art 3.1.

[32] J Pauwelyn, 'The End of Differential Treatment for Developing Countries? Lessons from the Trade and Climate Change Regimes' (2013) 22 *Review of European Community and International Environmental Law* 29.

[33] On shifts at the 2011 Durban COP, see L Rajamani, 'The Durban Platform for Enhanced Action and the Future of the Climate Regime' (2012) 61 *International and Comparative Law Quarterly* 501.

[34] Decision 1 CP/16 *The Cancun Agreements: Outcome of the Work of the Ad Hoc Working Group on Long-Term Cooperative Action under the Convention* and 1/CMP 6 *The Cancun Agreements: Outcome of the Work of the Ad hoc Working Group on Further Commitments for Annex I Parties under the Kyoto Protocol*.

[35] And the gap is growing, United Nations Environment Programme (UNEP), 'The Emissions Gap Report 2012: A UNEP Synthesis Report' (UNEP, 2012).

[36] On the intervening Durban COP, see Rajamani (n 33).

[37] Decision 1/CMP.8 *Amendment to the Kyoto Protocol (the Doha Amendment)*; M Grubb, 'Doha's Dawn?' (2013) 13 *Climate Policy* 281.

domestic product (GDP), which allows total emissions to continue to rise. A new, more global treaty is supposed to be agreed by 2015, to enter into force in 2020.

The expectation that a new and adequate global agreement will be reached by 2015 feels rather like the triumph of hope over experience, and global carbon emissions continue to rise. The limits of the UNFCCC 'model' of top-down global solutions have been much discussed.[38] Aside from being difficult to reach agreement on, a single global, legally binding emissions reduction target is not likely on its own to provide a 'solution' to the wicked problem of climate change. From different perspectives, Prins and Rayner argue that 'silver buckshot' of multiple approaches is better than the purported silver bullet of Kyoto;[39] Keohane and Victor argue for a 'regime complex' of loosely coordinated actions by different and overlapping groups of actors, since any global political agreement is likely to be weak, as well as less flexible and adaptive than alternatives.[40] These and other critiques of the UNFCCC emphasise the importance of iteration and social learning, of 'constant course corrections and improvements which, by definition cannot be prescribed precisely beforehand'.[41] These lessons about flexibility, learning and diversity apply at the EU level.[42] We see below that EU policy on climate change takes a range of different approaches, and in some respects has evolved in an iterative manner; whether it is sufficiently adaptive is open to question.

EMISSIONS TRADING

The EU Emissions Trading Scheme (EU ETS) is the centrepiece of the EU response to climate change. It was introduced by the 2003 Emissions Trading Directive, and amended significantly in 2009.[43] The ETS applies primarily to industry and power

---

[38] From a vast literature, see R Keohane and D Victor, 'The Regime Complex for Climate Change' (2011) 9 *Perspectives on Politics* 7; Prins and Rayner (n 10); D Helm, 'Climate-Change Policy: Why has So Little Been Achieved?' (2008) 24 *Oxford Review of Economic Policy* 211.

[39] Prins and Rayner (n 10) vi.

[40] Keohane and Victor (n 38). A 'regime complex' falls between 'fully integrated institutions that impose regulation through comprehensive, hierarchical rules' and a 'highly fragmented collection of institutions with no identifiable core and weak or non-existent linkages', 3–4, and includes, eg, bilateral agreements, organisations like the G8, non-FCCC UN bodies, and indeed the EU. H Osofsky, 'Is Climate Change "International"? Litigation's Diagonal Regulatory Role' (2009) 49 *Virginia Journal of International Law* 585 argues from a US perspective for a 'multi-scalar' approach of action at all levels.

[41] Prins and Rayner (n 10).

[42] Although there is also a virtue in 'stickiness', in the sense of legal commitments that are not vulnerable to short-term economic priorities, see RJ Lazarus, 'Super Wicked Problems and Climate Change: Restraining the Present to Liberate the Future' (2008) 94 *Cornell Law Review* 1153, to set alongside the discussion of flexibility in this chapter and ch 4.

[43] Directive 2003/87/EC establishing a scheme for greenhouse gas emission allowance trading within the Community ('Emissions Trading Directive') [2003] OJ L275/32; Directive 2009/29/EC amending Directive 2003/87/EC so as to improve and extend the greenhouse gas emission allowance trading scheme of the Community OJ [2009] L140/63. References will be to the consolidated version of the Directive, dated 25 June 2009, ec.europa.eu/clima/policies/ets/documentation_en.htm.

generation, and covers around 40 per cent of the EU's greenhouse gas emissions.[44] The overall 20 per cent emissions reduction target covers all greenhouse gas emissions, but a greater proportion is borne by the traded sector, where reductions are thought to be simpler, leaving a 10 per cent target for the non-traded sector. National obligations in non-traded sectors (for example transport,[45] waste, agriculture and buildings) are contained in the Effort Sharing Decision, which sets national annual emissions allocations, tradeable between the Member States.[46]

The literature and debate generated by this first supranational emissions trading scheme is enormous, and the Directive is dense and difficult. The basic scheme requires all covered installations to apply for a greenhouse gas permit,[47] which requires one EU allowance (EUA) to be surrendered for each tonne of carbon emitted.[48] Each operator can choose how many allowances to buy or sell in the market, depending on the price of allowances and the marginal cost of abatement for that particular operator.[49] The reduction of emissions should be achieved at a lower overall cost, as reductions take place where marginal abatement costs are lowest. There have been three 'phases' to the EU ETS (2005–07; 2008–12; 2013–20), with each phase attempting to respond to earlier problems.

Rather than attempt a comprehensive analysis of the ETS, this section focuses on three important issues: first, the setting of the 'cap' on overall carbon emissions; secondly, the allocation of allowances to operators; and thirdly, the use of credits from outside the EU. This section will then turn flexibility within the ETS, before concluding with a tentative examination of effectiveness.

The Cap

The acceptable overall level of pollution, the 'cap' on pollution up to which permits will be allocated, determines the level of environmental protection.[50] This 'quantity-based approach'[51] should create certainty as to ultimate environmental

---

[44] Directive 2009/29/EC, ibid, Annex I. The 2009 Directive made important extensions to coverage for the third phase. In particular, the ETS was controversially extended to aviation, which for reasons of space will not be discussed here. See J Scott and L Rajamani, 'EU Climate Change Unilateralism' (2012) 23 *European Journal of International Law* 469; Case C-366/10 *The Air Transport Association of America v Secretary of State for Energy and Climate Change* not yet reported in the ECR. The application of the ETS to flights into and out of the EU has been deferred to allow for further international progress, specifically at the meeting of the International Civil Aviation Organisation (ICAO) in September/October 2013, Decision 377/2013/EU derogating temporarily from Directive 2003/87/EC establishing a scheme for greenhouse gas emission allowance trading within the Community [2013] OJ L113/1.

[45] Except aviation, ibid.

[46] Effort Sharing Decision (n 20). Certain credits under the CDM, discussed below, are also available.

[47] Emissions Trading Directive (n 43) Arts 4–6.

[48] Ibid Art 6(2)(e).

[49] See ch 4 above.

[50] It is possible to have a system with no cap, see JH Lefevere, 'Greenhouse Gas Emission Allowance Trading in the EU: A Background' (2003) 3 *Yearbook of European Environmental Law* 149.

[51] D Driesen, 'Economic Instruments for Sustainable Development' in B Richardson and S Wood (eds), *Environmental Law for Sustainability* (Oxford, Hart Publishing, 2006).

performance. The cap is also essential to the operation of the market; if too many permits are issued, the price collapses and no trading takes place. The level of the cap is a political decision, a matter of acceptable risk and acceptable costs, shaped by scientific evidence. The cap in the EU ETS is related to the broader overall carbon emission reduction targets, the eight per cent Kyoto obligation up to 2012 and the 20 per cent target to 2020.

In the first phase of trading, the Member States were responsible for setting their own national cap. Each Member State drew up a 'National Allocation Plan' (NAP) setting out its overall level of emissions, and the initial allocations of allowances. The NAP had to be based on 'objective and transparent criteria', 'including' criteria set out in the Directive, supplemented by complex Commission guidance.[52] Member States were reluctant to disadvantage their own industry, and governments were dependent on industry for information about both current and achievable carbon emissions. Industry had strong incentives to state the highest case for current emissions, and the highest cost for mitigation. The result was a huge over-allocation of allowances by the Member States, leading to the collapse of the market in 2006. The Member States did not have a free hand, but the Commission's powers to accept or reject national plans turned out to be legally narrow.[53] Whilst the NAPs were less problematic in the second than the first phase, the economic crisis in the EU meant that there was still an enormous surplus of allowances on the market by the end of Phase II,[54] due to reduced output rather than long term structural change towards a low carbon economy.[55] The price of a tonne of carbon fell from around €30 in mid-2008, to under €3 in early 2013.[56]

NAPs have been abolished for the third trading phase. Instead, the Commission has set an EU-wide cap on emissions. A central cap cannot completely eliminate the information asymmetry or concern about international competitiveness that led to over-allocation by the Member States. But many of the decisions are made in the legislation itself, which does render the third phase cap more impervious to industry lobbying (although also too inflexible environmentally, discussed below). The starting point for the cap was allowances allocated in 2008–12, adjusted to

---

[52] Emissions Trading Directive (n 43) Art 9(1). European Commission, 'Guidance to Assist Member States in the Implementation of the Criteria Listed in Annex III to Directive 2003/87/EC Establishing a Scheme for Greenhouse Gas Emission Allowance Trading within the Community and Amending Council Directive 96/61/EC, and on the Circumstances in which Force Majeure is Demonstrated' COM (2003) 830 final.

[53] Case C-504/09 P *Commission v Poland* not yet reported in the ECR; Case C-505/09 *Commission v Estonia* not yet reported in the ECR. See J van Zeben, 'Emissions Trading Schemes and Division of Competence between Commission and Member States' (2013) 50 *Common Market Law Review* 231.

[54] European Commission, 'Information Provided on the Functioning of the EU Emissions Trading System, the Volumes of Greenhouse Gas Emission Allowances Auctioned and Freely Allocated and the Impact on the Surplus of Allowances in the Period up to 2020 SWD' (2012) 234 final.

[55] Sandbag, 'Losing the Lead? Europe's Flagging Carbon Market' (2012) sandbag.org.uk/reports/.

[56] P Clark, J Chaffin, J Blas, 'EU Carbon Prices Crash to Record Low' *Financial Times* 24 January 2013. Prices have been increasing in September 2013.

take into account the expansion of the ETS to additional sectors and new Member States, and reduced every year 'in a linear manner' by 1.74 per cent,[57] so that there is an overall reduction of 21 per cent by 2020.[58] However, over-allocation in the second phase continues to damage the ETS's potential: the surplus EUAs in the second phase can be banked and carried forward, so that if nothing is done, excess allowances will continue to reduce the need for real abatement action.[59] We return to the flexibility of the cap below.

Allocation of Allowances

How and to whom allowances are allocated is not, in theory, relevant for environmental or efficiency purposes: environmental protection is ensured by the cap, and the allowances end up in the possession of those who value them most highly, whoever starts out with them.[60] But because allocation involves the distribution of significant economic goods, it is controversial in practice. Some trading schemes provide for allowances to be auctioned to the highest bidder, which is a simple form of allocation that generates revenue and allocates resources where they are most valued economically. Auctioning also creates an incentive for polluters to calculate their emissions and abatement costs correctly,[61] overcoming some of the information asymmetries mentioned above. Industry generally resists auctioning, perceived to be an obligation to pay for something that was previously free. On the other hand, free allocation ('grandfathering') involves windfalls for established industry, which receives a valuable commodity free.

For the third phase, auctioning is presented as the basic means of allocation within the EU ETS.[62] However, that basic proposition is subject to so many exceptions that full auctioning is not expected before 2027.[63] The approach to allocation depends on which of three categories the operator is in: power generation, industry generally, or industry subject to 'significant risk of carbon leakage'.

---

[57] Emissions Trading Directive (n 43) Art 9.

[58] To accommodate less abatement in non-traded sectors.

[59] And indeed post-2020, see Sandbag, 'Drifting Towards Disaster: The ETS Adrift in the EU's Climate Efforts' (2013); and 'Cap or Trap: How the EU ETS Risks Locking in Carbon Emissions' (2010) sandbag.org.uk/reports/.

[60] Subject to transaction costs. See eg RB Stewart, 'Economic Incentives for Environmental Protection: Opportunities and Obstacles' in RL Revesz, P Sands and RB Stewart (eds), *Environmental Law, The Economy and Sustainable Development: the United States, the European Union and the International Community* (Cambridge, Cambridge University Press, 2000).

[61] R Baldwin, 'Regulation Lite: The Rise of Emissions Trading' (2008) *LSE Law, Society & Economy Working Papers* 3/2008.

[62] Emissions Trading Directive (n 43) Art 10(1).

[63] The Commission is to review free allocation on conclusion of an international agreement, ibid, Art 10(a)(1).

The power sector is in principle subject to full auctioning from 2013.[64] Electricity generators in the first two phases (especially the first phase) received windfall profits by passing on 'opportunity costs' to consumers. Essentially, EUAs, whether allocated free or purchased, can either be sold or used. Foregone sale receipts represent the 'opportunity cost' of *using* the EUAs. Normal accounting practice allowed the power generators to pass this opportunity cost on to consumers even when allowances had been allocated free of charge; when the power sector purchased allowances from over-allocated industry, electricity consumers also indirectly subsidised industry as well.[65]

Auctioning is to be phased in for industry. Eighty per cent of allowances will be allocated free of charge in 2013, reducing to 30 per cent in 2020, 'with a view' to 100 per cent auctioning in 2027. Sectors subject to significant risk of carbon leakage will receive free allowances until 2020.[66] Carbon leakage refers to the possibility that energy intensive production will be replaced by production in a jurisdiction that does not regulate carbon emissions. Concerns about competitiveness are often raised around environmental regulation, but the global effect of carbon emissions means that carbon leakage is especially problematic: carbon emitted inside or outside the EU is exactly the same, and slightly less stringently regulated emissions within the EU may be environmentally preferable to unregulated emissions elsewhere. The Commission (through comitology, chapter two above) keeps a (lengthy) list of industries at significant risk of carbon leakage.[67] Whether an industry should be placed on that list is obviously controversial, and the criteria in the Directive focus on proportionate additional production costs associated with the price of carbon, and the value of exports and imports;[68] third country commitments to carbon emission reductions may mean that a sector or company can be removed from the list.[69]

Free allocation takes place according to standard rules, based on 'ex ante benchmarks so as to ensure … incentives for reductions in greenhouse gas emissions'.[70] The 'starting point' is to be 'the average performance of the 10% most effective

[64] Derogations are provided for some Member States to 2020, to support the modernisation of electricity generation, Emissions Trading Directive, ibid, Art 10c.

[65] Sandbag (2010) (n 59). It is complicated, but opportunity cost should in theory not be passed on if the industry is subject to competitive pressures, J Sijm, K Newhoff and Y Chen, 'CO2 Cost Pass through and Windfall Profits in the Power Sector' (2006) 6 *Climate Policy* 49. Sandbag (n 55), notes that industries claiming competitiveness concerns have nevertheless passed on opportunity costs.

[66] Emissions Trading Directive (n 43) Art 10(a)(12). Carbon leakage due to increased *electricity* prices can be addressed by 'financial measures' at the national level, Art 10(a)(6). European Commission, 'Guidelines on certain state aid measures in the context of the greenhouse gas emission allowance trading scheme post-2012' SWD (2012) 130 and 131 final.

[67] Commission Decision 2010/2/EU determining a list of sectors and subsectors which are deemed to be exposed to significant risk of carbon leakage [2010] OJ L1/10.

[68] Emissions Trading Directive (n 43) Art 10a(14), (15), (16).

[69] Ibid Art 10a(18).

[70] Ibid Art 10a(1); Commission Decision 2011/278/EU determining transitional Union-wide rules for harmonised free allocation of emission allowances [2011] OJ L130/1.

installations in a sector or sub-sector' in 2007-08.[71] This should go some way to avoiding the rewards for heavy polluters and penalties for early movers that would be associated with using existing permits or emissions as a reference.[72]

Each Member State's auctions are open to operators from anywhere in the EU. One of the advantages of auctioning is the generation of funds for government, and so the Directive divides the auctioning between the Member States. Most allowances are allocated according to the Member State's earlier emissions.[73] This raises the obvious difficulty of favouring Member States who had made little progress in the second phase, so two per cent of allowances are distributed between early movers.[74] In addition, for the purposes of 'solidarity and growth', 10 per cent of allowances are allocated to less prosperous Member States.[75] The Directive also provides guidance on how the funds shall be used. Whilst 'Member States shall determine the use of revenues', at least 50 per cent of the proceeds from auctioning 'should' be used to fund various specified mitigation and adaptation measures; some scrutiny is provided by the obligation to report on the use of revenue.[76]

Mitigation beyond the EU

The incorporation of the Kyoto Protocol's CDM into the EU ETS allows climate change mitigation action in the developing world to count towards EU targets.[77] One purpose of incorporating the CDM is to allow mitigation to take place where it costs least, stimulating the development of new low carbon power infrastructure in the developing world, where existing infrastructure is poor, before prematurely retiring existing high carbon infrastructure in the industrialised world.[78] Even if the CDM does not survive the 'global' agreement in 2015, some way of trading between developed and developing countries is highly likely. The lessons of the CDM need to be learned.

A number of concerns have been raised about the CDM. The broader social and environmental impacts of CDM-funded projects have sometimes been controversial, for example the impacts on local people and environments of some large hydro-electricity projects. Land use, land use change and forestry (LULUCF) projects have to be sensitive to local ecosystems and social needs, and because their carbon reduction is temporary, require careful monitoring. Further,

---

[71] Emissions Trading Directive (n 43) Art 10a(2).
[72] Five per cent of the total cap is set aside for new entrants, ibid, Art 10a(7).
[73] Ibid Art 10(2)(a).
[74] Ibid Art 10(2)(c).
[75] Ibid Art 10(2)(b), Annex IIa.
[76] Ibid Arts 10(3), 10(4).
[77] For detail on the CDM process, see M Netto and K Barani Schmidt, 'The CDM Project Cycle and the Role of the UNFCCC Secretariat' in D Freestone and C Streck (eds), *Legal Aspects of Implementing the Kyoto Protocol Mechanisms: Making Kyoto Work* (Oxford, Oxford University Press, 2005).
[78] Wara (n 28).

the requirement that CDM projects be 'additional',[79] reducing carbon emission beyond business as usual does not seem to have been strictly applied in every case. For example, some question whether, given the country's extraordinary growth, the gas and hydroelectric generation supported by the CDM in China really replaces coal generation, or would have taken place anyway.[80] HFC-23, a gas produced during the manufacture of refrigerants, has been notorious. Although it is a potent greenhouse gas, HFC-23 is a small part of the climate change problem, compared to, say, power generation. And yet, up to 2007, it accounted for the majority of CDM credits. Moreover, preventing HFC-23 from entering the atmosphere is relatively straightforward, so even real and additional reductions are achieved at unnecessary cost.[81] This market does indeed seem to 'invite sharp and corrupt practices',[82] and new examples may continue to emerge. There have however been some responses to these particular problems within the EU. For example, hydroelectric projects are subjected to standards additional to those applied within the UN system.[83] The Directive allows the Commission, through comitology, to limit 'specific credits from project types', and the use of credits from industrial gas (including HFC-23) projects has been restricted.[84] Credits from LULUCF projects are no longer allowed into the EU system.[85] The Commission also intends to develop a new market mechanism addressing whole economic sectors in developing countries, rather than just projects.[86]

As well as a tool for least cost abatement, the CDM is also supposed to be a mechanism for 'assisting' non-Annex I countries 'in achieving sustainable development and in contributing to the ultimate objective of the Convention'.[87] The main developing country beneficiaries of the CDM in the EU ETS are the more prosperous ones, with China providing 59 per cent of the credits surrendered in 2008–11.[88] From 2013, although those credits already accrued will remain in the system, new credits will only be accepted in the EU ETS if they originate in states that are party to an international agreement on climate change, or, in the absence of an adequate international agreement, a bilateral agreement. This does

---

[79] Kyoto Protocol (n 26).

[80] Wara (n 28); D Campbell, M Klaes and C Bignell, 'After Copenhagen: The Impossibility of Carbon Trading' (2010) *London School of Economics Law, Society and Economy Working Papers* 22/2010.

[81] Wara, ibid.

[82] Prins and Rayner (n 10) v; also Campbell et al (n 80).

[83] Emissions Trading Directive (n 43) Art 11b(6), sets vague standards developed through guidance, J Scott, 'In Legal Limbo: Post-Legislative Guidance as a Challenge for European Administrative Law' (2011) 48 *Common Market Law Review* 329. See also ch 4 on the elaboration of vague standards.

[84] Commission Regulation 550/2011/EU on determining, pursuant to Directive 2003/87/EC, certain restrictions applicable to the use of international credits from projects involving industrial gases [2011] OJ L149/1. Any credits accrued to the end of 2012 can be exchanged for EU allowances, carrying the difficulties over into the third phase. Sandbag (n 28); Sandbag (2013) (n 59) 14, argues that the limits came too late.

[85] Emissions Trading Directive (n 43) Art 11a(3)(b).

[86] ec.europa.eu/clima/policies/ets/linking/index_en.htm.

[87] Kyoto Protocol (n 26) Art 12.

[88] Sandbag (n 28).

not apply to Least Developed Countries, who are thus privileged in an effort to re-emphasise the 'sustainable development' objectives of the CDM.[89]

Even if the CDM operated perfectly in terms of *quality*, there would be concerns about the *quantity* of carbon reduction obligations being satisfied outside the EU. Unlimited availability of CDM credits would mean that no mitigation need take place in the EU, and since the host countries have no mitigation targets under the Kyoto Protocol, that allows for an increase in emissions.[90] The Phase I NAPs did not limit the use of CDM credits; in Phase II, the limits varied. In the third phase, external credits can make up no more that 50 per cent of the EU wide reductions.[91]

Flexibility in the ETS

Reliance on the market means that fluctuation in demand, for reasons unrelated to environmental protection, can leave regulation impotent. The Commission has acknowledged that 'the economic crisis is clearly the major cause' of emission reductions since 2008.[92] Successful direct regulation can also affect demand. For example, the EUAs that might have been bought by activities captured by the Energy Efficiency Directive (EED), discussed below, are now available to activities not captured by that Directive. The need to monitor the effect of the EED on the ETS is recognised.[93]

The EU ETS cap cannot, however, easily be tightened in response to events. The Directive does allow for the number of allowances to be increased if there is a restriction of supply and the price goes too high,[94] but there is no corresponding power to tighten the cap for environmental reasons. The Commission has proposed the 'backloading' of some of the allowances due to be auctioned in Phase III, which involves auctioning them later than planned, when it is hoped that demand will have picked up.[95] In addition to this 'short term measure', the Commission has consulted on various options for 'structural measures' that would reduce the cap, including increasing the emissions reduction target to 30 per cent even in the absence of an international agreement; retiring allowances; early revision of the annual linear reduction factor; extending the ETS to other sectors; and changing access to international credits.[96] The Commission is also considering 'discretionary

---

[89] Emissions Trading Directive (n 43) Art 11a(4), (5), (7).
[90] Campbell et al (n 80).
[91] Emissions Trading Directive (n 43) Art 11(a)(8). This applies to JI and CDM credits.
[92] European Commission, 'The State of the European Carbon Market in 2012' COM (2012) 652 final, 3.
[93] Directive 2012/27/EU on energy efficiency ('Energy Efficiency Directive') [2012] OJ L315/1, Recital 55; Art 24(4).
[94] Emissions Trading Directive (n 43) Art 29a.
[95] European Commission, 'Proposal for a Decision of the European Parliament and of the Council Amending Directive 2003/87/EC Clarifying Provisions on the Timing of the Auctions of Greenhouse Gas Allowances' COM (2012) 416 final.
[96] Commission (n 92).

price mechanisms' (such as a minimum price for carbon), but is concerned that this would completely change the nature of the ETS, from a 'quantity based' to a 'price based' mechanism[97]—essentially to a tax. Reform of the ETS is proving extraordinarily sensitive,[98] and proposals from the Commission are still pending.

As suggested in the discussion of the international context, flexibility, an ability to revisit and improve, can be a great virtue in climate change governance. The changes introduced to the ETS in the third phase, as well as the legislation discussed below on renewable energy and energy efficiency, suggest an appreciation of the need for evolution. Whether the ETS is adequately flexible is, however, still open to question, and the Commission's proposals for structural change to the ETS, as discussed in the previous paragraph, are still uncertain. The ability of the Member States to move independently on climate change mitigation is also constrained. The Industrial Emissions Directive (IED), discussed in the previous chapter, prohibits the inclusion of emission limit values for carbon in IED permits.[99] However, EU legislation agreed under Article 192 of the Treaty on the Functioning of the European Union (TFEU), like the ETS Directive, lays down a *minimum* threshold of environmental protection. As discussed in chapter one, Member States retain the option of enacting more stringent standards. This suggests that an emissions standard set independently of the IED, could in principle be lawful. However, there is a question as to whether these standards really would provide more stringent environmental protection, as required by Article 193, given their potentially negative impact on the EU scheme.[100] The UK, for example, has a unilateral carbon price floor for electricity generation, which works as a tax if the price of carbon falls below a certain level. Not only does this create the possibility of 'carbon leakage' within the EU, but the EUAs that are freed up may be purchased elsewhere in the EU, leaving overall emissions unchanged. But if the EU ETS remains subject to such high levels of over-allocation, action by individual Member States may turn out to be necessary.

Concluding Comments

The EU was a late convert to the role of trading in climate change policy,[101] which the US had pressed for before it withdrew from the Kyoto Protocol. Even at home, the EU preferred a carbon tax, which, as discussed in chapter one, proved

---

[97] Ibid 10.

[98] Parliament, eg, only accepted the relatively modest backloading proposal on 3 July 2013, having rejected an earlier proposal.

[99] Directive 2010/75/EU on industrial emissions (integrated pollution prevention and control) ('Industrial Emissions Directive' (IED)) [2010] OJ L334/17, Art 9.

[100] J Scott, 'The Multi-Level Governance of Climate Change' in P Craig and G de Burca (eds), *The Evolution of EU Law* (Oxford, Oxford University Press, 2011) 821–24.

[101] See C Damro and P Luaces Méndez, 'Emissions Trading at Kyoto: From EU Resistance to Union Innovation' (2003) 12 *Environmental Politics* 71.

impossible because of the EU's constitutional arrangements. The dominance and embedding of the second choice policy of emissions trading is interesting in itself.

The ETS demonstrates that far from being de-regulatory, market instruments demand intense administrative activity. Some of the other benefits claimed for market instruments over direct regulation, discussed in chapter four, are also proving elusive. A lack of dynamic response to changing conditions is one of the core criticisms of direct regulation; ETS demonstrates that whilst neither market instruments nor direct regulatory instruments are necessarily inflexible, either can be. In addition, the ETS has shown itself to be subject to lobbying, to complexity, to uncertainty and delay, just as command instruments are.[102] Even the ability of emissions trading to stimulate innovation more effectively than direct regulation is open to doubt. There may be benefits to turning pollution prevention from a 'burden' into a 'business'.[103] But Driesen argues that there is less incentive to innovate than there would be if carbon emissions were subject to direct regulation: the primary purpose of emissions trading is to reduce compliance costs, and lower compliance costs reduce the incentives for costly innovation.[104] Emissions trading also raises serious questions of distributive fairness, both within the EU, and globally through the CDM.[105] The danger is that the rich continue to enjoy the economic advantages of pollution, whilst the poor limit their ability to develop in the same way by selling their allowances. It seems unlikely that ensuring a fair price for that sale (including longer term costs) and ensuring a minimum level of mitigation by rich industry and consumers, can be left entirely to the market.

Assessing the effectiveness of the EU ETS, even in simple terms of whether it has reduced carbon emissions, is fraught. The 2012 Kyoto target will be met,[106] but it is not possible to say what would have happened in the absence of the ETS. Even if we allow that some of the reductions are attributable to the ETS, the reduction seems largely due to reduced output during the post-2008 recession, and earlier unrelated reductions such as a shift from coal to gas and migration of industry out of the EU. The EEA attributes reductions in 2011 (in a growing economy) primarily to a mild winter, and says that high energy prices (notwithstanding a low carbon price) also had some effect.[107]

There are certainly problems with the EU ETS and it is difficult to muster up much enthusiasm. But it has at least normalised the regulation of carbon. The limits of the ETS are recognised not only by the changes to the ETS itself, but

---

[102] Baldwin (n 61).

[103] Lefevere (n 50) 166–67.

[104] See Driesen (n 51). One of the key differences between climate change and the US sulphur trading regulation that was its inspiration, is that the latter demanded a low innovation technical response.

[105] Baldwin (n 61).

[106] EEA (2012) (n 27).

[107] EEA (2013) (n 27). The fall was mainly located in the residential/commercial sector, which falls outside the ETS. Also Sandbag (n 55).

also by EU measures specifically designed to tackle renewable energy and energy efficiency, discussed next.

THE RENEWABLE ENERGY DIRECTIVE

Renewable energy, including energy from wind, wave, hydro, tidal, solar, geothermal and biomass sources, is expected to play an indispensable role in the move to a low carbon society, and takes a central place in the *20 20 by 2020* policy. Energy security is an increasingly important driver of the political will for renewable energy, emphasised by high oil and gas prices, and political volatility, as witnessed for example in the 2006 and 2009 gas disputes between Russia and Ukraine.[108] Renewables are also central to the 'green economy' strand of EU policy, discussed in chapter three.[109]

The Renewable Energy Directive (RED) imposes a target for the proportion of renewable energy used in the EU, which by 2020 should be 20 per cent of final energy consumption.[110] This target is designed in part to increase industry's confidence that there will be a consistent focus on a particular policy objective, reducing the risks associated with long term investment.[111] Individual targets are allocated to each Member State, calculated by reference to its 2005 proportion of renewable energy, and GDP.[112] Sweden has the highest target, of 49 per cent by 2020, up from 39.8 per cent in 2005; Malta has the lowest at 10 per cent, up from zero. The UK's 2020 target is 15 per cent, up from 1.3 per cent in 2005. These targets are a basic command instrument, and the Member States are subject in principle to the enforcement action by the Commission for failure to comply.[113] One of the downsides of long-term targets, however, is that they postpone formal judgment of compliance to the target date, in this case 2020. But whilst it would be extremely difficult to challenge any particular national decision or development,[114] Member States are not free from legal and political scrutiny. Generally, they are obliged to 'refrain from taking any measures liable seriously to compromise the attainment of the result' set out in a directive.[115] And specifically, Member States must submit a National Renewable Energy Action Plan (NREAP), which must,

---

[108] M Nilsson, LJ Nilsson and K Ericsson, 'Rapid Turns in European Renewable Energy Policy: Advocacy and Framing in the Proposed Trading of Guarantees of Origin' *FNI Report 9/2008*, 21.

[109] Energy security and economic competitiveness are not new motivations, R Hildingsson, J Stripple and A Jordan, 'Renewable Energies: A Continuing Balancing Act?' in Jordan et al (n 3).

[110] Directive 2009/28/EC on the promotion of the use of energy from renewable sources ('Renewable Energy Directive' (RED)) [2009] OJ L140/16.

[111] Ibid Recital 14, Art 3.

[112] Ibid Recital 15.

[113] RED's predecessor, Directive 2001/77/EC on the promotion of electricity produced from renewable energy sources in the internal electricity market [2001] OJ L283/33, set an *indicative* target that for 2010 22% of *electricity* would be from renewable sources.

[114] See eg *Case C-165/09 Stichting Natuur en Milieu v College van Gedeputeerde Staten van Groningen* [2011] ECR I-4599 [45] (in respect of obligations under waste legislation).

[115] Eg Case C-129/96 *Inter-Environnement Wallonie v Régione Wallone* [1997] ECR I-7411.

amongst other things, set out 'adequate measures' to achieve the national overall targets.[116] The Commission can issue recommendations in response to NREAPs. Any Member State falling below its *indicative* trajectory ('tracing a path towards' the mandatory targets[117]) must submit an amended NREAP, 'setting out adequate and proportionate measures to rejoin, within a reasonable timetable, the indicative trajectory'.[118] So, there is at least the potential for public and peer scrutiny, pending formal assessment of compliance in 2020.[119]

The RED applies to all energy use, including electricity and heating and cooling, and applies a specific target of 10 per cent renewable energy to transport. I will focus on electricity here. Far more than 20 per cent of *electricity* needs to be decarbonised to meet the 20 per cent target in *energy*. Moreover, even with successful energy efficiency measures, electricity demand will go up in a decarbonising world, as sectors like transport and heating turn to renewable electricity as an alternative to fossil fuel.

The Member States are likely to need to use support schemes if they are to meet their targets.[120] Whilst some renewable technologies in some circumstances are able to compete with fossil fuels, the Commission does not expect subsidies to be phased out before 2020.[121] The cost of the support scheme is generally paid by electricity consumers, inevitably raising distributive concerns with respect to poor consumers of electricity, and possibly wealthy recipients of subsidy.[122] The Commission's preference was initially for a harmonised, EU-wide approach to support, with heated debate around which of two main options was preferable.[123] The first, 'feed in tariffs', pioneered by Germany, sets a guaranteed long term price for energy from renewable sources when it is fed into the electricity grid. The second option is to require electricity suppliers to supply a quota of their electricity from renewable sources, demonstrated by the surrender of certificates issued to generators of renewable energy. Electricity suppliers can acquire certificates by generating their own renewable energy, purchasing both energy and certificates from other generators, or purchasing just the certificates. The detailed application

---

[116]   RED (n 110) Art 4. See ec.europa.eu/energy/renewables/action_plan_en.htm.

[117]   Required by RED, ibid, Art 3; Recital 19. Annex I, Part B contains a formula for calculating the indicative trajectory.

[118]   Ibid Art 4(4).

[119]   The NREAPs have been submitted, see ec.europa.eu/energy/renewables/action_plan_en.htm. If implemented, the plans will meet the 20% target, LWM Beurskens, M Hekkenberg and P Vethman, *Renewable Energy Projections as Published in the National Renewable Energy Action Plans of the European Member States* (ECN and European Environment Agency, 2011).

[120]   RED (n 11) Art 3(3).

[121]   Commission Staff Working Document, 'Review of European and national financing of renewable energy in accordance with Article 23(7) of Directive 2009/28/EC' SEC (2011) 131 final, 4.

[122]   The potential for support of solar photovoltaics to transfer funds from poor electricity consumers to those with large, south facing roofs suitable for solar panels, has been controversial in the UK, see G Monbiot, 'Are we Really Going to Let Ourselves be Duped into this Solar Panel Rip-Off?' *The Guardian* 1 March 2010.

[123]   See D Toke, 'The EU Renewables Directive—What is the Fuss About Trading?' (2008) 36 *Energy Policy* 3001.

of both quotas and feed in tariffs varies, and hence so does their effectiveness and cost; most obviously, the level of the quota and of the feed in tariff is crucial. But generally, quotas are thought to be less expensive, since holders of certificates compete and so have incentives to keep costs down.[124] However, this method is also thought to lead to less innovation, since the cheapest certificates will be generated by established technology.[125] Feed in tariffs seem to have been the more effective mechanism for driving renewable energy development in the EU, with countries using feed in tariffs seeing a dramatic growth in renewable energy production.[126]

The Commission's preference, as it began to prepare the RED, was for an EU-wide system of support for renewable energy. It initially intended to establish a system of quotas plus certificates, which would be tradeable throughout the entire EU.[127] The aim would have been to build an internal market in renewable energy, incentivising renewable energy projects where they are least expensive. In the end, the RED did not establish a harmonised scheme of support. Article 15 does require the Member States to issue 'guarantees of origin' (certificates) to generators of renewable energy. However, these cannot be used to meet the national renewable energy targets, but simply to satisfy requirements that bills and advertising disclose the proportion of electricity supplies from renewable sources, in support of voluntary green markets.[128] The RED allows Member States to pursue their own support systems, targeted at national suppliers only. Recital 25 makes the following statement:

> The majority of Member States apply support schemes that grant benefits solely to energy from renewable sources that is produced on their territory. For the proper functioning of national support schemes it is vital that Member States can control the effect and costs of their national support schemes according to their different potentials.[129]

Article 3 also provides that Member States 'have the right to decide … to which extent they support energy from renewable sources which is produced in a different Member State'. The RED, however, must remain subject to the internal market rules found in the Treaty, and discussed a little further in chapter 10.[130] The ECJ in *PreussenElektra AG v Schhleswag AG* confirmed the legality of an approach to feed in tariffs that required electricity suppliers to purchase, at a specified price,

---

[124] Toke, ibid, however argues that, with a genuinely very ambitious target, there will be a shortage of certificates, which will in turn be punishingly expensive in the absence of regulatory price limits.

[125] V Lauber, 'REFIT and RPS: Options for a Harmonised Community Framework' (2003) 32 *Energy Policy* 1405.

[126] R Haas et al, 'Efficiency and Effectiveness of Promotion Systems for Electricity Generation from Renewable Energy Sources—Lessons from EU Countries' (2011) 36 *Energy* 2186.

[127] Toke (n 123); European Commission Staff Working Document, 'The Support of Electricity from Renewable Energy Sources' SEC (2008) 57 final.

[128] RED (n 110) Recital 52.

[129] Ibid Recital 25

[130] Art 3 is explicitly subject to state aid rules.

all of the renewable energy generated in their area.[131] This obligation to 'buy local' was justified by its pursuit of environmental objectives, but also because, once electricity is in the system, 'it is difficult to determine its origin and in particular the source of energy from which it was produced'.[132] The approach taken in *PreussenElektra* to discrimination between national renewable energy and renewable energy generated by other Member States will not necessarily survive the development of more reliable ways of identifying the source of electricity.[133] But the terms of the RED nevertheless suggest that ensuring robust national support schemes is at least a legitimate objective for the Member States to pursue,[134] albeit demanding some careful arguments about the necessity of control of national expenditure if EU environmental targets are to be met.[135] Their measures will also of course have to be proportionate.

The Commission continues to press for a full internal market in renewable energy, and for 'consistency of approach' in support schemes,[136] arguing that there would be cost savings to a single European market in renewable energy.[137] The RED does contain three 'flexibility'[138] or 'cooperation'[139] mechanisms.[140] First, Article 6 provides for 'statistical transfers', allowing trading between Member States (not companies). High levels of renewable energy, and hence the existence of surpluses for statistical transfer, are likely to mean that there have been high levels of state or consumer financial support in that Member State, and Member States are unlikely to be willing to sell without recouping that cost.[141] Secondly, Article 7 allows for 'joint projects',[142] in which two or more Member States agree

---

[131] Case C-379/98 *PreussenElektra AG v Schhleswag AG* [2001] ECR I-2099.

[132] Ibid [79]. F Jacobs, 'The Role of the European Court of Justice in the Protection of the Environment' (2006) 18 *Journal of Environmental Law* 185.

[133] G van Calster, 'Topsy-Turvy: The European Court of Justice and Border (Energy) Tax Adjustments—Should the World Trade Organisation Follow Suit?' in *Critical Issues in Environmental Taxation: International and Comparative Perspectives (Volume I)*, (London, Richmond Law and Tax, 2003). A case on an obligation to surrender locally generated green energy certificates is pending, Case C-204/12 *Essent Belgium*; Bot AG found the measures in breach of EU free movement of goods (the opinion is not yet available in English).

[134] See the discussion in N Nic Shuibhne and M Maci, 'Proving Public Interest: The Growing Impact of Evidence in Free Movement Case Law' (2013) 504 *Common Market Law Review* 965 of national health systems.

[135] See the discussion of Case C-120/95 *Decker* [1998] ECR I-1831 and Case C-203/96 *Chemische Afvalstoffen Dusseldorp BV v Minister Van Volkshuisvesting, Ruimtelijke Ordening en Milieubeheer* [1998] ECR I-4075 in ch 10. See also Nic Shuibhne and Maci, ibid.

[136] European Commission, 'Renewable Energy: A Major Player in the European Energy Market' COM (2012) 271 final, 5.

[137] Commission (n 121) 11; the Commission will review in 2014, ibid 12.

[138] RED (n 110) Recital 36.

[139] Ibid Recital 25, also Commission (n 121) 12.

[140] For detailed discussion, see C Klessmann et al, 'Design Options for Cooperation Mechanisms under the New European Renewable Energy Directive' (2010) 38 *Energy Policy* 4679.

[141] Ibid.

[142] RED (n 110) Art 9 allows for joint projects outside the EU. In this case, the trade is a physical trade in electricity, rather than a virtual trade, although credit can be granted early for projects with long lead in times.

that the renewable energy from a specific project in one Member State is credited (in whole or in part) in the other. This effectively allows one Member State to fund renewable energy development outside of its jurisdiction, in return for counting the renewable energy towards its target. Thirdly, Article 11 allows for joint support mechanisms between two or more Member States. They can join or partially coordinate their support mechanisms, and agree to some pooling of credit for the renewable energy produced. This creates a bigger physical space for renewable energy generation, so that support should go to the most effective projects.

The cooperation mechanisms, especially joint support mechanisms, are a form of experimentation that allows incremental steps to be taken towards an internal market in renewable energy, and the Commission is eager to encourage them.[143] So far, however, the Member States remain largely national in their approach to renewables.[144]

The RED contains a number of other provisions that are supposed to ensure a smooth transition to renewable energy. All Member States are required to 'promote and encourage energy efficiency and energy saving'.[145] Article 16 provides for 'priority' or 'guaranteed' access of renewable energy to the grid for distribution. Member States must ensure that adequate information on support measures is made available to 'all relevant actors, such as consumers, builders, installers, architects, and suppliers',[146] and that 'suitable information, awareness-raising, guidance or training programmes' are available to citizens.[147] The Directive requires building regulations and codes to contain 'appropriate measures' to 'increase the share of all kinds of energy from renewable sources', including 'where appropriate', mandatory minimum levels of renewable energy in new buildings and buildings undergoing major renovation.[148] Public buildings are to 'fulfil an exemplary role'.[149]

The RED is also concerned with general administrative arrangements for the authorisation of renewable energy projects. Any national rules are to be 'proportionate and necessary', with 'transparent timetables' and 'streamlined and expedited' administrative procedures. 'Smaller projects and decentralised devices' should benefit from 'simplified and less burdensome authorisation procedures', 'where appropriate'.[150] This is not the place for a detailed review of the authorisation processes for renewable energy, especially since the regulatory approach and the social context varies around the EU,[151] but there are some cross-cutting issues.

---

[143] European Commission, 'Renewable Energy Progress Report' COM (2013) 175; the Commission is to issue guidance.
[144] Commission (n 136), explores the barriers.
[145] RED (n 110) Art 3.
[146] Ibid Art 14.
[147] Ibid Art 14.
[148] Ibid Art 13(4).
[149] Ibid Art 13(5).
[150] Ibid Art 13(1).
[151] See D Toke, S Breukers and M Wolsink, 'Wind Power Deployment Outcomes: How Can We Account for the Differences?' (2008) 12 *Renewable and Sustainable Energy Review* 1129.

First, there may be tension between a swift move to renewables and other environmental values. A preliminary reference to the ECJ from Italy involved a regional blanket prohibition on windfarm development in areas protected for nature conservation under the Habitats Directive.[152] As discussed in chapter one, the Court interpreted the Italian measures as providing more stringent environmental protection than is required under the Habitats Directive, and upheld them under Article 193 TFEU. It also said that the ban was compatible with the RED's objectives of 'streamlining and reducing administrative barriers'.[153] The Court did not engage with the potential for conflict (at least in the short term) between wind energy and conservation objectives. It simply observed that 'European Union policy on energy must have regard for the need to preserve and improve the environment', and that in any event, the Italian measure was not 'in view of its limited scope, liable to jeopardise the European Union objective of developing new and renewable forms of energy'.[154] Whilst it is reassuring to hear that climate change objectives need not sweep away all other environmental concerns, the Court does not engage at all with the scale of the renewables challenge, or the potential cumulative effect of such decisions. The fact that any particular project makes a tiny contribution to an enormous problem, or its solution, is a perennial issue in climate change litigation.[155]

Secondly, there may be some tension between the perceived urgency of action on climate change and a commitment to allowing people to shape their own environments, as reflected, for example, in rights granted by environmental impact assessment to participate in infrastructure development.[156] Even if a move to renewable energy in general is welcome, the specific projects can raise local concerns.[157] With any major infrastructure development, including renewable energy, some groups are asked to bear burdens in the broader public interest. The environmental and social costs are concentrated in a locality (sometimes balanced by benefits such as employment), whilst the energy and climate benefits are diffused; any financial profits often leave the area. Consistently high levels of support for renewable energy in general, coupled with local opposition to actual projects have frequently led to public concerns being dismissed as NIMBYism (not in my backyard). NIMBYism however is not an adequate explanation for resistance to

---

[152] Case C-2/10 *Azienda Agro-Zootecnica Franchini Sarl v Regione Puglia* [2011] ECR I-6561; Directive 1992/43/EEC on the conservation of natural habitats and of wild fauna and flora ('Habitats Directive') [1992] OJ L206/7.

[153] Case C-2/10 ibid [63]. The Commission is critical of progress in this respect, above (n 143).

[154] Ibid [56], [57]. See also Mazák AG [48] and [49].

[155] On 'death by a thousand cuts', see J Peel, 'Issues in Climate Change Litigation' (2011) 5 *Carbon and Climate Law Review* 15.

[156] M Lee et al, 'Public Participation and Climate Change Infrastructure' (2013) 25 *Journal of Environmental Law* 133; Directive 2011/92/EU on the assessment of the effects of certain public and private projects on the environment (codification) [2012] OJ L26/1; ch 7 below.

[157] Most of the literature below refers to wind, but eg P Devine-Wright, 'Enhancing Local Distinctiveness Fosters Public Acceptability of Tidal Energy: A UK Case Study' (2011) 39 *Energy Policy* 83.

development.[158] Support for renewable energy is likely to be qualified in ways that may not be captured by a general 'pro' renewable energy opinion survey,[159] so local opposition does not necessarily conflict with (qualified) general support. And NIMBY allegations overly simplify, as pure self-interest, what may be complex and multifaceted reasons for local opposition.[160] As a pejorative term, it can be used to dismiss perfectly reasonable local concerns.[161] There is some evidence that ensuring that the local community shares in the benefits from the development can enhance local support for a project.[162] In Denmark, famously, community ownership was an important element of the early development of wind energy, although large corporations are now increasingly dominant.[163] In the UK, it is more or less routine for payments to be made to local communities. The role of 'community benefits' (and the meaning of 'community' and 'benefits'[164]) is not, however, straightforward.[165] This is not unconnected to the misrepresentations inherent in 'NIMBYism'. If concern is understood as pure self-interest, a simplistic approach to community benefits may be taken, and if benefits are interpreted as an attempt to bribe the local community, they might actually increase resistance. Resistance to development is not about simply the physical facts of development, but about who benefits and how, and who controls the development. The distributive questions raised by a large scale shift to renewable energy have been especially visible in the turn to biofuels, with the concern that growing fuel for the rich, can increase the scarcity and price of food, affecting the poor most harshly.[166] Even if less dramatic in other cases, there will be winners and losers in any successful decarbonisation of the economy.

---

[158] P Devine-Wright, 'Beyond NIMBYism: Towards an Integrated Framework for Understanding Public Perception of Wind Energy' (2005) 8 *Wind Energy* 125.

[159] D Bell, T Gray and C Haggett, 'The "Social Gap" in Wind Farm Siting Decisions: Explanations and Policy responses' (2005) 14 *Environmental Policies* 460.

[160] Ibid.

[161] M Wolsink, 'Invalid Theory Impedes our Understanding: A Critique on the Persistence of the Language of NIMBY' (2006) 31 *Transactions of the Institute of British Geographers* 85.

[162] Toke, Breukers and Wolsink (n 151).

[163] With a consequential rise in public scepticism, A McHarg and A Ronne, 'Reducing Carbon-Based Electricity Generation: Is the Answer Blowing in the Wind?' in DN Zillman et al (eds), *Beyond the Carbon Economy: Energy Law in Transition* (Oxford, Oxford University Press, 2008) 302–03.

[164] G Walker and P Devine-Wright, 'Community Renewable Energy: What Should it Mean?' (2008) 36 *Energy Policy* 497. On the variety of 'benefits', see R Cowell, G Bristow and M Munday, 'Acceptance, Acceptability and Environmental Justice: The Role of Community Benefits in Wind Energy Development' (2011) 54 *Journal of Environmental Planning and Management* 539.

[165] Eg N Cass, G Walker and P Devine-Wright, 'Good Neighbours, Public Relations and Bribes: The Politics and Perceptions of Community Benefit Provision in Renewable Energy Development in the UK' (2010) 12 *Journal of European Public Policy* 255.

[166] European Commission, 'Proposal for a Directive Amending Directive 98/70/EC Relating to the Quality of Petrol and Diesel Fuels and Amending Directive 2009/28/EC on the Promotion of the Use of Energy from Renewable Sources' COM (2012) 595 final, aims, inter alia, to divert attention from 'conventional' (crop-based) biofuels to 'advanced' biofuels, made eg from waste or algae.

ENERGY EFFICIENCY

Amory Lovins, a great advocate of energy efficiency, describes energy efficiency as 'generally the largest, least expensive, most benign, most quickly deployed, least visible, least understood and most neglected way to provide energy services'.[167] Energy efficiency is a central element of the *20 20 by 2020* policy, which sets a target of a 20 per cent reduction in energy use by 2020, relative to projections. Member States are required by the EED to set an 'indicative national energy efficiency target', taking into account the overall EU target.[168] Like renewable energy, energy efficiency pursues multiple objectives, including security of supply and 'the competitiveness of industry in the Union, boosting economic growth and creating high quality jobs in several sectors related to energy efficiency'.[169] EU legislation defines energy efficiency as 'the ratio of output of performance, service goods or energy, to input of energy'.[170] For example, energy efficiency might allow a building to provide the same light, temperature control or entertainment, with less energy.

Although in some cases energy efficiency might be ignored because energy is cheap, it is also well established that economically efficient measures to save energy are routinely neglected.[171] First, the necessary skills, knowledge or information to make the change may be missing. Secondly, notwithstanding the overall advantages of investment in energy efficiency, cost may be a problem. The party who would benefit from the change may not have the capital required for investment, or 'split incentives' might mean that the party making the capital investment does not benefit sufficiently from the energy savings. Split incentives are most striking for landlord and tenant, but could also apply to the separate management of capital and current accounts in large organisations, or for example the electrician who competes for a job on price rather than cost of operation.[172] Thirdly, hidden costs, such as disruption to a business or home, may have been missed by economists calculating the rationality of energy efficiency measures, but are nevertheless real.

The EU addresses energy efficiency in numerous pieces of environmental regulation. For example, some product regulation makes information on energy consumption available through labeling, or introduces design or performance standards.[173] Energy efficiency can also be relevant in permitting, for example in

---

[167] AB Lovins, *Energy End-Use Efficiency* (Rocky Mountain Institute, 2005) 1.

[168] EED (n 93) Art 3(1)(a).

[169] Ibid Recital 1.

[170] Ibid Art 2(4).

[171] For a taxonomy of barriers, see eg B Barton, 'The Law of Energy Efficiency' in Zillman et al (n 163); MJ Grubb, 'Energy Efficiency and Economic Fallacies' [1990] *Energy Policy* 783.

[172] Lovins (n 167). If energy efficient wires are slightly more expensive, the electrician will be undercut by a competitor.

[173] See the Commission's energy efficiency webpages, ec.europa.eu/energy/efficiency/index_en.htm.

the IED.[174] The ETS should incentivise energy efficiency by increasing the price of energy. But I focus here on the energy efficiency of buildings, regulated by both the EED, which applies to 'buildings, transport, products and processes',[175] and the Buildings Directive.[176] Buildings represent 40 per cent of the EU's final energy consumption,[177] and are thought to have the greatest energy saving potential.[178] Their carbon emissions are not directly traded under the ETS, although the emissions from, for example, electricity generation will have been. It is not possible to cover the Directives comprehensively here, but they make interesting use of direct and informational approaches to regulation.

Under Article 4 of the Buildings Directive, Member States must set minimum energy performance standards for buildings, reviewed at least every five years, for new buildings and existing buildings undergoing 'major renovation'.[179] The Directive is interested in missed cost-effective opportunities, requiring levels of energy use to be 'cost-optimal'.[180] New buildings must be 'nearly zero-energy buildings' by the end of 2020 (2018 for public buildings, consistent with the 'exemplary role' of the public sector).[181] A 'nearly zero-energy building' is defined in an open-ended way, as 'a building that has a very high energy performance', with the energy that is required 'covered to a very significant extent' by renewable energy, including energy 'produced on-site or nearby'.[182] These enforceable minimum energy performance standards are a basic direct regulatory tool.

Secondly, the Directives both emphasise information as a regulatory tool. The EED requires Member States to 'establish a long-term strategy for mobilising investment in the renovation of the national stock of residential and commercial buildings, both public and private', starting with an overview of national building stock, and the identification of cost effective renovation for building type and climatic zone.[183] Member States have to ensure that information on 'available energy efficiency mechanisms and financial and legal frameworks is transparent', and information should be 'widely disseminated to all relevant market actors, such as consumers, builders, architects, engineers, environmental and energy auditors, and

---

[174] IED (n 99).

[175] EED (n 93) Recital 7.

[176] Directive 2010/31/EU on the energy performance of buildings (recast) ('Buildings Directive') (2010) OJ L153/13. R Dawes, 'Building to Improve Energy Efficiency in England and Wales' (2010) 12 *Environmental Law Review* 266.

[177] EED (n 93) Recital 16, Buildings Directive, ibid, Recital 3.

[178] European Commission, 'Energy Efficiency Plan' COM (2011) 109 final.

[179] Buildings Directive (n 176) Arts 6 and 7. Major renovation is either (at the option of the Member State) cost of renovations (over 25% of total value) or building envelope (increase of more than 25%), Art 2(10).

[180] Buildings Directive, ibid, Art 2(14).

[181] Ibid Art 9.

[182] Ibid Art 2(2). See Ecofys et al, *Towards Nearly Zero-Energy Buildings: Definition of Common Principles under the EPBD* (Ecofys, 2012); note the 'soft' elaboration of open-ended definitions, Scott (n 83) and ch 4.

[183] EED (n 93) Art 4.

installers of building elements'.[184] The usual peer and public scrutiny opportunities are provided by reporting, mainly through the National Energy Efficiency Action Plans,[185] reviewed by the Commission. These must include information on the national indicative target mentioned above, and on progress to meeting it. The Commission also has to assess progress towards the EU target; its preliminary view is that the Member States are not on track.[186]

The Buildings Directive requires 'energy performance certificates', with a simple rating of a building, to be provided to owners of new (or modified) buildings, and to prospective owners and tenants.[187] An important strand of market thinking on environmental protection relies on the 'green consumer', who consciously purchases on environmental grounds. But in this case, the potential educative effect (for example on the way the building is used or on investment) may be more important than the influence on purchasing decisions.[188] The certificates contain recommendations for improvement, and indicate where further information can be found. Buildings over a particular size that are 'frequently visited by the public' have to display their energy performance certificates.[189] The recitals to the Directive see this as '[setting] an example', which rather assumes good performance in those buildings. Whilst it seems unlikely at the moment, this disclosure could also lead to public pressure to reduce energy consumption. Other information measures include moves to introduce 'individual' metering for multi-apartment and multi-purpose buildings, and 'intelligent' metering to provide consumers with detailed information on precisely how, when and at what price, they use electricity.[190]

A more ambitious approach to information can be found in the EED's encouragement of energy management and auditing.[191] Management systems and audits are in part designed to fill information gaps, so that an organisation understands its energy use in detail. But they also have the potential to encourage active engagement and self-critical reflection on energy performance. Rather than dictating the objectives to be achieved, or principles to be followed, management systems and audits create structures and enhance opportunities for reflection and self-criticism.[192] Environmental auditing and management systems are usually voluntary, relying on reputational effects and financial savings to encourage

---

[184] Ibid Art 17. I will not discuss the EED's approach to financing here, but information plays an important role.

[185] Ibid Art 24.

[186] Ibid Art 3. European Commission, 'Green Paper: A 2030 Framework for Climate and Energy Policies' COM (2013) 169 final, 5.

[187] Buildings Directive (n 176) Art 12.

[188] Although there does seem to be some positive relationship between energy efficiency ratings and price, see BioIntelligence Service, R Lyons and IEEP, 'Energy Performance Certificates on Buildings and their Impact on Transaction Prices and Rents in Selected EU Countries: Final Report' (European Commission, 2013).

[189] Buildings Directive (n 176) Art 13(1)(2).

[190] EED (n 93) Arts 9–11.

[191] On minimum quality criteria, ibid, Annex VI.

[192] In accordance with some of the principles of 'reflexive law', EW Orts, 'Reflexive Environmental Law' (1995) 89 *Northwestern University Law Review* 1227.

take up. By contrast, energy audits are mandatory for large enterprises under the EED.[193] The frequent neglect of cost-effective efficiency measures, discussed above, may explain the compulsion. It also captures non-consumer oriented business, which tend to face lower reputational pressures and so be less engaged in these types of activities. With respect to other final consumers and the public sector, Member States are variously to 'promote' and to 'encourage' audits and management systems.[194]

Energy efficiency of buildings is more important, and more legally challenging, than it sounds. Putting energy efficiency measures in place is only the start; converting them into actual carbon savings is also difficult. The 'rebound effect' means that at least some energy saving is 'spent' in the consumption of more energy. At a banal level, if I use the savings from a more fuel efficient car to make more journeys, energy use does not shrink. Even if the amount I travelled was never constrained by fuel costs, and so I travel the same amount, I might spend the savings on other energy intensive goods. And even if I reduce my personal energy consumption, reduced energy demand lowers the price of energy, stimulating demand elsewhere in the economy. The existence and extent of the rebound effect is empirically controversial.[195] It seems to be the case that some of the energy efficiency is 'spent' in other energy use, but not necessarily the whole saving.[196] And some of the 'rebound' may be put to socially beneficial uses: converting efficiency from residential insulation to comfort (warmer houses) may also reduce the health effects of cold and damp housing for those living in fuel poverty. However, on its own, energy efficiency will probably not reduce carbon emissions a great deal. But alongside other measures it has a contribution to make, and may also help to make price or regulatory limits on consumption more palatable, and less disruptive.

CONCLUSIONS

A lot has changed in EU environmental law and scholarship since I finished writing the first edition of this book in the summer of 2004, but in no area as dramatically as climate change. Phase I of the ETS had not yet started; policy on renewables and energy efficiency was slowly evolving, but with nothing like its current legal clout. The scholarship on climate change law, including carbon trading, was modest compared to the ocean of material available now. This reflects to some extent the changing political salience of climate change, and it is probably fair to say that climate change became a high profile mainstream political issue in

---

[193] Enterprises 'that are not SMEs', EED (n 93) Art 8(4).

[194] EED, ibid, Arts 5(7) and 8. Financial support is permissible, Art 8(2).

[195] S Sorrell, 'Jevons' Paradox Revisited: The Evidence for Backfire from Improved Energy Efficiency' (2009) 37 *Energy Policy* 1456. The 'Jevons paradox' is the observation that historically, energy saving has led to more energy consumption overall.

[196] Barton (n 171).

2005/06. Whilst cause and effect are difficult to allocate, this followed news-worthy events that included the success of Al Gore's documentary, *An Inconvenient Truth*, the devastation of New Orleans by Hurricane Katrina,[197] and the powerful message in the Stern Report that mitigating climate change is economically preferable to doing nothing.[198] We might even consider whether the search by the EU for a way to connect with the European public in the wake of the failure of the Constitution for Europe increased the salience of climate change. But public enthusiasm comes and goes, and climate change seems to have slipped back down the agenda, perhaps in part due to frustration at lack of progress, as well as the economic downturn.[199] Nevertheless, climate change seems unlikely to disappear from the legal and policy agenda.

This chapter has given an indication of the wealth of regulatory approaches applying to climate change. Notwithstanding the scale of the problem, the legal response to climate change has been measured. Whilst complex and extensive, law approaches climate change as a number of more or less manageable problems— abatement in particular industries, renewable energy, energy efficiency, to take the examples used here. This might indicate a fundamental failure to engage with the urgency of the challenge, and a misunderstanding of the overarching dilemma posed by the 'carbon economy'. But it might also be the only way to make progress. The legal arrangements are a combination of the almost unimaginably ambitious with the almost laughably banal.[200] ETS has proven a fateful choice, since additional regulatory interventions fit awkwardly into the market. And yet there clearly has been considerable evolution of the legal approach to climate change. What really matters is the stringency and practicality of regulatory standards, rather than the beauty of the arrangements; one of the worrying things about climate change is how often the core questions of effectiveness are obscured by the decision-making tools of economics and science. The effectiveness of the legal response to climate change is, at best, still to be seen.[201]

---

[197] It is of course impossible to attribute particular events to climate change, but the devastation of such a large city in such a wealthy and powerful country was evocative.

[198] HM Treasury, *The Stern Review on the Economics of Climate Change* (UK Treasury, 2006), see ch 2 above.

[199] See Commission (n 186), referring to 'the consequences of the on-going economic crisis', including 'the budgetary problems of Member States and businesses', 'concerns of households about the affordability of energy and of businesses with respect to competitiveness', 2.

[200] I would not want to suggest that the banal is unnecessary, eg the obligations to service air conditioning units under the Buildings Directive (n 176) Art 15.

[201] For a scathing account, see D Campbell, 'After Doha: What has Climate Change Policy Accomplished?' (2013) 25 *Journal of Environmental Law* 125.

7

Participation in Environmental Decision-Making in the Member States: Environmental Assessment

INTRODUCTION

A REMARKABLE CONSENSUS emerged towards the end of the twentieth century, that public participation is a necessary part of good environmental decision-making. Obligations on Member States to provide opportunities for public participation became routine in EU environmental law. As with many other things discussed in this book, however, whilst there is broad agreement that public participation is a 'good thing', what 'public participation' means in any particular case is ambiguous. It might involve simple consultation, or more ambitious shared problem solving; a relatively narrow group of participants, or a more open process. The Environmental Impact Assessment (EIA) and Strategic Environmental Assessment (SEA) Directives arguably mark the high point of participatory environmental governance,[1] particularly if that phrase is understood as including broad, lay, 'public' participation, as well as elite 'stakeholder' participation. This chapter will both explore the role of public participation in EU environmental law, and provide an outline of the substantive law on environmental assessment. Environmental assessment is about much more than public participation. It is also a systematic attempt to gather information on the environmental impact of a project, plan or programme, before authorisation or implementation. The tension between these two (lay and expert) modes of reasoning, and the challenges of successfully engaging lay publics, are of broad relevance to environmental decision-making.

A range of justifications and explanations are claimed for public participation, some of which are particularly attractive in the environmental sphere. The final section of this chapter turns to possible reasons for the enthusiasm for public participation in environmental decision-making, and to certain challenges. First,

---

[1] Directive 2011/92/EU on the assessment of the effects of certain public and private projects on the environment (codification) ('EIA Directive') [2012] OJ L26/2; Directive 2001/42/EC on the assessment of the effects of certain plans and programmes on the environment ('SEA Directive') [2001] OJ L197/30.

however, and before examining the law on environmental assessment, this chapter introduces the three closely connected and mutually supportive 'pillars' of public participation (access to environmental information, public participation in decision-making and access to justice), found in the United Nations Economic Commission for Europe (UNECE) Aarhus Convention.[2] This chapter focuses on the participatory demands made of the Member States by EU environmental law; chapter eight addresses the EU level.

THE AARHUS CONVENTION

The Aarhus Convention is well known to environmental lawyers, and I do not propose to rehearse its provisions at length.[3] Although public participation was an important part of EU environmental law before the Aarhus Convention, amendments of detail and perspective have been made in response to its demands. There has been an interesting symbiotic relationship between EU law and the Convention. The Convention was signed by all Member States and by the EU itself, creating a strong normative case for routinely embedding participation in environmental law; in turn EU law added a hard, enforceable edge to the sometimes equivocal language of the Convention.[4]

One of the most significant elements of the Aarhus Convention is its clear valuing of environmental interest groups as bearers of the environmental or public interest. The 'public' is defined as 'natural or legal persons, and, in accordance with national legislation or practice, their associations, organisations or groups'; the 'public concerned', which features in most of the harder participatory rights, is 'the public affected or likely to be affected by or having an interest in, the environmental decision-making ... non-governmental organizations promoting environmental protection and meeting any requirements under national law shall be deemed to have an interest'.[5]

The Aarhus Convention is built of three pillars. The first requires access to environmental information. The definition of 'environmental information' is broad, explicitly including, as well as information on air, water and soil, information inter alia on 'biological diversity and its components', energy, noise and radiation,

---

[2] United Nations Economic Commission for Europe (UNECE) *Convention on Access to Information, Public Participation in Decision-making and Access to Justice in Environmental Matters* (1998) 38 ILM 517 (1999).

[3] For a detailed outline of implementation measures, see European Commission implementation reports, most recently, 'Aarhus Convention Implementation Report' COM (2011) 208 final. For discussion, see M Lee and C Abbot, 'The Usual Suspects? Public Participation under the Aarhus Convention' (2003) 66 *Modern Law Review* 80.

[4] The Convention's Compliance Committee, unusually, can take submissions directly from the public, as well as from a party or the Secretariat, see UNECE, *Guidance Document on the Aarhus Convention Compliance Mechanism* (Geneva, United Nations, not dated). Its findings are not binding, but nevertheless have the potential to be influential.

[5] Aarhus Convention (n 2) Arts 2(4) and (5).

and measures such as environmental agreements and policies and legislation affecting or likely to affect the elements of the environment. It also recognises the importance of administrative techniques of environmental decision-making, including 'cost-benefit analysis and other economic analyses and assumptions used in environmental decision-making', allowing participants to look behind the official reasons for a decision.[6] The Access to Environmental Information Directive provides a basic right of access to environmental information held by a public authority in a Member State, without an interest having to be stated, subject to certain exceptions.[7] Environmental information is broadly defined, and has been generously interpreted by the Court of Justice.[8] The importance of information in environmental governance was discussed in chapter four, and the sorts of issues that arise in access schemes are explored in the next two chapters.

The middle pillar of the Aarhus Convention divides its obligations on participation into three stages. Article 6 addresses 'decisions on specific activities', which are either listed in the Annex (for example chemicals installations, intensive farming) or 'may have a significant effect' on the environment. Article 7 addresses 'plans, programmes and policies relating to the environment', and Article 8 'the preparation of executive regulations and/or generally applicable legally binding normative instruments'. The most detailed requirements on public participation, for example as to timing and information provision, are contained in Article 6. 'Due account' must be taken of the outcome of the public participation. The EIA Directive and the Industrial Emissions Directive (IED)[9] are the most important pieces of legislation for the implementation of Article 6 in the Member States, and whilst they have always had a participatory element, that participation is now framed around the Convention.

Article 7 requires 'appropriate practical and/or other provisions for the public to participate during the preparation of plans and programmes relating to the environment, within a transparent and fair framework, having provided the necessary information to the public'; provisions on timing and taking due account of results apply. The SEA Directive is the most significant EU legal instrument with respect to plans and programmes. Article 7 also imposes a weak obligation to 'endeavour' to provide opportunities to participate, 'to the extent appropriate' in respect of 'policies relating to the environment'. 'Due account' has to be taken of the outcome of the public participation. The distinction between 'plans and programmes' and 'policies' is not defined, but that does not seem to have caused

---

[6] Ibid Art 2(3). On the need for transparency within expert assessments, see ch 2.

[7] Directive 2003/04/EC on public access to environmental information [2003] OJ L41/26.

[8] Eg Case C-266/09 *Stichting Natuur en Milieu v College voor de Toelating van Gewasbeschermingsmiddelen en Biociden* [2010] ECR I-13119 on information on the levels of pesticides in food, submitted during authorisation processes.

[9] Directive 2010/75/EU on industrial emissions (integrated pollution prevention and control) (IED) [2010] OJ L334/17. See ch 5.

problems in practice.[10] Article 8 provides for rule-making ('executive regulations and/or generally applicable legally binding normative instruments') that 'may have a significant effect on the environment': 'each party shall strive to promote effective public participation at an appropriate stage, and while options are still open'. Time-frames sufficient for effective participation, publication of draft rules, and the opportunity to comment directly or through representative consultative bodies are required. Again, the Aarhus Convention specified that 'the result of the public participation shall be taken into account', but this time 'as far as possible'.

The third pillar of the Aarhus Convention, access to justice in environmental matters, is contained in Article 9. It is largely tied to the other provisions of the Convention, providing first for review of a refusal or failure to respond to a request for access to information, and for the challenge of substantive or procedural legality in any decision subject to Article 6 (decision-making on projects), and also 'where so provided for under national law' any decision subject to 'other relevant provisions' of the Convention. Article 9(3) provides for a more general, but less tightly defined, obligation on members to ensure that 'where they meet the criteria, if any, laid down in its national law', the public has access to administrative or judicial procedures to challenge acts and omissions by private and public bodies that contravene domestic law relating to the environment.

The Convention requires the provision of 'adequate and effective remedies, including injunctive relief as appropriate' and the process must be 'fair, equitable, timely and not prohibitively expensive'. Any of these requirements can cause difficulties; the costs of litigation are proving a knotty problem in some EU Member States, including the UK.[11] The broad approach taken in the Convention to standing before the courts is most important for current purposes. Many jurisdictions have traditionally only allowed standing before the courts to guard against harm to individual interests or rights. This approach rarely captures the collective and diffuse nature of environmental harms, which may well affect one person very severely, but often, as for example with chronic air pollution or loss of biodiversity, affect large numbers of people in ways that are not easily perceptible. There is insufficient space to deal with access to justice here,[12] but three points about standing should be noted. First, the EIA Directive implements the Aarhus

---

[10] J Jendroska, 'Public Participation in the Preparation of Plans and Programmes: Some Reflections on the Scope of Obligations under Article 7 of the Aarhus Convention' (2009) 6 *Journal of European Environmental and Planning Law* 495 points out that the distinction has not been taken to the Aarhus Compliance Committee; UN ECE, *The Aarhus Convention: An Implementation Guide* (Geneva, United Nations, 2013) describes these terms as having a 'common-sense ... meaning', 178.

[11] See the discussion of the costs system in Case C-260/11 *R* (*on the application of Edwards*) *v Environment Agency*, not yet reported in the ECR: 'the cost of proceedings must neither exceed the financial resources of the person concerned nor appear, in any event, to be objectively unreasonable' [40]. The case concerned the requirement in the IED (n 9) (implementing Art 6 of the Aarhus Convention), that access to justice should not be 'prohibitively expensive', Art 25; see also the EIA Directive (n 1) Art 11(4).

[12] M Lee, 'Access to Justice at EU Level in Environmental Law' (2012) papers.ssrn.com/sol3/papers.cfm?abstract_id=2062252.

Convention requirements on access to justice in respect of decisions subject to Article 6. The EIA Directive provides that any person having 'sufficient interest' or able to 'maintain the impairment of a right' can bring a challenge to the 'substantive or procedural legality' of decisions before the national courts. Environmental interest groups, in accordance with the Aarhus Convention, are explicitly capable of holding rights and interests.[13] Friends of the Earth in Germany, denied standing to challenge the authorisation of a power station, challenged the German law that required an individual right to be at stake. The ECJ emphasised the importance of environmental interest groups, in this 'branch of law', given that the public interest was at stake, 'and not merely the protection of the interests of individuals as such'.[14] The Member States must liberalise their standing regime, in respect of decisions covered by the EIA Directive,[15] to allow environmental interest groups access to courts.[16] Secondly, and by stark contrast, the Court of Justice, through a narrow interpretation of the Treaty requirement that a party be 'directly' or 'directly and individually' concerned by a challenged measure,[17] has resisted any expansion of standing to allow environmental interest groups to bring judicial review actions at the EU level. As a result, whilst challenges to environmental measures from industry are often possible,[18] direct challenges from a pro-environmental perspective are not.[19]

Thirdly, the Regulation implementing the Aarhus Convention at EU level, to which chapter eight returns, has introduced a right for environmental interest groups to request internal review by an EU institution or body of an 'administrative act under environmental law'.[20] The restriction of this internal review to measures of 'individual scope' has been almost overwhelming, given that many environmental measures are of general application. The General Court has ruled this restriction to be incompatible with the Aarhus Convention.[21] The Commission

---

[13] EIA Directive (n 1) Art 11; also IED, see n 11.

[14] Case C-115/09 *Bund fur Umwelt v Bezerksregierung Arnsburg* [2011] ECR-I 3673 [46].

[15] Or the IED (n 9). EU law has not attempted to implement Art 9(3) of the Convention (n 2), in the Member States, but the ECJ has required 'consistent interpretation' of national law, Case C-240/09 *Lesoochranárske Zoskupenie v Ministerstvo životného prostredia Slovenskej republiky (Slovakian Brown Bears)* [2011] ECR I-1255. For criticism of the Court's approach to interpretation, see JH Jans, 'Who is the Referee? Access to Justice in a Globalised Legal Order' (2011) papers.ssrn.com/sol3/papers.cfm?abstract_id=1834102.

[16] Case C-24/09 *Djurgården-Lilla Värtans Miljöskyddsförening v AB Fortum Värme amägt med Stockholms stad* [2010] ECR I-35 prohibits the restriction of the right to groups with at least 2000 members.

[17] Art 263 of the Treaty on the Functioning of the European Union (TFEU), see eg Case C-50/00P *Unión de Pequeños Agricultores v Council (UPA)* [2002] ECR I-6677.

[18] Especially following the changes made by the Lisbon Treaty, see Lee (n 12).

[19] For a review of the limitations of the preliminary reference procedure in this respect, see the Opinion of Jacobs AG in *UPA* (n 17).

[20] Regulation 1367/2006/EC on the application of the provisions of the Aarhus Convention on Access to Information, Public Participation in Decision-making and Access to Justice in Environmental Matters to Community institutions and bodies ('Aarhus Regulation') [2001] OJ L197/30, Art 10.

[21] Case T-338/08 *Stichting Natuur en Milieu and Pesticide Action Network Europe v European Commission* not yet published in ECR. The Commission has appealed, Joined Cases C-404 and 405/12 P.

has appealed, but if unsuccessful, more generous rights of internal review will need to be created to comply with the Aarhus Convention. Internal review can be very important, but does not necessarily guarantee access to courts.[22]

Something should be said in conclusion on reason-giving, which although not a specific principle of the Aarhus Convention, does feature in support of other rights, and also features elsewhere in this chapter and the next. Whilst there is obviously a danger that 'boiler plate' reasons will be attached to any decision simply with an eye to judicial review,[23] there is a range of broadly accepted benefits to an enforceable obligation to give reasons. Reason-giving could contribute to countering 'bias, self-interest, insufficient reflection or simply excess haste',[24] since it encourages attention to be paid to the factors that should influence a decision. The discussion below indicates how particular issues can be singled out as requiring explanation. We might also expect a level of commitment to reasons provided, which even in the absence of a strict system of precedent may apply in later cases.[25] A record of reasons also provides a means for challenging a decision, whether politically or judicially.[26] Reasons can even form part of the deliberative process, as participants respond to reasons. What sorts of reasons are seen as legitimate can be very significant, as discussed in chapter two, and also below. Open participation assumes the relevance of a range of reasons, rather than a prioritisation of particular expert technical criteria. Over the longer term, 'repeat players' may influence what sorts of factors can be seen as a good reason.[27]

ENVIRONMENTAL ASSESSMENT

Environmental assessment is an important part of efforts to 'integrate' environmental considerations into other policy areas, requiring the systematic evaluation of the environmental impacts of certain projects, plans and programmes, before they are authorised. Environmental assessment also has the potential to reduce the

---

[22] The Aarhus Regulation provides for the internal review decision to be appealed to the General Court (n 20) Art 12. Because it is addressed specifically to the environmental interest group, there will be no difficulty with standing, but that does not grant the environmental interest group standing to challenge the underlying substantive decision. The legality of the underlying decision may be raised indirectly in some cases, but that cannot be taken for granted.

[23] Note also the discussion of boiler plate reasons in SEA, A McLauchlan and E Joao, 'The Inherent Tensions Arising from Attempting to Carry Out Strategic Environmental Assessments on All Policies, Plans and Programmes' (2012) 36 *Environmental Impact Assessment Review* 23.

[24] F Schauer, 'Giving Reasons' (1995) 47 *Stanford Law Review* 633 reviews some of the rationales for reason-giving obligations, 657.

[25] Ibid, focusing primarily on courts and adjudication, sees the commitment model as the most significant issue.

[26] Parties should be able to decide 'with a full knowledge of the relevant facts, whether there is any point in applying to the courts', Case C-75/08 *R (on the application of Mellor) v Secretary of State for Communities and Local Government* [2009] ECR I-3799 [59].

[27] S Owens, 'Siting, Sustainable Development and Social Priorities' (2004) 7 *Journal of Risk Research* 101.

fragmentation of regulatory consideration of the environmental media, although it has been criticised for using a reductionist methodology that fails to recognise the 'richness and diversity' of ecological systems.[28] Opinion is divided on the success of environmental assessment as a technique of environmental protection.[29] The success of 'impact assessment' as a policy technique is, however, undisputed. From its earliest formal manifestation in the US National Environmental Policy Act of 1969, environmental assessment has become a widely used tool of environmental protection, and assessments of a range of other impacts, such as health and inequality, are also now required in domestic and international law.[30]

Environmental assessment legislation was first introduced in the EU in 1985, with the EIA Directive, requiring EIA of individual projects. Environmental assessment has been revised and expanded since then, including by the introduction of the SEA Directive, applying to broader plans and programmes. The Commission expects its Proposal for further changes to EIA to be agreed in 2014.[31] This section will begin with EIA, although much of the discussion is also relevant to SEA. The legal obligations in both cases are wholly procedural,[32] without any requirement for more environmentally benign decisions.[33] The line between substance and procedure, however, is not a clear one, and environmental assessment is often seen as 'a procedural tool that aims to achieve substantive outcomes'.[34] Through environmental assessment, public authorities are presented with environmental information from a range of sources, and have an opportunity to reflect on the impact of their decision; the developer of a particular project produces and receives environmental information, and similarly has an opportunity to reflect upon it: 'making not just bureaucracy, but also governments and firms "think"'.[35] We return to the substantive impacts of environmental assessment in the final part of this section.

---

[28] J Holder, 'The Prospects for Ecological Impact Assessment' in J Holder and D McGillivray (eds) *Taking Stock of Environmental Impact Assessment: Law, Policy and Practice* (Abingdon, Routledge-Cavendish, 2007) 257, giving also examples of isolated consideration of impacts on different species.

[29] D McGillivray and J Holder, 'Taking Stock' in Holder and McGillivray (n 28).

[30] On impact assessment of Commission proposals, see ch 2.

[31] European Commission, 'Proposal for a Directive Amending Directive 2011/92/EU on the Assessment of the Effects of Certain Public and Private Projects on the Environment' COM (2012) 628 final. At the Environment Council on 21 March 2013, 'member states pointed out the risk of increased administrative burden and additional costs. Many delegations considered it not to be appropriate to establish a very prescriptive system at EU level. Most delegations were in favour of flexibility left to member states to cater for specific situations and to adapt to the existing provisions', Press Release 7640/13.

[32] SEA Directive (n 1) provides that 'this Directive is of a procedural nature', Recital 9.

[33] For criticism of 'aimless' environmental assessment, see W Howarth, 'Substance and Procedure in Strategic Environmental Assessment and the Water Framework Directive' in Holder and McGillivray (n 28).

[34] R Therivel, 'The Use of Sustainability Appraisal by English Planning Inspectors and Judges' (2013) 38 *Environmental Impact Assessment Review* 26, 26. See also Case C-474/10 *Department of the Environment for Northern Ireland v Seaport (NI) Ltd* not yet reported in the ECR [27] (Bot AG).

[35] McGillivray and Holder (n 29) 5, quoting S Taylor, 'Making Bureaucracies Think: The Environmental Impact Assessment Strategy of Administrative Reform' (Stanford, Stanford University Press, 1984).

Environmental Impact Assessment

The EIA Directive requires the environmental effects of projects likely to have significant effects on the environment to be assessed before authorisation. Projects listed in Annex I, (mainly major industrial and infrastructure developments), are always subject to environmental assessment; projects listed in Annex II (smaller industrial and infrastructure developments, as well as other activities) must be assessed if the Member State determines that they are 'likely to have significant effects on the environment by virtue, *inter alia*, of their nature, size or location'.[36] This leaves the Member States considerable discretion over Annex II projects, but the Court polices that discretion carefully.[37] The Member States are subject to an 'unequivocal obligation' to require EIA of projects likely to have a significant effect on the environment;[38] in particular, entire categories of project cannot be exempted in advance, unless the category as a whole is not likely to have significant environmental effects,[39] and EIA cannot be avoided by dividing projects into parcels that individually fall below the 'significant effects' threshold.[40] Furthermore, the Court has interpreted the same phrase, 'likely to have significant effects', in the Habitats Directive in accordance with the precautionary principle, requiring an assessment 'if it cannot be excluded, on the basis of objective information, that it will have a significant effect'.[41] The need for and scope of the EIA is not subject to any obligation of consultation, limiting the opportunity for outsiders to influence the shape of the assessment.[42] The Commission has not proposed that public participation be introduced at this stage, although a more formal 'scoping' stage to individual EIAs would include consultation of interested (for example environmental) authorities.[43] Any decision not to subject an Annex II project to EIA 'is made available to the public'.[44] The Court has held that an interested party is entitled to the reasons, relevant information and documents on request;[45] the Commission has proposed the introduction of a legislative obligation to publish a reasoned decision on whether an environmental assessment is necessary.[46]

---

[36] EIA Directive (n 1) Art 4. Annex III provides 'screening criteria'.

[37] A Ryall, *Effective Judicial Protection and the Environmental Impact Assessment Directive in Ireland* (Oxford, Hart Publishing, 2009) ch 4.

[38] Case C-431/92 *Commission v Germany* [1995] ECR I-2189 [39].

[39] Case C-72/95 *Aanemersebedrijf PK Kraaijeveld BV v Gedeputeerde Staten van Zuid-Holland (Dutch Dykes)* [1996] ECR I-5403; see Ryall (n 37).

[40] Case C-392/96 *Commission v Ireland* [1999] ECR I-5901.

[41] Case C-127/02 *Landelijke Vereniging tot Behoud van de Waddenzee v Staatssecretaris van Landbouw, Natuurbeheer en Visserij (Waddenzee Cockle Fishers)* [2004] ECR I-7405 [41] and [45]; Directive 1992/43/EC on the conservation of natural habitats and of wild fauna and flora ('Habitats Directive') [1992] OJ L206/7. See ch 1.

[42] The Commission (n 31), proposes that developers of projects listed in Annex II should be required to provide information for a more thorough screening exercise, proposed new Annex IIA.

[43] Commission, ibid proposed new Art 5(2).

[44] EIA Directive (n 1) Art 4(4).

[45] C-75/08 *Mellor* (n 26).

[46] Commission (n 31) proposed new Art 4(5).

The EIA 'shall identify, describe and assess in an appropriate manner ... the direct and indirect effects of a project' on '(a) human beings, fauna and flora; (b) soil, water, air, climate and the landscape; (c) material assets and the cultural heritage; (d) the interaction between the factors referred to in points (a), (b) and (c).'[47] Proposed amendments to this provision would explicitly emphasise biodiversity and climate change, responding to concern that they have not been adequately considered in EIA to date.[48] The EIA report must at least include a description of the project and proposed mitigation measures (the 'measures envisaged in order to avoid, reduce and, if possible, remedy significant adverse effects'); the data required to identify and assess the main effects; an outline of 'the main alternatives studied by the developer and an indication of the main reasons for his choice'.[49]

The developer is required to provide the primary information for the EIA.[50] As discussed elsewhere in this book, the information available to regulated parties can be crucial. Further, the engagement by the developer at an early stage with the environmental implications of the project (knowing that there will be scrutiny) creates potential for improved outcomes, even for 'cultural change' as the developer becomes more ecologically aware.[51] But there are real concerns that a process of information provision largely in the hands of a developer will be subject to manipulation, and Jane Holder explores the ways in which developers use their environmental statements as presentational tools, putting a positive gloss on their projects.[52] The presentation of information is important if it is to be properly scrutinised: 'a disparate collection of documents produced by parties other than the developer and traceable only by a person with a good deal of energy and persistence' is not adequate according to the UK courts.[53] The Directive also requires a non-technical summary of the relevant information. Whilst some effort to engage with the lay public is necessary if information is to be genuinely accessible, the developer is not necessarily the best person to control the non-technical summary. The non-technical summary provided by those proposing a wind farm on the Isle of Lewis, for example, 'adopted the language of environmental impact assessment ("significance", "impact", "fragility") in describing the *socio-economic* impacts of the project but with a positive spin', emphasising job creation and economic benefits.[54]

In an effort to improve the quality of the information provided by developers, the Commission has proposed that their information (to be called the environmental report) is either prepared by 'accredited and technically competent experts'

[47] EIA Directive (n 1) Art 3.
[48] Commission (n 31), proposed new Art 5; European Commission, *Guidance on Integrating Climate Change and Biodiversity into Environmental Impact Assessment* (2013).
[49] EIA Directive (n 1) Art 5.
[50] Ibid Art 5, Annex IV.
[51] J Holder, *Environmental Assessment: The Regulation of Decision-Making* (Oxford, Oxford University Press, 2004), discussed below.
[52] Ibid.
[53] *Berkeley v Secretary of State for the Environment* [2001] 2 AC 603, 617.
[54] Holder (n 28) 273.

or verified by 'accredited and technically competent experts and/or committees of national experts', in order to 'guarantee the completeness and sufficient quality of the environmental reports'.[55] Environmental consultants are already frequently responsible for preparing reports on behalf of developers, but the difference here is the subjection of those consultants to some sort of national accreditation scheme. The possibility that specialist 'committees' will verify the reports is also interesting. Some Member States do have an expert public body tasked with evaluating the quality of the information provided in environmental assessment, but extending that has not found favour in the past.[56] Consistent, detailed and expert scrutiny of the information provided by developers, by a publicly accountable body, would be a major achievement, especially in the current economically pressed environment.

Outsiders are given the 'opportunity to express their opinion' on the information provided by the developer and the application for development consent. First, this applies to 'authorities likely to be concerned by the project by reason of their specific environmental responsibilities', for example nature conservation or environmental agencies,[57] allowing expert engagement with the information provided.[58] Secondly, the 'public' is informed of the request for development consent, and given details about the decision-making procedure.[59] And thirdly, the 'public concerned'[60] is given 'early and effective opportunities to participate', and is 'entitled to express comments and opinions when all options are open' and before the decision is taken. The information provided by the developer and the reports of the 'authorities likely to be concerned' are 'made available'.[61] Member States have considerable discretion in respect of the 'detailed arrangements' for public participation, which could be very ambitious, or a simple opportunity to provide written comments.[62] The Court has even confirmed the possibility of levying a charge for participation, subject to the proviso that this does not create 'an obstacle to the exercise of the rights of participation'.[63] The EIA Directive also provides for transboundary participation (as does the SEA Directive).[64]

All of the information gathered during the EIA, including the results of the consultations, 'shall be taken into consideration' in the decision.[65] Both public

---

[55] Commission (n 31), proposed new Art 5(3).

[56] See eg, *The Government's Response to the Royal Commission's Twenty-third Report on Environmental Planning* (2003) Cm 5887, 12.

[57] EIA Directive (n 1) Art 6(1).

[58] See ch 4 on the importance of expert scrutiny.

[59] EIA Directive (n 1) Art 6(2).

[60] Defined broadly: those 'affected or likely to be affected' or having 'an interest in' the procedures; environmental interest groups are 'deemed to have an interest', ibid Art 1(2)(e).

[61] Ibid Art 6(4).

[62] Commission (n 31) proposes minimum and maximum time limits.

[63] C-216/05 *Commission v Ireland* [2006] ECR I-10787 [33]. See Ryall (n 37) 148–53. In this case, fees of €45 were not found to constitute such an obstacle.

[64] Ibid Art 7; SEA Directive (n 1) Art 7. R Macrory and S Turner, 'Participatory Rights, Transboundary Environmental Governance and EC Law' (2002) 39 *Common Market Law Review* 489.

[65] EIA Directive (n 1) Art 8.

participation and environmental protection feature explicitly in the reason-giving obligation: the decision and 'the main reasons and considerations on which the decision is based, including information about the public participation process' and 'a description, where necessary, of the main measures to avoid, reduce and, if possible, offset the major adverse effects' are to be made available to the public.[66]

The EIA Directive is undoubtedly in part a 'technical-rational' aid to decision-making,[67] and specialised expertise, including information from the developer and the consultation of public bodies with an interest in the environment, features highly. Environmental assessment does not necessarily demand *public* participation. The Habitats Directive for example, requires the 'appropriate assessment' of a plan or project likely to have a significant effect on a site listed for nature conservation purposes under the Directive, but focuses on technocentric information gathering. Public participation is not mandatory, simply subject to the bare requirement that 'the opinion of the general public' be obtained 'if appropriate'.[68] But the participation of lay publics clearly is important in the EIA Directive. Discussions of public participation frequently distinguish between 'substance' and 'process' rationales for participation. This is explored below, but essentially, participation may be an inherent (democratic) good, or a way to improve decisions. Both rationales feature in the EIA Directive. Broader participation by the lay public can be part of an information provision model; information on local priorities and values, for example, provides decision-making resources. The opportunity for scrutiny and review, and for the contestation of information, is crucial, not just to respond to deliberate 'spin' (or worse), but also to the likelihood that the professionals in the environmental assessment process share values and understandings, and that these might exclude some local or ecological perspectives.[69]

In a theme that is familiar elsewhere in this book, the capacity of 'public' participation truly to match the participation of regulated parties, here the developers, is questionable.[70] The highly technical nature of environmental assessment may tend to exclude non-specialists, who may feel unable to contribute to a technical debate. Contributions not framed in the terms of that technical debate may in turn not resonate very loudly. The explicit empowerment of environmental interest groups in the EIA Directive (following the Aarhus Convention in this respect) is significant, potentially providing competing expert contributions.

---

[66] Ibid Art 9(1)(c). Enhanced reason-giving obligations are proposed by the Commission (n 31), in proposed new Art 8.

[67] S Jay et al, 'Environmental Impact Assessment: Retrospect and Prospect' (2007) 27 *Environmental Impact Assessment Review* 287; J Petts, 'Environmental Impact Assessment—Overview of Purpose and Process' in J Petts (ed), *Handbook of Environmental Impact Assessment* (Oxford, Blackwell Science, 1999); S Owens, T Rayner and O Bina, 'New Agendas for Appraisal: Reflections on Theory, Practice, and Research' (2004) 36 *Environment and Planning A* 1943.

[68] Habitats Directive (n 41).

[69] C O'Faircheallsigh, 'Public Participation and Environmental Impact Assessment: Purposes, Implications and Lessons for Public Policy Making' (2010) 30 *Environmental Impact Assessment Review* 19. See also ch 2.

[70] See the case studies provided by Holder (n 51).

Again though, there are questions around the capacity of environmental interest groups to fill this role adequately; in particular, lack of resources is a persistent barrier.[71] The public body responsible for authorising (or not) the project plays a vital scrutiny role. Whether all of these bodies have the resources (including time and expertise) to perform this role adequately every time is open to question; the Commission's proposal, mentioned above, to introduce additional expert scrutiny has the potential to strengthen public scrutiny, but will only do so if those experts are properly resourced.[72]

But in any event, the ideal of rational, technical decision-making leading to the 'best' result in the public interest is, as discussed in chapter two, subject to criticism. EIA could, in the words of the English House of Lords, also be about providing an 'inclusive and democratic procedure ... in which the public, however misguided or wrongheaded its views may be, is given an opportunity to express its opinion on the environmental issues'.[73] EIA is not a simple linear process in which facts predate and inform policy, there is instead an 'interweaving of facts and values' in environmental assessment.[74] The evolving recitals to the EIA Directive suggest increasing concern with process. The recitals to the initial Directive and the 1997 amendments made very little of public participation, which was apparently simply an opportunity to obtain extra information; the 2003 amendments, with their express aim of implementing the Aarhus Convention and also in line with the focus on public participation around the turn of the century, shift the focus. But just as value-free decision-making is questioned, so the role of publics is not straightforward or cost-free. And actually creating institutions and situations in which meaningful public participation or genuine deliberation can take place is challenging.[75] The costs do not just fall on public authority and developer. There may be considerable immediate costs to participating individuals (time, learning about the issues for example), whilst any benefits are delayed and diffused.[76]

The tension between a technical approach to environmental assessment and adequate lay participation is not addressed by the legislation. Even in the strong stance of the English House of Lords, cited above, the language of 'misguided' and 'wrongheaded' suggests a struggle for those who do not express themselves in the terms of the dominant framework. Jane Holder concludes that 'the emphasis upon modelling and quantitative information and the objectification of information in developers' environmental statements mean that a range of values and viewpoints are not fully represented by the environmental assessment process'.[77]

---

[71] See the discussion of Ballindalloch Muir in O Hamlyn, 'Reassessing Environmental Impact Assessment: A Role for Wild Law?' (2011) 23 *Environmental Law and Management* 7. Ch 8 returns to the role of environmental interest groups.

[72] Commission (n 31).

[73] *Berkeley* (n 53) 15 (Lord Hoffmann).

[74] Owens et al (n 67) 1946.

[75] G Smith, *Deliberative Democracy and the Environment* (London, Routledge, 2003).

[76] Y Rydin and M Pennington, 'Public Participation and Local Environmental Planning: The Collective Action Problem and the Potential of Social Capital' (2000) 5 *Local Environment* 153.

[77] Holder (n 51) 184.

Strategic Environmental Assessment

There are serious limitations to assessing the environmental impact of projects, and allowing public participation, only after overall needs and priorities have been determined. The SEA Directive is designed to fill this gap, by requiring the environmental assessment at the earlier stage of preparing plans and programmes.[78] A plan or programme[79] covered by the SEA Directive is one that is adopted or prepared by an 'authority', and 'required by legislation, regulation or administrative provisions'.[80] Taking a purposive approach to the objective of achieving a high level of environmental protection, the Court has interpreted 'required' to mean that plans and programmes must be *regulated* by legislation, regulation or administrative provisions, even if not mandatory.[81] Planning obligations imposed on the Member States throughout EU environmental law, for example in the Water Framework Directive,[82] will in many cases fall under the SEA Directive.[83] The precise scope of 'authority' is not entirely clear,[84] but it is thought to apply to, for example, private water companies making long-term plans with significant environmental implications.[85]

Environmental assessment is required of plans and programmes in three categories: plans and programmes prepared for particular sectors such as agriculture or transport if they 'set the framework for' projects subject to EIA; plans or programmes that are subject to assessment under the Habitats Directive 'in view of the likely effect on sites';[86] other plans and programmes 'likely to have significant environmental effects' and 'which set the framework for future development consent of projects'.[87] As with EIA, national discretion for

---

[78] SEA Directive (n 1). The Directive refers to the adoption or modification of plans or programmes, and applies to repeal, Case C-567/10 *Inter-Environnement Bruxelles ASBL v Brussels-Capital Region* not yet reported in the ECR.

[79] The terms are not defined. Kokott AG prefers a broad approach to what constitutes a plan or programme, emphasising the environmental effects, Joined Cases C-105/09 and C-110/09 *Terre Wallonne ASBL v Région Wallonne* [2010] ECR I-5611 [29]–[35].

[80] SEA Directive (n 1) Art 2(a).

[81] *Inter-Environnement Bruxelles* (n 78) [28]–[32].

[82] Directive 2000/60/EC establishing a framework for the Community action in the field of water policy ('Water Framework Directive') [2000] OJ L 327/1, see ch 4.

[83] *Terre Wallone* (n 79) confirms that an 'action programme' adopted pursuant to Art 5(1) Directive 91/676/EEC concerning the protection of waters against pollution caused by nitrates from agricultural sources [1991] OJ L375/1, is subject to SEA.

[84] This is the same language as in the Aarhus Convention, Jendroska (n 10); UNECE (n 10) 178.

[85] This is consistent with the purposive approach taken by the Court, but European Commission, 'Implementation of Directive 2001/42 on the Assessment of the Effects of Certain Plans and Programmes on the Environment' (undated) also refers to C-188/89 *Foster v British Gas* [1990] ECR I-3313 to look beyond legal form, ec.europa.eu/environment/eia/pdf/030923_sea_guidance.pdf [3.12].

[86] Habitats Directive (n 41). The Court has held that this applies unless it 'can be excluded, on the basis of objective information, that that plan or project will have a significant effect on the site concerned', Case C-177/11 *Sillogos Ellinon Poleodomon kai Khorotakton v Ipourgos Perivallontos, Khorotaxias kai Dimosion Ergon*, not yet reported in the ECR [24].

[87] SEA Directive (n 1) Art 3.

this third category is restricted by the overriding requirement to carry out an assessment if the plan or programme is likely to have significant environmental effects.[88] Kokott AG has said that 'framework' is a 'very broad concept' that is to be 'construed flexibly'.[89]

A decision not to undertake an environmental assessment must be reasoned and made public.[90] If SEA is required, an 'environmental report' must be produced, in which 'the likely significant effects on the environment' of implementing the plan or programme have to be 'identified, described and evaluated'.[91] The minimum prescribed contents of the report include a non-technical summary and a requirement to consider 'reasonable alternatives'.[92] The report must include information 'that may reasonably be required taking into account current knowledge and methods of assessment', but does not demand an ambitious approach to information generation.[93]

As with EIA, those authorities which 'by reason of their specific environmental responsibilities are likely to be concerned' are consulted.[94] In this case they are consulted not only on the contents of the report, but also on the need for SEA, and its 'scope and level of detail'.[95] This earlier intervention provides greater opportunity to shape the approach to environmental assessment. The proponent of the plan is also often the public authority that prepares the SEA, and so the consultation of authorities with 'specific environmental responsibilities and proven skills'[96] is an important opportunity for alternative issues to be raised. There is no need to set up a special body for the purpose of consultation, but the consultee must have 'real autonomy', with 'administrative and human resources of its own' so that it is able to provide an 'objective opinion'.[97] The SEA Directive also provides for wider public consultation, including transboundary participation, after preparation of the environmental report. Both the draft plan or programme and the environmental report are made available to the public,[98] which is to be given 'an early and effective opportunity within appropriate time frames to express their opinion'.[99]

The environmental assessment of projects is often forced to be reactive to developers' proposals, with public participants reduced to the role of objectors.

[88] Case C-295/10 *Valčiukienė v Pakruojo Rajono Savivaldybė* [2011] ECR I-8819 [46].
[89] *Terre Wallone* (n 79) [64], [65].
[90] SEA Directive (n 1) Art 3(7).
[91] Ibid Art 5.
[92] Ibid Annex I. Guidance has been issued on climate change and biodiversity, as for EIA (n 48), European Commission, 'Guidance on Integrating Climate Change and Biodiversity into Strategic Environmental Assessment' (2013).
[93] SEA Directive, ibid, Art 5.
[94] Ibid Art 6(3).
[95] Ibid Art 5(4). Some Member States do consult on scoping, European Commission, 'Report on the Application and Effectiveness of the Directive on SEA' COM (2009) 469 final.
[96] *Seaport* (n 34) [34].
[97] Ibid [42].
[98] SEA Directive (n 1) Art 6.
[99] Ibid Art 6(2). 'Appropriate time frames' can be determined on a case by case basis, *Seaport* (n 34).

Done well, earlier environmental assessment can be more proactive, and allow more constructive engagement. A broader range of issues arises at the earlier stage, making the obligation to consider alternatives potentially much more powerful,[100] and it is more likely to be feasible to seek to reduce or eliminate negative impacts.[101] The environmental report and the opinions expressed 'shall be taken into account during the preparation of the plan or programme'.[102] This obligation is reinforced by the requirement for a statement of reasons, including not only a summary of how the environmental report and the results of consultations have been taken into account, but also a summary of how environmental considerations have been 'integrated' into the plan or programme.[103] This goes beyond a simple instruction to take environmental considerations into account. This framing of reason-giving should not however be allowed to sideline public concern on non-environmental issues. Public participation on narrow environmental issues only, excluding social or economic issues, would be a restricted and potentially frustrating exercise, even more so at the strategic level than at the project stage: 'the very nature of those decisions is invariably more qualitative, less detailed and with higher levels of uncertainty and a wider range of options available … and more political than rational'.[104] A broad scope for public participation is important.

There are clear potential benefits to earlier participation (and earlier assessment of environmental impacts), but it does also throw up some new challenges. The complexity of public participation increases as the scale of the decision expands. In particular, the non-specialist public will rarely be easily engaged by large-scale debates. Strategy can seem rather abstract, whilst the actual distributional effects only become clear at the stage of concrete projects. The intensity of interests increases as specific outcomes (the waste incinerator, the airport extension) get closer. The effect of plans and programmes on individual interests, whilst important, is not readily perceived; nor is it obvious to individuals what they can contribute. Domination by organised interest groups is to some extent inevitable, but has a major impact on what can be claimed for public participation. In particular, there is nothing inherently more 'democratic' about public participation in these circumstances. The Directive tries to prevent authorities treating public participation as a passive exercise.[105] As in the Aarhus Convention, Member

---

[100] This is 'one of the few issues' where the Member States report implementation problems, European Commission, 'Study Concerning the Report on the Application and Effectiveness of the SEA Directive (2001/42/EC): Final Report' (2009, study prepared by Cowi) 11.

[101] W Sheate, 'The EC Directive on Strategic Environmental Assessment: A Much-Needed Boost for Environmental Integration' (2003) *European Environmental Law Review* 331.

[102] SEA Directive (n 1) Art 8.

[103] Ibid Art 9.

[104] W Sheate, 'Purposes, Paradigms and Pressure Groups: Accountability and Sustainability in EU Environmental Assessment, 1985–2010' (2012) 33 *Environmental Impact Assessment Review* 91, 92.

[105] C Scott, 'Governmentality and Strategic Environmental Assessment: Challenging the SEA/Good Governance Nexus' (2011) 13 *Journal of Environmental Assessment Policy and Management* 67 identifies poor practice, especially failure to provide information on how to contribute to decision-making, 87.

States are expected to identify the 'public' for participation in particular cases, 'including relevant non-governmental organisations, such as those promoting environmental protection'.[106] This raises inevitable concerns about the potential for arbitrary or self-interested selection of the 'public'. It does however recognise that some effort should be made to ensure inclusion.

The Success of Environmental Assessment?

Identifying the purposes of environmental assessment, the criteria against which its success should be judged, is contentious.[107] Conclusions look very different depending on whether our criterion for success is democratic decision-making, speedy infrastructure development, or environmental quality, and different participants in the process have different objectives.[108] There is some consensus that environmental assessment has substantive environmental aims (whether or not it also has democracy enhancing aims). The expressed objective of the SEA Directive is to 'provide for a high level of protection of the environment and to contribute to the integration of environmental considerations ... with a view to promoting sustainable development'.[109] This is reflected in the ECJ's approach to a programme that had incorrectly been adopted without SEA. The Court confirmed that generally, if a plan or programme is adopted without SEA, national courts must suspend or annul the plan or programme.[110] But in this case, the contested Wallonian action programme on nitrates in water would be significantly better for the environment than removing it: 'given the existence of an overriding consideration relating to the protection of the environment', the national court may 'exceptionally' maintain certain effects of an annulled plan.[111]

Evaluating the substantive (environmental) success of environmental assessment is extremely difficult.[112] Not only are we comparing against a hypothetical,

---

[106]   SEA Directive (n 1) Art 6(4).

[107]   M Cashmore et al, 'The Interminable Issue of Effectiveness: Substantive Purposes, Outcomes and Research Challenges in the Advancement of Environmental Impact Assessment Theory' (2004) *Impact Assessment and Project Appraisal* 295; Jay et al (n 67).

[108]   The benefits identified by the Member States are resource saving through better integration of environmental issues, better project design and increased public acceptability of projects, GHK, *Collection of Information and Data to Support the Impact Assessment Study of the Review of the EIA Directive* (2010).

[109]   SEA Directive (n 1) Art 1.

[110]   Case C-41/11 *Inter-Environnement Wallonie ASBL and Terre Wallonne v Region Wallonne* not yet reported in the ECR [46]; by analogy with the EIA Directive, Case C-201/02 *R (on the application of Wells) v Secretary of State for Transport, Local Government and the Regions* [2004] ECR I-723.

[111]   Ibid [57], [58]. 'Economic grounds' would not constitute such an overriding consideration, ibid. On the broader implications of this decision, see T Lock, 'Are There Exceptions to a Member State's Duty to Comply with the Requirements of a Directive?' (2013) 50 *Common Market Law Review* 217.

[112]   M Cashmore, 'The Role of Science in Environmental Impact Assessment: Process and Procedure versus Purpose in the Development of Theory' (2004) 24 *Environmental Impact Assessment Review* 403 is critical of the relative lack of attention to this.

that is what would have happened in the absence of assessment, but the effects of environmental assessment are likely to be subtle and complex.[113] There is also sometimes legitimate disagreement about what environmental protection requires in any particular case, given the trade-offs and uncertainties involved in environmental protection. Nor should we think that substantive effects are invariably positive in an environmental sense. Jane Holder argues that EIA has 'important substantive consequences', but highlights the ability of EIA 'to advance and legitimise a particular project on a particular site'.[114]

There does however seem to be some agreement that there are modest environmental benefits to environmental assessment, in the sense of environmental information being taken into account in the decision-making process.[115] There may also be more subtle, longer term benefits of environmental education.[116] 'Learning' can imply a routine sense of the generation and gathering of information. Even in this routine sense, information is not easy, but needs active governance. Daniel Farber describes as a 'paradox' the creation of huge amounts of information, knowledge and expertise, only for it to then be buried 'in inaccessible archives'.[117] There is no legal obligation to maintain the information gathered during an environmental assessment exercise, to ensure that it is accessible and searchable, to revisit and review the approach taken in any particular case. Learning could also be seen as more radically transformative. In this respect, Jane Holder distinguishes between 'cultural' and 'information' approaches to environmental assessment: whether environmental assessment is about providing decision-makers with all relevant information, or whether it is about inspiring ecological values among those taking decisions, including developers.[118] However we view environmental learning, the ability to adapt is important. The SEA Directive includes an obligation to monitor the significance of the environmental effects of the implementation of a plan or programme,[119] and the Commission has proposed introducing such an obligation to the EIA Directive.[120] Not only does this allow for 'appropriate remedial action' to be taken, as suggested by the SEA Directive,[121] but is also crucial to any ideal that regulation should 'learn' from experience. SEA follow up seems, however, to be fairly poor in practice.[122]

---

[113] Jay et al (n 67).

[114] Holder (n 51) 8.

[115] Jay et al (n 67) review the literature. C Jones et al, 'Environmental Assessment: Dominant or Dormant' in Holder and McGillivray (n 28) review the literature on both EIA and SEA.

[116] Jay et al, ibid.

[117] D Farber, 'Bringing Environmental Assessment into the Digital Age' in Holder and McGillivray (n 28) 219.

[118] Holder (n 51) 22.

[119] SEA Directive (n 1) Art 10.

[120] Commission (n 31), specifically 'to monitor the significant adverse environmetnal effects, in order to assess the implementation and the expected effectiveness of mitigation and compensation measures, and to identify any unforeseeable adverse effects', proposed new Art 8(2).

[121] SEA Directive (n 1) Art 10.

[122] M Gachechiladze-Bozhesku and TB Fischer, 'Benefits of and Barriers to SEA Follow up—Theory and Practice' (2012) 34 *Environmental Impact Assessment Review* 22.

Environmental assessment provides one of the most important legislative frameworks for public participation in environmental decision-making. A legal command to allow for public participation does not, however, tell us much about what public participation will consist of, or what it might contribute to the decision.[123] The context within which the legislative command sits in respect of local consultation around nationally significant (assessed by size) windfarms in the UK, amounts to a legal and policy background that leaves relatively little for local participation to latch on to.[124] Many of the most controversial issues have been addressed: noise, aesthetics, the impact on protected sites, the existence of alternative sites, are all unlikely to influence the decision, since the higher level policy claims to have already taken these issues into account.[125] Providing the trappings of engagement, when the most important decisions have already been taken, is problematic and may undermine trust in consultation processes. A partial solution to the potential dislocation in EIA between the issues at stake and the issues open for consideration may be found in earlier public participation during SEA. However, aside from any other difficulties, the constituency changes between SEA (where the lay public is unlikely to take part) and EIA (where local publics may well be interested). The theoretical opportunity to participate at the strategic stage does not necessarily compensate for lack of influence at the project stage.

Adequate institutional responses to this dilemma are not obvious. Many of the people reading this book are likely to have some sympathy for the claim that climate change infrastructure is indeed necessary, and urgent, although we also know very well that many projects subject to environmental assessment are less attractive. Nevertheless, it must be legitimate to make decisions in the national or global interest; but equally it is legitimate for people to seek to shape their local environment. One, far from adequate response to this dilemma is to make it clear to those invited to participate locally precisely what is open to debate, and to explain why that is the case. The credibility of the explanation is likely to depend on more general credibility in pursuing climate change objectives, or the other broader global or national objectives.[126]

EXPLAINING PARTICIPATION

There are diverse and complex motivations and rationales for public participation in environmental decision-making. The first edition of this book looked at two main categories of rationale for public participation, that is 'substantive'

---

[123] Nor does it tell us anything about the equally important possibility of protest in the absence of legal protection, or in contravention of the law.

[124] M Lee et al, 'Public Participation and Climate Change Infrastructure' (2013) 25 *Journal of Environmental Law* 33.

[125] It is not quite straightforward, ibid. There is possibly adequate wriggle room to satisfy the legalistic point that 'all options' have to be open, but that is hardly the point.

[126] Lee et al, ibid.

and 'process' rationales (in the EU, often called 'input' and 'output' legitimacy, to which we return in the next chapter). This simplified categorisation is a useful way of thinking about public participation. In broad outline, substantive rationales make a link between participation and improved outcomes, so that participation contributes to the quality and substance of a decision. Process rationales see public participation as an inherently beneficial (indeed necessary) contribution to democracy; citizens have a right to be involved in decisions that shape their world. Each of these rationales is multifaceted, and the line between them is blurred. So for example, because environmental decision-making is political as well as technical, substantively good decisions (and deciding what is 'good'), require non-expert contributions. Similarly, democracy itself can be understood as a substantive problem-solving exercise.[127]

The next chapter examines the call on participation at the EU level, including its role in responding to the EU's 'democratic deficit'. The prospect of enhancing the legitimacy of EU environmental legislation through *national* participation is also appealing to the EU institutions. National participatory mechanisms can, however, only partially reverberate at EU level. National discussion of policies that are subsequently developed at EU level can only tenuously be reflected in a debate between 28 Member States and the EU institutions. And domestic participation in the implementation of EU law takes place after crucial policy decisions have been taken, when the national or local body may be subject to binding legal obligations. The EU does not have a monopoly on 'democratic deficits', however. The relationship between green political thought and democratic traditions is also complicated, albeit more abstract (the EU exists, but there is no 'green state'). Elements of ecological thought query whether the environmental crisis is too grave to leave to democracy, certainly liberal democracy.[128] We sometimes hear calls for 'strong leadership', or for a wartime footing, to respond to climate change; this is not necessarily authoritarian (and leadership may well be a crucial part of collective action), but has the potential to nod in that direction. But even if the authoritarian streak of green politics has been exaggerated,[129] the sometimes tense relationship between representative democracy and environmentalism has led to an emphasis on various forms of participatory or deliberative democracy. There should be no expectation that public participation will necessarily lead to green outcomes, but deliberation and participation are an important way to allow the expression of green values alongside other priorities.[130] This approach is also able to acknowledge the plurality of values within what can only loosely be called 'the' environmental movement.[131]

---

[127] JS Dryzek, *The Politics of the Earth: Environmental Discourses* (Oxford, Oxford University Press, 2005).

[128] See the discussion in A Dobson, *Green Political Thought* (London, Routledge, 2000) 114–24.

[129] Dobson, ibid, warns against too hasty a link between green thought and authoritarianism, 114–24.

[130] Eg Smith (n 75).

[131] Ibid.

Another dimension to the green democratic deficit is the very common delegation of environmental decision-making to administrative bodies, including environmental agencies, with at best only indirect and weak links to electoral processes. The delegation is most commonly justified by the need for technical and scientific expertise in environmental decision-making. However, as discussed especially in chapter two above, environmental decisions are not simply technical questions, but involve political value judgments and divided interests. The most common response to the distance between administrative decision-making and the electorate is to turn to participatory mechanisms, including transparency, consultation and review.[132] Even when decisions are the responsibility of elected officials, including many decisions involving EIA in the UK,[133] broader perspectives and alternative values offered by participating outsiders can temper the expert input to representative decision-making, and the influence of economic actors.

The approach to public participation that seeks improved substantive results, at its most basic aims simply to increase the information available to decision-makers. Public participation provides otherwise dispersed expertise, including local knowledge, and a wider range of perspectives, including environmental perspectives. This could involve quite minimal levels of consultation, with little interaction between participants and decision-maker. An attempt jointly to resolve controversial problems in the public interest could go beyond gathering information on technical matters and pre-formed interests, to a more deliberative and collective approach.[134] More ambitious hopes for environmental assessment include the development of a potentially transformative approach, through a cultural model of ecological learning.[135] Environmental education and awareness-raising are also said to contribute to environmental citizenship, an environmental reflection of the argument that deliberative democracy more generally raises democratic and civic awareness.[136] This too could be potentially transformative in the long term, and embraced by the 'cultural' understanding of environmental assessment.[137]

The discussion so far implies an acknowledgement that the responsible authority does not have all the answers. A different perspective on substantive rationales for public participation concentrates on the implementation of decisions. Public involvement may aim to enhance public acceptance of a decision that is considered self-evidently necessary, either reducing conflict in infrastructure development (such as wind energy projects), or persuading individuals to change

---

[132] Although see the discussion of socio-economic analysis in ch 9.
[133] Decisions falling within the town and country planning system are in many cases made by elected local officials.
[134] J Steele, 'Participation and Deliberation in Environmental Law: Exploring a Problem-solving Approach' (2001) 21 *Oxford Journal of Legal Studies* 415.
[135] Holder (n 51).
[136] A Dobson, *Citizenship and the Environment* (Oxford, Oxford University Press, 2003).
[137] Holder (n 51).

their behaviour. Along similar lines, it is sometimes suggested that consensus on regulation improves implementation; whilst this is often a concern about the acceptability of regulation to the regulated industry, easing relationships between an installation's operators and neighbours can be an advantage of a fully participative process.[138] Consensus is not however a straightforward good, especially if it leads to self-censorship or a limitation on who can participate, and participation falling short of a search for consensus could attempt to capture some of these benefits.[139] Still in the realm of implementation, many regulation scholars see third party involvement and transparency as a way to keep regulators and regulated on the straight and narrow.[140] Specifically, European preoccupations with national participatory arrangements build on the long-standing instrumental benefits of individual rights through the direct effect of EU law.[141] Access to information allows the public to police the environmental performance of polluters and public regulators, who in turn are aware that their decisions are subject to public scrutiny.

The substantive effect of public participation should be testable by reference to the actual outcomes of decisions. But as with environmental assessment, measuring the substantive effect of public participation is a contentious, normative question, rather than a simple empirical inquiry. Assessing quality assumes some agreement about the environmental objectives of the decision, and so what constitutes a 'good' outcome. Even if the objective of a particular decision is clear, judgment is difficult. Moreover, a 'good' decision will inevitably incorporate other facets of the public interest than the purely environmental, and trade-offs may well be necessary. If the desire is simply to fit decision-making processes to the nature of the decisions, recognising that environmental decisions involve a wide range of values and perspectives points towards the inclusive processes, even if positive environmental outcomes cannot be guaranteed.

Different understandings of the purpose of public participation are often used interchangeably and simultaneously. In some cases, the different rationales can cumulatively emphasise the importance of public participation. But the objectives are not always consistent. A search for 'good' decisions may have a narrower conception of the public than a search for more democracy; the nature of the debate within the participatory exercise is also likely to be different. And just as the role of public participation is unclear, so is its form. Public participation that allows for

---

[138] Eg J Petts, 'Waste Management Strategy Development: A Case Study of Community Involvement and Consensus-Building in Hampshire' (1995) 38 *Journal of Environmental Planning and Management* 519.

[139] Eg C Coglianese, 'Is Consensus an Appropriate Basis for Regulatory Policy?' in EW Orts and K Deketelaere (eds), *Environmental Contracts: Comparative Approaches to Regulatory Innovation* (The Hague, Kluwer, 2000).

[140] See eg I Ayres and J Braithwaite, *Responsive Regulation: Transcending the Deregulation Debate* (Oxford, Oxford University Press, 1992); M Gunningham and P Grabosky, *Smart Regulation: Designing Environmental Policy* (Oxford, Clarendon, 1998).

[141] Case 26/62 *Van Gend en Loos* [1963] ECR 1; ch 5.

competition between, and aggregation of, individual interests, has been described as a 'thin' approach to public participation, which can be contrasted with a 'thick', more deliberative approach to decision-making.[142] The challenging ideal of 'deliberative democracy' is sophisticated and extensive, and subject to considerable internal and external critique.[143] The key thing for current purposes is that deliberation involves rational argument, including the provision of reasons that are capable of recognition as 'reasons' by others who disagree. Deliberative processes could provide decision-makers with information on the reasons behind public opinions and values. There is also an assumption that values can be transformed by deliberation, by contrast with the pre-formed and static private interests elicited in 'thin' forms of participation.[144] Deliberation is contentious theoretically and its conditions are almost impossibly difficult to achieve in practice. Many environmentalists make an appeal to deliberation without significant theoretical ambition, but on the basis that the provision of reasons and argument, within a process open to diverse perspectives, is the best way to capture ecological values. We should note though that deliberative democracy does not necessarily imply direct citizen involvement (experts or representative politicians can deliberate); nor does direct citizen involvement necessarily imply deliberation.

The EIA and SEA Directives do not demand any particular institutional arrangements for public participation. The detail of the public participation has been tightened in some respects by the implementation of the Aarhus Convention, but the type of participation remains unspecified. Nothing is said on the risk of exclusion, for example the drowning out of lay participation by expertise. Nor is there any commitment to deliberation or dialogue, but simply to an information gathering exercise. Whilst the reasons behind public views may be explored and challenged in a way that can be used to explain and support decision-making, there is no requirement for such an approach, which remains at the discretion of the Member States. It is perhaps appropriate that these sensitive issues should be left to the Member States; however, any thought that we now have a brave new world of environmental democracy should be resisted.

CONCLUSIONS

Rights to participate in environmental decision-making are now thoroughly embedded in law, and environmental assessment is at the heart of that. This is positive, but not straightforward. Those who see environmental assessment as a 'hindrance to fast implementation of their projects' are more likely to apply environmental assessment as a bureaucratic hurdle, a 'mandatory checklist', than

---

[142] See J Black, 'Proceduralizing Regulation' (2000) 20 *Oxford Journal of Legal Studies* 597 and (2001) 21 *Oxford Journal of Legal Studies* 33.
[143] See eg Smith (n 75); Dobson (n 136).
[144] Black (n 142).

those who believe that environmental assessment can 'help to develop more environmentally sound decisions'.[145] If the former perspective dominates, we are not likely to see genuine opportunities for the public to influence development. And paying lip service to consultation when decisions can only be influenced at the extreme margins, may be actively pernicious. Legislative requirements such as those in the environmental assessment Directives tell us relatively little about public participation. The ways in which they are implemented case by case is crucial.[146]

Donald McGillivray and Jane Holder suggest that whilst some think environmental assessment 'a potent, perhaps even radical, regulatory mechanism', others think it 'a deceit of no substance (and perhaps even of some mischief)'.[147] The potential for environmental assessment to disrupt established ways of doing things can be glimpsed in the slow and controversial process of negotiation for both EIA, which was almost 10 years in the drafting, and SEA. The ways in which environmental assessment has been amended and expanded over the years is suggestive of an iterative approach to regulatory processes.[148] For the purposes of this chapter we might usefully think about the two, closely related, aspects of environmental assessment, process and substance. In neither case could we claim overwhelming success. But institutionalised obligations to include a range of actors in decisions, and to consider environmental impact early in the process, have advantages that we would be loathe to abandon.

---

[145] H Runhaar et al, 'Environmental Assessment in the Netherlands: Effectively Governing Environmental Protection? A Discourse Analysis' (2013) 39 *Environmental Impact Assessment Review* 13.

[146] On the diversity of implementation, see Commission (n 100).

[147] McGillivray and Holder (n 29).

[148] J Scott and J Holder, 'Law and New Environmental Governance in the European Union' in J Scott and G de Búrca, *Law and New Governance in the EU and US* (Oxford, Hart Publishing, 2006).

8

Participation in Environmental Decision-Making at the EU Level

INTRODUCTION

A TURN TO more participatory processes, in all its complexity, is now almost an instinctive response to concerns about the legitimacy of decision-making, concerns that arise with some regularity in EU law. Ambiguity as to the purpose and role of public participation is at least as intense at EU level as nationally. As discussed in chapter seven, participation can respond to disparate sources of anxiety about environmental decision-making: the dilemma of non-majoritarian decision-making; an apparent loss of faith in the ability of representative democracy to achieve environmental ends; the fear of 'green authoritarianism'; the quality and implementation of environmental measures; the pragmatic desire to see particular developments introduced with the minimum of public complaint. Add to this the 'democratic deficit' in the EU, and the place of 'public participation' as an orthodox part of 'good' EU decision-making is easily understood.

This chapter addresses the law and policy applying to public participation in environmental decisions taken at EU level. The presence, nature or absence of consultation requirements in individual pieces of legislation determines consultation in much EU level administration, as discussed in respect of chemicals in the next chapter. This chapter tries to draw some more general lessons about EU participation. I begin with an examination of the role of participation in the Treaties. Certain relatively unchallenging demands are made of the institutions. The Treaty on the Functioning of the EU (TFEU) also provides for a potentially more far reaching 'citizens' initiative', which will be addressed separately. I then turn to the consultation requirements contained in the Aarhus Regulation,[1] which implements the 1998 Aarhus Convention on *Access to Information, Public Participation in Decision-Making and Access to Justice in Environmental Matters*[2] at EU level. A crucial and complex issue in this area is 'who' participates, and the

---

[1] Regulation 1367/2006/EC on the application of the provisions of the Aarhus Convention on Access to Information, Public Participation in Decision-making and Access to Justice in Environmental Matters to Community institutions and bodies ('Aarhus Regulation') [2006] OJ L264/13.
[2] (1999) 38 ILM 517.

role of 'civil society', an examination of which follows. The discussion of national decision-making in the previous chapter observed that the more distant the process is from an actual activity or project, the more difficult it is to engage 'ordinary' publics. At EU level, the scale of the decisions means that we are generally concerned with the participation of a particular sort of expert outsider, especially organised interest groups, public and private. Whilst there are optimists in the search for real direct engagement of the lay public in decision-making, and the failed European Constitution did for a while focus attention on *citizen* involvement, the challenges of transnational citizen participation, with its diverse politics and languages, are immense. This raises serious questions about which interests and which groups are represented, and about how and even whether participatory mechanisms can contribute to the democratic legitimacy of the EU.

The final topic of this chapter is access to environmental information in the EU, a crucial element of participatory mechanisms.

PUBLIC PARTICIPATION IN THE TREATIES

European integration was, in its early years, a predominantly elite project, pursued in relative isolation from public concerns.[3] But public debate on the 'democratic deficit' emerged relatively early in the life of the EEC, and remains fundamentally unresolved. Indeed, public attention to the democratic deficit has only increased over the years, and concern has intensified following the 2008 financial crisis and the associated sovereign debt crisis in the Euro zone.

The debate about EU democracy is broad, deep and sophisticated, and we will only touch on it here. The meaning of democracy is complicated and contested, as is the character of the 'democratic deficit' in the EU.[4] Some deny the existence of a democratic deficit,[5] and EU membership may be to some extent democracy-enhancing, in the sense of forcing national governments to consider concerns beyond the immediate constituency of the nation state.[6] But certain well under-

---

[3] Ch 1 above.

[4] There is an enormous literature on the subject. See eg, P Craig, 'Integration, Democracy and Legitimacy' in P Craig and G de Búrca (eds), *The Evolution of EU Law* (Oxford, Oxford University Press, 2011); A Follesdal and S Hix, 'Why There is a Democratic Deficit in the EU: A Response to Majone and Moravcsik' (2006) 44 *Journal of Common Market Studies* 533.

[5] To simplify, Moravcsik sees the EU as fundamentally under the control of the Member States, eg A Moravcsik, 'In Defence of the "Democratic Deficit": Reassessing Legitimacy in the European Union' (2002) 40 *Journal of Common Market Studies* 603. Others positively embrace the non-majoritarian aspects of EU decision-making, focussing on the potential for better decisions, see especially G Majone (ed), *Regulating Europe* (London, Routledge, 1996). See the discussion in Craig and in Follesdal and Hix (n 4).

[6] A Menon and S Weatherill, 'Democratic Politics in a Globalising World: Supranationalism and Legitimacy in the European Union' *LSE Working Papers Series* 13/2007. On comitology, see ch 2 above; in other deliberative fora, see eg CF Sabel and J Zeitlin, 'Learning from Difference: The New Architecture of Experimentalist Governance in the EU' in CF Sabel and J Zeitlin (eds), *Experimentalist Governance in the European Union: Towards a New Architecture* (Oxford, Oxford University Press, 2010).

stood features dominate debate on the democratic deficit. At the most basic level, the people on whose behalf laws are passed and implemented are unable to reject or influence legislators or government by popular vote.[7] The Commission and Council have significant legislative powers, but only the European Parliament is subject to elections; nor is the Commission subject to full democratic control by Parliament. And even for Parliament, elections are not a simple competition over European policy and leadership, since voting continues at least in part along national lines.[8] There is no solid European political party system, and most fundamentally, there is a lack of perceived shared interests among the European electorate.[9] The EU may suffer a little from unfavourable comparisons between flawed EU institutions and somewhat idealised notions of national parliamentary democracy. But there are real issues. The democratic deficit has led to great soul searching over many years, especially in the lead up to, and unfortunate aftermath of, the European Constitution. Whilst most discussions of the democratic deficit focus on legislation-making, this book is more concerned by administrative decision-making; the legitimacy of the legislation on which it is based is of course one aspect of administrative legitimacy. Moreover, similar ideas apply, and the democratic deficit is reinforced by the obscurity of the EU's (administrative) activities to many of its citizens.

In the early years of the new millennium, the resistance of the gaps in the EU's democratic accountability to the solutions offered by representative democracy[10] created space, and a real demand, for thinking about more participatory forms of democracy. The Treaty on European Union (TEU) contains a title on the 'democratic principles' of the Union, including Article 11 TEU, which provides for participation in decision-making. The Treaty status of the provisions in Article 11 could indicate an emphasis on the democratic rather than instrumental advantages of participation.[11] However, the focus of the treaties seems to be on rep-

---

[7] Follesdal and Hix see political competition over leadership and policy, 'conspicuously absent' in the EU, as 'an essential element of even the "thinnest" theories of democracy' (n 4) 534. See also Craig (n 4).

[8] Although on the increasing salience of European issues, see eg L Hooghe and G Marks, 'A Post-Functionalist Theory of European Integration: From Permissive Consensus to Constraining Dissensus' (2008) 39 *British Journal of Political Science* 1.

[9] The 'no demos' argument, for discussion see especially JHH Weiler, 'Does Europe Need a Constitution? Demos, Telos and the German Maastricht Decision' (1995) *European Law Journal* 217.

[10] Eg, giving unitary legislative power (currently shared) to the European Parliament, would be more 'democratic', but would mean a transfer of power away from the Council (more accountable to its national constituencies), and implies the *acceptability* of binding minorities to the majority will in the EU. At the other extreme, giving unitary legislative power to Council acting unanimously, relying on national democratic processes to provide democratic legitimacy would not only run the risk of paralysing decision-making, but without the corresponding reform of national parliaments, would increase the strength of the executive over parliament at the domestic level. For discussion of the importance of national resources of legitimacy, see JHH Weiler, 'In the Face of Crisis: Input Legitimacy, Output Legitimacy and the Political Messianism of European Integration' (2012) 34 *European Integration* 825.

[11] J Mendes, 'Participation and the Role of Law after Lisbon: A Legal View on Article 11 TEU' (2011) 48 *Common Market Law Review* 1849.

resentative mechanisms. Article 10 provides that 'The functioning of the Union shall be founded on representative democracy'; and the 'twin conceptions of legitimacy'[12] embodied in the TEU are representation of the people through the European Parliament, and the Member States through the Council and European Council, in turn 'democratically accountable either to their national Parliaments, or to their citizens'.[13]

The first three paragraphs of Article 11 TEU provide that:

1. The institutions shall, by appropriate means, give citizens and representative associations the opportunity to make known and publicly exchange their views in all areas of Union action.
2. The institutions shall maintain an open, transparent and regular dialogue with representative associations and civil society.
3. The European Commission shall carry out broad consultations with parties concerned in order to ensure that the Union's actions are coherent and transparent.

The emphasis seems to be on groups rather than individuals, by contrast with the Article on representative democracy.[14] There is one reference to citizens in paragraph 1, but paragraph 2 addresses representative associations and civil society,[15] rather than individuals, or even formally representative democratic institutions. And whilst the 'parties concerned' in paragraph 3 could include individuals, it is as likely to engage with groups, especially given the expressly instrumental objective. The language does however leave open the possibility of a thicker form of deliberative involvement in the EU.[16] I am sympathetic to the continued arguments that we should be ambitious in our hopes for participatory forms of democracy in the EU, and interpret the Treaty in a demanding way.[17] But the language is bland, and in the absence of any specific requirements on processes of involvement, does not demand any systematic or particularly challenging participatory processes.

Calls have been made for deliberative or republican democracy in the EU, and the notion of deliberation has also been used to explain and justify the workings of different EU institutions.[18] Participatory approaches are a necessary part of

---

[12] Craig (n 4) 37.

[13] Art 10 (1)(2) TEU.

[14] Art 10(3) TEU provides that 'Every citizen shall have the right to participate in the democratic life of the Union. Decisions shall be taken as openly and as closely as possible to the citizen.' Art 9 TEU provides that citizens 'shall receive equal attention from [the EU's] institutions, bodies, offices and agencies.'

[15] The distinction between a 'representative association' and 'civil society' is not clear; nor indeed is the real difference between the first three paragraphs of Art 11 TEU, Mendes (n 11).

[16] See the discussion in ch 7.

[17] Mendes (n 11).

[18] Most famously, C Joerges and J Neyer, 'From Intergovernmental Bargaining to Deliberative Political Processes: The Constitutionalisation of Comitology' (1997) 3 *European Law Journal* 273, discussed in ch 2. C Lord and P Magnette, 'E Pluribus Unum? Creative Disagreement about Legitimacy in the EU' (2004) 42 *Journal of Common Market Studies* 183 discusses deliberation in a number of institutions.

'democratic striving' at the transnational level.[19] There does however seem to have been something of a retreat from democratic rationales for public participation in the EU in recent years. Even if the search for 'a new form of supranational, participatory democracy' was just a 'wild goose chase',[20] however, the demands for participatory and collaborative governance are still considerable.

The third paragraph of Article 11 highlights in particular Commission responsibilities for consultation.[21] The Commission is of course not the only institution or body that consults or allows for participation. But the Commission does have a central role in environmental administration and the development of EU environmental regulatory standards. The Commission's processes for the involvement of outsiders have been increasingly formalised over recent years. A rhetoric of participation was central to the Commission's 'White Paper on European Governance', which was the response to a period of intense concern about the legitimacy of the Commission,[22] and as part of this exercise, the Commission also committed to minimum standards of consultation.[23] In addition, although regulatory impact assessment is often criticised for encouraging a reductive technical approach to environmental problems, as discussed in chapter two, in the case of the EU, impact assessment also encourages consultation, and reviews by the Impact Assessment Board provide some insight into and scrutiny of consultation.[24] As mentioned in chapter four, legitimacy in the EU is often discussed in terms of 'output' legitimacy, emphasising the quality of decisions, and 'input' legitimacy, concerned with the democratic quality of the 'inputs' to decision-making.[25] Whilst the Commission demonstrates some concern with the input legitimacy-enhancing potential of openness, it is probably fair to say that the emphasis of the relevant documents is substantive, an instrumental approach to gathering information and to enhancing the substantive quality of proposals.

Before moving on to the Citizens' Initiative (CI), Article 298 TFEU should be mentioned. This provides that 'the institutions, bodies, offices and agencies of the

---

[19] G de Búrca, 'Developing Democracy Beyond the State' (2008) 46 *Columbia Journal of Transnational Law* 101, in the global rather than EU context.

[20] C Harlow, *Accountability in the European Union* (Oxford, Oxford University Press, 2002) 179.

[21] *Protocol No 2 to the TFEU, on the Application of the Principles of Subsidiarity and Proportionality* also requires the Commission to 'consult widely'.

[22] European Commission, 'White Paper on European Governance' COM (2001) 428 final. Committee of Independent Experts, *Allegations Regarding Fraud, Mismanagement and Nepotism in the European Commission* (1999) led to the resignation of the entire Commission in 1999.

[23] European Commission, 'Towards a Reinforced Culture of Consultation and Dialogue—General Principles and Minimum Standards for Consultation of Interested Parties by the Commission' COM (2002) 704 final. They are to be revised, although not apparently in a radical way, see European Commission, 'Review of Commission Consultation Policy' SWD (2012) 422 final. A failure to comply with the minimum standards can be maladministration, see A Alemanno, 'The Better Regulation Initiative at the Judicial Gate: Trojan Horse within the Commission's Walls or the Way Forward?' (2009) 15 *European Law Journal* 382.

[24] See eg the criticism of consultation in the annual reports, European Commission, 'Impact Assessment Board Report for 2012' (no number).

[25] Weiler (n 10).

Union shall have the support of an open, efficient and independent European administration', and provides for the possibility of adopting a regulation to that end. This obviously has implications far beyond questions of public participation. The advantages of minimum administrative standards are clearest if one considers the vast array of mechanisms for generating rules and standards in the EU. Diverse processes, such as the Seville and CIS processes discussed in chapters four and five, as well as Commission or agency guidelines, are subject to ad hoc and patchy guarantees of transparency and openness. In addition, although in principle 'soft' and 'not binding', these norms can have considerable authority, as also discussed in chapter four. Applying transparent and easily accessible minimum standards to these processes would be an important step forward.[26] In this respect, we might also note the limited scope of the Commission's minimum standards on consultation, which apply essentially to 'major policy initiatives' subject to extended impact assessment; impact assessment applies to 'the most important Commission initiatives and those which will have the most far-reaching impacts',[27] as identified by the Commission.

THE CITIZENS' INITIATIVE

Article 11(4) TEU provides for the novel instrument of a 'citizens' initiative' (CI).

> Not less than one million citizens who are nationals of a significant number of Member States may take the initiative of inviting the European Commission, within the framework of its powers, to submit any appropriate proposal on matters where citizens consider that a legal act of the Union is required for the purpose of implementing the Treaties.[28]

This is potentially a significant institutional commitment. In the absence of actual decision-making powers for citizens (there is no obligation on the institutions to act), it is not a true form of direct democracy, nor indeed is it what would conventionally be called an initiative. It is more like a right to petition, similar to (if more ambitious than) citizen entitlement to petition the European Parliament.[29] The hope for these sorts of measures is that they will stimulate deliberation between and beyond participants, energising democratic debate, in this case across national borders. As discussed in the previous chapter, public participation is no guarantee of 'green' outcomes, and one of the currently open citizens' initiatives is a call to

---

[26] D Curtin, H Hofmann and J Mendes, 'Constitutionalising EU Executive Rule-Making Procedures: A Research Agenda' (2013) 19 *European Law Journal* 1. P Craig, 'A General Law on Administrative Procedure, Legislative Competence and Judicial Competence' (2013) 19 *European Public Law* 503 considers the applicability of such a general law to national bodies acting in EU administration.

[27] Commission (2002) (n 23); European Commission, 'Impact Assessment Guidelines' SEC (2009) 92, 6.

[28] See M Dougan, 'What Are We to Make of the Citizens' Initiative' (2011) 48 *Common Market Law Review* 1807.

[29] Art 227 TFEU. Dougan ibid.

suspend the 2009 Climate Package, in order to 'stop EU climate policy wasting hundreds of billions of euros on ineffective unilateral action on the climate at a time of economic crisis'.[30] The main potential benefit of CIs from an environmental perspective is said to be in side-stepping the official agenda, often dominated by economic questions.[31] As indicated by the climate change example, this can be a double-edged sword if environmental protection is in fact part of the official agenda. 'End Ecocide in Europe: A Citizens' Initiative to give the Earth Rights' fits better with this narrative of breaking with the official agenda. It aims to 'criminalise Ecocide and ensure that natural and legal persons can be held responsible for committing Ecocide according to the principle of superior responsibility'.[32]

The Treaty is fairly sparse on the criteria for a CI: one million citizens, from a 'significant number of Member States', can 'invite' the Commission to take action. The detail has now been filled in by the Citizen's Initiative Regulation.[33] The original proposal was criticised for the high burdens imposed on those seeking to organise an initiative, and whilst they were relaxed a little, the balance between ease of use and institutional efficiency is still contentious.[34] The 'organisers' of the initiative must form a 'citizens' committee', of at least seven people (not companies or organisations), who are citizens of the EU and resident of at least seven different Member States.[35] Organisers of a CI are required to register 'regularly updated information on the sources of support and funding for the proposed citizens' initiative'.

The CI must be registered by the Commission.[36] The Commission can refuse to register the proposed initiative, if, inter alia, it is 'manifestly contrary to the values of the Union as set out in Article 2 TEU'.[37] Some 'manifestly' racist or sexist initiatives can easily be imagined, although refusal to register is not likely to kill the sentiment. But identifying the consistency of a proposed CI with the values of the Union, for example with human dignity,[38] is potentially difficult ground for the Commission (and indeed for the Court). We might expect that 'manifestly' means that the CI will be registered if there is any doubt, leaving the argument to the public debate. The Commission can also refuse to register if the

---

[30] Commission registration number: ECI (2012) 10, see the official register at ec.europa.eu/citizens-initiative/public/initiatives/ongoing. The initiative has received some support from the 'Europe of Freedom and Democracy' group in the European Parliament, ibid.

[31] G Smith, *Deliberative Democracy and the Environment* (London, Routledge, 2003) 93–98.

[32] Commission registration number: ECI (2013) 2.

[33] Regulation 211/2011/EU on the citizens' initiative ('CI Regulation') [2011] OJ L65/1, as required by Art 24 TFEU.

[34] Dougan (n 28).

[35] CI Regulation (n 33) Art 3. Members of the European Parliament (MEPs) cannot count in the seven.

[36] Ibid Art 4.

[37] 'The Union is founded on the values of respect for human dignity, freedom, democracy, equality, the rule of law and respect for human rights, including the rights of persons belonging to minorities. These values are common to the Member States in a society in which pluralism, non-discrimination, tolerance, justice, solidarity and equality between women and men prevail.'

[38] Dougan (n 28).

proposed initiative is 'manifestly abusive, frivolous or vexatious'. Again, there may be some difficult judgments. So far, the usual reason for refusing to register an initiative is that it 'manifestly [falls] outside the framework of the Commission's powers to submit a proposal for a legal act of the Union for the purpose of implementing the Treaties'.[39] Any decisions refusing to register a proposed initiative will be addressed to the organisers and subject to judicial review.

After registration, the committee has 12 months to gather the necessary 'statements of support'.[40] This is essentially a petition, organised online.[41] The Regulation requires the supporters of a CI to come from a minimum of one quarter of Member States.[42] This is explicitly to ensure that the initiative is 'representative of a Union interest', avoiding purely national concerns. A minimum number of participants from each Member State is required, calculated by reference to the number of that State's Members of the European Parliament (MEPs).[43]

The CI has not been rapturously received. It promises only 'a relatively frail instrument',[44] even a 'toothless, pseudo-direct and pseudo-democratic tool'.[45] It is possible that the CI may in some cases foster shared European political debate.[46] However, divides between supporters in different Member States, including between small and large Member States or geographically clustered Member States, are possible, as is greater use of the CI in some Member States than others. Whilst the CI is an interesting effort to stimulate a European democratic mood, a 'European public' is no more imminent in participatory democracy than it is for the purposes of representative democracy.

The desirability of this sort of exercise is not absolutely straightforward. CIs will not necessarily involve collective debate and deliberation, but could simply involve the aggregation of individual interests. The protection of minorities is also always an issue. And if driven or even manipulated by political and economic elites, a CI could weaken rather than enhance legitimacy. More prosaically, institutions might be concerned about the coherence of legislative agendas, and conflicting initiatives. In any event, from an environmental perspective, the popularity of environmental protection measures, especially in times of economic hardship, does not go without saying, as witnessed by the effort to gather support for the abandonment of the climate change package.

---

[39] All the rejected initiatives listed in the register on 14 September 2013, for which reasons were given in English, French or Spanish, were rejected for that reason, ec.europa.eu/citizens-initiative/public/initiatives/non-registered. Registration can also be refused if the citizens' committee is not properly set up, CI Regulation (n 33) Art 4.

[40] Ibid Art 4. ec.europa.eu/citizens-initiative/public/welcome.

[41] Ibid Art 2(2), Art 5, Annex III.

[42] Ibid Recital 5, Art 7(1). This is actually rather complicated, see Dougan (n 28).

[43] Ibid Art 7(2).

[44] Dougan (n 28) 1807.

[45] B de Witte et al, *Legislating after Lisbon: New Opportunities for the European Parliament* (European Union Democracy Observatory, Florence, 2010) www.eui.eu/Projects/EUDO/Documents/EUDO-LegislatingafterLisbon(SD).pdf.

[46] Dougan (n 28) is optimistic.

The Treaty is silent on what should be done with a 'successful' CI. At the time of writing, no CI has gone past the 12-month deadline, and so there is no experience.[47] The Regulation provides that organisers are entitled to present the initiative at a public hearing at the European Parliament,[48] putting the initiative on the broader political agenda. They are also able to present the CI to the Commission 'at an appropriate level'.[49] The rejection of initiatives 'manifestly' in conflict with the EU's values are dealt with at a prior stage; at this stage any disagreement over values between the organisers and the EU institutions should in principle be subject to open political debate. The Regulation requires the Commission to 'set out in a communication its legal and political conclusions on the citizens' initiative, the action it intends to take, if any, and its reasons for taking or not taking that action'.[50] This reason-giving obligation could require the Commission to reflect upon its decision and provide an accountability trail, although the expressed aim is more superficial, that is to 'demonstrate' that the CI has been 'carefully examined'.[51]

As at 15 September 2013, only 17 open CIs were listed on the register. Commission and European Parliament willingness to engage with CIs will largely determine the future of CIs, although the willingness of public interest groups to organise and support CIs is also open to question. In many cases interest groups are already able to engage with EU institutions, and have established strategies for engaging public and media debate.[52]

THE AARHUS REGULATION

Chapter 7 introduced the Aarhus Convention. Formal implementation of the public participation 'pillar' of the Aarhus Convention at EU level concentrates on Article 7 of the Convention, which requires arrangements 'for the public to participate during the preparation of plans and programmes relating to the environment, within a transparent and fair framework, having provided the necessary information to the public'.[53] There have been no formal steps to implement the very soft provisions of Article 8, which applies to 'executive regulations and other

---

[47] According to a note on the webpage, the deadline was extended for some of the early CIs, due to problems finding hosts for the collection of signatures.

[48] CI Regulation (n 33) Art 11.

[49] Ibid Recital 20, Art 11; Art 10.

[50] Ibid Art 10(1)(c).

[51] Ibid Recital 20.

[52] Empirical work suggests limited initial enthusiasm for the CI on the part of civil society groups, see L Bouza Garcia, 'Anticipating the Attitudes of European Civil Society Organisation to the European Citizens' Initiative: Which Public Sphere May it Promote?' *Bruges Political Research Papers 2012-24.*

[53] For discussion see J Jendroska, 'Public Participation in the Preparation of Plans and Programmes: Some Reflections on the Scope of Obligations under Article 7 of the Aarhus Convention' (2009) 6 *Journal for European Environmental and Planning Law* 495; United Nations Economic Commission for Europe (UNECE), *The Aarhus Convention: An Implementation Guide* (New York, United Nations, 2013). 'Policies' are also addressed in Art 7: 'to the extent appropriate, each party shall endeavour to provide opportunities for public participation in the preparation of policies relating to the environment'.

generally applicable legally binding rules that may have a significant effect on the environment'. Article 6 applies to specific activities and projects, and so generally (not exclusively) applies at the national level, since that is where the relevant projects and activities are authorised.[54]

The Aarhus Regulation implements the Convention at EU level.[55] It requires all EU institutions and bodies to make arrangements for 'early and effective opportunities for the public to participate' during the preparation, modification or review of 'plans and programmes relating to the environment'. As important as this is, the focus on plans and programmes is not likely to fill the gaps left by the Commission's 'Minimum Standards on Consultation'.[56] The plans and programmes affected are those 'required under legislative, regulatory or administrative provisions' that 'contribute to or are likely to have significant effects on, the achievement of the objectives of Community environmental policy'.[57] 'Financial or budget plans or programmes' are explicitly excluded, according to the explanatory memorandum on the basis that they 'do not as such have a significant direct effect on the environment'.[58] Given the recurrent controversy over funding of environmentally damaging initiatives, and the general policy of integration of environmental considerations into other areas, this is a blunt conclusion.

Participation must be possible at a point 'when all options are still open',[59] for a minimum of 12 weeks.[60] 'Due account' must be taken of the outcome of the participation, the public must be informed of the plan or programme, 'and of the reasons and considerations upon which the decision is based, including information on public participation'.[61] Reason-giving about consultation processes has the potential to be an important tool of scrutiny and accountability. Reason-giving not only provides some accountability mechanisms to participants, but allows everyone to see 'details of how, who and on what' the Commission has consulted,[62] responding to a concern about consultation that has been touched on in earlier chapters: 'which interests [participants] represent' and 'how inclusive that representation is'; 'who is being consulted and why'.[63] But in general, this sort of reason-giving obligation seems to be poorly implemented.[64] The Impact

---

[54] Activities to which Art 6 applies are listed in Annex I of the Convention (n 2) (Art 6(1)(a)). Annex I covers physical developments (such as chemicals installations). Art 6 also applies to activities 'which may have a significant effect on the environment', 'in accordance with its national law'. But it is provided that 'Parties shall determine whether such a proposed activity is subject to these Provisions'.

[55] The Aarhus Regulation (n 1).

[56] See nn 26–27.

[57] See ch 7 on strategic environmental assessment.

[58] The Aarhus Regulation (n 1) Art 2(1)(e) 9.

[59] Ibid Art 9.

[60] The Commission has extended its normal consultation period from eight to 12 weeks, see Commission (2012) (n 23).

[61] The Aarhus Regulation (n 1) Art 9(5).

[62] Commission (n 22) 20. Commission (2012) (n 23) 16.

[63] Commission (2002) (n 23) 17.

[64] See also Mendes (n 11). Note also participants' dissatisfaction with feedback, Commission (2012) (n 23) 16.

Assessment Board, which reviews impact assessments carried out during the legislative process, has expressed some concern, and 'often recommended a more transparent reflection of the views expressed, especially those which were opposed to the preferred approach'.[65]

One of the most significant elements of the Aarhus Convention is its inclusion of environmental interest groups in the rights that it grants.[66] The 'public' under the Regulation includes individuals, and associations, organisations and groups, with a clear role for environmental interest groups, providing a valuable alternative input. The Aarhus Regulation requires the EU institution or body to 'identify the public affected or likely to be affected by, or having an interest in' the plan or programme. The selection of participants, as discussed in the previous chapter, raises obvious concerns about the extent of institutional control over 'public' participation, but equally recognises that public participation does not simply happen, and that some thought should be paid to who needs to be involved.

WHO PARTICIPATES?

Participation at the EU level largely revolves around organised interest groups. Some experiments in lay participation have taken place, but seem to have made relatively little contribution to policy development, or to the development of meaningful participatory processes.[67] A possible exception to the absence of individual citizens is the CI, which should be directly inclusive, escaping some of the concerns that the demands of participation actually enhance exclusion. Its simplicity means that it does not, like more demanding participatory exercises, favour the highly educated and the time-rich, or those professional lobbies best able to access the very complex EU system of decision-making. The high demands placed on the organising committee, however, suggest that the CI is unlikely to be set in motion by 'ordinary' citizens or groups of citizens. The committee must have members from at least seven Member States, bear the costs of translation (not mandatory, but probably necessary for gathering support), and be responsible for data protection issues, and for ensuring Member State verification of signatures. All of this requires high levels of organisation. In addition, whilst one million supporters is a low threshold as a proportion of the EU population, compared to

---

[65] Commission (n 24) 4; European Commission, 'Impact Assessment Board Report for 2010' SEC (2011) 126 final, 15; European Commission, 'Impact Assessment Board Report for 2011' SEC (2012) 101 final, 4. The voluntary 'Transparency Register', ec.europa.eu/transparencyregister/info/homePage. do?locale=en, is a further effort to provide information on 'consultees', but remains incomplete.

[66] Aarhus Convention (n 2) Arts 2(4) and 2(5).

[67] On the failures and (limited) successes of participatory experiments, see A Fischer-Hortzel, 'Democratic Participation? The Involvement of Citizens in Policy Making at the European Commission' (2010) 6 *Journal of Contemporary European Research* 335.

similar processes in European states,[68] generating such numbers across a quarter of Member States requires a high level of pan-European organisation.

Given the challenges of language, technical complexity and diverse cultures and politics, it is probably not realistic to expect widespread direct participation of individual citizens in EU decision-making. The inclusion of interest groups is, however, like the inclusion of citizens, thought to be capable of improving 'input' legitimacy. Vibrant public interest groups can be an important part of healthy democratic debate. In a specifically European approach to arguments that membership of collective interest organisations enhances political or civil awareness, and encourages 'active citizenship',[69] the Commission hopes that the involvement of civil society will 'Europeanise' society, channelling public views to decision-makers, getting 'citizens more actively involved in achieving the Union's objectives', and indeed raising European consciousness generally.[70] This is not straightforward. Aside from anything else, 'civil society' may be unable or unwilling to perform an awareness-raising role.[71] A 'representative' role for 'civil society' is attractive, but may assume close connections with its members and with citizens that are difficult to maintain.[72] A representative of the European Environment Bureau (EEB) has been quoted as saying that 'While ideally it would be good to get people involved … my role is not to encourage the most participatory governance but to ensure the best results for the environment.'[73]

Whether the EEB alone can identify what is 'best' for the environment is doubtful. But in any event, and notwithstanding any potential contribution to democratic culture, the greatest role for environmental interest groups is focussed on *substantive* (output) legitimacy. They provide information and knowledge, much needed in complicated governance processes. They provide an alternative

[68] V Cuesta-Lopez, 'A Preliminary Approach to the Regulation on European Citizens' Initiative from Comparative Constitutional Law' (Bruges, College of Europe, 2011).

[69] B Kohler-Koch, 'Civil Society Contribution to Democratic Governance: A Critical Assessment' in B Kohler-Koch, D De Bièvre, W Maloney (eds), *Opening EU-Governance to Civil Society Gains and Challenges* CONNEX Report Series No 05 (2008) calls this the 'Scandinavian model' and describes it as declining even in Scandinavia.

[70] Eg Commission (2002) (n 23), especially 15.

[71] A Warleigh, '"Europeanising" Civil Society: NGOs as Agents of Political Socialisation' (2001) 39 *Journal of Common Market Studies* 619.

[72] For a nice review of these issues, see K-O Lindgren and T Persson, *Participatory Governance in the EU: Enhancing or Endangering Democracy and Efficiency?* (Basingstoke, Palgrave MacMillan, 2011) ch 1. On a declining concern with the representativeness of individual interest groups, see N Perez-Solorzano Borragan and S Smismans, 'Representativeness: A Tool to Structure Interest Intermediation in the European Union?' (2012) 50 *Journal of Common Market Studies* 403.

[73] W Maloney, 'The Professionalisation of Representation: Biasing Participation' in Kohler-Koch, de Bièvre and Maloney (n 69), citing I Sudbury, 'Bridging the Legitimacy Gap in the EU: Can Civil Society Help Bring the EU to its Citizens?' (2003) 26 *Collegium* 7. The EEB is an environmental interest group based in Brussels that brings together national environmental groups, in a 'federation'. For details, see the EEB website at www.eeb.org/.

perspective to dominant economic interests. In this respect they have the potential to keep the deals honest.[74]

The political dynamics of early European integration are thought to have favoured interest groups by comparison with national systems.[75] Fragmented decision-making processes meant that there were a number of different points at which decision-makers could be accessed, the relative weakness of the European Parliament meant that legitimacy was sought outside of the institutions, and the small size of the Commission meant that there was a demand for external exper-tise. Those factors favouring outside intervention remain to a greater or lesser degree. Whether they have favoured public or private interest groups historically is controversial, and highly variable depending on context.[76] There is a large and growing literature on the presence, representation and influence of interest groups in the EU.[77] Studies of the open online consultation during the negotia-tion of the EU-level chemicals regulation (REACH),[78] suggested that industry and the larger Member States were at least quantitatively better represented; leading to the conclusion that consultation may be open and broad, without necessarily being equal.[79] But Lindgren and Persson's examination of the same legislation suggest that both environmental and industrial interest groups were happy with the process; industry only slightly happier. And whilst industry had advantages over environmental interest groups in terms of influence, industry was not allowed to dominate.[80]

The precise relationships of influence are difficult to measure and are highly variable,[81] depending for example on diverse institutional (Parliament, Commission, etc) and functional (trade, social, environmental) contexts. Different resources are likely to be mobilised over a matter of high politics than routine administra-tion, and we might be as interested in the day to day application of REACH as its

---

[74] Eg I Ayres and J Braithwaite, *Responsive Regulation: Transcending the Deregulation Debate* (Oxford, Oxford University Press, 1995).

[75] S Mazey and J Richardson, 'Environmental Groups and the EC: Challenges and Opportunities' (1992) 1 *Environmental Politics* 109.

[76] C Quittkat and B Finke, 'The EU Commission Consultation Regime' in Kohler-Koch, de Bièvre and Maloney (n 69), see the 'first generation' of Commission consultation as focussed on industrial sectors, employers and trade unions. In their case study of DG Employment's consultation regime, 'EU-level business associations are much more present ... than EU-level NGOs', 213.

[77] See the material cited in this section.

[78] Regulation 1907/2006/EC concerning the Registration, Evaluation, Authorisation and Restriction of Chemicals (REACH), establishing a European Chemicals Agency [2006] OJ L396/1.

[79] T Persson, 'Democratizing European Chemicals Policy: Lessons from the Open Consultation on REACH' (2005) *Paper Prepared for the Workshop on the Institutional Shaping of EU-Society Relations*. In consultation on the Environmental Action Programme, out of 164 organisational responses, 57 were from companies or business, and 47 were from non-governmental organisations (NGOs), European Commission, 'Impact Assessment of Proposal for a Decision on a General Union Environment Action Programme to 2020, "Living Well, within the Limits of our Planet"' SWD (2012) 398 final, Annex I, 1.

[80] Lindgren and Persson (n 72), especially chs 4 and 5.

[81] A Dur and D de Bievre, 'The Question of Interest Group Influence' (2007) 27 *Journal of Public Policy* 1.

initial negotiation.[82] So it is difficult to draw conclusions about the strength of environmental interests in EU participation. But environmental interest groups do face clear weaknesses relative to industry, even once they have been included in the process.[83] The classic literature on collective action predicts that diffuse interests (such as environmental protection) find it more difficult to organise than focused interests, such as economic interests,[84] and so are less well represented in decision-making. Environmental interest groups have fewer resources than industrial actors, both financially, and in terms of access to the information most valued by decision-makers.[85] These issues were touched on in respect of the Industrial Emissions Directive (IED) in chapter five.[86] Public funding achieves some parity of resources with industry groups, but enhances concerns about independence and autonomous priority setting,[87] not to mention vulnerability to changes in priorities. Environmental interest groups also have less influence on the sections of institutions that are not explicitly 'environmental' (such as the Enterprise and Industry Directorate General of the Commission).[88]

There is a danger that formal equality between environmental interest groups and economic and industry actors, coupled with practical inequalities, creates simply an illusion of full involvement. The rhetorical emphasis of the Commission on engagement with 'civil society' does nothing to bring this out into the open; 'civil society' is a phrase suggesting a focus on the 'public interest', but clearly includes economic interests.[89] The Commission 'does not always resist the temptation to use civil society as a legitimating discourse for all its existing interactions, including those with all sorts of private lobby actors'.[90]

[82] For example, it would appear that many NGOs diverted their limited resources away from chemicals to other priorities once the Regulation had been passed, O Fuchs, 'REACH: A New Paradigm for the Management of Chemical Risks' *Health and Environment Reports No 4* (IFRI, 2009).

[83] Lindgren and Persson (n 72).

[84] M Olson, *The Logic of Collective Action: Public Goods and the Theory of Groups* (Harvard, Harvard University Press, 1965).

[85] Although see C Adelle and J Anderson, 'Lobby Groups' in A Jordan and C Adelle (eds), *Environmental Policy in the EU: Actors, Institutions and Processes* (London, Routledge, 2012) on the extensive resources enjoyed by some environmental groups.

[86] Directive 2010/75/EU on industrial emissions (integrated pollution prevention and control) [2010] OJ L334/17.

[87] The EU does fund environmental interest groups, ec.europa.eu/environment/ngos/list_ngos97_07.htm. The Commission is an important source of funding for the EEB, see C Knill and D Liefferink, *Environmental Politics in the European Union* (Manchester, Manchester University Press, 2007) 72.

[88] W Grant, D Matthews and P Newell, *The Effectiveness of European Union Environmental Policy* (Basingstoke, Macmillan Press, 2000).

[89] D de Bièvre, 'Assessing Interest Group Politics in EU Governance' in Kohler-Koch, de Bièvre and Maloney, (n 69). Commission (2002) (n 23), is explicit: '"civil society organisations" are the principal structures of society outside of government and public administration, including economic operators not generally considered to be "third sector" or NGOs', 6.

[90] S Smismans, 'European Civil Society: Shaped by Discourses and Institutional Interests' (2003) 9 *European Law Journal* 482, 491.

Much of the Commission's consultation activity takes place with participants, including environmental interest groups, which it identifies.[91] This leads to an additional concern that some groups are privileged, and that stakeholder identification will be self-interested. Groups with challenging ecological viewpoints could easily be excluded as unhelpful or unconstructive, and notwithstanding the Commission's acknowledgement of the value of the non-Brussels standpoint,[92] it is clear that the Commission prefers to work with pan-European organisations. Aside from the perhaps legalistic point that the Aarhus Convention does not permit discrimination as to 'citizenship, nationality or domicile',[93] the marginalisation of the local, ad hoc, or poorly resourced organisations, by transnational, highly bureaucratic organisations, may increase the distance between organised groups and citizens.[94] The representation of the environmental interest is also difficult. It is multi-dimensional, and there might be tensions between protecting different aspects of the environment—habitats versus climate change, for example. Nor can it be assumed that local and European environmental groups share a view on what is most environmentally progressive, especially if something that has global environmental benefits imposes an environmental burden on a particular and identifiable community.[95]

The 'overall rationale' of the Commission's minimum standards on consultation 'is to ensure that all relevant parties are properly consulted'.[96] The Commission should ensure 'adequate coverage' in a consultation process of 'those affected by the policy; those who will be involved in implementation of the policy; or bodies that have stated objectives giving them a direct interest in the policy', also taking into account 'the wider impact of the policy on other policy areas, eg environmental interest', as well as 'the need to involve non-organised interests, where appropriate'.[97] There is also an emphasis on the 'proper balance' between representatives of 'social and economic bodies', 'large and small organisations or companies', 'wider constituencies … and specific target groups'.[98] A similar concern can be seen in the Commission's Impact Assessment Guidelines, which observe that 'an open consultation is unlikely to provide a fully representative picture of opinions', so that 'specific efforts' may be needed to ensure that all relevant stakeholders are both aware of and able to contribute to the consultation.[99]

---

[91] Note also the institutionalised role of the Committee of the Regions and the Economic and Social Committee, Commission (2002) and (2012) (n 23).

[92] Commission, ibid (2002) 11–12.

[93] Aarhus Convention (n 2) Art 3(9).

[94] See K Armstrong, 'Rediscovering Civil Society: the European Union and the White Paper on Governance' (2002) 8 *European Law Journal* 102, suggesting that transnational organised civil society may suffer from the same sorts of legitimacy problems as transnational governance more generally.

[95] For example energy from waste incinerators, rail freight depots and wind farms.

[96] Commission (2002) (n 23) 3.

[97] Ibid 19–20.

[98] Ibid 20.

[99] Commission (n 27). The Annexes to the Guidelines emphasise further the need to resist calling only on the 'usual suspects', and to be proactive in seeking out stakeholders, 15.

The Commission is at least aware of the potential problems. The risk that it will only speak to a narrow section of self-consciously European society is nevertheless real.

ACCESS TO ENVIRONMENTAL INFORMATION AT THE EU LEVEL

Access to information is a specific application of the broader value of transparency in EU decision-making, also discussed in terms of 'openness' in the EU.[100] Touching, as it does, on 'every intellectual neurosis of the contemporary age',[101] great claims are made for transparency. The objective of the requirement in Article 15 TEU that the 'Union's institutions, bodies, offices and agencies shall conduct their work as openly as possible', for example, is to promote 'good governance' and ensure 'the participation of civil society'.[102] Article 15 also provides a 'right of access to documents', reiterated in Article 42 of the Charter of Fundamental Human Rights. The Access to Documents Regulation sees 'openness' as something that 'enables citizens to participate more closely in the decision-making process', which 'guarantees' a more legitimate, effective and accountable administration and 'contributes to strengthening the principles of democracy and respect for fundamental rights'.[103] The language of democracy and of good and accountable administration is also rehearsed by the judiciary.[104] These great expectations may assume too much, since there is no necessary or automatic link between transparency and other values. But transparency, specifically access to information, is often a first step, a precondition of basic rights such as the right to vote, the right to free speech, the right to participate in decision-making. Transparency also serves more instrumental purposes, touched on in earlier chapters. In particular, careful scrutiny by those external to the decision-making process may identify errors and improve outcomes. But again, there is no simple link between access to information and improved outcomes, and ensuring the real transparency of information to which access is provided can be complex.[105]

Moreover, whilst the principle of access to information is enthusiastically recognised, its implementation remains controversial. It is not self-evident where lines should be drawn, and when there may be good reasons to maintain

---

[100] Although openness may be broader, also including 'open' in the sense of inclusive, processes, A Alemanno, 'Unpacking the Principle of Openness in EU Law: Transparency, Participation and Democracy' (2013) *European Law Review* (forthcoming).

[101] E Fisher, 'Transparency and Administrative Law: A Critical Evaluation' (2010) 63 *Current Legal Problems* 272, of transparency generally, 272.

[102] See also Arts 1, 10(3) and 11.

[103] Regulation 1049/2001/EC regarding public access to European Parliament, Council and Commission documents ('Access to Documents Regulation') [2001] OJ L145/43, Recital 2

[104] Eg Case C-353/99P *Council v Hautala* [2001] ECR I-9565; Case T-211/00 *Kuijer v Council* [2002] ECR II-485; Case C-39/05P *Sweden and Turco v Council* [2008] ECR I-4723.

[105] Fisher (n 101); S Jasanoff, 'Transparency in Public Science: Purposes, Reasons, Limits' (2009) 69 *Law and Contemporary Problems* 21.

secrecy.[106] An obvious example might be concerns about reduced candour when meetings are held in public, and Jasanoff also discusses the ability of opponents to 'manufacture uncertainty' when they have access to detail of scientific decision-making.[107] Rules on public access to documents held by the EU institutions are laid down by the Access to Documents Regulation, which provides a right of access, within specified time limits, and a requirement for reasoned decisions.[108] A negative response can be appealed internally through a 'confirmatory application' and is subject to judicial review.[109] The right of access applies not only to documents produced by the institution, but also those received:[110] the public have a right to know not only the position of the institutions, but in principle also who is communicating with them and how. The Aarhus Regulation applies the Access to Documents Regulation to 'environmental information', with a few small extensions to comply with the Convention.[111] Proposals to amend the Regulation further proved to be extremely controversial, with major disagreement within and between the European Parliament and the Council, raising concerns about a possible retreat on access principles.[112]

Rights of access to information are subject to exceptions to allow for the protection of competing public interests. A Member State can 'request the institution not to disclose a document originating from that Member State without its prior agreement', but the grounds for refusal still need to be found in the exceptions in the Regulation.[113] Judicial interpretation of the exceptions has been fraught with difficulties, and remains unpredictable,[114] illustrating the complexity of

---

[106] Jasanoff, ibid.

[107] Ibid.

[108] Access to Documents Regulation (n 103) Arts 2 and 7. Applications must be handled promptly, and within 15 working days, Art 7(1), extendable in exceptional circumstances by a further 15 working days.

[109] Ibid Art 7.

[110] Ibid Art 2.

[111] Aarhus Regulation (n 1). The Access to Documents Regulation (n 103), applies to documents, rather than information, but the broad definition of 'document', extending to any medium including 'sound, visual or audiovisual recordings', Art 3(a), means that this is less problematic than might be expected.

[112] MZ Hillebrandt, D Curtin and A Meijer, 'Transparency in the EU Council of Ministers: An Institutional Analysis' (2013) *European Law Journal* (forthcoming). European Commission, 'Proposal for a Regulation Regarding Public Access to European Parliament, Council and Commission Documents' COM (2008) 229, which would have made some substantive changes; a further Commission, 'Proposal for a Regulation Amending Regulation (EC) No 1049/2001 Regarding Public Access to European Parliament, Council and Commission Documents' COM (2011) 137 is more modest. Both proposals are extant, European Commission, 'Report on the Application in 2011 of Regulation (EC) No 1049/2001 Regarding Public Access to European Parliament, Council and Commission Documents' COM (2012) 429 final [1].

[113] Access to Documents Regulation (n 103) Art 4(5); C-64/05P *Sweden (IFAW) v Commission* [2007] ECR I-11389.

[114] See especially D Adamski, 'Approximating a Workable Compromise on Access to Official Documents: The 2011 Developments in the European Courts' (2012) 49 *Common Market Law Review* 521; P Leino, 'Just a Little Sunshine in the Rain: The 2010 Case Law of the European Court of Justice on Access to Documents' (2011) 48 *Common Market Law Review* 1215. Commission reports on the Regulation give an indication of the scale of the litigation, see Commission (2012) (n 112).

transparency, and the inconsistent rights and interests involved.[115] The grounds for refusing access to documents are set out in three main categories in the Access to Documents Regulation,[116] and the Aarhus Regulation introduces a further exception 'where disclosure of the information would adversely affect the protection of the environment to which the information relates, such as the breeding sites of rare species'.[117] The Aarhus Regulation requires the exceptions to be 'interpreted in a restrictive way' in respect of environmental information, 'taking into account the public interest served by disclosure and whether the information requested relates to emissions in the environment'.[118] The case law generally provides for restrictive interpretation of the exceptions.[119]

The *first* category of exception is that access shall be denied if it would undermine protection of the public interest in public security, defence and military matters, international relations or the financial, monetary or economic policy of the EU or a Member State,[120] or if it would undermine the protection of the 'privacy and integrity of an individual'.[121] The potential inconsistency of a strong interpretation of this latter exception with scrutiny of collaborative governance mechanisms is discussed in chapter five.

The *second* category of exceptions to the right of access applies if access would undermine the protection of commercial interests, court proceedings and legal advice, or the purpose of inspections, investigations and audits, subject to a test of overriding public interest in disclosure.[122] The Aarhus Regulation provides that in respect of commercial interests, inspections and audits (not investigations), 'an overriding public interest in disclosure shall be deemed to exist where the information required relates to emissions into the environment'.[123] It has been suggested that the disapplication or more restrictive interpretation of exceptions in respect of emissions, reflects the fact that emissions lose 'their proprietary

---

[115] Adamski, ibid.

[116] Access to Documents Regulation (n 103) Art 4; those parts of a document not subject to an exception should be severed and disclosed, ibid Art 4(8). For statistical information on the use of the exceptions, see Commission (2012) (n 112).

[117] Aarhus Regulation (n 1) Art 6(2).

[118] Ibid Art 6(1).

[119] Eg *Kuijer* (n 104); although not uniformly, see P Craig, *EU Administrative Law* (Oxford, Oxford University Press, 2012) ch 13.

[120] Access to Documents Regulation (n 103) Art 4(1)(a), indents 1 to 4. Note that the Aarhus Convention (n 2) contains no exception relating to 'financial, monetary or economic policy', a point not addressed by the Aarhus Regulation (n 1). This exception may arise only rarely in an environmental context, but clarity (transparency even) would be welcome.

[121] Access to Documents Regulation (n 103) Art 4(1)(b). See Commission (n 112, 2012), on the increased use of this exception.

[122] Ibid Art 4(2), indents 1 to 3.

[123] Ibid Art 6(1). This goes a little further than the Aarhus Convention, which requires in most cases just that the fact that the information requested relates to emissions into the environment be taken into account; only in respect of commercial or industrial confidentiality does the Aarhus Convention state that information on emissions 'shall be disclosed'.

character' once they are emitted into the environment.[124] It may also recognise greater public concern about this type of environmental impact, and greater potential for direct effects on human health.

Thirdly, access to documents relating to a matter in which the decision has not been taken, or preparatory documents after the decision has been taken, shall be refused if disclosure would 'seriously undermine the institution's decision-making process', unless there is an overriding public interest in disclosure. The Courts have emphasised that this is not a general assumption of no access. In *Sweden v MyTravel*, a case about access to evidence on mergers, the General Court had upheld the Commission's refusal to release the documents, and emphasised concerns that self-censorship within the administration could lead to loss of independence and frank speaking;[125] the Court rejected abstract claims, and required 'detailed evidence ... allowing it to be understood why disclosure would have been likely seriously to undermine the Commission's decision-making process'.[126] The Commission must genuinely balance the interest of citizens in gaining access to its documents against any interest of its own.[127]

Only harm to a recognised interest justifies denial of access; the exceptions are not about the convenience of government, but about very specific conflicting interests. The institution must consider 'reasonably foreseeable' risks to the protected interest, and not the 'purely hypothetical'.[128] The limitation of the third category of exceptions to cases where the relevant interest is 'seriously undermined' emphasises that access is not to be lightly denied. The Commission has however observed the difficulty of distinguishing between 'undermining' an interest and 'seriously undermining' that interest,[129] particularly given that in either case, the harm to the recognised interest should nevertheless be incurred if the public interest in disclosure is overriding. Both the second and third categories of exception are conditional exceptions, requiring disclosure if the public interest in disclosure is overriding.[130] This is welcome, although the EU Courts have never relied on the overriding public interest to justify not applying an exception.[131]

As has been discussed on a number of occasions, simple access to complicated information may not actually enhance transparency, and the right to access is

---

[124] UNECE (n 53) 83. This guidance borrows the definition of 'emissions' contained in the Industrial Emissions Directive (n 86): 'direct or indirect release of substances, vibrations, heat or noise from individual or diffuse sources in the installation into air, water or land'.

[125] T-403/05 *Sweden v MyTravel* [2008] ECR II-2027.

[126] Case C-506/08P *Sweden v MyTravel* [2011] ECR I-6237 [89].

[127] Case T-19/96 *Carvel and Guardian Newspapers Ltd v Council* [1996] ECR II-1519, so dating back to the first decision in this area. See also eg *Sweden and Turco* (n 104).

[128] *Kuijer* (n 104) [56]; Case T-233/09 *Access Info Europe v Council* [2011] ECR II-1073; this has been appealed, Case -280/11P.

[129] Commission (2012) (n 112) 23.

[130] The public interest can be an interest in transparency, *Sweden and Turco* (n 104).

[131] Adamski (n 114).

simply to information that already exists and has been recorded.[132] The audience is important. Some information may be accessible only to experts, or only to the highly educated and highly motivated. Most applications to the Commission under the Access to Documents Regulation are from academics, followed by law firms, and by 'civil society'.[133] The absence of any obligations on the institutions to make the information in documents 'transparent' to more general publics suggests that environmental information will be used, or mediated, by environmental interest groups.

As well as the right of access to existing information, the Aarhus Convention imposes duties on public authorities actively to collect and disseminate environmental information.[134] The obligation in the Access to Documents Regulation to list documents in a public register goes some way to reinforcing third party involvement in decision-making, although the content of the register is rather unspecified in the Regulation.[135] Anyone reading this book is probably aware of the vast number of documents made available online. Under the Aarhus Regulation, environmental information is to be organised 'with a view to its active and systematic dissemination to the public, in particular by means of computer telecommunication and/or electronic technology'.[136] The sort of information that should be available is set out a little more clearly,[137] including an obligation on the Commission to publish reports on the state of the environment, including information on the quality of, and pressures on, the environment, at least every four years.[138] The Aarhus Convention 'where appropriate' also requires parties to establish 'publicly accessible' and standardised pollution registers,[139] implemented in the EU by the European Pollutant Release and Transfer Register (E-PRTR).[140]

CONCLUSIONS

There are many compelling reasons to enhance public participation in environmental decision-making. Most of the indications point to substantive rationales

---

[132] Also the Aarhus Regulation 'any information in written, visual, aural, electronic or any other material form', (n 1) Art 2(d). See Case T-264/04 *World Wildlife Fund UK* [2007] ECR 2007 II-911, in which it sufficed for the Council to say that minutes of certain meetings (preparing for World Trade Organisation negotiations) did not exist. The institutions must, however, 'in so far as possible, and in a non-arbitrary and predictable manner, draw up and retain documentation relating to their activities' [61].

[133] Commission (2012) (n 112) [4.4]. Reports are published for each institution.

[134] Aarhus Convention (n 2) Art 5.

[135] Access to Documents Regulation (n 103) Art 11.

[136] Aarhus Regulation (n 1) Art 4(1).

[137] Eg international treaties and their implementation, data on activities and authorisations, environmental impact assessments, ibid Art 4.

[138] Ibid Art 4.

[139] Aarhus Convention (n 2) Art 5(9); *Protocol on Pollutant Release and Transfer Registers.*

[140] Regulation 166/2006/EC concerning the establishment of a European Pollutant Release and Transfer Register [2006] OJ L33/1, Recital 4, as amended, prtr.ec.europa.eu/.

for the participation of external actors in EU decisions, although concerns about democratic legitimacy are often apparent in the background. Even in its substantive guise, public participation has an important constitutional dimension, sanctified by the call on participatory mechanisms in Article 11 TEU. The real limits to citizen participation at EU level mean that public participation is primarily a matter for interest groups. The empowerment of environmental interest groups is crucial, since the industry view is well embedded in EU environmental decision-making, and environmental interest groups can bring an important balance and a potentially richer range of perspectives into the process. Whether environmental interest groups can really bear the weight they are expected to shoulder is open to question. Adequate public resources still need to be devoted to regulation.

Participatory mechanisms bring with them considerable challenges. The concern with effectiveness, that 'output legitimacy' will be sacrificed to 'input legitimacy', is valid, and a balance must inevitably be drawn. The tension between public participation and reasonably swift and decisive regulation is acute; environmental interest groups should be particularly concerned that making regulatory activity more onerous can serve simply to strengthen the status quo. However, to argue that environmental decisions can be made well without some breadth of participation, involves a mistaken understanding of environmental issues, which are rarely one-dimensional technical decisions. There should also always be concern for the risk of exclusion. Participatory mechanisms may further exclude the poor, poorly educated and unorthodox from institutions of decision-making; in the current context, one might also be anxious about the inadequately 'European'. Exclusion can be direct, in the sense of restricted access to the forum. More insidious forms of exclusion can be found in obscure decision-making structures and specialised information and discourse. It is far from unusual to see limitations placed on what counts as 'legitimate' reasoning in environmental debate: most obviously, a narrow approach to 'sound science' or efficiency can lead to the dismissal of every other concern as irrational or self-interested. Actually creating institutions and situations in which meaningful public participation or genuine deliberation can take place is extremely challenging and demands vigilance.[141]

---

[141] See Smith (n 31).

9

Authorising Products in the Internal Market: The Regulation of Chemicals in the EU

INTRODUCTION

THE EXTRAORDINARY REACH (Registration, Evaluation, Authorisation and Restriction of Chemical Substances) Regulation, finally agreed in 2006, was years in the negotiation, and controversial within the EU and beyond.[1] Urgent interests conflict: chemicals are an important part of the EU economy, employing thousands of people, but it is also all too easy to call to mind chemicals banned or regulated only after years of damage.[2]

A number of themes can be explored through the REACH framework. First, information plays an absolutely central role in REACH. A core concern is to remedy our brutal ignorance of the impacts of chemicals on people and the environment. The responsibility for filling the knowledge gap is placed primarily on the 'industry' (loosely speaking). Information also plays a regulatory role, and the hope that the availability of information will allow third parties to put economic and political pressure on the industry bears considerable weight in the regulation of chemicals. Secondly, chemicals are products, and hence their regulation is fundamentally connected to the internal market. Whilst environmental and human health protection is, according to the Court, REACH's main objective,[3] free movement of goods in the internal market is central. Accordingly, the focus of REACH is on harmonised decisions, taken at the EU level. The European Chemicals Agency (ECHA), responsible for 'the technical, scientific and administrative aspects' of the Regulation,[4] is at the heart of the institutional arrangements

---

[1] Regulation 1907/2006/EC concerning the Registration, Evaluation, Authorisation and Restriction of Chemicals (REACH), establishing a European Chemicals Agency [2006] OJ L396/1 (consolidated version published 9 October 2012). On the debate around REACH, see E Fisher, 'The "Perfect Storm" of REACH: Charting Regulatory Controversy in the Age of Information, Sustainable Development and Globalization' (2008) 11 *Journal of Risk Research* 541.

[2] European Commission, 'General Report on REACH' COM (2013) 49 final.

[3] The European Court of Justice (ECJ) has found that the protection of human health and the environment is REACH's main objective, Case C-558/07 *R (on the application of SPCM SA) v Secretary of State for Environment, Food and Rural Affairs* [2009] ECR I-5783.

[4] REACH (n 1) Art 75; also Art 77.

created by REACH.[5] However, as with other EU agencies, neither Member States nor the Commission were willing to hand control over to an autonomous agency.[6] Centralisation is mediated by Member State intervention at all points in decision-making, and many final decisions are taken by the Commission, with the involvement of the Member States through comitology (discussed in chapter two). Thirdly, REACH is ambivalent about public participation: outsiders are expected to use information to influence the production and use of chemicals, but space for public involvement in regulatory decision-making is restricted. And finally, risk assessment plays an important role in the regulation of chemicals, in particular in the processes for authorisation and restriction, and so many of the issues discussed in chapter two can be seen in operation. In particular, the question of what 'counts' as a 'good' reason for a decision is worth exploring further. 'Socio-economic' assessment, essentially a cost benefit analysis (CBA), plays an unusually explicit role in the risk regulation of chemicals.

This chapter begins by outlining very briefly the key steps in REACH (registration, evaluation, authorisation and restriction) before turning to each of the four themes set out above in turn. Before proceeding, it should be noted that risk regulation, especially of products, has global implications. Chemicals are globally traded, and imported and exported chemicals are caught by REACH. There is insufficient space to discuss the international context here, but we might note that in addition to concerns about the compatibility of REACH with World Trade Organisation rules, the EU self-consciously presents its regulation as a model for other national jurisdictions, perhaps because of a conviction that REACH is superior to other approaches, but also out of concern for EU companies competing on the global market.[7]

THE REGULATORY REGIME

REACH ends the practice in the EU, common to many jurisdictions, of regulating 'existing' chemicals less heavily than 'new' chemicals. This tended to incentivise the continued use of old chemicals, creating disincentives to innovate, with potentially negative economic and environmental effects. 'New' (post–1981) chemicals had to be notified and tested; 'existing' chemicals, which in most cases had not been adequately tested when they were put on the market, were to be evaluated case by case.[8] Between 1996 and 1998, only four existing chemicals went through

---

[5] Ibid, title X.

[6] See M Martens, 'Executive Power in the Making: The Establishment of the European Chemicals Agency' *Arena Working Paper 2009–08* on the institutional pressures in the creation of the ECHA; and ch 2 on agencies.

[7] On the complexities of 'rules globalisation', see V Heyvaert, 'Globalizing Regulation: Reaching beyond the Borders of Chemical Safety' (2009) 36 *Journal of Law and Society* 110.

[8] See V Heyvaert, 'The EU Chemicals Policy: Towards Inclusive Governance?' in E Vos (ed), *European Risk Governance: Its Science, Its Inclusiveness and Its Effectiveness* (Mannheim, CONNEX report series, 2008).

full assessment.[9] REACH applies to all 'substances'[10] imported or manufactured in the EU,[11] on their own or in mixtures, and in some cases also when contained in articles.[12] Much of the discussion of the Regulation will be integrated into the rest of this chapter, and so what follows is a brief introduction to some of the key terms and important stages of the regulatory process.

The first obligation in REACH is one of registration. Manufacturers or importers of more than one tonne of any substance per year must register that substance.[13] The ECHA performs a completeness check on registration dossiers, and in the absence of any indication to the contrary, manufacture or import can start in three weeks.[14] Quantity is used as a crude guide to significance, and more information (as set out in Annexes VI to X) is required as the 10, 100 and 1000 tonne threshold is passed.[15] No risk assessment is required unless a substance is imported or manufactured over the crucial 10 tonne threshold.[16] At this point a chemical safety report, which assesses the risks of the substance's specified uses, based on individual chemical safety assessments, must be included.[17] The registrant also has to 'identify and apply the appropriate measures to adequately control the risks'.[18] For substances imported or manufactured in annual quantities over 100 tonnes, if all necessary information is not available, proposals for testing have to be submitted to the ECHA.

The next stage of REACH is the ECHA's responsibility for evaluation, both 'dossier evaluation', and 'substance evaluation'. Dossier evaluation involves the evaluation of all registrants' testing proposals,[19] as well as a 'compliance' evaluation of

---

[9] ES Williams, J Panko and DJ Paustenbach, 'The European Union's REACH Regulation: A Review of its History and Requirements' (2009) 39 *Critical Reviews in Toxicology* 553. For detail on the information gap, see European Commission, 'White Paper: Strategy for a Future Chemicals Policy' COM (2001) 88 final.

[10] Definitions can be found in REACH (n 1) Art 3.

[11] Certain uses are exempted from all or some of the obligations because they are regulated elsewhere, eg cosmetics, food contact materials, plant protection products, biocides, medicines, as are substances for use in research and development. Polymers are excluded primarily for pragmatic reasons, see the discussion in *SPCM* (n 3).

[12] REACH (n 1) Art 3(1); Arts 6–7.

[13] Ibid Art 6. Registration applies to substances in articles if the substance is present in quantities over one tonne, and is intentionally released 'under normal or reasonably foreseeable conditions of use', see also Williams et al (n 9). A lesser notification requirement applies if an article contains a substance not intended for release which is included on the Candidate List (discussed below), unless the producer or importer is able to 'exclude exposure to humans or the environment during normal or reasonably foreseeable conditions of use including disposal', Art 7(2), (3).

[14] Ibid Art 20; this is explicitly not a check of quality or adequacy, Art 20(2).

[15] Ibid Art 12.

[16] F Fleurke and H Somsen, 'Precautionary Regulation of Chemical Risk: How REACH Confronts the Regulatory Challenges of Scale, Uncertainty, Complexity and Innovation' (2011) 48 *Common Market Law Review* 357.

[17] REACH (n 1) Art 14, Annex I. The threshold is subject to review, Art 138.

[18] Ibid Art 14.

[19] Ibid Art 40. As above, testing proposals have to be submitted at the 100 tonne threshold if the information is not available.

at least five per cent of dossiers submitted.[20] The ECHA is also responsible for ensuring the evaluation of *substances*. A 'rolling action plan', prioritising substances for evaluation when 'there are grounds for considering ... that a given substance constitutes a risk to human health or the environment', is updated annually.[21] Substance evaluations are performed by a national competent authority: Member States 'choose' substances, but the ECHA 'shall ensure' that any substance not chosen is evaluated.[22] The evaluating competent authority 'shall consider how to use the information obtained' for the purposes of the other elements of the Regulation, including whether the substance should be considered of very high concern, and whether restrictions should be considered.[23]

The obligation to seek authorisation for the use of 'substances of very high concern' (SVHC) is the 'command and control' element of REACH.[24] The authorisation obligation applies regardless of the quantity of the substance. SVHCs are substances meeting the criteria for classification as CMRs (carcinogenic, mutagenic or toxic for reproduction), PBTs (persistent, bioaccumulating and toxic) and vPvBs (very persistent and very bioaccumulating), as well as substances 'for which there is scientific evidence of probable serious effects to human health or the environment which give rise to an equivalent level of concern', as the other substances, identified on a case-by-case basis.[25] A 'Candidate List' of SVHCs is held by the Commission,[26] and a final list of SVHCs is found in Annex XIV.[27] The circumstances in which authorisation will be granted are discussed below, as is the process for identifying an SVHC. Authorisations are granted for a fixed period, and can also be reviewed if changed circumstances affect the risk assessment or socio-economic impact of the substance, or 'new information on possible substitutes becomes available'.[28]

In addition to registration, evaluation and authorisation, REACH provides for restrictions to be imposed when any substance poses 'an unacceptable risk' or an uncontrolled risk, to human health or the environment.[29] A decision on a

---

[20] Ibid Art 41.

[21] Ibid Art 44. See also ECHA, *Evaluation under REACH: Progress Report 2012* (Helsinki, ECHA, 2012) 28.

[22] Ibid Art 45.

[23] Ibid Art 48.

[24] Ibid Art 56. The General Court has rejected the proposition that a substance must be registered before it can be placed on the Candidate List, Case T-96/10 *Rütgers v European Chemicals Agency*, not yet reported in the ECR, appealed to the ECJ, Case C-290/13 P.

[25] Ibid Art 57.

[26] Ibid Art 59. The General Court has confirmed that the Candidate List has binding legal effects, *Rütgers*, (n 24), eg (n 13) above.

[27] Ibid Art 58.

[28] The breach of environmental quality standards contained in other legislation can also trigger a review, and if there is 'a serious and immediate risk for human health or the environment', the Commission can suspend authorisation, ibid Art 61.

[29] Ibid Art 68(1); Art 69(1). Restriction and authorisation processes are not mutually exclusive; on the need for coordination, see European Commission, 'Staff Working Document Accompanying General Report on REACH' SWD (2013) 25. Authorisation cannot relax a restriction, Art 60(6).

restriction must 'take into account the socio-economic impact of the restriction, including the availability of alternatives'.[30] There is no quantitative threshold, and the substance need not have been registered. By contrast with authorisation of SVHCs, the regulator bears the burden of justifying a restriction. Restrictions are listed in Annex XVII to the Regulation.

INFORMATION

Information is central to REACH. This section begins by discussing the central role of the industry in information provision, before turning to the potential of information as a regulatory tool. It then goes on to explore the limitations on the role of information in REACH.

Privatisation of Information

The 'privatisation' of information provision has been identified as one of the key characteristics of REACH.[31] Lack of information paralyses regulation, and prevents markets from competing on safety.[32] But unless they are required to do so through regulation, manufacturers of chemicals have no incentive to take on the costs of producing safety information. In fact, the incentives are for them not to do so:[33] not only does the production of information literally cost money, but finding negative safety information may at the extreme destroy their market. Relying on information produced by regulators has been painfully slow. REACH therefore operates the principle of 'no data, no market',[34] under which failure to register a substance meets with the substantial penalty of denial of access to the market. But although severe penalties are associated with failure to register, and downstream users have an interest in ensuring that suppliers have registered their substances,[35] registrants have considerable incentives to underestimate the risk associated with their substance.[36] The structure of the Regulation tries to enhance the opportunities for what Joanne Scott calls 'hierarchical' and 'peer' oversight.[37]

---

[30] Ibid Art 68(1).

[31] Fisher (n 1). V Heyvaert, 'Regulating Chemical Risk: REACH in a Global Governance Perspective' in J Eriksson, M Gilek, and C Rudén (eds), *Regulating Chemical Risks: European and Global Challenges* (Dordrecht, Springer, 2010).

[32] Fisher, ibid.

[33] Fisher, ibid; J Scott, 'REACH: Combining Harmonization and Dynamism in the Regulation of Chemicals' in J Scott (ed), *Environmental Protection: European Law and Governance* (Oxford, Oxford University Press, 2009).

[34] REACH (n 1) Art 5.

[35] V Heyvaert, 'No Data, No Market. The Future of EU Chemicals Control under the REACH Regulation' (2007) 9 *Environmental Law Review* 201.

[36] C Hey, K Jacob and A Volkery, 'Better Regulation by New Governance Hybrids? Governance Models and the Reform of European Chemicals Policy' *FFU Report 02/2006*.

[37] Scott (n 33).

The evaluation of dossiers by the ECHA, the importance of which is emphasised by the poor initial quality of registrations so far,[38] provides for clear 'hierarchical' oversight.[39] Joint registration and data sharing provisions may mean that other operators in the sector actually share responsibility for the data, enhancing peer review. Competitors may also have an interest in scrutinising the registration: they may have alternative substances, or want to compete on safety, or they may simply be interested in the reputation of the sector.[40] Much of the information provided on registration is made public, so that consumer groups, trade unions and environmental groups also have opportunities for scrutiny. There is still no guarantee that registrants will be open handed with information,[41] and the resources available for regulatory scrutiny are particularly important. But the provision of data is not entirely in the hands of self-interested commercial operators.

Registration is not the end of the information obligations imposed on the private sector. Obligations of information communication up and down the supply chain are described by the Commission as 'a central cross-cutting theme of REACH'.[42] Registrants have to pass information to downstream users,[43] and downstream users are expected to pass 'new information on hazardous properties' and 'any other information that might call into question the appropriateness of the risk management measures identified in a safety data sheet' back upstream.[44] They are able to provide information on their use of a substance to assist in registration. If their use of a substance is not included in their supplier's material, they must provide the ECHA and others with information (or find a new supplier).[45] The definition of a 'downstream user' catches a wide range of actors who use a substance in industrial or professional activities (expressly not including consumers or distributors), beyond the 'chemicals industry'.[46] Many have never before had obligations under chemicals regulation, an element of REACH that poses significant challenges.[47]

Finally, a range of information must be submitted with the application for authorisation, including a chemical safety report (which will already have been

---

[38] ECHA (n 21) claims that registration quality is improving, 7. European Environmental Bureau (EEB) and Client Earth, *Identifying the Bottlenecks in REACH Implementation: The Role of ECHA in REACH's Failed Implementation* (2012) criticises the ECHA for accepting poor dossiers.

[39] REACH (n 1) Arts 40 and 41.

[40] See ch 4; N Gunningham, 'Corporate Environmental Responsibility—Law and the Limits of Voluntarism' in D McBarnet, A Voiculescu and T Campbell (eds), *The New Corporate Accountability: Corporate Social Responsibility and the Law* (Cambridge, Cambridge University Press, 2007).

[41] Scott (n 33).

[42] Commission (n 29) 44.

[43] Generally a 'safety data sheet', including information on the identification of the substance, hazards, first aid, fire fighting and accidental release measures, advice on exposure control and disposal, REACH (n 1) Art 31, Annex II. If a safety data sheet is not required, the information set out in Art 32 applies. More modest obligations apply with respect to substances in articles, Art 33.

[44] Ibid Art 34.

[45] Ibid Art 37.

[46] Ibid Art 3(13).

[47] Commission (n 29) 56.

submitted on registration for chemicals reaching the 10 tonne threshold), and an 'analysis of alternatives, considering their risks and the technical and economic feasibility of substitution'; if 'suitable alternatives' are 'available', the application must include a 'substitution plan'.[48] We return to alternatives and substitution in the final section below.

Information as a Regulatory Tool

In part, the role of information in REACH is to provide regulators with the information necessary for decisions. But it is also more than that. It enables outsiders to demand action from retailers, politicians, regulators or sometimes the courts, and creates the potential for the market to operate around safety, even in the absence of direct regulatory intervention.[49]

The interpretation of some of this information will of course be difficult; even the highly politically resonant language of 'very high concern' means nothing if we do not know where the chemical might be found. This means that the information generated and released with the REACH framework is generally dependent on some sort of translation if it is to be used by lay audiences.[50] There are some signs of this. Non-governmental organisations (NGOs), critical of the time being taken to identify SVHCs,[51] have produced a SIN ('substitute it now') list, listing substances that they say meet the regulatory criteria for qualification as a SVHC.[52] It contained 626 substances in September 2013; the candidate list contained 144, and Annex XIV, 22.

We should also note that the information on the ECHA's website is available globally, to market actors, as well as to regulators and those seeking regulatory change through political activism. News that a chemical is deemed to be 'of very high concern', or has not been authorised in the EU, or is subject to restrictions, may well demand a response elsewhere. American NGOs are demonstrating their potential for 'translation' of this information into politically accessible terms,[53] and parts of the 'SIN list' are being translated for easier use by the market in

---

[48] REACH (n 1) Art 62(4).

[49] Fisher (n 1).

[50] Eg S Jasanoff, 'Transparency in Public Science: Purposes, Reasons, Limits' (2006) 69 *Law and Contemporary Problems* 21.

[51] EEB, *The Fight to Know? Substances of Very High Concern and the Citizens' Right to Know under REACH* (EEB, 2010).

[52] www.chemsec.org/what-we-do/sin-list. J Scott, 'From Brussels with Love: The Transatlantic Travels of European Law and the Chemistry of Regulatory Attraction' (2009) 57 *American Journal of Comparative Law* 897. The Commissioner for the Environment has suggested that the SIN list indicates the substances to be considered for inclusion in the Candidate List, J Potočnik, *Reaching for Resource Efficiency and Innovation in the Chemicals Sector*, speech to Chemicals Forum (Helsinki, 19 May 2011), europa.eu/rapid/press-release_SPEECH-11-344_en.htm. Environmental interest groups can empower environmental regulators in debate within an institution.

[53] See Scott, ibid, for a discussion of the activities of Moms Rising and the Environmental Defense Fund.

China.[54] In the absence of any demands on the ECHA to make the available information more transparent, the impact of information is to a considerable extent dependent on the continued resources and attention of NGOs.

Obligations to produce information also have the potential to generate more self-reflection, and more safety conscious organisations, as discussed in chapter seven.[55] At the moment, REACH as a tool of cultural transformation seems a little far-fetched. But important elements of REACH attempt to direct the industry's attention and knowledge towards safety, and industry responsibility is a general feature of REACH. A registrant must update the registration 'on his own initiative' and 'without undue delay', providing information on 'new knowledge of the risk of the substance to human health and/or the environment of which he may reasonably be expected to have become aware',[56] as well as keeping chemical safety reports 'available and up to date',[57] and updating safety data sheets 'without delay'.[58] Industry ('manufacturers, importers and downstream users'), rather than regulators, have the primary responsibility to ensure that their substances 'do not adversely affect human health or the environment';[59] and in respect of authorised substances, 'notwithstanding any conditions of an authorisation, the holder shall ensure that the exposure is reduced to as low a level as is technically and practically possible'.[60]

Limitations on Information in REACH

Notwithstanding the centrality of information to the regulatory regime imposed by REACH, there are some real limitations on the availability of information. The need for 'translation' of technical information has come up on numerous occasions in this book.[61] Here, there is also a literal translation issue: the ECHA's working language is English, and whilst there is an effort to translate, some of the information on the ECHA website is published only in English.[62] The amount of information produced is also likely to be a barrier to unmediated utility: in September 2013, the ECHA's register contained 9,952 unique substances and information from 40 329 dossiers.[63] This is not just a challenge for lay people.

---

[54] www.chemsec.org/what-we-do/sin-list/latest-on-sin/1113-making-it-easier-for-chinese-companies-to-use-the-sin-list.

[55] M Führ and K Bizer, 'REACH as a Paradigm Shift in Chemical Policy: Responsive Regulation and Behavioural Models' (2007) 15 *Journal of Cleaner Production* 327.

[56] REACH (n 1) Art 22(1).

[57] Ibid Art 14(7).

[58] Ibid Art 31(9).

[59] Ibid Art 1(3).

[60] Ibid Art 60(10).

[61] Above n 50.

[62] Echa.europa.eu/about-us/the-way-we-work/multilingual-practice. Safety data sheets do have to be translated, raising cost and quality issues, Commission (n 29) 47.

[63] Echa.europa.eu/web/guest/information-on-chemicals/registered-substances.

Even for commercial users, there is some concern that 'important information is diluted in purely formal information', with safety data sheets doubling in length since the introduction of REACH.[64] Ensuring that this vast body of information is available to be used properly is a major challenge. The importance of the challenge is enhanced by the possibility that information gathered in REACH could be used in other regulatory exercises, and vice versa.[65]

It is surprising that information for consumers plays such a limited role in REACH.[66] The presence of even a SVHC in a consumer article (such as shoes or wallpaper[67]) is not subject to a labelling obligation.[68] The Classification, Labelling and Packaging (CLP) Regulation, also administered by the ECHA, provides for simple hazard labelling: for example, labelling of a substance classed as 'acute toxicity category 1 (oral)' will include the hazard statement 'fatal if swallowed', the word 'Danger' and a pictogram with a skull and crossbones.[69] But the CLP Regulation does not generally apply to articles, with the exception of flammability.[70] Under Article 33 of REACH, the consumer of an article on the Candidate List for SVHCs is entitled, on request, to be provided with 'sufficient information, available to the supplier, to allow safe use of the article including, as a minimum, the name of that substance'.[71] Research by the European Environmental Bureau (EEB), however, suggests that even this very limited provision, requiring proactive requests from the consumer, is poorly understood by the industry, and poorly implemented.[72]

A large amount of information is made freely available on the ECHA's website. The most significant exception to access is made with respect to information that would undermine somebody's commercial interests. The scope of this exception is likely to be increasingly controversial,[73] and could be crucial to the regulatory potential of information under REACH. Article 119 of REACH provides for the proactive publication of information. It lists information that will always be released, including the identification of the substance, physico-chemical data and pathways, and the results of toxicological and ecotoxicological studies. Other information will be made available unless the party that submitted it provides a 'justification ... accepted as valid' of why publication would be harmful to its,

---

[64] Commission (n 29) 45. Williams et al (n 9).
[65] Commission, ibid, 13 onwards.
[66] Scott (n 33).
[67] The examples are taken from EEB (n 51).
[68] Scott (n 33); Fleurke and Somsen (n 16).
[69] Regulation 1272/2008/EC on classification, labelling and packaging of substances and mixtures, as amended [2008] OJ L353/ 1. The example is taken from echa.europa.eu/web/guest/regulations/clp/understanding-clp
[70] Scott (n 33).
[71] If it is contained in the article over 0.1% by weight.
[72] 158 requests were made to 60 retailers or brands in five EU countries. 50% did not answer, and the EEB thought that half of the responses made were inadequate, (n 51).
[73] Environmental interest groups are challenging the refusal to release certain information that the ECHA claims is commercially confidential, see Case T-245/11 *ClientEarth and International Chemical Secretariat v ECHA*.

or someone else's, commercial interests.[74] This includes other information on the safety data sheets, information on purity of a substance, tonnage bands (eg 10–100 tonnes), and study summaries. Article 118 further provides that some information will 'normally be deemed' to undermine the protection of commercial interests, unless 'urgent action is essential to protect human health, safety or the environment, such as emergency situations'. This category comprises details of the full composition of a mixture; the precise use, function or application of a substance or mixture; the precise quantity of the substance or mixture manufactured or placed on the market; links between a manufacturer or importer and his distributors or downstream users.[75]

The ECHA is subject to the EU's rules on providing access to documents on request, discussed in chapter eight, including the Aarhus Regulation, and has published a Decision on how that legislation will apply.[76] The Access to Documents Regulation provides an exception to the obligation to provide documents when disclosure 'would undermine the protection of … commercial interests of a natural or legal person', but subject to 'an overriding public interest in disclosure'.[77] The Aarhus Regulation provides that for commercial interests, an overriding public interest in disclosure shall be deemed to exist where the information relates to emissions into the environment.[78] Presumably the ECHA means to satisfy these constraints on the commercial interests exception on a case-by-case basis, but it is surprising that the relationship between the different provisions on access has not been dealt with explicitly by the ECHA. Protection of commercial confidentiality has the potential to be a major restriction on the availability of information under REACH. Vigilance will be necessary.

The more general limitations on information, discussed in chapter two, remain. Chemicals are subject to pervasive and inevitable uncertainty.[79] Epidemiology only reliably detects fairly large effects,[80] and its usefulness is also limited by

---

[74] 1,300 confidentiality claims had been made by March 2011, ECHA, *The Operation of REACH and CLP* (Helsinki, ECHA, 2011) 23. ECHA, *Access to Documents at ECHA—2012 Key Figures* (Helsinki, ECHA, 2013) shows rough figures (without distinguishing between reasons) for decisions: around 50 documents were disclosed, nearly 400 partially disclosed.

[75] REACH (n 1). Note also Art 120, on release to third countries.

[76] Regulation 1049/2001/EC regarding public access to European Parliament, Council and Commission documents [2001] OJ L145/43; Regulation 1367/2006/EC on the application of the provisions of the Aarhus Convention on access to information, public participation in decision-making and access to justice in environmental matters to Community institutions and bodies [2006] OJ L264/13 ('Aarhus Regulation'); ECHA, *Decision on the Implementation of Regulation 1049/2001/EC Regarding Public Access to Documents* (Helsinki, ECHA, 2009). The relationship between the three sets of provisions is not entirely clear, M Bronckers and Y van Gerven, 'Legal Remedies under the EC's New Chemicals Legislation REACH: Testing a New Model of European Governance' (2009) 46 *Common Market Law Review* 1823.

[77] Ibid Art 4.

[78] Aarhus Regulation (n 76), Art 6(1).

[79] See eg D Farber, 'Five Regulatory Lessons from REACH' (2008) *UC Berkeley Public Law Research Paper No 1301306* and W Wagner, 'The Science Charade in Toxic Risk Regulation' (1995) 95 *Columbia Law Review* 1613 for detailed discussion.

[80] Eg Swedish Chemicals Agency, *The Substitution Principle* (Report No 8, 2007).

latency (long delays between exposure and effect) and confounding background factors (for example those exposed to a chemical may differ from the population in other ways, such as diet). Epidemiological studies of the general population are rare, and difficult to interpret, and extrapolating from groups who have been exposed to high levels of a chemical, for example those working with a chemical, to 'safe' levels, is also difficult. Animal studies are the main alternative to epidemiology, and again, extrapolating is problematic. The problem of indeterminacy discussed in chapter two is also significant. Testing many chemicals, acting together in complex ecosystems and complex social systems is virtually impossible; Heyvaert describes the approaches to testing in REACH as 'notoriously feeble' in respect of ecosystems.[81]

Information: Concluding Comments

Information plays an enormously important role in REACH. The intense resistance of industry to the negotiation of REACH demonstrates that information tools are not 'de'-regulatory in any ordinary sense. The information requirements of REACH make enormous demands on the industry. But nor is reliance on industry an easy option for regulators, whose role in ensuring the quality and accessibility of information cannot be taken for granted.

CENTRALISATION AND THE ROLE OF THE MEMBER STATES

As product regulation, REACH is highly concerned with the internal market, and was passed on the basis of what is now Article 114 of the Treaty on the Functioning of the European Union (TFEU). There can be tension between the free trade values at the heart of the EU and the protection of the environment. National measures to protect the environment may interfere with the free movement of goods, and need to be justified if they are to survive, as discussed in chapter 10; once an area has been harmonised, these justifications are not available. In chapter four, 'flexibility' was identified as a key theme of 'new' environmental governance. REACH provides for exhaustive harmonisation, and shows no particular concern for national flexibility. Whilst REACH undoubtedly does centralise relative to earlier legislation,[82] the approach taken is 'more complex, more subtle, and certainly more promising' than asserting any simple centralisation of power would suggest.[83]

---

[81] Heyvaert (n 8). See also European Commission, 'Proposal for a Decision of the European Parliament and of the Council on a General Union Environment Action Programme to 2020, "Living Well, within the Limits of our Planet"' COM (2012) 710 final, eg 22–23.

[82] Eg Heyvaert (n 31).

[83] Scott (n 33) 56.

First, the centralisation inherent in the empowerment of an EU agency is mediated by a strong institutional role for the Member States within the ECHA. The ECHA's Management Board, for example, is composed of a 'representative' from each Member State.[84] Although members are appointed for 'relevant experience and expertise in the field of chemical safety or the regulation of chemicals', they are not subject to an explicit requirement that they act independently of their Member States. The ECHA also has a Member State Committee, whose consensus-seeking role (it is 'responsible for resolving potential divergences of opinions on draft decisions proposed by the Agency or the Member States'[85]) is distinctive compared with other agencies, and provides deliberate space for the representation of national interests. The members of the Member State Committee are appointed directly by the Member States.[86]

The two other ECHA committees are responsible for risk assessment and socio-economic assessment. These committees are not supposed to represent the Member States, which are prohibited from issuing instructions that are 'incompatible with the individual tasks of those persons or with the tasks, responsibilities and independence of the Agency'.[87] When acting as rapporteurs on particular tasks, members of the Committees 'undertake' to act 'in the interests of the Community'.[88] But even these independent committees have important links with the Member States. Member States nominate members, and the ECHA Management Board appoints at least one, and no more than two, members from each nominating Member State to each committee. Committee members are also to 'ensure' 'appropriate coordination' between the ECHA and the national competent authority,[89] and the Member States are required to 'provide adequate scientific and technical resources' to their nominees.[90] The ECHA committees have been criticised for being too close to national policy.[91]

The interaction between the national and the European in the ECHA's complex institutional structure is not entirely predictable. Member States are strongly represented in the ECHA, even compared for example with the European Food Safety Authority (EFSA).[92] For example, members of EFSA's scientific panels are recruited by calls for expression of interest, rather than by national nomination,[93] and nor are all Member States represented on EFSA's Management Board.

---

[84] The Management Board has extensive responsibilities, REACH (n 1) Art 83.
[85] Ibid Art 76(1)(e).
[86] Ibid Art 85(3).
[87] Ibid Art 85(7). No such bar applies to the Member State Committee.
[88] Ibid Art 87.
[89] Ibid Art 85(5).
[90] Ibid Art 85(6).
[91] Commission (n 29) 86, suggesting that this could be explained by inexperience.
[92] See ch 2.
[93] See eg EFSA, *Call for Expressions of Interest for Membership of the Scientific Panels of the European Food Safety Authority* (EFSA/E/2013/001), advertised on the EFSA website. Four members of the 19-member genetically modified organisms panel are British, see www.efsa.europa.eu/en/gmo/gmomembers.htm.

The precise role of the different parts of the ECHA, the EU institutions, and the Member States themselves, varies in the different stages of REACH, but the Member States are involved in evaluation, authorisation and restrictions. Starting with the evaluation of dossiers, the Member States have the opportunity to comment on the ECHA's draft evaluation. In the absence of any Member State proposals, the ECHA may adopt its decision; if a Member State does make a proposal, the ECHA may amend its draft, which it can only adopt on unanimous agreement of the Member State Committee. In the absence of unanimity, the decision is taken by the Commission, with comitology maintaining national input.[94] The ECHA's draft Rolling Action Plan for the prioritisation of *substances* for evaluation can be adopted with the majority support of the Member State Committee.[95] Substance evaluation is actually carried out by a volunteering Member State, so that Member States who had taken a strong interest in particular chemicals before REACH retain their influence.[96] Substance evaluation is potentially resource intensive, and EFSA has sometimes experienced difficulty persuading Member States to take on risk assessment obligations for genetically modified organisms (GMOs).[97] No such difficulties have yet been reported in respect of chemicals, although competent authorities are concerned about resources.[98] The adoption of a decision on substance evaluation is subject to the same process as dossier evaluation, so disagreement triggers a need for unanimity in the Member State Committee, or the decision goes to comitology.[99]

Authorisation obligations apply to SVHCs, the identification of which falls into two stages, as mentioned above. Including a substance in the Candidate List depends in the first place on the submission of a dossier by a Member State, or a request from the Commission to the ECHA to prepare a dossier. The ECHA has no independent power to identify SVHCs.[100] In the absence of comments from 'interested parties', the ECHA, or a Member State, the substance on which a dossier has been prepared is added to the Candidate List. If there are comments, either the unanimous decision of the Member State Committee, or a Commission decision with comitology is necessary.[101] Inclusion of a substance in Annex XIV of REACH starts with a Recommendation from the ECHA to the Commission; Annex XIV is drawn up by a Commission Regulation, subject to comitology.[102]

---

[94] REACH (n 1) Art 51.

[95] Ibid Arts 45(5) and 85(8).

[96] Martens (n 6).

[97] European Commission, 'Report on the Implementation of Regulation 1829/2003 on Genetically Modified Food and Feed' COM (2006) 626 final, 10.

[98] Commission (n 29) 95.

[99] REACH (n 1) Art 52.

[100] *Rütgers* (n 24) [94].

[101] On practice, see Commission (n 29).

[102] Eg Commission Regulation 348/2013 amending Annex XIV to Regulation 1907/2006 on the Registration, Evaluation, Authorisation and Restriction of Chemicals (REACH) [2013] OJ L108/1. The 'regulatory procedure with scrutiny' (under which Council or Parliament can oppose a Commission draft, regardless of the view of the committee) survives Lisbon, Regulation 182/2011/EU laying down the

Applications for authorisation are submitted to the ECHA, and scrutinised by the Committee for Risk Assessment and the Committee for Socio-Economic Analysis. The Committees' 'draft opinions' are sent to the applicant, who has an opportunity to comment; the Opinions are finalised, 'taking this argumentation into account where appropriate', and sent to the Commission and Member States. The Commission then makes the final decision, through the comitology procedure.[103] Finally, the restrictions process is initiated either by a Member State preparing a dossier, or by a Commission request to the ECHA to prepare a dossier.[104] The two Committees each produce an opinion. The Commission decides, with Member State involvement through comitology.[105]

It should be clear that there are opportunities for the introduction of national concerns and interests at every stage of the REACH process. The Member States retain some powers of initiative, and their comments can trigger a search for consensus (albeit that there is ultimately no veto for any Member State). The Member States also have a further opportunity to provide input to an explicitly political process of decision-making in comitology. This means that sensitive or difficult issues, whether because of economic interests or because of the sensitivity of risk or uncertainty in a particular national context, have the opportunity to be aired. The lessons of GMOs and neonicitinoids, as discussed in chapter two, indicate that in some cases, deliberation to a decision that everyone is happy to live with is just impossible. But in most cases, any disagreement between the different actors should be identified early on in REACH, providing at least the opportunity for deliberation and consensus.

PUBLIC PARTICIPATION IN DECISION-MAKING

REACH is careful to provide opportunities for input from the registrant or applicant, and third party contributions are sought at various points in the process. For example, the identification of SVHCs, at both the Candidate List and the final Annex XIV stages, is subject to the invitation of comments from interested parties; restriction dossiers are available on the ECHA website, and interested parties are invited to comment, and to submit a socio-economic analysis.[106] REACH also requires the publication of the opinion of the Committee on

---

rules and general principles concerning mechanisms for control by Member States of the Commission's exercise of implementing powers (2011) OJ L55/13, Recital 21, Art 12. The regulatory procedure with scrutiny applies to the imposition of restrictions, and the listing of SVHCs in Annex XIV.

[103] REACH (n 1) Art 64(8). Recall the difficulty of distinguishing between 'implementing acts' (subject to comitology) and 'delegated acts' (not subject to comitology), ch 2. REACH would need to be amended if any of the current comitology provisions were to be shifted to delegation.

[104] Ibid Art 69. The ECHA can also prepare a dossier if the substance is contained in Annex XIV (SVHC), and the sunset date for authorisation has passed, Art 69(2).

[105] Applying the regulatory procedure with scrutiny (n 102).

[106] Ibid Art 69(6)

Socio-Economic Analysis (on authorisation, although the ECHA has undertaken to publish all Committee opinions[107]) and comments are sought.[108] The ECHA is also concerned to consult 'stakeholders' and what it calls 'institutional interested parties' (meaning the Commission, Member State competent authorities and third country representatives) when it drafts guidance on REACH. Its particular concern in this case is to achieve 'high certainty' that action in line with guidance will be acceptable to other actors.[109]

Public participation is, however, clearly limited.[110] In respect of authorisation, for example, the ECHA makes available on its website 'broad information on uses', and both committees have to 'take into account' information submitted by third parties.[111] Third parties are however only explicitly invited to provide information on 'alternative substances or technologies',[112] rather than on more general issues. There is no opportunity for third party intervention in review of authorisations.[113] External input into the evaluation of dossiers is also subject to interesting limitations. It will be recalled that the ECHA evaluates registrants' testing proposals. Interested parties are invited to make comments, but only on animal testing, not on other testing proposals.[114] Animal welfare is a well-established ethical consideration in EU law,[115] and REACH provides that animal testing 'shall be undertaken only as a last resort'.[116] Consultation in principle provides an opportunity for the ethical concerns about animal testing to be expressed. However, only 'scientifically valid information and studies', rather than ethical concerns, must be taken into account.[117] Anyone hoping that REACH will provide an opportunity to deliberate the circumstances in which we are prepared to tolerate animal experiments may be disappointed. In part, this is a reflection of the prioritisation of safety, in the sense that in the absence of reliable alternative testing methodologies, animal testing is not just permitted, but required. But equally, any argument that an alternative to animal testing would be not to *use* a banal substance (a particular colouring for soft furnishings, for example), is out of bounds.[118]

The allocation of public participation rights in REACH is slightly miserly: the legal entitlements to contribute are limited to particular moments, and the nature of the contribution is framed around technical and specialised information. There

---

[107] Ibid Arts 70 and 71; ECHA (n 76) Art 8.
[108] Ibid Art 71.
[109] ECHA, *(Revised) Consultation Procedure on Guidance* (Helsinki, ECHA, 2011) 2.
[110] See also Heyvaert (n 8).
[111] REACH (n 1) Art 64(3).
[112] Ibid Art 64(2).
[113] Fleurke and Somsen (n 16).
[114] Commission (n 29) 13, suggests that this is not only the limit of legally required consultation, but also of consultation in practice.
[115] Animal welfare has a place in the Treaty (Article 13 TFEU). On limitations of animal testing of cosmetics, see European Commission, *Communication on the Animal Testing and Marketing Ban and on the State of Play in Relation to Alternative Methods in the Field of Cosmetics* COM (2013) 135 final.
[116] REACH (n 1) Art 25; in particular for human toxicity, Art 13.
[117] Ibid Art 40(2).
[118] Although that is effectively the position on cosmetics in most cases (n 115).

are also opportunities for limited outsider input *within* the ECHA institutions. This could provide outsiders with a more profound opportunity to influence, but in terms of public accountability, is especially prone to the risk that the elite participants will develop shared interests that blunt accountability.[119] The Commission is allowed up to six representatives on the Management Board, including three individuals from 'interested parties' (currently representing the chemicals industry, trade unions and environment and consumer NGOs[120]), who do not have voting rights. The Parliament can also appoint two 'independent persons'.[121] In addition, the Management Board shall 'in agreement with the Commission', 'develop appropriate contacts' with 'relevant stakeholder organisations'.[122] Stakeholder organisations have been invited to send a regular observer to the Committees, judged a 'positive' experience, which 'helps guarantee the credibility and transparency of the decision-making process'.[123] In respect of Member States and 'stakeholders', especially industry, the balance between independence and responsiveness is a fine one. Some concern has been expressed about the ECHA's 'strong engagement with industry stakeholders'.[124] The Commission attributes this to the need to ensure industry compliance,[125] and the 'shift' in 'the responsibility to manage chemical risks from public authorities to industry'.[126]

REACH takes an instrumental understanding of public participation, revealed, for example, by the concern to 'improve the quality of the contributions from interested parties',[127] and in the concentration on particular pieces of information (such as animal testing[128] and alternatives). The engagement of outsiders is a source of information.[129] This is valuable, especially given the privatised nature of information generation, but might be contrasted with any more political opportunity to shape chemicals regulation in the EU.

---

[119] C Harlow and R Rawlings, 'Promoting Accountability in Multilevel Governance: A Network Approach' (2007) 13 *European Law Journal* 542.

[120] echa.europa.eu/web/guest/about-us/who-we-are/management-board/management-board-members.

[121] REACH (n 1) Art 79(1). The Parliament has appointed a professor of applied environmental science, and a consultant engineer who is also a former MEP.

[122] Ibid Art 108.

[123] ECHA (n 74) 62. See the list of 'accredited stakeholder organisations', echa.europa.eu/about-us/partners-and-networks/stakeholders/echas-accredited-stakeholder-organisations. Accredited stakeholders must have a 'legitimate interest', have activities at European Union level, be 'representative of their field of interest' and be non-profit making, ECHA, *ECHA's Approach to Engagement with its Accredited Stakeholder Organisations* (Helsinki, ECHA, 2011).

[124] See Commission (n 2) [4].

[125] Ibid, also on the challenges of implementation.

[126] Ibid [1].

[127] Ibid 70, in respect of the inclusion of a substance in Annex XIV.

[128] The ECHA reports that so far no animal test has been deemed unnecessary as a result of third party information, ECHA (n 74) 29. By 2012, some of the comments were 'more case specific', possibly triggering withdrawal by proponents, ECHA (n 21) 18, 19.

[129] For example, on restrictions, Commission (n 29) 75.

AUTHORISATION: BEYOND RISK?

However constrained, REACH does allow different viewpoints to be introduced into the decision-making process. But even when there is an opportunity to speak, whether outsiders are heard depends in part on what counts as a 'good' reason for the final decision.[130] The most pressing issues about chemicals revolve around 'risk', the likelihood of harms to people and the environment. It is not then a matter of criticism that the Regulation revolves around technical scientific input. But who bears risks, who benefits from risks, and which risks are 'acceptable', are important political questions. Decisions in this area may also have enormous economic consequences for one of the EU's most successful industries. None of the key steps in REACH (registration, evaluation, authorisation, restriction) is without politics. This section focuses on authorisation.

Certain aspects of REACH clearly take us into the politics beyond 'risk' to the environment or human health.[131] Authorisation 'shall be' granted if the 'risk to human health or the environment ... is adequately controlled'.[132] 'Adequate control' is open-ended, but basically means that particular 'safe' exposure levels have been identified and will not be exceeded, and the likelihood of an event such as an explosion is negligible.[133] In some cases, authorisation will not be possible under this provision, however, either because exposure cannot be reduced sufficiently or because a safe threshold cannot be set for that substance.[134] An authorisation can nevertheless be granted 'if it is shown that socio-economic benefits outweigh the risk to human health or the environment arising from the use of the substance and if there are no suitable alternative substances or technologies'.[135] Decisions on restrictions also 'take into account the socio-economic impact of the restriction'.[136]

This inclusion of socio-economic questions acknowledges the importance of issues other than risk. Annex XVI provides that a socio-economic analysis 'may' include a wide range of issues (including the impact of (non) authorisation or restriction on those in the supply chain, on consumers, on employment, on trade, competition and economic development, on human health and the environment), plus a catch all 'any other issue that is considered to be relevant'. A turn to public participation has long been the first response to the recognition that a broader range of information is necessary than can be provided by expert risk assessment. REACH takes a diametrically different approach, and instead seeks

---

[130] See the discussion in M Lee, 'Beyond Safety? The Broadening Scope of Risk Regulation' (2009) 62 *Current Legal Problems* 242; ch 2.

[131] REACH (n 1) Art 76(3) provides that 'the Committees ... may, if they consider it appropriate, seek advice on important questions of a general scientific or ethical nature from appropriate sources of expertise'; this is the only reference to general ethical concerns.

[132] Ibid Art 60(2).

[133] Ibid Art 60(2) refers to s 6.4 of Annex I.

[134] Ibid Art 60(3).

[135] Ibid Art 60(4).

[136] Ibid Art 68(1).

another form of expertise to go alongside risk assessment, specifically expertise in CBA. As we saw above, public participation is not conceptualised in REACH primarily as a way of incorporating public values into decision-making, but as a way to gather specific types of information.

Even the briefest of glances at the ECHA's hundreds of pages of guidance on socio-economic analysis indicates how difficult and evaluative the exercise is. In line with the discussion in chapter two, at virtually every step of the way, choices have to be made. The phrase 'based on judgment' peppers the Guidance, which emphasises that these judgments should be transparent in the published analysis, as well as the need to record uncertainty.[137] Impacts should be quantified 'to the extent possible, practicable and proportionate',[138] and often monetised,[139] although the things that can be quantified should not be prioritised over the things that cannot.[140] Uncertainty and judgment (rather than technical inevitability) are apparent from the very beginning, when the socio-economic analysis identifies the 'likely response' of relevant actors, before '[finding] and [using] the right data to estimate the impacts under each of these foreseen responses'.[141] The more obvious limitations of the process are clear in the (admittedly simplified) approach to carbon emissions:

> ... if refusal of the application leads to a first crude estimate that an additional 200 tonnes per year of CO_2 emissions will occur, one can use the information about market price of CO_2 (which at the time of writing is about €20/tonne CO_2) and deduct the significance of reducing emissions by 200 tonne CO_2 being worth about €4,000. Even though the 200 tonne CO_2 estimate may be highly uncertain at this point of the analysis, it may give a feel for whether this impact is significant.[142]

In this extract, both the price (as discussed in chapter six, the price of carbon is highly contingent on non-environmental factors, and has fallen well below €20) and the thing being priced (the quantity of emissions) are highly uncertain.

The EU institutions resist the language of CBA, reflecting their insistence that there is no need to monetise all costs and benefits. Nevertheless, the strong critique of CBA by those concerned about the political acceptability of decisions affecting the environment (discussed in chapter two) provides important warnings for the development of socio-economic assessment in the EU. There is a risk that CBA could transform a political decision on which we might reasonably disagree, into an obscure, but apparently inevitable technical judgment. However carefully the expert opinion is caveated, there are real questions about the capacity for autonomous political judgment to be exercised. It is important to guard against the possibility

---

[137] Eg ECHA, *Guidance on Socio-Economic Analysis: Restrictions* (Helsinki, ECHA, 2008) 103.
[138] ECHA, *Guidance on the Preparation of Socio-Economic Analysis as Part of an Application for Authorisation* (Helsinki, ECHA, 2011) 66.
[139] Although this will not always be possible, ECHA, ibid 55.
[140] Ibid 66.
[141] Ibid 10.
[142] Ibid 59.

that CBA will lead to an over-emphasis of and over-confidence in prediction (of what manufacturers, downstream users and consumers will do, for example), and a focus of decision-makers on the narrow range of information subject to expert pronouncement. CBA can also create distance from publics, and there is nothing in REACH suggesting any strong efforts to counteract that tendency.

The role of the industry is again important. The 'first draft' of the socio-economic analysis for authorisation is generally drafted by the 'industry'; third parties also have the opportunity to submit a socio-economic analysis.[143] The Committee uses this information to reach its own opinion. Industry applicants are seeking authorisation of substances that have already been found to be of 'very high concern', explaining 'whether the socio-economic benefits of continued use of the substance outweigh the risks of continued use'.[144] There is no suggestion that socio-economic concerns, for example about who bears and who benefits from a risk, could tip the balance in the other direction, and *prevent* the marketing of a substance. The point is not to deny the possibility that 'dangerous' substances may bring benefits, simply to observe the way that the legislation is structured.

Authorisation also goes beyond risk in its aim to ensure that SVHCs 'are progressively replaced by suitable alternative substances or technologies where these are economically and technically viable'.[145] The 'principle of substitution' attempts to reverse the implicit incentive, pre-REACH, to persist with established chemicals.[146] The energy spent on gathering information about risk, and trying to identify an 'acceptable' risk could on this approach be devoted to exploring alternatives to the risky substance. Substitution eliminates the risk posed by the substituted chemical (although of course the new substance or process may bring its own risks with it). 'Suitable alternative' is not defined in the legislation, which provides for the consideration of 'all relevant aspects', including 'overall risks to human health and the environment, taking into account … risk management measures', and 'the technical and economic feasibility of alternatives for the applicant'.[147] According to the ECHA, an alternative will not be 'suitable' if it is not 'technically feasible and available', 'not economically feasible for the applicant', or does not actually reduce the risk.[148]

The substitution requirement does not apply to chemicals across the board. First of all, the obligations apply only to SVHCs; substituting other substances with less hazardous alternatives is not addressed. Second, substitution is not necessary for all SVHCs; in some cases, risks will be 'adequately controlled'. ECHA guidance

---

[143] Member States are 'strongly recommended' to prepare a socio-economic analysis when they propose restrictions, ECHA (n 137).

[144] ECHA (n 138) 1.

[145] REACH (n 1) Art 55. See also Recital 12.

[146] 'Substitution' is also a feature of other legislation, for example, 'the use of less hazardous substances' is one of the 'criteria' for determining 'best available techniques' under Directive 2010/75/EU on Industrial Emissions (Integrated Pollution Prevention and Control) [2010] OJ L334/17.

[147] REACH (n 1) Art 60(5).

[148] ECHA (n 138) 38.

suggests that the 'adequate control' route to authorisation will only be satisfied if there is no 'alternative', or the applicant has a 'substitution plan'.[149] The applicant is indeed required to submit such a plan with the application. But there is no regulatory requirement for substitution as part of the conditions of authorisation. Implicitly recognising the gap, the Commission observes that 'substitution is the ultimate objective for both routes to authorisation', and says that it is 'evaluating the appropriate procedure to reflect this requirement'.[150] Pending more direct intervention, the ECHA has attempted to encourage good analyses of alternatives by providing that the robustness of the analysis, and information on research and development into alternatives, will affect the review date for any authorisation.[151] And whilst regulation may be the strongest driver of substitution,[152] requiring the applicant to consider alternatives does generate information. Public concern is a potentially strong driver of substitution,[153] especially if backed by a strong NGO campaign. The Commission has concluded that, five years after the entry into force of REACH, there were 'increased moves towards the substitution of [SVHCs] through the supply chain'.[154]

Finally, the opportunities for 'political' input into decision-making could take authorisation 'beyond risk'. The Commission and comitology take the final decision, consistently with the orthodox view on limited delegation to an agency, and the purported dichotomy, discussed in chapter two, between risk assessment and risk management.[155] In most cases, the comitology committee will probably quietly agree with the Commission. It is not inconceivable however that some decisions on chemicals will prove controversial and high profile, and be escalated through comitology. Political input through this procedure could potentially raise any number of different issues. There are, however, limited grounds for refusing authorisation, as set out above. Similarly, restrictions can only be imposed if the substance poses an unacceptable, or uncontrolled, risk; and a substance can only be placed on Annex XIV if it meets the criteria for a SVHC. There is no single 'technically' correct answer in many cases, so there is room for political input. But equally, not all reasons count as 'good' reasons.

CONCLUSIONS

REACH raises many questions about risk regulation in the internal market. Its complexity is legendary, and this chapter has only scratched the surface of

---

[149] Ibid 4.
[150] Commission (n 29) 71.
[151] Ibid.
[152] J Lohse et al, *Substitution of Hazardous Chemicals in Products and Processes: Final Report Prepared for the European Commission* (Hamburg, 2003).
[153] Ibid.
[154] Commission (n 2) [2.1.2].
[155] Commission (n 29) says that the key risk management issue is risk acceptability, 85.

the doctrinal position. The primary actors in REACH are industry, the ECHA (including a strong role for Member States) and the Commission (including a role for Member States through comitology). Third parties, especially environmental or consumer interest groups are enormously empowered by the release of information through REACH, although that release of information is limited in some respects. By contrast, there is rather little space for outsider engagement when decisions are taken within the REACH framework.

REACH only came into force in the middle of 2007, and given the long process of implementation, it is still too early to assess its success, or even to draw too many lessons from it. The authorisation process, for example, is in its very earliest stages, and at the time of writing, only one application had been placed on the ECHA's register, and consultation was open.[156] The relationships between the different actors in the process will be interesting to watch, as will the relative reliance on different sources of information. For example, if the Commission relies on ECHA opinions in the same way as it does on EFSA opinions, we will see another step on the (controversial) journey towards a common EU approach to risk assessment. It also remains to be seen whether the Committee on Socio-Economic Analysis provides a model towards the building of a similar common EU approach to CBA.

---

[156] echa.europa.eu/web/guest/addressing-chemicals-of-concern/authorisation/applications-for-authorisation. See Annex XIV for the 'sunset date' by which authorisation must be sought. An application has been made in respect of Bis(2-ethylhexyl) phthalate (DEHP).

10

After Authorisation in the Internal Market: GMOs and National Autonomy

INTRODUCTION

THE DEVELOPMENT AND content of EU environmental norms, and the role of different actors in that process, have been central to the discussion of EU environmental law in this book. But a full understanding of the governance of environmental protection in the EU also demands an examination of the authority of different actors after regulation, and the grounds on which that authority can be exercised. The scope of national autonomy in an area regulated by EU law, which is the extent to which Member States can adopt different or additional measures to those taken by the EU, is the focus of this chapter. This chapter explores national autonomy in the specific context of genetically modified organisms (GMOs), an area in which the disputed nature of EU authority brings the scope and strength of national autonomy into sharp relief.[1]

GMOs have been subject to an authorisation process since 1990, but public alarm at the prospect of their widespread marketing meant that between 1998 and 2004, the EU essentially abandoned its regulatory framework. What amounted to a de facto moratorium on the marketing of GMOs in the EU was condemned under international trade law,[2] of doubtful legality under EU law, and at odds with the Union's self-image as an economy built on scientific progress. Rather than insisting that the 1990 legislation be implemented, the pause in authorisations was used to negotiate an elaborate legislative package that was put in place in the early years of the twenty first century. The Member States, however, and the EU institutions, remain deeply divided. The first authorisation of a GM product in 2004 heralded merely a trickle of further authorisations, in controversial circumstances.[3]

---

[1] The formal responsibilities in EU law are on the Member State, but that is not to deny the significance of sub-national action in this area, see J Hunt, 'Ploughing their Own Furrow: Subnational Regions and the Regulation of GM Crop Cultivation' (2010–2011) 13 Cambridge Yearbook of European Legal Studies 135.

[2] World Trade Organisation (WTO) EC—Measures Affecting the Approval and Marketing of Biotech Products (DS291, 292, 293, 29 September 2006).

[3] Commission Decision 2004/657/EC authorising the placing on the market of sweet corn from genetically modified maize line Bt11 as a novel food or novel food ingredient under Regulation (EC) No 258/97 of the European Parliament and of the Council [2004] OJ L300/48.

This chapter briefly outlines the authorisation process applying to GMO food and feed crops. Many of the issues discussed in chapter two are relevant to the authorisation of GMOs.[4] The aim in this chapter is to complete the story, in respect of what happens *after* a product has been regulated in the EU. An authorised GMO in principle enjoys free movement in the internal market, but the internal market is not utterly inflexible to national concerns, and four issues will be considered. Member State action can be taken first under Article 114 (formerly Article 95) of the Treaty on the Functioning of the European Union (TFEU) itself. GMOs are regulated as products under the internal market provisions of the Treaty, not under the environment Title, so freedom of action under Article 193, discussed in chapter one, is not available. Secondly, the 'safeguard clauses' contained in the legislation may allow Member States to restrict individual GMOs, on a case by case basis. Thirdly, the failure of the authorisation process to lead to the smooth progress of GMOs on to the market has led the Commission to propose a 'new approach' to the cultivation of GMOs, under which Member States would be free, subject to internal market law, to restrict or prohibit the cultivation of GMOs, but only on grounds other than the protection of health or the environment. Whether this is *de*-harmonisation, or the non-environmental, non-health aspects of GMOs were simply never harmonised, is discussed below.

This discussion is relevant beyond the specific field of GMOs. Safeguard clauses are a common feature of EU environmental and internal market legislation; Article 114 derogations apply to all legislation adopted under Article 114 TFEU (measures 'which have as their object the establishment and functioning of the internal market'); and national decisions on non-harmonised (or de-harmonised) issues are subject to the basic provisions of internal market law discussed below. In addition, there is a recognised need to regulate the cultivation of GMOs in order to ensure the co-existence of GM, conventional and organic agriculture. This is a fourth category of national autonomy that applies only to GMOs.

AUTHORISATION

All GMOs must be authorised before they are released into the environment or placed on the market in the EU. This is a complicated process, attempting to distribute authority between the scientific and the political, and the centre and the Member State. Authorisation processes subtly vary depending on the intended function of the GMO. For current purposes, the most effective way to consider the key issues to is assume that the GMO in question will have (human) food or (animal) feed uses, and will be grown commercially in the EU. An application for authorisation of this GMO is made under the 2003 Food and Feed Regulation,

[4] For a detailed discussion of the authorisation process, see M Lee, *EU Regulation of GMOs: Law and Decision-making for a New Technology* (Cheltenham, Edward Elgar, 2008).

subject to some provisions of the 2001 Deliberate Release Directive.[5] The first substantive stage of the process, following the application for authorisation, is a risk assessment opinion from the European Food Safety Authority (EFSA), Depending on the precise content of the application, national risk assessors are involved in the risk assessment process to varying degrees, from consultation to actually carrying out an environmental risk assessment. In some cases this involvement is mandatory, in others at the discretion of EFSA. In a phenomenon familiar from earlier chapters, the risk assessment process is highly dependent on the applicant's provision of information for the risk assessment.[6] When EFSA states the reasons for its opinion, it must include the information on which the opinion is based, including the responses of consulted competent authorities.[7] The EFSA opinion is passed to all Member States and the Commission, and made public.[8]

Following this risk assessment stage, the final decision on authorisation is taken by the Commission, together with the Member States in comitology, discussed in chapter two. The Commission submits a draft decision to the comitology committee, 'taking into account the opinion of [EFSA], any relevant provisions of Community law and other legitimate factors relevant to the matter under consideration'.[9] As discussed in chapter two, the Member States have been consistently unable to reach a qualified majority either to support or to reject the Commission's draft decisions on GMOs. All authorisations of GMOs under the current legislation have been granted by the Commission, adopting its decision in the absence of a decision in comitology.[10] Commission decisions are based overwhelmingly on EFSA scientific opinions rather than on competing evidence from the Member States or environmental or consumer groups, or on the 'other legitimate factors' criterion (discussed briefly in chapter two).[11] The central and autonomous role of the Commission, distant from European publics, raises questions about the legitimacy of the process for an issue that raises such profound

---

[5] Directive 2001/18/EC on the deliberate release into the environment of genetically modified organisms ('Deliberate Release Directive') [2001] OJ L106/1; Regulation 1829/2003/EC on genetically modified food and feed ('Food and Feed Regulation') [2003] OJ L268/1. See Case C-58/10 to 68/10 *Monsanto v Ministre de l'Agriculture et de la peche* [2011] ECR I-7763 on the relationship between the pieces of legislation. Commission Decision 2009/244/EC concerning the placing on the market, in accordance with Directive 2001/18/EC, of a carnation (*Dianthus caryophyllus L.*, line 123.8.12) genetically modified for flower colour [2009] OJ L72/18 was made under the Deliberate Release Directive alone.

[6] See chs 5 and 9.

[7] Food and Feed Reg (n 5) Art 6(6).

[8] Ibid Art 6(7).

[9] Ibid Art 7(1).

[10] Deliberate Release Directive (n 5); Food and Feed Reg, ibid. Authorisation decisions can be found on the GMO register, ec.europa.eu/food/dyna/gm_register/index_en.cfm, and the recitals indicate the outcome of comitology, eg Commission Decision 2010/135/EU concerning the placing on the market, in accordance with Directive 2001/18/EC of a potato product (Solanum tuberosum L. line EH92-527-1) genetically modified for enhanced content of the amylopectin component of starch [2010] OJ L53/11, Recitals 21 and 22.

[11] For more detail, see Lee (n 4).

concerns among clearly divided Member States. The authority of these decisions is resisted, with some Member States refusing to allow GMOs in their territory, relying on measures of doubtful legality.[12]

Most of the GMOs authorised so far are imported for use in animal feed.[13] There is very little cultivation of GM crops in the EU, although some GM seeds were authorised for cultivation under the pre-moratorium legislation. Only one GMO was authorised for cultivation in the EU between 2004 and September 2013, a potato (Amflora) with a high starch content, for use in industry. Just how controversial and difficult the Amflora process was is indicated by the fact that five years,[14] and the threat of legal action by BASF, passed between the final EFSA opinion and authorisation (by the Commission in the absence of a decision in comitology).[15]

In principle, subject to conditions in the authorisation, an authorised seed can be grown anywhere in the EU, and GM food and animal feed can be sold anywhere in the EU. This goes some way to explaining the high stakes in the authorisation process, and the difficulty of finding a compromise. The Commission's 'new approach' to national freedom of action in respect of cultivation, discussed below, is supposed to reduce disagreement in comitology, and make authorisation easier, although its limits are significant. The rest of this chapter explores the authority of Member States to restrict the use of GMOs after authorisation. Finding a route to enhance national autonomy, whilst respecting the internal market, is proving to be very difficult.

ART 114 TFEU: THE 'ENVIRONMENTAL GUARANTEE'

As discussed in chapter one, Article 114 TFEU provides a legal base for measures designed with the aim of establishing or ensuring the functioning of the internal market. Article 114 provides a so-called 'environmental guarantee', introducing the possibility of derogating from measures passed under that Article, to reassure those Member States who were concerned that the move away from unanimity in this area would compromise their high standards in areas such as the environment and public health. Measures must be notified to the Commission, and are not

---

[12] ec.europa.eu/food/food/biotechnology/gmo_ban_cultivation_en.htm.

[13] Although not all, eg, the Amflora potato is for industrial use, Decision 2010/135/EU (n 10). Note that there are no labelling obligations in respect of meat, eggs or dairy products from animals fed with GM feed.

[14] European Policy Evaluation Consortium Report to DG Sanco, *Evaluation of the EU legislative Framework in the Field of Cultivation of GMOs under Directive 2001/18/EC and Regulation (EC) No 1829/2003 and the placing on the market of GMOs on or in products Under Directive 2001/18/EC; Final Report* (2011) 51.

[15] Decision 2010/135/EU (n 10). Hungary is seeking annulment of this decision, challenging the sufficiency of the risk assessment, particularly with respect to the antibiotic resistance gene, Case T-240/10 *Hungary v Commission*.

effective until the Commission has accepted them (or failed to take action within the appropriate time limits).[16]

Article 114(4) allows for the *maintenance* of *existing* national measures after the adoption of EU measures, on the 'grounds of major needs referred to in Article 36 [discussed below], or relating to the protection of the environment or the working environment'. National measures on GMOs have so far been dealt with as *new* measures under Article 114(5), which allows for the *introduction* of *new* national measures for the protection of (only) 'the environment or the working environment'.[17] This paragraph is stricter than paragraph 4, on the basis that new measures are thought more likely to jeopardise harmonisation, because existing measures will have been taken into account in the harmonisation.[18] New national measures must be 'based on new scientific evidence relating to the protection of the environment or the working environment on grounds of a problem specific to that Member State, arising after the adoption of the harmonisation measure'. These conditions are cumulative.[19] Austrian measures banning the use of GMOs in the Upper Austria region allow us to examine this provision in some detail. The Austrian measures, which aimed to protect organic agriculture, as well as nature and the environment, were rejected by the Commission on a number of grounds; Austria's appeal was rejected by both the General Court and the Court of Justice.[20]

The requirement that the measure be based on 'new' scientific evidence has the potential to be highly restrictive. Austria relied on a report published after the adoption of the legislation, but the Commission rejected the use of this report because the data it contained 'were for a large part available prior to the adoption' of the Directive and 'the vast majority of the sources ... were published prior to the adoption' of the Directive.[21] This demand for new data places a heavy burden on Member States, excluding, for example, evidence that exists before the EU measures but was not taken into account, as well as suggesting that only a particular type of evidence suffices; not the 'broad compilation' of evidence provided by

---

[16] Case C-319/97 *Kortas* [1999] ECR I-3143. The Commission has six months to accept or reject the measure, 12 months '[when] justified by the complexity of the matter and in the absence of danger for human health', Art 114(6) TFEU.

[17] Art 114(8) TFEU provides for a 'specific problem on public health' to be brought to the attention of the Commission, which must 'immediately examine' whether to propose an 'adaptation' of those measures.

[18] Eg Case C-512/99 *Germany v Commission* [2003] ECR I-845.

[19] Case T-182/06 *Netherlands v Commission* [2007] ECR II-1983.

[20] Commission Decision 2003/653 relating to national provisions on banning the use of genetically modified organisms in the region of Upper Austria notified by the Republic of Austria pursuant to Article 95(5) of the EC Treaty [2003] OJ L230/34; Case T-366/03 and 235/04 *Land Oberosterreich and Austria v Commission* [2005] ECR II-4005; Case C-439 and 454/05 *Land Oberosterreich and Austria v Commission* [2007] ECR I-7141. FM Fleurke, 'What Use for Article 95(5) EC? An Analysis of *Land Oberosterreich and Austria v Commission*' (2008) 20 *Journal of Environmental Law* 267.

[21] Decision 2003/653, ibid [65].

Austria.[22] The requirement for new data might be compared with the approach taken to Article 114(4), under which a Member State may rely on its 'divergent assessments' of risks, without necessarily any 'new or different scientific evidence'.[23] Importantly, Sharpston AG took a similar approach when the Austrian case was appealed to the European Court of Justice (ECJ), concluding that 'new conclusions drawn from existing data *may* constitute new scientific evidence within the meaning of Article [114](5)'.[24] Although Austria could not provide such evidence in this case, this is a more realistic understanding of what might provoke a change in national policy, and allows greater scope for national diversity.

The capacity and willingness of the Commission to subject the nature and quality of the evidence relied on by the Member States to 'centralised' scrutiny is also significant. In the Austrian decision, EFSA assessed the Austrian science from scratch, and the Commission (with two layers of Court approval) relied heavily on EFSA's dismissal of Austria's competing evidence. EU level 'review' of national science on GMOs is not uncommon. For example, a decision on a notification by Portugal, relating to the specific ecological and agricultural conditions of Madeira, was delayed by the Commission to allow for an EFSA opinion: 'a thorough scientific risk assessment is necessary'.[25] Whilst it is important to subject complex evidence to scrutiny, in many cases the Member State by definition draws different conclusions from those drawn by EFSA during the authorisation process. An implicit scientific hierarchy may be developed through the reliance on EFSA.

Secondly, the requirement that a problem be 'specific to the Member State' is also potentially highly restrictive. In the same Austrian case, citing EFSA, the Commission held that Austria had failed to establish either that 'small-structured farming systems' are specific to this region, or to provide scientific evidence establishing that 'this area of Austria had unusual or unique ecosystems that required separate risk assessments from those conducted for Austria as a whole or for other similar areas of Europe'.[26] Both the General Court and the Court of Justice rather abruptly rejected Austria's appeal on the basis of lack of evidence identifying a problem specific to the Member State.[27] The ECJ provided an important clarification when it reminded us that the requirement is not that the problem should be 'unique' to the Member State, but that it should be 'specific'.[28] The question

---

[22] M Doherty, 'The Application of Article 95(4)-(6) of the EC Treaty: Is The Emperor Still Unclothed?' (2008) 7 *Yearbook of European Environmental Law* 48. See also Doherty's discussion of the *collection* of the data.

[23] Case C-3/00 *Denmark v Commission* [2003] ECR I-2643 [63].

[24] *Austria* (n 20) [124]. This point was not pursued by the Court, given its findings on a 'specific problem' and the cumulative nature of the requirements.

[25] Commission Decision 2009/828/EC relating to the draft regional legislative decree declaring the Autonomous Region of Madeira to be an area free of genetically modified organisms, notified by the Republic of Portugal pursuant to Article 95(5) of the EC Treaty [2009] OJ L294/16.

[26] Decision 2003/653 (n 20) [71].

[27] *Austria* (General Court) (n 20) [68]. Neither Court considered all conditions of Art 114(5), which are cumulative.

[28] *Austria* (ECJ) (n 20) [65]–[68].

remains as to how extensive the problem might be: 'a specific problem clearly lies somewhere between one which is unique and one which is common, generalised or widespread'.[29] In *Netherlands v Commission*, the General Court puts the question in context: specificity should be looked at 'from the angle of the aptness or inaptness' of harmonisation: if harmonisation would be inappropriate, national measures are appropriate.[30] The problems must also be 'so acute as to distinguish them significantly' from those elsewhere.[31] This is helpful to understanding, and emphasises the exhaustive nature of the harmonisation. But it is very restrictive. There is a danger that specificity completely precludes higher national standards in respect of shared environmental problems,[32] for example climate change. The 'specific' problem must furthermore arise after the adoption of the EU measure. Sharpston AG considered this in *Austria*. Small increases in the proportion of agriculture devoted to organic farming would not demonstrate the existence of a 'newly arisen problem'. However, a problem that was 'latent' at the time of the legislation, and 'only subsequently revealed' could fall within Article 114(5),[33] although the Advocate General links this 'revelation' with the requirement for new scientific evidence.

Thirdly, the only interests that can be pursued under Article 114(5) are the protection of the environment or the working environment. Efforts to avoid negative impacts on organic farming are deemed to relate 'more to a socio-economic problem than to the protection of the environment or the working environment'.[34] This understanding of the values of organic farming is contentiously narrow, as discussed further below. And finally, the measures must not constitute 'a means of arbitrary discrimination', 'a disguised restriction on trade between Member States' or 'an obstacle to the functioning of the internal market'.[35] The first two requirements are familiar from Article 36 TFEU.[36] For current purposes, it suffices to say that they are connected with proportionality, discussed below, and the need to establish the genuineness of the pursuit of the protected objective. Since the third criterion could in principle thwart any application under Article 114(5), it must also be a matter of proportionality.[37]

---

[29] Ibid [110] (Sharpston AG).

[30] Relating to air pollution see *Netherlands* (n 19) [64].

[31] Ibid [53].

[32] The Netherlands, ibid, wanted to regulate particulates from diesel vehicles more strictly than the EU legislation; comparisons were drawn with other Member States, 'such as Belgium, Austria, Greece, the Czech Republic, Lithuania, Slovenia and Slovakia' [67]. The ECJ overturned the General Court on the basis of the Commission's failure to take account of relevant information, without discussing the substance of 'specificity', Case C-405/07P *Netherlands v Commission* [2008] ECR I-8301.

[33] *Austria* (n 20) [131], [132] (Sharpston AG). Austria did not attempt to provide evidence about the novelty of the impact on small structured farming.

[34] Commission Decision 2003/653/EC (n 20) [67].

[35] Art 114(6) TFEU.

[36] Although they have been little examined, see J Jans and H Vedder, *European Environmental Law: After Lisbon* (Groningen, Europa Law Publishing, 2012) 273.

[37] Doherty (n 22) 65, citing the Commission. See also N de Sadeleer, 'Procedures for Derogations from the Principle of Approximation of Laws under Article 95 EC' (2003) 40 *Common Market Law Review* 889, 906.

We can conclude that the opportunities for national autonomy under Article 114(5) TFEU are narrow, especially in the requirements for 'new' scientific evidence and specificity. The interpretation of these two issues could be more generous,[38] and Sharpston AG suggests a very slightly more progressive approach. But it is clear that Article 114 does not accommodate disagreement about the adequacy of a risk assessment, or political or cultural differences of opinion, such as the possibility that more certainty on safety might be demanded where uncertainty is particularly sensitive. Article 114(5) applies only to the protection of the environment or the working environment, whilst GMOs raise much broader issues. Over its years of operation, the ambition that Article 114 might provide an 'environmental guarantee' to EU citizens has become rather distant.[39]

SAFEGUARD CLAUSES

EU directives and regulations often contain safeguard clauses, allowing Member States to take action to respond to problems emerging after authorisation. The use of safeguard clauses is explicitly authorised by the Treaty for those measures passed under Article 114 TFEU;[40] this Treaty authorisation sidesteps any legal or conceptual concerns about whether a 'harmonising' measure can allow for derogation in this way.

Article 23(1) of the Deliberate Release Directive,[41] headed 'Safeguard clause', provides that:

> Where a Member State, as a result of new or additional information made available since the date of the consent and affecting the environmental risk assessment or reassessment of existing information on the basis of new or additional scientific knowledge, has detailed grounds for considering that a GMO as or in a product which has been properly notified and has received written consent under this Directive constitutes a risk to human health or the environment, that Member State may provisionally restrict or prohibit the use and/or sale of that GMO as or in a product on its territory.

The only permissible objectives of safeguard action under this clause are to protect the environment or human health, so that any broader social, ethical and political questions are excluded. The Deliberative Release Directive makes high demands in terms of scientific evidence, although it takes a slightly broader approach than Article 114(5). Reassessment of earlier evidence is possible, and the reference to 'new or *additional* information' suggests that information that existed, but was not considered, during authorisation, may form the basis for a decision.

---

[38] See also Doherty, ibid; H Sevenster, 'The Environmental Guarantee after Amsterdam: Does the Emperor Have New Clothes?' (2000) 1 *Yearbook of European Environmental Law* 291.

[39] Doherty, ibid; Sevenster, ibid.

[40] Art 114(10) TFEU. There is a similar provision for measures adopted under the environment Title, Art 191(2) TFEU.

[41] Deliberate Release Directive (n 5).

Information can also be 'reassessed', but only 'on the basis of new or additional scientific knowledge'. A disagreement about the interpretation of the evidence, or about the appropriate level of safety, is not likely to be tolerated.

A decision to take safeguard measures under the Deliberate Release Directive must be notified to the Commission and all other Member States. The Commission, through comitology, can request a Member State to withdraw its measure, but it has been reluctant to resist national safeguard measures on GMOs.[42] When it has pressed Member States, things have not always gone well, since the Council has reached qualified majority decisions to reject Commission proposals that challenge national safeguard measures restricting the cultivation of GMOs.[43] Given how difficult it has been to reach qualified majorities on GMOs, this amounts to a strong statement that Member States are not content to impose the cultivation of GMOs on their reluctant peers. The Council has justified its position with the argument that 'the different agricultural structures and regional ecological characteristics in the European Union need to be taken into account in a more systematic manner in the environmental risk assessment of GMOs'.[44] Member States have been unable to reach a qualified majority in either direction in respect of Commission proposals for the lifting of safeguard measures that do not involve cultivation, leaving the Commission free to adopt its proposals.[45]

In fact, the safeguard clause in the Deliberate Release Directive is now of limited practical significance, since most GMO authorisations are for animal feed. Applications for use as animal feed are made under the Food and Feed Regulation.[46] The Food and Feed Regulation appears to restrict dramatically the possibility of national safeguard action. 'Emergency measures' (not safeguard measures) may be triggered either by an opinion from EFSA, or where 'it is evident' that authorised

---

[42] Similarly, the Commission allowed its deadline for rejecting Portugal's notification of measures declaring the island of Madeira to be GM-free under Art 114 TFEU (n 25) to pass by, with the result that Portugal was able to introduce its restrictions. The period within which the Commission could object expired on 4 May 2010; presumably this is connected with the 'new approach' announced by the Commission in July 2010. Equally, however, the Commission finds it difficult to exercise its authority in this area.

[43] Eg 2773rd Council meeting, 18 December 2006, European Commission, *Proposal for a Council Decision concerning the provisional prohibition of the use and sale in Austria of genetically modified maize (Zea mays L. line T25) pursuant to Directive 2001/18/EC* COM (2006) 510 final; 2785th Council meeting, 20 February 2007, European Commission, *Proposal for a Council Decision concerning the provisional prohibition of the use and sale in Hungary of genetically modified maize (Zea mays L. line MON810) expressing the Bt cryIA(b) gene, pursuant to Directive 2001/18/EC* COM (2006) 713; 2928th Council meeting, 2 March 2009, European Commission, *Proposal for a Council Decision concerning the provisional prohibition of the use and sale in Austria of genetically modified maize (Zea mays L. line MON810) pursuant to Directive 2001/18/EC* COM (2009) 56 final.

[44] See Council meetings, ibid.

[45] Commission Decision 2008/495/EC concerning the provisional prohibition of the use and sale in Austria of genetically modified maize (*Zea mays L.* line MON810) pursuant to Directive 2001/18/EC [2008] OJ L172/25; Commission Decision 2008/470/EC concerning the provisional prohibition of the use and sale in Austria of genetically modified maize (*Zea mays L.* line T25) pursuant to Directive 2001/18/EC [2008] OJ L162/31.

[46] Deliberate Release Directive and Food and Feed Regulation (n 5).

products 'are likely to constitute a serious risk to human health, animal health or the environment', and 'the need to suspend or modify urgently an authorisation arises'.[47] The ECJ has interpreted the emergency measures provision as 'referring to a significant risk which clearly jeopardises human health, animal health or the environment'.[48] Whilst this is no more precise a threshold for emergency action than that set in the legislation, it does confirm that the evidential threshold is a high one. The Court went further, adding the requirement, not explicit in the Food and Feed Regulation, that the risk 'must be established on the basis of new evidence based on reliable scientific data'.[49]

The safeguard clause in the Deliberate Release Directive cedes to sectoral legislation on food and feed (so the Food and Feed Regulation) if it contains 'a safeguard clause at least equivalent to that laid down in this Directive'; the Food and Feed Regulation, however, provides that the Deliberate Release Directive's safeguard clause shall not apply to authorisations granted under that Regulation.[50] *Monsanto v Ministre de l'Agriculture et de la peche ('Monsanto (France)')* arose out of litigation over whether France could restrict the availability of GM animal feed on the basis of the safeguard clause in the Deliberate Release Directive.[51] The Court found that only the emergency measures under the Food and Feed Regulation were available.

The emphasis in *Monsanto (France)* was on the similarities between the two provisions. In *Monsanto Agricoltura Italia SpA v Presidenza del Consiglio dei Ministri ('Monsanto (Italy)')*, the Court had held that safeguard clauses 'must be understood as giving specific expression to the precautionary principle'.[52] Mengozzi AG, in *Monsanto (France)*, explains that the precautionary principle 'makes a decisive contribution to standardising the conditions laid down in the directive and the regulation';[53] the Court confirms that measures 'cannot validly be based on a purely hypothetical approach to risk, founded on mere assumptions which have not yet been scientifically verified', and 'may be adopted only if they are based on a risk assessment which is as complete as possible'.[54]

---

[47] Food and Feed Regulation, ibid, Art 34.

[48] *Monsanto (France)* (n 5) [76]: 'the specification that the risk must be "serious" ... must, in my view, be construed as meaning that the probability of a harmful event occurring is real and not within the normal limits of the risk inherent in any human activity' [66] (Mengozzi AG).

[49] Ibid [76].

[50] Deliberate Release Directive (n 5) Art 12(1); Food and Feed Regulation, ibid, Art 5(5).

[51] Above n 5.

[52] Case C-236/01 *Monsanto Agricoltura Italia SpA v Presidenza del Consiglio dei Ministri ('Monsanto (Italy)')* [2003] ECR I-8105 [110], citing Case C-6/99 *Greenpeace France v Ministère de l'Agriculture et de la Pêche* [2000] ECR I-1651.

[53] *Monsanto (France)* (n 5) [64], [66] (Mengozzi AG).

[54] Ibid [77] (ECJ). See chs 1 and 2 above. M Weimer, 'The Right to Adopt Post-Market Restrictions of GM Crops in the EU—A Shift from de-Centralised Multi-Level to centralised Governance in the Case of GM Foods' (2012) 3 *European Journal of Risk Regulation* 467 argues that the decision departs from the conclusion on the role of the precautionary principle in safeguard clauses in *Monsanto (Italy)*, (n 52).

Given its recognition of the importance of uncertainty, we might have expected the precautionary principle to, if anything, relax the evidential demands associated with use of safeguard clauses. *Monsanto (France)*, however, seems to tighten evidential requirements, for example as to risk assessment and new evidence. More importantly for current purposes, once emergency measures have been triggered by an 'evident … serious risk', under the Food and Feed Regulation, the centralised procedure set out in the General Food Law applies.[55] This provides for action by the Commission, with comitology. A Member State can take independent action only where it has informed the Commission of the need to take emergency measures, and the Commission has not acted; again, the national measures go to comitology. The Court in *Monsanto (France)* could not be clearer about the absence of national autonomy under the Food and Feed Regulation. It states that the objective of the legislation is precisely 'avoiding artificial disparities in the treatment of a serious risk' (begging the question as to when differences are 'artificial'). In that context, 'the assessment and management of a serious and evident risk ultimately come under the sole responsibility of the Commission and Council, subject to review by the European Union Courts'.[56] In deciding that the provisions in the Directive and Regulation are 'equivalent', Mengozzi AG is able to assert that 'the only significant difference' between them 'is the party called on to adopt a measure',[57] the implication being that it makes no difference who makes decisions based on a risk assessment. This is convenient for internal market values, but, as discussed in chapter two, risk assessments are not simply objective assessments that are universally applicable, but are tied up with cultural and political values and assumptions. *Monsanto (France)* is completely unconcerned with the national autonomy provided by safeguard clauses. The Treaty however, whilst not requiring safeguard clauses (they should be included only 'in appropriate cases') does make clear that they are directed at Member States.[58]

THE 'NEW APPROACH' TO GMO CULTIVATION

The regulation of GMOs in the EU seems to be in a state of perpetual reform. The original Directive[59] was replaced by the Deliberate Release Directive in 2001, and almost immediately amended by the Food and Feed Regulation in 2003.

---

[55] Food and Feed Regulation (n 5); Regulation 178/2002/EC Laying down the general principles and requirements of food law, establishing the European Food Safety Authority and laying down procedures in matters of food safety ('General Food Law') [2002] OJ L31/1 Arts 53 and 54.

[56] *Monsanto (France)* (n 5) [78].

[57] Ibid [42] (Mengozzi AG).

[58] Art 114(10) TFEU: 'The harmonisation measures referred to above shall, in appropriate cases, include a safeguard clause authorising the Member States to take, for one or more of the non-economic reasons referred to in Article 36, provisional measures subject to a Union control procedure'.

[59] Directive 1990/220 on the deliberate release into the environment of genetically modified organisms [1990] OJ L117/15.

This regulatory regime has not provided for the peaceful authorisation and commercialisation of GMOs in the EU, and the Commission is seeking further reforms. This includes a general review of the authorisation process.[60] Particularly interesting for current purposes is the package of measures published by the Commission in summer 2010,[61] including a proposal for the insertion of a new Article 26b into the Deliberate Release Directive.[62] Even if this proposal, currently objected to by a number of Member States, never enters into law,[63] it provides interesting insights into the nature of harmonisation and autonomy in the EU. Proposed Article 26b, headed 'cultivation' provides:

> Member States may adopt measures restricting or prohibiting the cultivation of all or particular GMOs authorised in accordance with … this Directive or [the Food and Feed Regulation], … in all or part of their territory, provided that:
> (a) those measures are based on grounds other than those related to the assessment of the adverse effect on health and environment which might arise from the deliberate release or the placing on the market of GMOs; and,
> (b) that they are in conformity with the Treaties.

This proposal looks like a profound shift away from a very determined effort on the part of the Commission to harmonise GMOs, and to resist national and sub-national independence. The expectation is that greater flexibility after authorisation will make the authorisation process less fraught, suggesting that a divided market in GMOs might be a price to pay for cultivation in favourable Member States.[64] Measures must be 'reasoned', and communicated in advance.[65] Three other conditions are imposed on national autonomy: first, it only applies in respect of cultivation; secondly, that the measures are 'based on grounds other than those related to the assessment of the adverse effect on health and environment'; and thirdly, that they conform with the treaties.

The limitation of the proposed liberalisation to cultivation may restrict its ability to reduce controversy over GMOs. Cultivation is certainly especially

---

[60] ec.europa.eu/food/food/biotechnology/evaluation/index_en.htm.

[61] European Commission, 'Freedom for Member States to Decide on the Cultivation of Genetically Modified Crops' COM (2010) 380 final.

[62] European Commission, 'Proposal for a Regulation Amending Directive 2001/18/EC as Regards the Possibility for the Member States to Restrict or Prohibit the Cultivation of GMOs in their Territory' COM (2010) 375 final.

[63] Council *Progress Report*, 6 June 2012, register.consilium.europa.eu/pdf/en/12/st10/st10883-re01. en12.pdf.

[64] 2912th Council meeting, 4 December 2008, *Council Conclusions on Genetically Modified Organisms* are attributed by the Commission and others with provoking reform, but their literal content is simply rather anodyne encouragement for the improved implementation of the legal framework. Subsequently, Austria, supported by 12 other Member States, called for 'options to be considered that would 'allow Member States to decide for themselves as regards cultivation, without challenging the general authorisation procedure', *Genetically Modified Organisms—a Way Forward—Information from the Austrian Delegation*, 25 June 2009.

[65] The usual three-month 'standstill period' in Directive 1998/34/EC laying down a procedure for the provision of information in the field of technical standards and regulations [1998] OJ L204/37 will exceptionally not apply.

controversial, and stimulates the greatest Member State *unity* in the resistance to GMOs. But it is not the full extent of national antipathy to GMOs; proposed Article 26b seems to have no relevance to the continued comitology stalemate on applications that exclude cultivation from their scope.[66]

The limitation of reasons for restrictions on GMOs to non-environment/health concerns is significant. Risks to the environment and human health are deemed to have been satisfactorily addressed by the authorisation procedure. Whilst non-risk (non-health or environment) grounds are important in the resistance to GMOs, resistance is often at least *presented* in terms of risk. Perhaps this presentation is in part simply an effort to frame objections in the terms most readily heard by the regulatory regime,[67] and the recent *Evaluation* of the legislative framework concluded that 'there is a general understanding ... that the use of national safeguard measures, while presented as having a scientific justification, is sometimes an expression of non-scientific objections to GMO cultivation and of political circumstances.'[68] The Commission's legal opinion on its proposal similarly describes it as 'designed to tackle the issue of safeguard clauses adopted to address concerns not related to health and/or environment protection'.[69] But given the still significant disagreement over the risk assessment process, environment or health derogations should presumably be taken at face value in some cases.[70] These concerns will need to go through safeguard measures or Article 114 TFEU, the limitations of which are discussed above. A more generous approach, exceptionally recognising different appetites for risk and uncertainty, would be helpful.

However, allowing national restrictions on grounds that go beyond health and environmental protection is significant. GMOs raise fundamental questions about the sort of world in which we wish to live. Ethical concerns about the extent to which it is acceptable to interfere with nature; political questions about enhanced corporate control over the food sector; and distributional issues such as possible economic dislocation for small or organic farmers, all go beyond adverse effects on health and the environment.[71] These concerns are very likely to manifest themselves differently in different national and local contexts.[72] The argument that technological developments might tend to incentivise particular types of social and institutional arrangements is not unique to GMOs. Nuclear

---

[66] All authorisations in 2012 and until September 2013 (none of which was for cultivation) were made by the Commission, following failure to reach qualified majority either way in committee or appeal committee, see (n 10).

[67] M Lee, 'Beyond Safety? The Broadening Scope of Risk Regulation' (2009) 62 *Current Legal Problems* 242.

[68] EPEC (n 14) 6.

[69] European Commission, 'Considerations on Legal Issues on GMO Cultivation Raised in the Opinion of the Legal Service of the Council of the European Union of 5 November 2010' SEC (2010) 1454 final [20].

[70] Risk assessment is the issue on which views are 'most diverse' according to EPEC (n 14) 14.

[71] See the detailed discussion in Lee (n 4) ch 1.

[72] See S Jasanoff, *Designs on Nature: Science and Democracy in Europe and the United States* (Oxford, Princeton University Press, 2005).

power, for example, has been said to demand (or at least to be highly compatible with) more rather than less authoritarian and unequal social structures.[73] With GMOs, one concern is that insistence on the inclusion of GMOs in EU crop cultivation implies high capital costs, with possible disadvantages for traditional small, family farming systems, and organic production. GM agriculture may instead be highly compatible with a farming system dominated by big corporations farming intensively. Countries like Austria have so far found it difficult to find a space for these sorts of concerns in the regulatory system.

The third limitation on national autonomy is that measures taken under proposed Article 26b must be 'in conformity with the treaties'. Since secondary legislation cannot amend the Treaty, that would be the case whether or not explicitly stated. Goods are entitled to free movement in the internal market, and Article 34 TFEU prohibits quantitative restrictions on imports, and measures having equivalent effect. Sometimes there are difficult decisions about whether restrictions on use fall under Article 34, but it seems to be reasonably straightforward that a complete ban on cultivation would have 'a considerable influence on the behaviour of consumers', and 'greatly restrict' the use of GM seeds;[74] demand would probably completely disappear. So a cultivation ban would fall within Article 34.

Article 36 TFEU provides that Article 34 'shall not preclude' Member State restrictions that protect specified values: 'public morality, public policy or public security; the protection of health and life of humans, animals or plants; the protection of national treasures possessing artistic, historic or archaeological value; or the protection of industrial and commercial property'. In addition, the Court allows the pursuit of 'mandatory requirements' in the public interest, including environmental protection.[75] Article 36 and the mandatory requirements doctrine are available only in respect of areas that are not harmonised at EU level. Whether or not an area has been exhaustively harmonised is not always straightforward.[76] But the legislation on GMOs does by common consensus provide for exhaustive harmonisation at least in respect of environmental protection and human health, hence the turn to Article 114(5) as above. Proposed Article 26b purports to *de*-harmonise *non*-health and *non*- environment issues, allowing Member States to rely on Article 36 TFEU and mandatory requirements again for those unharmonised areas.[77]

It is possible that the 'other' (non-health, non-environment) issues were never harmonised at all, and so Article 36 and mandatory requirements always applied in any event. In practical terms, this is crucial if the proposal does not make it through the legislative process, or if Member States wish to rely on 'other' reasons

---

[73] Discussed in Lee (n 67).

[74] Case C-142/05 *Åklagaren v Mickelsson and Roos* [2009] ECR I-4273 [26] and [28].

[75] Case 120/78 *Rewe-Zentral AG v Bundesmonopolverwaltung fur Branntwein (Cassis de Dijon)* [1979] ECR 649; Case 302/86 *Commission v Denmark (Danish bottles)* [1988] ECR 4607.

[76] See the discussion in Jans and Vedder (n 36), ch 3.

[77] Referring to Art 2(2) TFEU, introduced at Lisbon: Member States 'shall again exercise their competence to the extent that the Union has decided to cease exercising its competence'.

to restrict GMOs that are not intended for cultivation. The Commission's position that de-harmonisation is needed is credible.[78] It is backed up by the possibility of incorporating 'other legitimate factors' (not just health and environment) into decisions under the Food and Feed Regulation, and for the consultation of an ethical committee under the Deliberate Release Directive.[79] Equally, however, the role of 'other legitimate factors' is, as discussed in chapter two, constrained by the legal context in which it sits, and so far unused; and the Deliberate Release Directive is explicit that its references to ethical issues do not affect the Directive's 'administrative procedures',[80] and that the Member States retain competence 'as regards ethical issues'.[81] The reach of the harmonisation in the existing legislation is not entirely clear, and the Court may yet need to decide on the scope of national freedom to address 'ethical', or more broadly non-environmental, non-health, issues.[82]

Whether never harmonised or de-harmonised, the approach is basically the same. To exercise autonomy, the Member State first needs to establish an 'other', non-environmental or health related objective that pursues a legitimate public interest objective under Article 36 TFEU or the mandatory requirements doctrine. The Commission proposal does not define the issues that fall under Article 26b, leaving all sorts of ethical and socio-economic issues up for consideration. Both European Parliament and the Commission (in a subsequent legal opinion) have provided examples of the sorts of issues that might be at stake: 'public order ... preserving cultural and social tradition or ... ensuring feasibility of controls or balanced rural conditions'.[83] There is no obvious legal effect to these lists, since they are non-exhaustive, and in any event measures still have to comply with the Treaties.

The Court does not always distinguish clearly between Article 36 and the mandatory requirements doctrine in this respect,[84] in particular the line between

---

[78] M Weimer, 'What Price Flexibility? The Recent Commission Proposal to Allow for National "Opt-outs" on GMO Cultivations under the Deliberate Release Directive and the Comitology Reform Post-Lisbon' (2010) *European Journal of Risk Regulation* 345.

[79] Deliberate Release Directive (n 5) Recital 57, Art 29; Food and Feed Regulation (n 5) Art 33.

[80] Deliberate Release Directive, ibid, Art 29(3). The same proviso applies to the consultation of scientific committees, Art 28.

[81] Ibid Art 29, see also Recital 9; Food and Feed Regulation (n 5) Recital 42.

[82] In Case C-165/08 *Commission v Poland* [2009] ECR I-6843, Poland sought to rely on ethical arguments, but the Court did not address the availability of this line of argument. Similarly, in Case C-313/11 *Commission v Poland*, not yet reported in ECR, the Court did not comment on Poland's argument that its prohibition of GM animal feed was justified by public morality under Art 36 TFEU, because the contested measures were not in force at the relevant time. More surprisingly, the Court did not address the argument that the existence of the ban in law, even when its application was being postponed, breached the principle of legal certainty. The Court held that the Commission had not made the case on legal certainty.

[83] Commission (n 69) [41].

[84] Eg Case C-244/06 *Dynamic Medien Vertriebs GmbH v Avides Media AG* [2008] ECR I-505, where the Court moves swiftly between public morality and public policy, and international legal instruments on the rights of the child; P Craig and G de Búrca, *EU Law: Text, Cases and Materials* (Oxford, Oxford University Press, 2011) 680.

open-ended 'public morality' and 'public policy' limbs of Article 36, and more specific mandatory requirements in the public interest. The significance of the distinction is that mandatory requirements in principle apply only to non-discriminatory measures. Determining whether bans on GMOs are discriminatory will not be straightforward, although national measures apply equally to domestic and imported GM seeds.[85] Moreover, the Court applies the requirement for non-discrimination inconsistently, often avoiding it, especially, although not exclusively, in environmental cases.[86]

The Court's case law suggests that a wide range of social and ethical objectives can legitimately be pursued by the Member States. The control of pornography is relatively straightforwardly recognised and understood as a legitimate question of 'public morality'.[87] Fundamental rights of freedom of expression and freedom of assembly were at stake in *Schmidberger v Austria*, a case in which the failure of Austria to prevent environmental protests that closed a motorway, impeded trade between Member States.[88] The *Sunday Trading* cases established that rules that 'reflect certain political and economic choices in so far as their purpose is to ensure that working and non-working hours are so arranged as to accord with national or regional socio-cultural characteristics' pursued legitimate objectives.[89] Restrictions on gambling can pursue legitimate objectives of protecting consumers (and specifically reducing gambling addiction), and control of fraud, or even of preventing 'private profit to be drawn from the exploitation of a social evil or the weakness of players and their misfortune'.[90] The Court considers the Austrian law on the abolition of the nobility to be 'an element of national identity', as well as being about the 'equality of Austrian citizens', and as such one of the 'legitimate interests' to be balanced as a matter of public policy.[91] It has been suggested that

---

[85] Whether (imported) GM seeds are 'like' (domestic) conventional seeds, and so should be treated alike, would be a fraught issue in WTO law, see most recently *United States—Clove Cigarettes* WT/DS406/AB/R. In the EU, it is reasonable to assume that the very different regulatory treatment of GM seeds in the EU means that they are different products, legitimately treated differently by the Member States.

[86] F Jacobs, 'The Role of the European Court of Justice in the Protection of the Environment' (2006) 18 *Journal of Environmental Law* 185; also C Barnard, 'Restricting Restrictions: Lessons for the EU from the US?' (2009) 68 *Cambridge Law Journal* 575; R Craufurd Smith, 'Culture and European Union Law: Always the Bridesmaid, Never the Bride?' in P Craig and G de Búrca (eds), *The Evolution of EU Law* (Oxford, Oxford University Press, 2011).

[87] Case C-34/79 *R v Henn and Darby* [1979] ECR 3795.

[88] Case C-112/00 *Schmidberger v Austria* [2003] ECR I-5659.

[89] Case 145/88 *Torfaen BC v B&Q Plc* [1989] ECR 3851 [14]. Note that this case pre-dates the line of case law arising out of Case C-267/91 and C-268/91 *Criminal Proceedings against Keck and Mithouard* [1993] ECR I-6097 on the capture of 'selling arrangements' by Art 34 TFEU.

[90] See the discussion in S Van den Bogaert and A Cuyvers, 'Money for Nothing: The Case Law of the EU Court of Justice on the Regulation of Gambling' (2011) 48 *Common Market Law Review* 1175; Case C-447 and 448/08 *Sjöberg* [2010] ECR I-6921 [43].

[91] Case C-208/09 *Sayn-Wittgenstein* [2010] ECR I-13693 [83].

the religious and ethical concerns associated with GMOs could form part of the Polish 'national identity', protected under Article 4(2) TEU.[92]

Whilst this is not a comprehensive discussion, these decisions demonstrate the potential diversity of the objectives that can in principle be pursued by Member States. Two final decisions are particularly pertinent for current purposes. First is a case about free movement of capital in the context of Austrian restrictions on the ownership of agricultural land. The Court showed some sympathy for the 'social objectives' of

> preserving agricultural communities, maintaining a distribution of land ownership which allows the development of viable farms and sympathetic management of green spaces and the countryside as well as encouraging a reasonable use of the available land by resisting pressure on land, and preventing natural disasters.[93]

In its submissions in this case, the Commission 'sees no reason to conclude that preserving, strengthening or creating a viable farming community are less important objectives than regional planning or protection of the environment'.[94] Secondly, in *Commission v Poland*, Poland tried to rely on ethical and religious requirements to justify a ban on GM seeds. The Court rejected Poland's argument on the basis that it had failed to establish that ethics and religion were the real basis for the Polish measures.[95] But the potential for restrictions to cultivation on ethical or religious grounds survived this decision, provided those grounds are properly made out.

The cases suggest that the Court might be reluctant to find that any genuinely pursued national objective is simply illegitimate. The cultivation of GMOs is arguably one of those areas where 'there are significant moral, religious and cultural differences between the Member States', so that in the absence of harmonisation, 'it is for each Member State to determine ... in accordance with its own scale of values, what is required to protect the interests in question'.[96] One significant exception to the Court's flexibility on the national definition of the public interest is the basic principle of internal market law that the Member States cannot use economic arguments to justify an interference with the free movement of goods.[97] This is in principle the case even when the Member State justified the economic protection offered to a national industry on the basis that the industry provides environmental benefits.[98] This latter point may now be applied less rigidly than

---

[92] A von Bogdandy and S Schill, 'Overcoming Absolute Primacy: Respect for National Identity under the Lisbon Treaty' (2011) 48 *Common Market Law Review* 1417; *Wittgenstein*, ibid.

[93] Case 452/01 *Ospelt v Schlössle Weissenberg Familienstiftung* [2003] ECR I-9743 [39].

[94] Ibid [98] (Geelhoed AG).

[95] *Commission v Poland* (Case C-165/08) (n 82). The Court explicitly declined to decide whether Poland *could* legislate on that basis, ibid [51].

[96] *Sjöberg* (n 90) [37] (of gambling).

[97] Case C-120/95 *Decker* [1998] ECR I-1831 [39].

[98] Case C-203/96 *Chemische Afvalstoffen Dusseldorp BV v Minister Van Volkshuisvesting, Ruimtelijke Ordening en Milieubeheer* [1998] ECR I-4075 [44].

it once was.[99] Nevertheless, it is important to establish that the protection of organic (or small family) farming pursues something more than economic objectives. Elsewhere, the Commission accepts that organic farming is a form of farming 'known to deliver public goods', including 'public health, social and rural development' and 'animal welfare', as well as environmental benefits.[100]

Whilst multiple objectives, with the exception of economic objectives, are legitimate, the Court still exercises tight control over national action. It is clear from *Poland* that a simple assertion of a public objective is not adequate; in that case, Poland 'failed … to establish that the true purpose of the contested national provisions was in fact to pursue the religious and ethical objectives'.[101] Poland failed to establish that 'public morality' was 'a separate justification', rather than part of protection of human health and the environment.[102] A Member State will need to identify very carefully its reasons for restricting cultivation. If the measures are about the support of a particular farming structure (small, family farms for example), or a particular form of farming (organic for example), the Member State would need to explain why this is important, as well as the role of the restrictions on GMOs in furthering these objectives. A consistent approach to the problem through other measures will help to establish the genuineness of the Member State's motivations.[103]

Allowing national flexibility on cultivation is in part about allowing the Member States to respond to the distinctive democratic concerns of their citizens. The Commission anticipates greater levels of public participation at the national level, with the Member States devoting 'more resources and time' to public participation: 'Social, economic and ethical aspects are expected to be put on the table and provide the platform for the respective decisions at national, regional or local level'.[104] It is unlikely that the Commission anticipates granting majorities a veto over decisions on GMOs, and a simple response to public concern—people just do not want GMOs—is not likely to satisfy the demands of internal market law. But public engagement might usefully allow the reasons for public views on

---

[99] N Nic Shuibhne and M Maci, 'Proving Public Interest: The Growing Impact of Evidence in Free Movement Case Law' (2013) 504 *Common Market Law Review* 965, particularly in respect of health services; see the discussion of the waste export cases, Jans and Vedder (n 36) 281–83. Note also the question of national support measures for renewable energy generation in ch 6.

[100] European Commission, 'European Action Plan for Organic Food and Farming' COM (2004) 415 final, s 1.4; Council Regulation 834/2007/EC on organic production and labelling of organic products [2007] OJ L189/1, Recital 1. Note also that organic products are one of the 'sustainable' products promoted in the EU's *Renewed Sustainable Development Strategy* (2006) 13. A very broad range of goals is associated with sustainable development in this document.

[101] *Commission v Poland* (Case C-165/08) (n 82) [52].

[102] Ibid [55], citing also Case C-1/96 *Compassion in World Farming* [1998] ECR I-1251.

[103] This is why allowing the legitimacy of preventing private profit from gambling is so important, because by contrast with an objective of tackling gambling addition, it allows even the encouragement of gambling provided that its proceeds are directed to public purposes, van den Bogaert and Cuyvers (n 90).

[104] Commission (n 61) [2.2.2].

GMOs to be explored, which in turn could help a national government to explain and defend its response to public opinion.

Importantly, an open explanation of why GMOs are being restricted allows others to challenge it (politically as well as legally), enhancing accountability. The Court has not yet spelled out what it requires in the way of evidence.[105] Evidence on public opinion may contribute to establishing the genuine connection between, for example, national identity or cultural specificity and restrictions on the cultivation of GMOs. Evidence on the economic impacts of GMOs may help the Member State establish the vulnerability of the particular approach to farming that it argues is valued nationally. It is however necessary to be alert to the possibility that demanding any particular form of evidence may limit the sorts of objectives that can legitimately be pursued.[106] A very stringent approach from the courts would be problematic.

If a Member State is able to establish that it is genuinely pursuing legitimate public interest objectives, it must further satisfy a proportionality test. The precise stringency of 'proportionality' in internal market cases is not straightforward.[107] The Member State may be required to satisfy proportionality 'proper', ie balancing the importance of the interest being pursued against the degree of interference with the internal market. The Member State will certainly have to establish first, a link between the measure introduced and the objective pursued, that is its effectiveness; and secondly the necessity of that measure, that is the unsuitability of less restrictive measures. In *Commission v Austria*,[108] a case about the prohibition, on environmental grounds, of certain heavy lorries from an Austrian motorway that was one of the main links between Germany and Italy, the measures at issue were, relatively unusually in the environmental sphere,[109] found to be disproportionate. But the Court said that if Austria had 'clearly established' that alternative means were inadequate to achieve the reduction of nitrogen dioxide pollution that were sought, it would have been lawful. The Member State would need to satisfy the Court that its restrictions on GM cultivation would actually contribute to the maintenance of traditional forms of farming (for example), and that no lesser measures would suffice. *Pioneer Hi Bred Italia Srl v Ministero delle Politiche Agricole Alimentari e Forestali* suggests that proportionality could be a major hurdle to national or regional bans on the cultivation of GM crops. Italy had banned cultivation of GMOs pending the agreement of measures to ensure the coexistence of conventional and organic crops with GM crops (discussed in the next section). Whilst Bot AG agreed that it is 'not inconceivable' that sometimes there will be a need to prohibit cultivation in parts of the national territory to

---

[105] See Nic Shuibhne and Maci (n 99) for analysis.
[106] See also ibid, on the difficulty of enhancing evidential requirements of public interest claims.
[107] The stringency of the approach can vary, see eg Jacobs (n 86). In preliminary references, the ultimate finding on proportionality should in principle be left to the national courts
[108] Case C-320/03 *Commission v Austria* [2005] ECR I-9871.
[109] Jacobs (n 86).

ensure coexistence, 'in accordance with the principle of proportionality, such a possibility would be subject to the provision of strict proof that other measures would not be sufficient'.[110]

Pioneer is a reminder that whilst the Court accepts the significance and legitimacy of public objectives in the internal market, we should not be complacent about the scope for action under proposed Article 26b. Cases like *International Transport Workers' Federation and Finnish Seamen's Union v Viking Line* and *Laval v Svenska Byggnadsarbetareförbundet* , which famously condemned national provisions on strikes and collective bargaining on labour conditions because of their impact on treaty economic freedoms, confirm that there is no guarantee of judicial sensitivity to social values.[111]

The Commission's proposal has been very controversial, and there is no guarantee that it will make its way through the legislative process. Even if it ultimately fails, the proposed Article 26b is worth examining for its illustration of the challenges of allowing national autonomy; these arguments will no doubt reach the courts in any event, alongside an argument that the legislation only harmonises risk to the environment and human health. Which leads to the question of why the Commission's proposal is so contentious. First, some are concerned that it is incompatible with internal market law. It is clearly capable of compatible interpretation. The problem is that such an interpretation is likely to provide only a narrow path for national autonomy. And that leads to a second concern, which is that this proposal is essentially pointless, or even a cynical attempt to hasten authorisation, in confident expectation that any autonomy will be meaningless in practice. Given the years of urging the EU institutions to find greater space for national autonomy, dismissing Article 26b out of hand would be a little churlish. Although only a very narrow opportunity, it could represent a change of philosophy, away from the very tenacious hold on central authority.

Of greater concern might be what de-harmonisation means for the role of 'other legitimate factors' in the authorisation process. As discussed in chapter two, authorisation decisions are not in principle limited to the outcome of risk assessment, but can also take account of 'other legitimate factors'. This is a potentially significant and positive opening up of EU risk management to the politics (politics as a noble enterprise) of risk. Other legitimate factors seems so far to have played no explicit role in the authorisation process, and a judicial and political context that prefers an apparently objective notion of risk, places serious constraints on the use of this criterion.[112] The division of responsibility implied

---

[110] Case C-36/11 *Pioneer Hi Bred Italia Srl v Ministero delle Politiche Agricole Alimentari e Forestali* not yet published in ECR [61] (Bot AG). Note that new Commission guidelines on co-existence, discussed below, do envisage restrictions on cultivation that cover 'large areas', European Commission, Recommendation on Guidelines for the Development of National Co-Existence Measures to Avoid the Unintended Presence of GMOs in Conventional and Organic Crops (no number) [2010] OJ C200/1.

[111] C-438/05 *International Transport Workers' Federation and Finnish Seamen's Union v Viking Line* [2007] ECR I-10779; Case C-341/05 *Laval v Svenska Byggnadsarbetareförbundet* [2007] ECR I-11767.

[112] See ch 2; Lee (n 4).

by the Commission's proposal seems to be that risk assessment stays with the EU, whilst other (legitimate) factors go to the Member State. This may imply a further downgrading of the status of other legitimate factors in authorisation.

Of course the EU itself is not wholly autonomous on these issues, and the potential impact within the free trade disciplines of the World Trade Organisation (WTO) also looms large.[113] This is not the place for a detailed consideration of the WTO rules, however.[114] As with the internal market, the WTO in principle allows some space for the pursuit of social values, but as with the internal market, that space is highly constrained and will not be simple to use. Expanding the range of values that can justify interruptions to free trade, within and beyond the EU, is extremely challenging. However, equally challenging to the legitimacy and sustainability of regulatory frameworks is the insistence that countries and regions cannot respond to the concerns of their citizens about the implications of GMOs.

CO-EXISTENCE

Total isolation of GM material, certainly once agricultural biotechnology is widespread in the EU, is impossible. There will inevitably be some level of mixing between GM and non-GM material, through for example natural cross-pollination by wind or insects, the survival of GM 'volunteers', and mixing by farm machinery, or in storage, distribution or processing. Article 26a of the Deliberate Release Directive provides that: 'Member States may take appropriate measures to avoid the unintended presence of GMOs in other products'. This 'co-existence' provision in principle allows considerable flexibility in the Member States, with different approaches to respond to their diverse conditions, for example as to the size of farms, different levels of commitment to organic farming and varied geographical and ecological conditions. Measures to ensure the co-existence of different forms of agriculture include staggered sowing, weed management and careful cleaning and maintenance of equipment. At the more interventionist end, separation distances or buffer zones between crops might amount to GM free zones on various scales.

As always, the bare provisions of the legislation, allowing Member State autonomy, operate within a broader legal and political context. The Commission issued

---

[113] European Commission, 'Complementary Considerations on Legal Issues on GMO Cultivation Raised in the Opinions of the Legal Service of the Council of the European Union of 5 November 2010 and of the Legal Service of the European Parliament of 17 November 2010—WTO Compatibility' SEC (2011) 551 final.

[114] The WTO context for GM regulation is discussed in Lee (n 4). Of a large literature, see J Scott, 'European Regulation of GMOs and the WTO' (2003) 9 *Columbia Journal of European Law* 213; R Howse and PC Mavroidis, 'Europe's Evolving Regulatory Strategy for GMOs: The Issue of Consistency with WTO Law: of Kine and Brine' (2000) 24 *Fordham International Law Journal* 317; J Peel, 'A GMO by Any Other Name … Might be an SPS Risk!: Implications of Expanding the Scope of the WTO Sanitary and Phytosanitary Measures Agreement' (2006) 17 *European Journal of International Law* 1009.

a *Recommendation and Guidelines on Co-existence* in 2003,[115] which were highly restrictive of national autonomy in respect of co-existence. 'GM free' zones, other than to the extent that they emerge spontaneously through farmers' decisions not to grow GMOs, were frowned upon. More focused approaches were preferred, such that co-existence measures should be specific to particular species and 'priority should be given to farm-specific management measures and to measures aimed at coordination between neighbouring farms'.[116] The Guidelines provided that proportionality required measures not to go further than would be necessary to comply with the 'tolerance thresholds' set in the legislation. In particular, this refers to the '0.9% exception' to obligations to label GMOs: the normal obligation to label food containing, consisting of or produced from GMOs,[117] is waived in the case of up to 0.9 per cent GM content that is adventitious or technically unavoidable, provided that 'appropriate steps' have been taken 'to avoid the presence of such material'.[118] The approach in the 2003 Guidelines was very restrictive.[119] The presence of GM material below this threshold has potentially negative effects on non-GM production, especially organic production. Some certifiers of organic produce take a 'zero tolerance' approach to the presence of GM material.[120] Given the higher costs of organic production, a loss of organic certification is disastrous for the individual farmer. Further, the long-term health of organic farming may have broader public benefits than the impact on individual farmers.[121]

Notwithstanding the restrictive approach in the 2003 Recommendation, a number of Member States introduced very strict co-existence measures, coupled with unforgiving liability regimes.[122] The Commission did not generally take formal legal action, although Pioneer did challenge the Italian refusal to allow the cultivation of GMOs pending the adoption of detailed co-existence rules.[123] One of the package of measures put forward by the Commission in its 'new approach'

---

[115] European Commission, Recommendation on guidelines for the development of national strategies and best practices to ensure the co-existence of genetically modified (GM) crops with conventional and organic farming [2003] OJ L189/36

[116] Ibid [2.1.5] and [2.1.6].

[117] Food and Feed Regulation (n 5) Art 12; non-food products are labelled if they contain or consist of GMOs, Regulation 1830/2003/EC concerning the traceability and labelling of genetically modified organisms and the traceability of food and feed products produced from genetically modified organisms [2003] OJ L268/24.

[118] Food and Feed Regulation, ibid, Art 12(3).

[119] The wording of which looks as if 0.9% presence is to be exceptional, after all efforts have been taken to avoid any GM presence at all in non-GM products; the Commission's approach presents 0.9% as a target, a normal level of GM presence. See Lee (n 4).

[120] GMOs cannot be *used* in organic agriculture, Regulation 834/2007/EC (n 100) Art 9, and a product that has to be labelled under the GMO legislation cannot also be labelled organic, Art 23(3). Those who certify products as organic can make more stringent demands.

[121] Commission (n 100).

[122] J Corti Varela, 'The New Strategy on Coexistence in the 2010 European Commission Recommendation' (2010) 4 *European Journal of Risk Regulation* 353.

[123] *Pioneer* (n 110). On a preliminary reference to the Court of Justice, it was held that Art 26a allows coexistence measures that give rise to restrictions, but not to a general ban on cultivation (which may in practice be indefinite) pending their adoption.

in summer 2010 was a new, somewhat more flexible, 'Recommendation on Guidelines on Coexistence', which emphasise 'the diversity of farming systems and natural and economic conditions in the EU'.[124] Rather undermining the potential significance of the new Guidelines, the Court in *Pioneer*, with no explanation, said that they simply 'describe and amplify' the 2003 Guidelines.[125] But the new Guidelines clearly are more flexible. In respect of the 0.9 per cent threshold, they recognise that 'in certain cases ... the presence of traces of GMOs in particular food crops—even at a level below 0.9%—may cause financial harm to the operator who would wish to market them as non-containing GMOs'.[126] And by contrast with the intolerance of GM free zones in the 2003 Recommendation, the Commission recognises that the exclusion of GM cultivation from 'large areas' may be necessary.[127] Again, these words need to be set in their legal context. The role of internal market law in constraining bans on cultivation was discussed above in respect of the proposed Article 26b. It is likely that any GM free zone will need to be justified under Article 36 TFEU or mandatory requirements. One would expect that ensuring the co-existence of different forms of farming is a valid objective. The comments of Bot AG on proportionality are not, however, encouraging.[128]

CONCLUSIONS

The context in which GMOs are marketed, cultivated and consumed is an important element of their regulation.[129] National autonomy in respect of authorised GMOs is fragmented, depending on the objectives being pursued. Article 26a addresses the presence of GMOs in other products; proposed Article 26b addresses restrictions on the cultivation of GMOs for reasons other than the protection of the environment or health; Article 114 TFEU addresses the environment and the working environment. The safeguard clauses, it turns out, are not about national autonomy at all. All of this plays out in the context of a powerful and controversial common agricultural policy, within which it can be difficult to reconcile agribusiness and small farming.[130] One obvious but important conclusion is that this complex legal framework is dramatically lacking in transparency. The very major limitations on national action on GMOs, discussed in this

---

[124] Commission (n 110) Recital 2.

[125] Above n 110 [13]. The timing of the case meant that the Court applied the 2003 recommendation [61].

[126] Commission (n 110) [1.1], [2.3.1].

[127] Ibid Recital 5, [2.4]—if other measures are not adequate and proportionate to the objective pursued.

[128] See (n 110).

[129] This is a theme in Lee (n 4), and a range of different issues are explored there.

[130] L Levidow and K Boschert, 'Coexistence or Contradiction: GM Crops versus Alternative Agricultures in Europe' (2008) 39 *Geoforum* 174.

chapter, are not easily appreciable, even to specialists, let alone to broader publics concerned about GMOs.

In a sense, the narrow scope for national autonomy is precisely what the internal market is supposed to achieve. It is not however necessary to interpret, for example, Article 114, quite as narrowly as it has been. Commission President Barroso agrees that 'it should be possible to combine a Community authorisation system, based on science, with freedom for Member States to decide whether or not they wish to cultivate GM crops on their territory.'[131] The internal market can cope with difference, up to a point, and can provide flexibility, as we have seen. The exercise of autonomy is highly demanding, but rather than writing it off, it should be pursued with great care.

---

[131] JM Barroso, *Political Guidelines for the Next Commission* (Brussels, European Commission, 2009) 39.

Conclusions

I T IS PROBABLY not possible to find uncontested common or unifying
principles of EU environmental law, or EU environmental law scholarship.[1]
We might advocate certain approaches (wide participation for example, a
high level of protection, or integration), but their meaning and role would be
uncertain and disputed. Rather than incoherence, the inevitable absence of unifying principles reflects multiple understandings of the 'environment', and what
it means to 'protect' it,[2] as well as the dependence on more developed legal sub-
disciplines (EU administrative and constitutional law, internal market law) to
achieve the aims of environmental law.[3]

Rather than trying to draw generic conclusions from the diverse body of law
discussed in this book, I would like to revisit some of the key themes that have
emerged. Environmental protection and environmental decision-making depend
intimately on detailed, specialised information about the physical state of the
world, information which is in the hands of technical experts; but it also depends
on political judgments about values and priorities, distributing goods and bads
between rich and poor, current and future generations, prioritising between different environmental goods, and between the environment and other social goods.
A lack of consensus around the values at stake may in some cases emphasise the
salience of pervasive uncertainty about the 'facts' of environmental protection.
Responses to the demands of environmental decision-making for the resources of
both expertise and political legitimacy, can be glimpsed throughout EU environmental law. The ways in which a strong emphasis is placed on the generation of
knowledge and information, coupled with an expectation of openness to scrutiny
and participation in decision-making, are especially significant.

Elaborate processes for ensuring the enhancement of knowledge and the availability of information are at the centre of much EU environmental governance,
for example the regulation of industrial pollution, chemicals, and environmental

---

[1] On environmental law generally, see eg O Pedersen, 'Modest Pragmatic Lessons for a Diverse and
Incoherent Environmental Law (2013) 33 *Oxford Journal of Legal Studies* 103; E Fisher et al, 'Maturity
and Methodology: Starting a Debate about Environmental Law Scholarship' (2009) 21 *Journal of
Environmental Law* 213. AD Tarlock, 'Is There a There There in Environmental Law?' (2004) 19 *Journal
of Land Use and Environmental Law* 213 is more concerned about the impact of 'incoherence'.

[2] Eg Pedersen, ibid, as well as the discussion in earlier chapters.

[3] Fisher et al (n 1).

assessment. The practice of sustainable development is also deeply engaged in trying to improve ways of measuring progress, and the elaborate institutional structure for impact assessment is premised around the organisation of information. Some of these information gathering processes are highly elaborate, involving institutionalised elite participation in problem-solving, most obviously the Common Implementation Strategy for water and the Seville process for industrial emissions. The primary concern in EU environmental law is to generate and gather information on the physical risks posed to the environment and human health by different economic activities. The role of economic information on the costs of harm to the environment and of regulation is, however, increasingly significant. We may even be seeing the beginnings of a common European approach to cost benefit analysis (CBA). It is important that CBA's judgment on whether regulatory measures are 'worthwhile', and implicit prioritisation of competing values, is not used to attempt to sanitise the messy and unpredictable role of politics in environmental decision-making.

All of this information is then in principle available to environmental governance, and although 'information' is far from straightforward, as discussed in chapter two especially, decisions should be taken in the context of improved understanding. The focus on information is in part about enabling regulators; it is also in some cases a tool of regulation in itself, placed in the hands of third parties so that they can scrutinise and exert pressure, and in the hands of the regulated so that they can reflect upon their own environmental impacts. Again, this is apparent in most of the chapters in this book, a feature of environmental assessment and energy efficiency, as well as more obviously of pollution registers and chemicals regulation.

EU environmental law is also resolute that the final decision, for which so much effort has been put into enriching knowledge, is a political decision, to be taken by politically legitimate administrative decision-makers. As discussed in chapter two, this 'solution' takes for granted the ability to maintain a clear separation between facts and values, when they are inextricably linked. It also pays too little attention to the difficulties faced by political decision-making trying to exercise autonomy when they have been provided with specialised and detailed expert advice. A further difficulty is that administrative decision-makers face their own legitimacy issues, the preferred institutional arrangements in the EU (Commission plus comitology), more so than many. The insistence that final decisions are political, for politically legitimate decision-making, is nevertheless valuable and important. The point is that it requires further attention. Environmental decision-making processes are not easily subjected to familiar democratic or legal processes of legitimacy and accountability. But trying to enhance the 'building blocks' of legitimacy,[4] for example by ensuring transparency, inclusion and opportunities

---

[4] See G de Búrca, 'Developing Democracy beyond the State' (2008) 46 *Columbia Journal of Transnational Law* on the importance of 'democratic striving' (in a different context).

for political and legal contestation in legislative frameworks is important. This applies to both the sometimes powerful expert processes feeding into the final decision, and to the political decision-making process itself.

'Public participation' is part of the mosaic of responses to weak political legitimacy at EU level, as well as a way of providing alternative perspectives on environmental issues, alternative sources of knowledge and information. Some of the great hope for 'public participation' as a route to democracy seems to have waned since the turn of the century, or is certainly less visible in the official discourse around environmental decision-making. The difficulties of enabling real public participation are also more painfully recognised. It is probably fair to say that an instrumental view of public participation dominates in EU environmental law, in which participation is valued for the contribution it makes to information-gathering and scrutiny, and the most valued information is often highly technical. The dangers of exclusion are considerable.

Identifying the actors involved in EU environmental decision-making is not always straightforward: the regulated industries, environmental interest groups, concerned citizens, EU level actors, Member States, all have a role to play. The institutional embedding of national actors and interests in EU level administration, in agencies and comitology for example, as well as other EU level fora such as the technical working groups dealing with industrial emissions, provides mechanisms for national political concerns to influence EU decisions. Even the line between harmonisation and national autonomy can be quite fuzzy, as illustrated by the regulation of industrial emissions, and by efforts to adjust national freedom of action in respect of genetically modified organisms. Information is often managed primarily by EU or national public administrations. But the prioritisation of information has also brought with it a central role for private actors in EU environmental governance. In many cases, for example industrial emissions, chemicals regulation, and environmental impact assessment, the industry (even the firm) being regulated has primary responsibility for providing the 'first draft' of the information on which regulatory decisions depend. Given industry's possession of the best information, or at least the best means to acquire it, putting incentives in place to pass the burden of evidence production to the private sector is valuable. But the importance of strong external scrutiny is also clear. Environmental interest groups play a central role in the provision of necessary alternative perspectives. But their ability to match the influence of industry is at least open to question, and regulators must still shoulder a considerable amount of the burden.

The focus of this book has been on environmental decision-making. Law can be used to indicate where and by whom decisions are taken, the information that is to be prioritised, who is able to contribute and how. But the broad legal context, for example the internal market rules or the judicial use of science to discipline administrative discretion, is as important as the words in the legislation. Nor does law have a free hand, since the broader governance context also matters. For example, changing the legal status of 'soft' rules in the regulation of industrial emissions is not a simple exercise; and the existence of a legal obligation to allow the public to participate tells us very little about the role of public participation in decision-making. But EU environmental law provides a means by which to look for an answer to environmental questions. The means and the answers are inevitably imperfect and flawed, but important nonetheless.

Perhaps the key theme in this book has been the way in which environmental decision-making rests on an inseparable amalgamation of politics and expertise, facts and values. The strong emphasis in EU environmental law and governance on both technical knowledge and information, and openness to scrutiny and participation in decision-making, is a way to attempt to rationalise and to respond to this. The divide between political and technical decision-making should not however be over-emphasised: virtually no one would advocate one without the other, and the inherently political nature of environmental decision-making is widely understood. But the tension between them is inevitable, sometimes acute, and will rightly be the subject of ongoing scrutiny.

Index